中国经济中长期发展和转型

国际视角的思考与建议

[英]林重庚
[美]迈克尔·斯宾塞 编著

余 江 等译

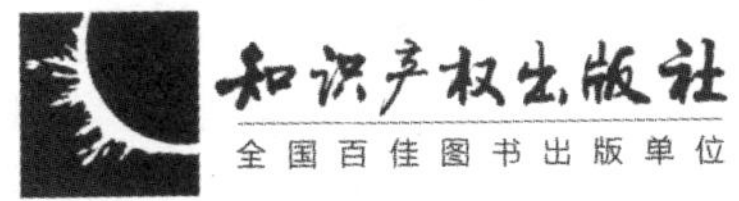

图书在版编目（CIP）数据

中国经济中长期发展和转型：国际视角的思考与建议：汉英对照 /（英）林重庚，（美）迈克尔·斯宾塞编著；余江等译．—北京：知识产权出版社，2020.1

ISBN 978-7-5130-4081-5

Ⅰ.①中… Ⅱ.①林… ②迈… ③余… Ⅲ.①中国经济—经济发展—文集—汉、英 Ⅳ.① F124-53

中国版本图书馆 CIP 数据核字（2018）第 267572 号

总 策 划：王润贵 **项目负责**：蔡 虹
套书责编：蔡 虹 石红华 **责任校对**：谷 洋
本书责编：蔡 虹 程足芬 **责任印制**：刘译文

中国经济中长期发展和转型：国际视角的思考与建议（汉英对照）

［英］林重庚 ［美］迈克尔·斯宾塞 编著
余 江 等译

出版发行：知识产权出版社有限责任公司 **网 址**：http：//www.ipph.cn
社 址：北京市海淀区气象路 50 号院 **邮 编**：100081
责编电话：010-82000860 转 8324 **责编邮箱**：caihongbj@163.com
发行电话：010-82000860 转 8101/8102 **发行传真**：010-82000893/82005070/82000270
印 刷：三河市国英印务有限公司 **经 销**：各大网上书店、新华书店及相关专业书店
开 本：787mm × 1092mm 1/32 **印 张**：13.5
版 次：2020 年 1 月第 1 版 **印 次**：2020 年 1 月第 1 次印刷
字 数：340 千字 **定 价**：68.00 元

ISBN 978-7-5130-4081-5

京权图字：01-2019-5231

出版说明

知识产权出版社自1980年成立以来，一直坚持以传播优秀文化、服务国家发展为己任，不断发展壮大，影响力和竞争力不断提升。近年来，我们大力支持经济类图书尤其是经济学名家大家的著作出版，先后编辑出版了《孙冶方文集》《于光远经济论著全集》《刘国光经济论著全集》和《苏星经济论著全集》等一批经济学精品力作，产生了广泛的社会影响。受此激励和鼓舞，我们和孙冶方基金会携手于2018年1月出版《孙冶方文集》之后，又精选再版孙冶方经济科学奖获奖作品。

“孙冶方经济科学奖”是中国经济学界的最高奖，每两年评选一次，每届评选的著作奖和论文奖都有若干个，评选的对象是1979年以来的所有公开发表的经济学论著。其获奖成果基本反映了中国经济科学发展前沿的最新成果，代表了中国经济学研究各领域的最高水平。这次再版的孙冶方经济科学奖获奖作品，是我们从孙冶方经济科学奖于1984年首次评选到2017年第十七届共评选出的获奖著作中精选的20多部作品。这次再版，一方面是为了缅怀和纪念中国卓越的马克思主义经济学家和中国经济改革的理论先驱孙冶方同志；另一方面有助于系统回顾和梳理我国经济理论创新发展历程，对经济学同人深入研究当代中国经济学思想史，在继承基础上继续推动我国经济学理论创新、更好构建中国特色社会主义政治经济学都具有重要意义。

在编辑整理“孙冶方经济科学奖获奖作品选”时，有几点说明如下。

第一，由于这20多部作品第一版时是由不同出版社出版的，所以开本、版式、封面和体例不太一致，这次再版都进行了统一。

第二，再版的这20多部作品中，有一部分作品这次再版时作者进行了修订和校订，因此与第一版内容不完全一致。

第三，大部分作品由于第一版时出现很多类似“近几年”“目前”等时间词，再版时已不适用了。但为了保持原貌，我们没有进行修改。

在这20多部作品编辑出版过程中，孙冶方经济科学基金会的领导和同事对本套图书的出版提供了大力支持和帮助；86岁高龄的著名经济学家张卓元老师亲自为本套图书作了思想深刻、内涵丰富的序言；这20多部作品的作者也在百忙之中给予了积极的配合和帮助。可以说，正是他们的无私奉献和鼎力相助，才使本套图书的出版工作得以顺利进行。在此，一并表示衷心感谢！

知识产权出版社

2019年6月

总　序

张卓元

知识产权出版社领导和编辑提出要统一装帧再版从 1984 年起荣获孙冶方经济科学奖著作奖的几十本著作，他们最终精选了 20 多部作品再版。他们要我为这套再版著作写序，我答应了。

趁此机会，我想首先简要介绍一下孙冶方经济科学基金会。孙冶方经济科学基金会是为纪念卓越的马克思主义经济学家孙冶方等老一辈经济学家的杰出贡献而于 1983 年设立的，是中国在改革开放初期最早设立的基金会。基金会成立 36 年来，紧跟时代步伐，遵循孙冶方等老一辈经济学家毕生追求真理、严谨治学的精神，在经济学学术研究、政策研究、学术新人发掘培养等方面不断探索，为繁荣我国经济科学事业做出了积极贡献。

由孙冶方经济科学基金会主办的“孙冶方经济科学奖”（著作奖、论文奖）是我国经济学界的最高荣誉，是经济学界最具权威地位、最受关注的奖项。评奖对象是改革开放以来经济理论工作者和实际工作者在国内外公开发表的论文和出版的专著。评选范围包括：经济学的基础理论研究、国民经济现实问题的理论研究，特别是改革开放与经济发展实践中热点问题的理论研究。强调注重发现中青年的优秀作品，为全面深化改革和经济建设，为繁荣和发展中国的经济学做出贡献。自 1984 年评奖活动启动以来，每两年评选一次，累计已评奖 17 届，共评出获奖著作 55 部，获奖论文 175 篇。由于孙冶方经济科学奖的评奖过程一直是

开放、公开、公平、公正的，在作者申报和专家推荐的基础上，由全国著名综合性与财经类大学经济院系和中国社会科学院经济学科领域研究所各推荐一名教授组成的初评小组，进行独立评审，提出建议入围的论著。然后由基金会评奖委员会以公开讨论和无记名投票方式，以简单多数选定获奖作品。最近几届的票决结果还要进行公示后报基金会理事会最终批准。因此，所有获奖论著，都是经过权威专家几轮认真的公平公正的评审筛选后确定的，因此这些论著可以说代表着当时中国经济学研究成果的最高水平。

作为17届评奖活动的参与者和具体操作者，我不敢说我们评出的获奖作品百分之百代表着当时经济学研究的最高水平，但我们的确是尽力而为，只是限于我们的水平，肯定有疏漏和不足之处。总体来说，从各方面反映来看，获奖作品还是当时最具代表性和最高质量的，反映了改革开放后中国经济学研究的重大进展。也正因为如此，我认为知识产权出版社重新成套再版获奖专著，是很有意义和价值的。

首先，有助于人们很好地回顾改革开放40年来经济改革及其带来的经济腾飞和人民生活水平的快速提高。改革开放40年使中国社会经济发生了翻天覆地的变化。贫穷落后的中国经过改革开放30年的艰苦奋斗于2009年即成为世界第二大经济体，创造了世界经济发展历史的新奇迹。翻阅再版的获奖专著，我们可以清晰地看到40年经济奇迹是怎样创造出来的。这里有对整个农村改革的理论阐述，有中国走上社会主义市场经济发展道路的理论解释，有关于财政、金融、发展第三产业、消费、社会保障、扶贫等重大现实问题的应用性研究并提出切实可行的建议，有对经济飞速发展过程中经济结构、产业组织变动的深刻分析，有对中国新型工业化进程和中长期发展的深入研讨，等等。阅读这些从理论上讲好中国故事的著作，有助于我们了解中国经济巨变的内在原因和客观必然性。

其次，有助于我们掌握改革开放以来中国特色社会主义经济理论发展的进程和走向。中国的经济改革和发展是在由邓小平开创的中国特色社会主义及其经济理论指导下顺利推进的。中国特色社会主义理论体系也是在伟大的改革开放进程中不断丰富和发展的。由于获奖著作均系经济理论力作，我们可以从各个时段获奖著作中，了解中国特色社会主义经济理论是怎样随着中国经济市场化改革的深化而不断丰富发展的。因此，再版获奖著作，对研究中国经济思想史和中国经济史的理论工作者是大有裨益的。

再次，有助于年轻的经济理论工作者学习怎样写学术专著。获奖著作除少数应用性、政策性强的以外，都是规范的学术著作，大家可以从中学到怎样撰写学术专著。获奖著作中有几套经济史、经济思想史作品，都是多卷本的，都是作者几十年研究的结晶。我们在评奖过程中，争议最少的就是颁奖给那些经过几十年研究的上乘成果。过去苏星教授写过经济学研究要“积之十年”，而获奖的属于经济史和经济思想史的专著，更是积之几十年结出的硕果。

是为序。

2019 年 5 月

序 言

刘 鹤

林重庚先生邀请我为这份研究报告作序，这实在是我的殊荣。这项关于中国中长期发展战略的研究，是北京凯恩克劳斯经济研究基金会（以下简称“凯恩克劳斯基金会”）接受中央财经领导小组办公室（以下简称“中财办”）与国家发展和改革委员会（以下简称“国家发改委”）的委托而开展的，林重庚（Edwin Lim）先生和诺贝尔经济学奖得主迈克尔·斯宾塞（Michael Spence）教授是课题的负责人，他们邀请了20多位来自国际不同机构的著名经济学家，参加了课题的研究，在各自的研究领域为该课题撰写了背景材料。这个国际专家组包括多个拥有不同背景和不同经验的顶级经济学家，例如，获得2010年诺贝尔经济学奖的彼得·戴蒙德(Peter Diamond)教授、“新增长理论之父”保罗·罗默（Paul Romer）教授、世界最大的资产管理公司之一PIMCO总裁穆罕默德·埃尔埃利安（Mohamed EL-Erian）先生等。中方委托开展这项课题研究的目的，是听取国际专家对中国第十二个五年规划制订的建议。

研究工作是2009年初开始的，2010年春节之前正式完成。

在此期间，参与研究的专家和我们多次见面，就研究的命题和具体内容交换意见。我认为，这是一份高质量的研究报告，凡是想从全球经济结构变化中理解中国的人，凡是想把握中国未来10年发展脉络的人，都有必要认真阅读，因为它以大师的视野和思想深度，准确描述了中国发展和改革的趋势、重点和优先顺序，具有重要的决策参考价值。

研究报告形成后，按照我们的建议，迈克尔·斯宾塞教授和林重庚先生联手保罗·罗默教授及前世界银行东南亚局局长伊恩·波特（Ian Porter）先生，亲笔归纳和提炼了一份简明的综合研究报告摘要，题为“从国际视角看中国的第十二个五年规划”。收到这份报告，感觉这里面充满对中国未来5年发展的真知灼见。不久后，报告分送到中国政府“十二五”规划建议起草组成员手中。起草组是一个以总理和副总理为首的极其重要的宏大团队，有70多位部长和专家学者参与了这项历史性的重要起草工作。毋庸置疑，国际专家们提交的研究报告对“十二五”规划建议的形成发挥了重要作用。

中国的“十二五”规划提出了未来中国经济社会的发展战略，这是在国际金融危机发生后、在中国迈向高收入国家的关键历史阶段的重大战略，它不仅指引中国全面建设小康社会，也将对全球经济平衡和人类福祉产生不可估量的影响。凡是能够参与“十二五”规划的人，从其影响意义而言，都是幸运和难得的，也是值得感谢的。借此机会，请允许我代表课题委托单位向以迈克尔·斯宾塞教授和林重庚先生为首的国际专家组表示由衷的感谢。我也提议，中国应设立一个特别贡献奖，对那些在中国改革开放中作出重要贡献的国际专家进行奖励，通过他们，中国获得了先进的发展理念和难得的他山之石。

由官方机构委托非官方国际专家进行国家发展战略的研究，这在中国可能没有先例。事实证明，这是一种独特而高质量、高效率的合作方式。我希望，我们能够继续以这种方式合作下去。

2011年3月10日

前　言

本研究项目由诺贝尔奖得主迈克尔·斯宾塞教授和世界银行驻华首任首席代表林重庚先生牵头负责的国际专家团队共同完成。本项研究由中财办和国家发改委委托开展，目的是从国际视角对中国中长期发展和“十二五”规划提出意见建议。

该国际团队的专家来自世界多国著名的大学、智库、国际机构及跨国公司，他们是：

K.Y. 阿莫阿科（K.Y.Amoako，联合国非洲经济委员会前执行秘书）；

A.B. 阿特金森（A.B.Atkinson，牛津大学教授）；

朱迪思·巴尼斯特（Judith Banister，美国经济咨商局全球人口研究所所长）；

尼古拉斯·巴尔（Nicholas Barr，伦敦经济学院公共经济学教授）；

大卫·布卢姆（David Bloom，哈佛大学经济学与人口学教授）；

蔡昉（中国社科院人口与劳动经济研究所所长）；

安德鲁·克罗克特(Andrew Crockett，JP 摩根大通集团国际部总裁，国际清算银行前总经理）；

彼得·戴蒙德（Peter Diamond，2010 年诺贝尔奖得主，麻省理工学院经济学教授）；

巴里·埃肯格林（Barry Eichengreen，加州大学伯克利分校经济学和政治学教授）；

穆罕默德·埃尔埃利安（Mohamed EL-Erian，PIMCO 太平洋投资管理公司总裁）；

樊胜根（Shenggen Fan，国际粮食政策研究所所长）；

理查德·弗里曼（Richard Freeman，哈佛大学经济学教授）；

霍华德·格伦纳斯特（Howard Glennerster，伦敦经济学院社会政策名誉退休教授）；

弗农·亨德森（J.Vernon Henderson，布朗大学经济学和城市研究教授）；

拉维·坎布尔（Ravi Kanbur，康奈尔大学应用经济学及管理学国际教授）；

霍米·卡拉斯（Homi Kharas，世界银行前东亚局首席经济学家）；

圣蒂亚戈·莱维（Santiago Levy，泛美开发银行副行长、墨西哥前财政部副部长）；

李实（北京师范大学教授）；

林重庚（Edwin Lim，世界银行驻华首任首席代表、中金公司首任总裁）；

让·皮萨尼－费里（Jean Pisani-Ferry，欧洲智库 Bruegel

主任）；

伊恩·波特（Ian Porter，世界银行前东南亚局局长）；

保罗·罗默（Paul Romer，斯坦福大学经济学教授）；

沈联涛（Andrew Sheng，中国银监会首席顾问）；

迈克尔·斯宾塞（Michael Spence，2001年诺贝尔奖得主，纽约大学、斯坦福大学教授）；

黄佩华（Christine Wong，牛津大学高级研究员）；

阿德里安·伍德（Adrian Wood，牛津大学国际发展教授）；

伊夫·泽诺（Yves Zenou，斯德哥尔摩大学经济学教授）；

张晓波（Xiaobo Zhang，国际粮食政策研究所高级研究员）；

香港利丰集团研究中心（Li & Fung Research Center）。

阿根廷前中央银行行长Mario Blejer博士、哈佛大学公共卫生学院萧庆伦（William Hsiao）教授、《金融时报》（Financial Times）首席经济评论员Martin Wolf等国际专家在课题研究过程中均有贡献。

这项研究课题得到了顾问团队的指导。他们是：刘仲藜、项怀诚、吴敬琏、周小川、楼继伟、郭树清、李剑阁、刘鹤以及冯国经（Victor Fung，中国香港）和郑国枰（Teh Kok-Peng，新加坡）。

在课题研究过程中，国际专家团队与中财办和国家发改委有关司局密切联系。在准备期间，课题组多次与中财办副主任刘鹤先生、国家发改委秘书长杨伟民先生进行交流，对形成写作提纲起到重要作用。中财办韩文秀局长、王志军副局长、蒙剑副局长，国家发改委规划司田锦尘副司长、张耕田处长为该课题的执行提供了必要的支持。国家发改委也拨课题经费予以支持。

该研究课题由凯恩克劳斯基金会资助并提供组织协调方面的支持。凯恩克劳斯基金会理事长赵人伟教授全面参与了该课题的准备、执行及推广工作，为课题提供了全面咨询。凯恩克劳斯基金会理事、项目主任林至人(Cyril Lin)博士和秘书长苏国利女士为该项研究课题的准备、执行及推广工作提供了全方位的组织和协调支持。

新加坡国立大学东亚研究所(East Asian Institute, National University of Singapore)为本研究课题提供部分资助及行政支持。自2004年起，东亚研究所为迈克尔·斯宾塞教授和林重庚先生共同主持的从社会保障改革到后来的城市化等中国政策问题研究项目提供了大力支持。这些课题的研究成果对现课题研究贡献良多。所长郑永年教授和高级副主任(Senior Associate Director)连伟莉女士为此提供了有力的支持。

参加综合报告讨论并提出意见的有：白重恩、丁宁宁、傅军、何迪、赖德胜、隆国强、卢锋、马晓河、钱颖一、王小鲁、吴晓灵、许善达、易纲、余永定、张维迎、张秀兰等。

在该课题研究过程中，中国人民银行、中国社会科学院人口与劳动经济研究所、中国国际金融有限公司和中国发展研究基金会为中外专家的交流组织了研讨活动。为国际专家介绍中国情况并为专题报告提出意见的专家有：陈佳贵、陈雨露、崔之元、都阳、高世楫、葛延风、哈继铭、韩俊、何平、何宇鹏、景天魁、李稻葵、李善同、李扬、刘国恩、刘国宏、卢迈、陆学艺、路英、单菁菁、申兵、司劲松、宋立、宋晓梧、苏明、汤敏、王德文、王建伦、王延中、王有强、王振耀、谢多、游钧、于法明、曾湘泉、张力、张秀兰、张振忠、赵殿国、郑秉文、郑功成、郑永年、朱玲、朱民、Louis Kuijs、Philip O'Keefe 和 Yvonne Sin 等。

余江负责《综合报告》终稿的翻译；成九雁、戴任翔、丁怡、房连泉、黄念、刘培林、齐传君、王美艳、宣晓伟、赵晓松、郑真真等翻译了背景论文及其他材料；《比较》杂志执行主编肖梦女士对课题研究成果的推广提供了建议，在报告的译文审稿、定稿、出版方面给予指导和大力协助。《比较》杂志编辑部主任吴素萍女士对报告译文做了审稿、编辑和定稿，从始至终为报告的出版提供了有力支持。

该研究课题主持人谨此对参与研究工作及提供支持的所有人员在课题中的贡献表示衷心的感谢。每篇背景论文的研究发现、诠释及所作出的结论均为作者个人观点。

目 录

第一篇 综合报告

执笔人：林重庆 伊恩·波特 保罗·罗默 迈克尔·斯宾塞

第一章 引言：经济增长的国际经验与比较 3
经济增长的历史 3
从中等收入向高收入国家的转型 6
对中国中长期发展的启示 8
本报告的概述 10
第二章 转变增长方式 15
新增长方式 15
产业和技术升级 18
投资体制 21
金融部门的发展 24

第三章　城市和地区发展　31
缩小城乡之间的收入差距　32
调整城市的规模和经济结构　35
促进有效率的城市发展　38
改革城市的财政和管理制度　41
缩小地区差异　43
第四章　增加国内消费和壮大中产阶层　48
增加国内消费的政策　48
中产阶层　53
中产阶层的重要性　55
中产阶层与可持续的经济增长：国际经验　56
对中国的中产阶层规模的估计　59
第五章　就业、教育与劳动力市场　62
就业增长、产业结构和调整　64
教育和技能开发　67
劳动力市场的制度和监管　72
第六章　加强养老金体系建设　81
经济学理论和国际经验的启发　82
中国养老金体系下一步改革的政策选择　89
中国养老金体系的整体管理　95
结论　100

第七章　社会政策　*102*

应对收入不平等的问题　*102*

改革的一般原则　*104*

教育　*107*

医疗卫生　*109*

低保制度　*111*

人口政策　*112*

社会政策的总体规划和管理　*113*

第八章　中国在世界经济中的角色　*117*

金融危机的后果　*118*

世界经济的重新调整　*120*

全球需求的再平衡　*124*

中国的再平衡　*125*

促进全球贸易和投资　*127*

向低碳经济转轨　*130*

全球治理　*135*

第九章　体制改革　*140*

增进政府的效率和应负的责任　*141*

改革国有企业的范围和功能　*148*

改革财政体制　*152*

结束语　*158*

第二篇　背景论文

（按作者姓氏首字母排序）

背景论文一　非洲国家对中国的期待

K.Y. 阿莫阿科

背景论文二　中国社会政策改革中的问题

A.B. 阿特金森

背景论文三　中国的人口老龄化与经济增长

朱迪思·巴尼斯特　大卫·布卢姆

拉里·罗森伯格

背景论文四　中国的养老金改革：问题、选择和政策建议

尼古拉斯·巴尔　彼得·戴蒙德

背景论文五　社会政策：中国发展中的一项中心内容

尼古拉斯·巴尔　霍华德·格伦纳斯特

背景论文六　中国就业政策的国际视角

蔡　昉　理查德·弗里曼　阿德里安·伍德

背景论文七　中国在世界经济中的角色：展望第十二个五年规划

安德鲁·克罗克特

背景论文八　世界期望中国担当什么样的经济和金融领导角色：两段历史的启示

巴里·埃肯格林

背景论文九　世界对中国的期待及中国应该做什么

穆罕默德·埃尔埃利安　拉曼·托鲁伊

背景论文十　中国的地区差距：经验和政策

樊胜根　拉维·坎布尔　张晓波

背景论文十一　中国的城市化：面临的问题及政策选择

弗农·亨德森

背景论文十二　中国向高收入国家转型：避免中等收入陷阱的因应之道

霍米·卡拉斯

背景论文十三　对拉丁美洲社会政策的有关评论

圣蒂亚戈·莱维

背景论文十四　中国工业生产的分散化和面向国内市场的制造业前景

香港利丰集团研究中心

背景论文十五　中国社会保障改革：争论与选择

李　实

背景论文十六　中国与世界经济：基于欧洲视角的分析

让·皮萨尼－费里

背景论文十七　中国新增长方式的最优化探析

保罗·罗默

背景论文十八　中国融入全球金融架构的路径选择

沈联涛　成九雁

背景论文十九　为中国和谐社会建设而进行的公共部门改革

黄佩华

背景论文二十　中国的住房政策：面临的问题和选择

伊夫·泽诺

作者介绍　*163*

英文部分　*175*

第一篇

1

综合报告

执笔人：林重庚　伊恩·波特
保罗·罗默　迈克尔·斯宾塞

第一章　引言：经济增长的国际经验与比较*

经济增长的历史

经济增长是人类历史上近期才出现的现象。该进程始于 18 世纪末的英国工业革命，到 19 世纪推广至欧洲和北美，并逐渐加速。进入 20 世纪（尤其是后半叶），经济增长再次拓展和加速，参见图 1-1。

随着经济的成长，社会的组织更加紧密，相互联系更为密集。一个增长中的经济体意味着活力得到更好的发挥，资源得到更好的配置，各种技术得到掌握和改进，而不仅仅是收入的增加。

今天的经济学家们用技术、资本和人力资本的三元方程来解

---

* 2006年，一群引领世界各国发展的政策实践者（包括前总理、部长、规划官员和商业人士，以及两位诺贝尔经济学奖获得者）共同组成了“增长与发展委员会”（Commission on Growth and Development），委员中包括中国人民银行周小川行长。本报告的作者之一迈克尔·斯宾塞（Michael Spence）教授担任委员会主席。本章内容基于该委员会于2008年发表的《增长报告：可持续增长与包容式发展的战略》。有关该报告、背景论文及该委员会的更多信息，参见www. growthcommission org。

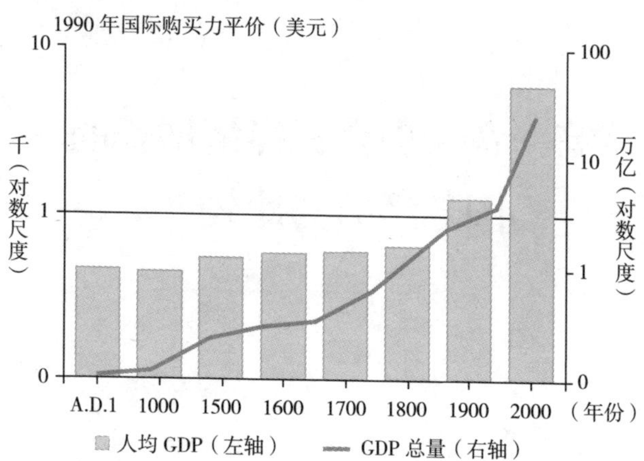

图 1-1 过去 2000 年中全球 GDP 和人均 GDP 的变化

资料来源：Commission on Growth and Development，*The Growth Report*，第 18 页（原始数据来自 Angus Maddison, 2007，*Gontours of the World Economy*，*1–2030AD*，Oxford University Press）。

释经济增长，但这些只是增长的近似原因，更深层的动力来自多重因素的作用，包括科学、金融、贸易、教育、医疗、公共健康和政府组织的进步。我们今天所说的世界经济在过去两个世纪经历了间歇性的扩张，在 20 世纪 30 年代出现中断和倒退，到 20 世纪 40 年代重建，并奠定了当前的世界经济所依赖的制度基础。在立法（削减关税和配额限制、放松资本管制等）和创新（运输和通信成本的下降）的帮助下，全球化自此之后加速推进。

全球化的复兴有助于解释 20 世纪后半叶世界经济增长的提速。随着世界经济开放度的提高和一体化程度的增强，技术和诀窍更容易传播到发展中国家。后来者吸收新技术的速度可以远远快于先进国家创新的速度，这就是落后国家能逐步“追赶”富裕国家的原因。

这些国家从外面得到的收获并不仅限于技术，例如，中国和印度对其严格管制的封闭经济体制进行了改革，这在一定程度上受到国际上其他成功案例的启发。中国的改革开放不但给自身带来了深刻的变化，也影响到世界经济的全貌。增长过程的加速也带来了新的挑战。第一个挑战是各国内部和国家之间的收入分配差距拉大。在地球上的60多亿人中，约有65%生活在高收入国家或高速增长的国家（而在30年前这个数字仅有不到1/5），其余的20亿人生活在收入水平停滞甚至倒退的国家。全世界的总人口预计到2050年还将增加30亿人，但不幸的是，其中的20亿人将出现在目前几乎没有经济增长的国家。因此，如果这一趋势保持不变，生活在低收入增长环境中的人口所占的比重可能上升。

第二个挑战是环境方面的，世界GDP总量的加速增长给地球的生态和气候造成了新的压力。这样的压力最终可能威胁过去200年以来的增长环境。如果经济增长停滞，人们改善自己生活的努力将变成对总量固定的资源的混乱争夺，生态方面的威胁会很快蔓延到社会和政治领域。

自第二次世界大战（以下简称二战）结束以来，许多国家和地区都经历过至少短期的快速增长，但只有13个经济体在25年或更长的时间段维持了年均7%及以上的持续增长，其中包括：博茨瓦纳、巴西、中国、中国香港、印度尼西亚、日本、韩国、马来西亚、马耳他、阿曼、新加坡、中国台湾和泰国。越南和印度可能将加入这一行列，希望其他国家和地区也会尽快加入。

取得过这样的经济成就的国家和地区包含各种各样的类型，东亚各经济体占据主体，但其他各个地区的发展中国家也都有自己的代表，包括非洲、拉丁美洲、中东和欧洲的新兴地区等。有些国家的自然资源丰富，例如博茨瓦纳、巴西、印度尼西亚、阿曼和泰国，其他国家则没有那么幸运。样本中包含一个10亿人口以上的大国（中国），也包含一个不足50万人口的小国（马耳他）。

这13个经济体各有自己的特色，但并不意味着它们之间没有共同点，或者说从它们的增长历程中不能得到适用于其他国家的经验教训。仔细分析这13个案例，可以发现如下5条惊人的相似之处：

1. 它们充分利用了世界经济；
2. 它们维护了宏观经济稳定；
3. 它们保持了高储蓄率和高投资率；
4. 它们通过市场来配置资源；
5. 它们拥有负责、可信和有能力的政府。

从中等收入向高收入国家的转型

这些国家的增长历史有若干共同点，但有趣的是，它们在达到中等收入水平后保持持续增长并力求向高收入转型的经历却大不相同。其中6个经济体（中国香港、日本、韩国、马耳他、新加坡和中国台湾）继续成长到高收入阶段，而其他一些国家则在距离发达国家还很远的时候就丧失了部分或全部增长动力。从中等收入向高收入转型失败并不是一个罕见的现象，相当多国家（包括若干拉丁美洲国家）在达到中等收入水平后，增长率就显著放缓。原因是多方面的。一个重要区别在于，与前一阶段的发展相比，对于从中等收入进入高收入的这第二个发展阶段，人们的理解没有那么深入，研究也明显不足。

没有人能查清某些经济体失去增长势头而其他一些可以保持的所有原因。但各国之间某些共同特征具有启发意义。随着一个国家成功从中等收入进入高收入行列，其经济结构会转入技术密集度更高的产业，服务业将加速成长，规模和财富不断积累的国内经济成为更重要的增长发动机。

中等收入国家的劳动力供给在早期曾具有无限的弹性，但这一优势将不再持续。随着富余劳动力的消失，某个产业雇用员工的机会成本将会提高，企业需要争夺员工，工资会相应上涨。工资的提升将制约劳动密集型产业的增长，于是，曾经引领增长的出口产业会出现下滑甚至消失。

高技能劳动力短缺的现象将会显现。它带来的一个结果是，政策会转向促进人力资本和技术进步。政策制定者的角色必须相应调整，在一个国家远远落后于世界先进水平的时候，它非常清楚必须做哪些事情，决策者可以像指挥军队一样引领国家前进。可是当发展水平接近领先者的时候，哪些事情应该做、未来的前途在何方就变得不够明确了。此时，必须把更多的决策交给私人投资者去博弈，让市场来进行集体判断。

政策制定者的首要任务应该是预见到这一转型，并给自己提出新的要求。许多国家的政府都有规划部门，它们关注经济的未来发展和变化，并预测需要为此提供怎样的公共政策和支出。例如，韩国在 20 世纪八九十年代就调整了政策和公共投资，帮助本国经济从以劳动密集型制造业为主转变为知识和资本密集度更高的类型。韩国向外国直接投资打开大门，对国有钢铁公司进行私有化，加入了经济合作与发展组织（OECD，以下简称经合组织），将劳动密集型制造业转移到了新的目的地。

政府的第二个并不轻松的任务是摒弃原来的某些政策，甚至那些曾取得过成功的政策。几个具体案例包括：出口加工特区、严格管理的汇率制度以及其他形式的产业政策。它们的执行时间都可能过长。这些政策当初所针对的问题已经逐步缓解，因此并不是永远需要。抗拒变革将会迟滞经济的结构调整，不利于人们对新的出口产业和面向国内市场的产业进行投资。

拉丁美洲出现过很多案例，许多国家在达到中等收入水平后未能持续增长。该地区的所有大经济体，特别是阿根廷、巴西、智利、哥伦比亚和墨西哥，都经历过快速增长期，但没有一个国家实现了更长时期的稳健增长，并最终完成跨入高收入国家行列的“毕业”。它们的进步是间歇性的：旺盛的增长被严重的宏观经济危机打断，然后是强劲复苏，重新进入增长。

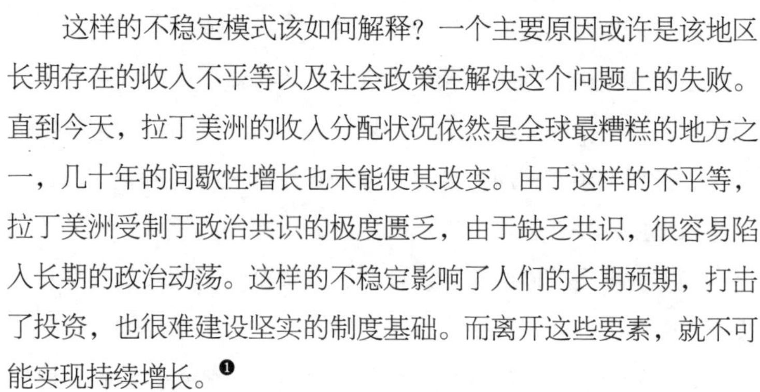

这样的不稳定模式该如何解释？一个主要原因或许是该地区长期存在的收入不平等以及社会政策在解决这个问题上的失败。直到今天，拉丁美洲的收入分配状况依然是全球最糟糕的地方之一，几十年的间歇性增长也未能使其改变。由于这样的不平等，拉丁美洲受制于政治共识的极度匮乏，由于缺乏共识，很容易陷入长期的政治动荡。这样的不稳定影响了人们的长期预期，打击了投资，也很难建设坚实的制度基础。而离开这些要素，就不可能实现持续增长。[1]

对中国中长期发展的启示

按照国际货币基金组织的说法，中国的人均收入在 2010 年已达到 4280 美元，[2] 按购买力平价计算则为 7520 美元（购买力

❶ 参见第四章“专栏4-1拉丁美洲的中产阶层”。感谢阿根廷中央银行前行长、国际货币基金组织前高级顾问马里奥·布雷杰博士(Mario Blejer)的贡献。

❷ 国家统计局2011年2月28日发布的2010年统计公报显示：2010年国内生产总值(GDP)为397983亿元，2010年年末全国总人口为13.41亿。按1美元等于6.5696元人民币计算，我国2010年的人均GDP为4517美元。

平价调整了各国的价格差异）。根据世界银行的分类标准，中国已跻身世界中等收入国家的行列。然而，全国的平均数掩盖了国内存在的巨大差异。贵州和甘肃等贫困省份相当于下中等收入国家的水平，而最发达的珠江三角洲和长江三角洲等地区则与上中等收入国家相当，城市地区更是接近高收入国家的水平。

这些地区差异不容忽视。不过，尽管还有很多落后地区，仍然有理由相信中国会在可预见的将来成为高收入国家，并应该为随之而来的挑战做好准备。政府已经制定了到2020年建成小康社会的远大目标。但那不应该是中国的终极目的，也不应该制约规划者的视野。政策制定者们还应该看得更远，瞄准成为高收入国家的最终目标。

一段时期以来，中国的政策制定者和经济学家们已经认识到了上述挑战，他们经常讨论到“转变增长方式”的必要性。这个转变通常包含三方面的内容：首先，从基于资本和劳动力积累的投资驱动型增长转向基于生产率提高的增长；其次，产业结构从以工业为主转向以服务业为主；最后，需求结构的调整，从外需转向内需。另外一个方面的挑战关系到建设“和谐社会”，并确保发展“以人为本”。中国确定的这些优先议题完全同国际经验相一致。

然而，中国也有两个特征使其面临的发展挑战具有特殊性。第一个特征是上文提到的差异性。不同地区之间以及城乡之间存在的差距，在设计新的增长方式及规划和谐社会建设所需要的社会项目时，必须充分考虑到这样大的差异。

第二个特征是中国本身的巨大规模。中国的规模使其与世界其他国家的相互作用显得不同寻常。虽然中国在过去20年的增长模式与之前的“亚洲四小龙”等并无太大差别，但其贸易盈余和汇率制度引起的关注却大得多。尽管中国仍处在相对低水平的

发展阶段，但其消耗的水泥几乎占全球的1/2，钢铁占1/3，铝约占1/4。

中国的规模表明，它永远不能模仿如今的发达国家曾采用的增长方式：因为地球没有足够多的自然资源来支撑这种增长。一个显而易见又颇具争议的例子是碳排放，它带来了灾难性的气候变化的风险。虽然中国的人均碳排放量只有美国的约1/4，但总排放量却已经是全球第一，而世界其他国家不可能忽视这个事实。总的来说，中国在人均收入水平和发展阶段相对较低的时候，就已经在世界经济中取得了相当大的份额和影响力（见图1–2）。与历史上的其他国家都不同，中国必须在完成向发达和富裕国家的艰难转型的同时，承担起一个超级经济大国的责任和义务。

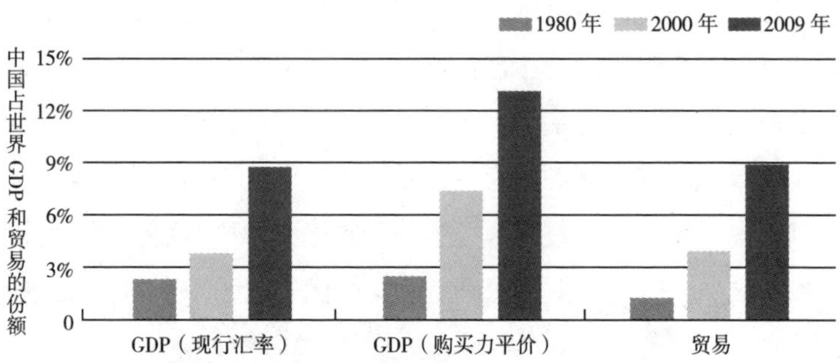

图1–2　中国占全球GDP的份额迅速上升

资料来源：IMF，Arora and Vamvakids，“Gauging China's Influence”，*Finance & Development*，December 2010，p.12，chart 1。

本报告的概述

在中国为制定“十二五”规划进行前期准备的过程中，中央财经领导小组办公室及国家发展和改革委员会邀请国外知名学者对未来中国发展问题进行研究和提出意见建议。出于这个目的，我们组织了20多位来自世界多国著名的大学、智库和国际机构及跨国公司的经济学家，在他们的专业领域撰写论文。我们还组织了一系列研讨会，从中国的经济学家和政府官员那里获得了大量的参考意见。

我们把为这一研究项目准备的所有论文结集成书。目录中列出了论文标题及其作者，并简要介绍了这个由多国经济学家组成的国际团队。本报告后面的八章即是根据这些论文和讨论中得到的主要发现和结论所做的综合报告。

接下来的第二章到第四章详细阐述了转变中国增长方式必须进行的内容。

第二章讨论中国的增长方式，过去，中国只需要将劳动力从农业转移到制造业，就可以获得迅速增长，这个过程虽然尚未结束，但在未来，中国的增长将更少依赖制造业的就业增加，而更多依靠生产效率的改进。这就要求进行“创造性破坏”（creative destruction），如同老牌企业被新兴的更有生产效率的企业取代一样。政府可以通过有利于新产业和新技术发展的政策来推动这个进程，同时不要排斥市场在发现最好的投资机会方面的核心作用。事实上，中国需要在资本配置方面给市场更大的发挥空间。在目前的投资中，有太多属于国有企业获得的普通银行贷款，或者用于再投资的国有企业留存利润。中国未来的增长将在很大程度上可以依靠有效动员储蓄、分散风险、把资本配置给更多类型企业的金融市场。

第三章分析中国增长战略的地理因素，指出中国的城市化程度不及同一发展阶段的其他许多国家，许多城市的规模缺乏效率（需要更多发展人口规模在100万~1200万的城市），经济结构陈旧（依赖制造业的时间太长）。中国的城市还容易受到市区蔓延和周边土地利用碎片化的双重问题的困扰。这一章认为，应该让中国的城市更自由地竞争人才和投资，而不要让地方保护主义阻碍统一的国内市场的运转。城市化水平的提高可以帮助缩小不同地区之间的巨大收入差距。政府在采纳向落后地区倾斜的开支不菲的区域发展政策之前，应该首先取消那些不利于落后地区的政策。

第四章从中国经济的增长惊人的供给方面转向相对滞后的需求方面。在下一个 10 年，中国应该更多依靠国内消费作为增长的发动机。然而，消费在 GDP 中所占的份额一直在下降，因为工资所得在国民收入中的份额在下跌。本章讨论了政府在提振消费方面可以采取的若干措施，包括对劳动收入的减税、放松消费信贷限制，以及将某些国有资产转让给公众等。为了继续保持增长动力，中国必须培养一个强大的中产阶层，给他们足够的安全感和对未来稳定的预期，使其可以更自由地选择消费项目。这一章比较了中国与其他国家的中产阶层规模，其中既包括成功实现了持续增长的国家，也包括不成功的案例。

从第五章到第七章涉及的是与政府的“以人为本”目标和“和谐社会”建设有关的话题。

第五章是就业、教育与劳动力市场，中国的劳动力市场正快速接近拐点：劳动力供给总量可能会在 10 年之内停止增长。过去，中国应对的挑战是将劳动力从农业转移到工业制造业，而未来的挑战则是将非农产业的劳动力从生产率较低的部门转向生产率较高的部门。非常关键的认识在于：物质资本存量的规模差异只能很有限地影响不同国家的生产率，最大的影响因素是人力资本，也就是国民的技能。这就要求提高大批员工和年轻人的技能，他们可能缺乏在高技术经济中取得成功必须具备的教育背景。

第六章加强养老金体系建设。养老金有多重功能：熨平消

费、提供保险、扶贫和收入再分配。由于各国对这些目标各有侧重，所以没有哪种养老金体系能适用于所有的国家。中国近期形成的养老金体系的三支柱——基本养老金、个人账户和自愿性养老金——打下了一个良好的制度基础。中国如今需要关注扩大覆盖面并改进对养老金体系的管理。应该把基本养老金扩展成普及性的国家养老金，对所有达到一定年龄标准的国民发放，并由此改变农村、城市和农民工的养老保险体系各自为政的局面。中国需要加强养老金体系的总体管理，可以从其他国家的失误和成功中学到很多做法。为进一步改革个人账户，可以考虑引进瑞典和其他国家先行采用的记账式个人账户体系[1]。

第七章社会政策，针对中国的快速增长伴随着收入不平等的扩大，用比较分析的视角描述了其他一些国家的政府，如何成功地利用社会政策来缓解不平等问题，而在中国，社会事务支出占GDP的比重偏低，社会项目的覆盖较为零散，福利不容易在地区和职业之间实现转移，制约了劳动力流动。贫富分化现象如果不能得到妥善解决，有可能导致更大的社会矛盾和社会动荡。成功的社会政策应该覆盖全国，哪怕是在较低的福利水平上。福利的提供应该尽可能本地化和分散化，但其筹资来源却应该主要由中央政府负责，以实现从富裕地区向贫困地区的再分配。

综合报告最后的第八章和第九章讨论的是中国在世界经济中的角色和未来应对挑战所需要进行的改革。

第八章中国在世界经济中的角色，强调全球化给中国带来了追赶式增长的两个关键要素：知识和市场。中国经济的成功发展使其具有了牵动全球经济大局的地位，影响到世界市场的价格，

---

❶ Notional individual account，有时候也译为名义个人账户，但后一种译法容易误导，有关记账式个人账户的概念，请参见第六章。

并引起全球的普遍关注。今天，其他国家期望中国承担起某些国际责任，如全球需求再平衡和控制碳排放等。但是，中国仍然是刚刚迈入中等收入水平的国家，一个经济体在如此早期的发展阶段就产生了如此全局性的影响力，这在世界历史上恐怕还没有先例。本章的分析指出，在其他国家对中国的期望与中国自身的发展目标之间，并不存在无法克服的矛盾。当然，就中国实现这些目标的方式和速度，的确有大量的不同看法。因此一个很重要的任务是，中国在各种各样的引导世界经济发展的国际论坛上需要发挥更积极的作用。

第九章体制改革，分析中国为成功实现中长期经济发展与转型所需要推行的体制改革。中央政府和地方政府都必须重新思考自己的角色，改进行政能力。此外，体制改革的内容还应该包含国有企业，它们目前面临的竞争不足，给政府提供的支持（分配的红利）太少。中国还必须改革财政体制，尤其是中央、省级和县级政府的收入与支出责任划分。这一章要回答的最重要的问题是，如何缩小中国的长期目标与实际实施效果之间的差距，这对任何国家而言都是极其复杂而具有挑战性的议题。本章应该被视为对这个议题的思考的开始，而非结论。

在迈向“小康”和更富裕社会的转型时期，中国将面临一系列艰巨挑战。当然，中国也有着非常有利的因素。我们认为，中国的长期目标与短期目标、实现可持续增长与建设和谐社会之间并不存在不可调和的矛盾，中国走向富强的梦想与世界其他国家的利益也没有根本冲突。中国过去 30 年来的伟大成就给了我们很强的信心，它完全有能力应对当前的挑战、抓住未来的机遇。

第二章　转变增长方式*

新增长方式

许多国家经历过突发性的快速经济增长，但正如第一章所指出的那样，其中很少能像中国这样持续 30 年时间。实际上，只是到了 20 世纪后半叶，每年 5%~10% 的高增长率才成为可能。以这样的速度成长需要一个开放的世界经济，通过贸易自由化、运输和通信技术的进步捆绑在一起。全球化使落后国家可以从先进国家那里引进观念和技术，并让它们进入广阔的国际市场，从而发挥单靠本国市场不足以支撑的规模经济和专业化效益。随着生产的迅速扩大，它们可以充分利用农业中滞留的大量富余劳动力。

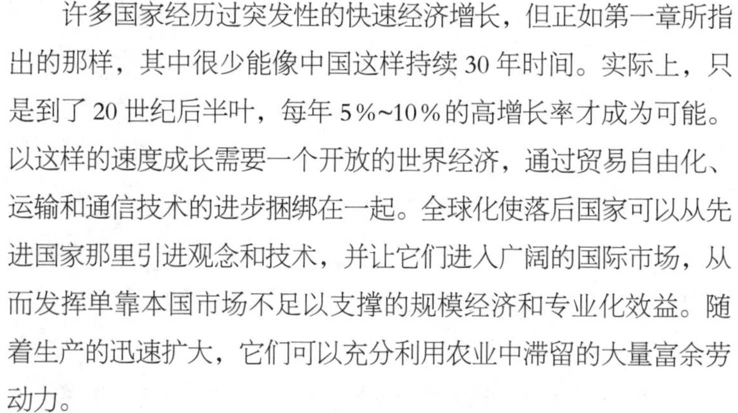

但是，在这些国家达到中等收入水平以后，如何最好地利用劳动力和资本的决策就变得复杂起来。一个国家的基本特征和资源禀赋可以为此提供某些参考，例如，是发展技术密集型为主的服务业，还是发展资本密集型为主的制造业等。但具体来说，应该发展哪个部门的制造业，使用什么类型的技术呢？很多问题的

* 本章主要参考了背景论文十七：保罗·罗默，《中国新增长方式的最优化探析》；背景论文七：安德鲁·克罗克特，《中国在世界经济中的角色：展望第十二个五年规划》。

答案依旧是不确定的。有些国家在过去将出口的成败视为对某个产品或某家企业的终极考验，如今则主要根据国内市场来判断。它们以前主要消化从海外引进的技术，如今则必须更多地依靠本地企业作为观念和技术创新的源泉。

在发展的早期阶段，取得进步的最佳指标是就业量的增加，尤其是正规部门和城市地区的就业。当一个国家步入中等收入水平后，成功的最佳指标变成了平均工资的提高。这是出于两方面的原因：首先，随着经济的发展，企业对拥有一定技能的员工的争夺会加剧，从而推高工资水平；其次，员工的技能也在提高，让他们可以从事更具有挑战性、回报也更高的工作。此时，那些依赖廉价劳动力的企业要么提升到全球供应链上附加价值更高的环节，要么退出，或者转移到其他国家，把廉价劳动力的就业机会送给发展水平更低的国家员工。

在各国经历上述的创造性破坏过程时，许多企业会抱怨说，它们负担不起雇用员工的成本了。在这种情况下，一个国家必须作出选择：是保护现有的企业，还是让员工的工资水平继续得到提高？那些保护企业的国家会停止增长，生产率会止步。而追求更高工资的国家则会继续增长。很明显，持续的增长要求在经济的供给面上进行深入的结构调整，特别是针对可贸易部门，尤其是出口部门。

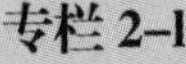

转变中国的增长方式：一个类比

阿尔弗雷德·马歇尔在 1890 年的经典著作《经济学原理》中把经济发展的突变比喻为森林的成长。中国的发展也可以借用类似的比喻。改革开放前的中国就像一片很早以前生长起来的松树林，所有的树木都已经停止生长。改革让人们得以引进生长速度远快于松树的红杉树苗，红杉树给森林带来了新的活力，就像新企业给中国经济带来的效果一样。

在下一个阶段，经济的持续增长会变得更为困难。挑战之一是每年都需要找到更好的树种，使得新一代的红杉树能长得更高。幸运的是，中国可以一方面借鉴其他国家已经尝试和应用过的大量理念，另一方面培养本国在技术前沿的创新能力。

第二个挑战是给那些更有生长效率的新树苗创造空间，这要求砍伐掉一些现有的树木，否则它们会遮蔽尚在幼年的小树苗的阳光。在所有人都希望森林长高的时候，很容易说服大家砍伐掉一些已经停止生长的较矮的松树。但是，要说服他们把一些较高的红杉树也砍掉，给后来会长得更高的小树预留空间的时候，就会困难一些。要让大家都同意把一些还在生长的红杉树砍掉，那就更困难了。但如果每一代的树苗都比上一代的好得多，就必须找到一个办法，每年都能栽种很多新树苗，这也就是经济学家们所说的创造性破坏。

当国家和企业身处绝境时，人们都会拥抱改革。不过在第一轮改革带来了增长率的爆发后，有人会很容易满足。他们会忽略，给新观念让路要求经常性的更新。

为了实现下一个五年规划中生产率持续提高的目标，中国不但需要鼓励新企业的加入，还要设法缩减甚至关闭那些曾经非常成功，但已开始落后的老企业。只有新老企业之间的积极竞争，才能确保一个社会最有价值的资源（人才）年复一年地进入更有生产率的企业组织。

资料来源：背景论文十七：保罗·罗默，《中国新增长方式的最优化探析》。

一个国家的工资水平要想持续提高，其生产率也必须跟上。有些老企业会开发新业务，要求拥有更高技能的员工，也能负担更高的工资。但有些老企业则不能跟上形势。在高收入国家，大量的收入更高的就业岗位是新企业创造的，它们起步时往往是小企业，其中许多会失败，但获得成功的企业将快速成长，并推动生产率的进步。

要让这一转型取得成功，投资必须迅速转向生产率最高的企业和业务。在经济发展越来越依赖观念、知识和创新精神的时候，投资（包括公共部门的投资）重点必须从物质资本转向人力资本。

产业和技术升级

有些经济学家会认为，中国目前还不需要新的发展方式，中国的比较优势仍然在劳动密集型产业。中国毕竟还有很多地区刚刚越过低收入水平的发展阶段，农村依然存在大量的富余劳动力。因此，他们认为劳动密集型的制造业还是中国的比较优势所在。

中国的制造业的确还有发展空间，也可以转移到国内较为贫困、劳动力更便宜的地区。但要持续提高工资水平，中国就必须在某一时点上采纳新的增长方式，而在沿海城市，这个时点可能已经到来。此外，新的增长方式是基于知识的积累和生产率的改进，它们要求新的制度和规则来支持，这些制度因素也需要一定的时间来培育。所以，中国应该尽可能迅速地启动转型的进程。

还有些经济学家赞成中国需要进行产业升级，但认为政府并不是推动这一进程的合适主体：产业政策很容易带来反作用，政府没有能力判断谁应该是胜利者。然而，包括中国在内的许多东亚经济体的经验说明，情况未必如此。日本、中国台湾、韩国和新加坡都通过对市场的干预成功实现了从中等收入阶段向更高发展阶段的过渡。鼓励转型的优惠政策不需要针对特定的企业甚至特定的产业，某些产业政策应当具有广泛的适用面，有利于各种类型的新技术和新企业，无论其所处的产业或部门。这些政策可以鼓励新企业的创建和老企业的创新，依然让市场来决定哪些企业或哪些产业会最终起飞。

这不是否认产业政策的制定和实施具有相当的难度。在这方面并没有统一的蓝图，每个国家必须根据自己的情况制定合适的制度模式。不过，亚洲和拉丁美洲国家的经验可以提供几方面的启示。

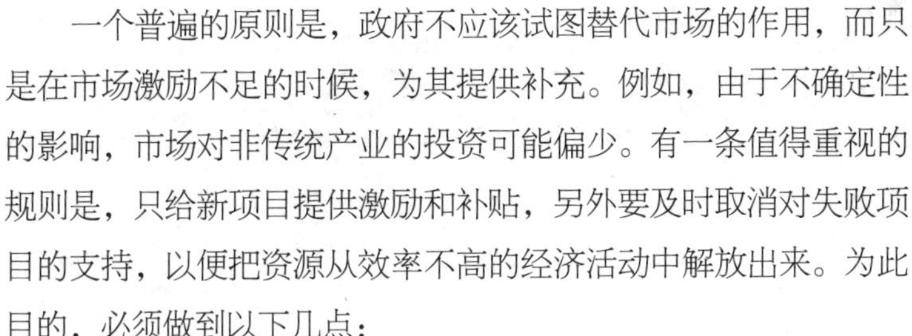

一个普遍的原则是，政府不应该试图替代市场的作用，而只是在市场激励不足的时候，为其提供补充。例如，由于不确定性的影响，市场对非传统产业的投资可能偏少。有一条值得重视的规则是，只给新项目提供激励和补贴，另外要及时取消对失败项目的支持，以便把资源从效率不高的经济活动中解放出来。为此目的，必须做到以下几点：

- 制定可以监测的判断成败的标准，并加入有关自动取消补贴的条款。
- 补贴的对象是特定的经济活动或者既定的技术变革（如低碳技术），而不是产业部门或企业。
- 只给那些具有潜在溢出效应或示范效应的活动提供补贴。
- 通过补贴用户等方式来保持不同创新阶段的企业的竞争，让多家企业争夺业务。
- 鼓励具有持续发展和自我更新潜力的活动，让政府支持的项目带来持续不断的创新循环。

负责执行产业政策的政府机构，如国家发展和改革委员会等，应该尽可能贴近市场，面向私人投资者和顾客建立起沟通和反馈的渠道。

通过这些方式，政府可以帮助企业借鉴和应用新的观念和技术，但政府还应该在更高层次上发挥关键作用，鼓励原创性的研究。在技术和研究的政策领域，中国可以借鉴从其国际经验中总结出来的若干原则。

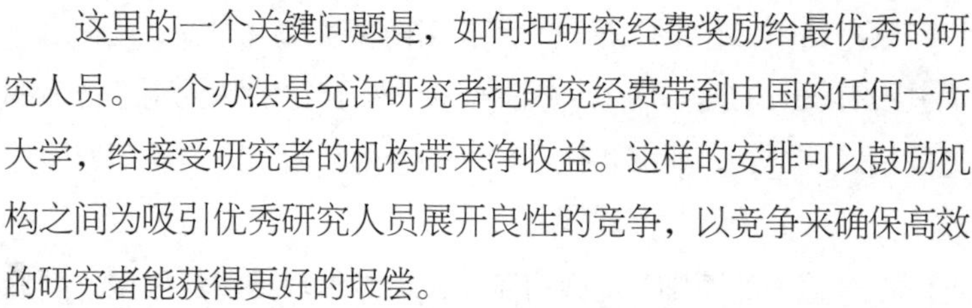

这里的一个关键问题是，如何把研究经费奖励给最优秀的研究人员。一个办法是允许研究者把研究经费带到中国的任何一所大学，给接受研究者的机构带来净收益。这样的安排可以鼓励机构之间为吸引优秀研究人员展开良性的竞争，以竞争来确保高效的研究者能获得更好的报偿。

政府还应该允许一些政府机构将研究任务外包出去。经验表明，政府机构可以资助对某些课题感兴趣的大学，让自己也受益颇多。外包的研究往往比政府机构自己开展的研究更有效率。这一模式还可以调整，让政府机构内部的研究和它们资助的外部研究进行竞争。

然而，政府不应该直接向企业提供研究经费，这一做法的缺陷在美国的清洁汽车创新项目中体现得非常突出。美国政府投入了数亿美元，试图让本国的汽车制造商开发混合能源汽车。但不幸的是，这些企业对于低能耗汽车的开发并不感兴趣，它们的利润主要来自大排量汽车，政府的研究经费无法改变原来的战略方针。如果政府希望实现特定的效果，就应该为相关的行为创造激励。更有效的办法或许是给新技术的消费者提供补贴，而不是给生产者。另一个办法是对没有采用新技术的竞争产品的消费征税（或者不提供补贴）。给企业划拨的研究经费当然对企业有利，但未必有助于政府希望达到的研究或技术目标。

所以，政府在促进新的增长方式上可以扮演关键角色，但资源配置的主要责任应该由金融部门来承担，这是本章后面部分的主题。

投资体制

如果没有强劲的投资率，中国不可能在过去 30 年取得如此高的增长速度。中国为投资而牺牲了部分消费，更看重未来，而非现在。这个困难的选择取得了巨大的成果，被广泛赞许和模仿。

然而，中国的投资率近年来已超过 GDP 的 45%，这在世界历史上前所未有。巨大的投资可以促进增长，但必要的前提是能获得足够的投资回报。有充分证据显示，中国的投资产出率正在衰减。增量资本产出率（Incremental Capital Output Ratios，ICORs）虽然是个不太可靠的指标，但它们也在一定程度上反映出，中国的投资效率已滑落到其他许多国家之下。自 20 世纪 90 年代早期以来，中国的增量资本产出率快速从 3 提高到 5 以上，而国际上的平均水平是 2。其他计量分析也表明，从 90 年代早期以来，资本回报率明显下降。在投资来源于国内储蓄的时候，这会挤压国内消费。由低投资回报创造的总需求不能给增长提供可持续的基础。

30 年的经济改革让供求力量在中国的劳动力市场和产品市场上成为主角，相比之下，市场力量在资本配置上的作用就小得多。[1]中国的固定资产投资有一半来自企业的自有资金，制造业的投资还与企业的流动资金量密切相关，它在很大程度上是未分

---

[1] 国际货币基金组织工作论文：Barnett和Brooks，“What’s Driving Investment in China? ”，2006年11月；以及*OECD Economic Surveys*：*China* 2010，第3章和第4章。

配利润的表现。如果企业有董事会或股东的严格监控，这个问题不会很严重。但严重依赖自有资金与企业治理薄弱的问题结合起来，就会导致自我增强的投资扩张。经理人会将企业留存的利润用于再投资，扩大资产总额与市场份额，而不是集中在创新和生产率改进上。

这个问题之所以越显突出，还有部分原因在于创造性破坏的一个惊人的副作用。许多利润非常丰厚的企业往往没有什么好的投资机会，这对于那些成熟行业或者衰退行业的老牌企业而言尤其如此。相反，投资机会多的企业却可能缺乏现金或资本，尤其是新产业中的创业企业。如果金融体系鼓励企业用利润进行再投资，前一类型的企业就会将大量投资投入回报较低的项目，新创的企业则不能充分利用它们发现的良好机遇。

传统的中央计划经济体制是通过压制消费来维持很高的投资率。30 年改革消除了“短缺经济”的许多特征，但所谓的“投资饥渴”现象还在延续。这样的饥渴来源于对风险的低估（由于软预算约束导致）和对企业规模的追求，规模扩大有助于提高企业、主管部门以及经理人的地位。

在中国，不但企业具有这样的投资饥渴，地方政府和官员们也同样如此。这正是地方政府热衷于绕开对政府借款的限制，利用国有企业开展基础设施投资，依靠银行贷款来提供支持的原因。巨大的投资规模，加上上述各种问题，导致了很多浪费。中国有大量的所谓面子工程的案例，导致了基础设施的重复建设和产能过剩。因此，尽管中央在努力扩大居民消费占 GDP 的份额，但在过去 10 年中，虽然投资回报率有所下降，投资所占据的资源份额却仍在继续提高。

国有企业在投资体制中的作用尤其值得注意，国有企业在经济中的分量在下降，私人企业和外资企业相应提高。但国有企业依然是重要的经济成分，可能会严重拖累整个经济转变发展方式的努力（参见第九章有关国有企业作用的详细讨论）。

资本配置的这些问题可能会随着中国经济增长方式的转变带来更大的影响。在早期的发展阶段，一个国家的产品结构相对简单，可以从许多先进国家那里汲取大量的经验，政府也比较容易发现提高生产率的机会，并将资源相应地引导过来。但随着中国经济复杂性的提高，政府很难将资源引向最好的用途。作出向制造业中哪一家企业进行投资的决策，要远远难于作出向制造业投资而不是向农业投资的决策。

只要投资资金由政府官员和高层经理人员掌控，他们就会倾向于投资那些有影响力的老牌大企业，而不太顾及生产效率。这不仅仅是所有权的问题。其他国家的经验显示，大型私人企业也会受到同样问题的困扰。例如，美国的汽车生产商就把很大一部分利润再投资于维持市场份额的项目，而抵制创新。假设通用汽车公司曾把更多的利润用于分红，而新企业能利用外来资金进行更多的投资，美国的汽车产业今天或许能有更好的结局。其中的关键在于，要确保经理人不能将利润仅仅用于再投资以建造他们的企业“帝国”。

增长方式的转变还要求完全不同的投资体制。需要培育一个独立的金融产业，让它在非国有企业之间乃至国有企业与私人企业之间的资本配置上发挥更大作用。应该根据风险调整后的回报率来引导投资，而不是主要根据哪些主体拥有资金。在某些重要的社会目标未能反映在私人回报上的时候，政府可以并且应该进行干预，改变投资激励。除此以外，则应该让市场评估和市场约束更多地引导投资过程。

以市场为基础的金融体系如果能顺利运行，那么中介机构就可以将居民储蓄和老企业的利润配置到最有前途的投资机会上。

由于金融中介机构在追求最高的回报，它们会努力搜寻那些最有创造性的企业。如果根据对新企业的潜在回报率的真实评估来配置资本，那些现金充裕但缺乏投资机会的企业就不能再无原则地向劣质项目投资。相反，它们的资金应该配置给那些能更好地利用资金的新企业，或者有更高回报的新业务。

当然，正如全球金融危机的案例所示，市场自身也可能犯重大错误。我们一方面认为中国应该让市场（包括金融市场）在资本配置方面发挥更大的作用，另一方面也相信应该对这些市场进行严格监管。或者说，中国应该将更多的投资交给市场，但不能对这些市场放任不管。有关的规范和监督将是下一节探讨的主题。

金融部门的发展

在市场经济中，金融部门是主要的控制中心：通过资产价格、利率和制度规范，引导资源在各种用途之间的配置。如果金融体系运行良好，整个经济都能获益，达到更高的生产率、增长和就业水平。同理，如果金融体系运行不佳，甚至完全停止运行，则会给更广泛的经济领域造成普遍打击。

高度发达的金融体系包含多个部分，这需要进行专门研究。下文是个概述：中国为促进增长方式的转变，需要对金融部门开展哪些关键的改革。我们还会讨论金融危机的情况以及从中获取的教训。

金融部门依然是中国经济中发展相对滞后的部分，即使与拉丁美洲和南亚的中等收入国家相比，情况也是如此。银行并不是产业投资的最适合的长期资本来源，还需要更多地培育股票市场和其他股权投资工具，如私募股权市场等。中国还需要扩大固定收益类型的金融工具的范围，让企业可以谨慎地使用财务杠杆。尽管近期推出了一些措施，但对中小企业和农村企业而言，信贷依然很难获得。公司债券市场虽已经有所扩大，但发行量相对而言还是太小。

如果中国的实体经济将走向以生产率为驱动、以知识为基础的增长方式，金融体系也必须进行相应的改造。其他国家的经验显示，金融部门可以帮助整个经济进入技能更复杂、更为多样性的经济活动。

中国的金融体系不但必须跟上本国经济的步伐，还要适应世界环境的变化。麦肯锡全球研究院最近的一项研究指出，全球廉价资本的时代即将终结。随着新兴经济体的成长以及投资率的提高，它们的资本支出将抵消发达国家的投资率下降。这将足以提高世界市场上的资本成本。简单地说，对储蓄的竞争会加剧。当然，中国是净资本输出国，再加上监管措施的帮助，受世界资本市场的影响不大。但随着全球资本成本的上升，本国投资的机会成本也必然提高。结果导致，资本的配置效率问题将显得愈加重要。金融部门必须被列入中长期发展的优先议题。

储蓄

要让中国的金融体系促进增长方式转变，就需要迅速开发出几个关键的功能。包括提供更丰富的储蓄工具，它们有合适的风险回报率，能鼓励谨慎的投资行为。共同基金的广泛出现也可以让中国的储户们受益，给他们提供除存款和房地产之外的投资选择。如果居民家庭拥有品种更为多样的股票和固定收益投资工具，他们面对的风险就能更好地分散。

不寻常的是，增加储户的收益还具有减少多余储蓄的附加效果。居民从储蓄和投资中得到的回报率提高后，就不需要将那么多的钱节余下来实现储蓄目标（例如，应付退休或者医疗开支等）。储户的回报率提高还可能具有减少轻率投资的第二附加效果，例如在目前的金融体系下，许多焦虑的储户在房地产投机中追求更高的回报，承担了太大的风险。

公司金融

除了提供广泛的储蓄工具外，金融体系还必须更好地引导资本流向各种规模和各个产业的新企业和成长中的企业。在早期发展阶段，银行是主要的融资来源，债务是主要的融资工具。随着国民经济转向更高附加价值的活动，服务业的成长，更多自有技术的开发，原来的金融体系的结构也需要改变。

在目前所处的发展阶段，中国可以从私募股权的资本和专业运作中获得巨大收益。私募股权包括为创业企业服务的风险资本，还包括帮助企业成长、家族企业所有权改造以及创办新服务的其他各类投资。私募股权投资机构需要对特定的产业和部门有深入了解，才能发挥作用，这些专长需要时间来积累。但政策制定者们应该借鉴国际经验，通过适当的监管和报告要求来鼓励该私募股权的发展。

为了推动这个进程，中国应该鼓励外国投资公司的加入，就像历史上对外国直接投资开放市场一样。当然，中国吸引外国资本的出发点不必是寻求资金，因为国内储蓄已经足以应付投资需要。但风险投资和私募股权投资通常与各类专业技能紧密结合，可以帮助很多产业领域（从农业到生物医药，再到环保产业等）的企业成长。苹果、太阳微系统、思科、谷歌、英特尔、甲骨文以及其他许多成功的企业，包括中国的几家新技术公司（如百度等），都得到过风险资本的帮助。“重新发明轮子”虽然可以，但更有效率的做法是有鉴别地从其他地方的成功经验中学习。

客观地说，中国在风险投资和私募股权投资领域的制度和能力建设上，已经取得了快速进步，吸引了大批外国私募股权投资经理与为数众多的国内公司开展合作和竞争。这些企业在募集资金方面没有什么困难：中国已经有足够多的财富供它们发展。挑战在于确保法律、监管和制度上的支持措施能跟上。60 年前，美国的风险投资还主要是少数富裕个人和家庭给创业企业提供的直接投资，但随着规模和范围的扩大，就需要设立新型的更大机构了。中国也会出现类似的模式。

为支持中国的经济转型，还需要其他一些金融部门的发展。中国将需要规模更大、流动性更好的债券市场，包括地方政府为支持城市的快速发展而发行的市政债券市场。土地出让可以作为城市基础设施的过渡性办法，但不能可持续地提供长期资金。与其他领域一样，这个市场的发展也需要法律和监管制度。

中国的银行监管者在培育银行与客户之间的“信用文化”方面取得了进步，但政府和其他公共机构，尤其是地方层级的机构，仍然对借贷决策发挥着影响力。在改革过程中，中国需要努力使银行的信贷决策摆脱非经济因素的干扰。如果中国的资本市场能更好地发展，银行监管者的任务可能会轻松一些。市场能在银行的监督和审核方面给监管者提供补充，通过卖出银行的股份或者购买其债券的信贷违约掉期产品，对银行的经营施加压力。

这些都是非常艰巨的任务，在行动中，中国无疑可以广泛借鉴其他国家的专业知识和经验教训，包括外资企业以及在华合资企业的人才和知识。当然，最终还是要靠自己的方式来应对这些挑战。

金融危机的教训

近年来的全球金融危机起源于发达国家（尤其是美国），揭

示了市场监管方面的若干错误和疏漏。危机爆发前，许多监管者相信金融机构可以比较准确地判断它们承受的大多数风险，因此金融体系具有自我监管的性质。这个看法目前已经被更为积极的监管思路所取代。但正在建设中的新监管体系还没有经过检验，在一段时期之内，我们并不清楚其实际效果如何。因此，危机的一些教训还需要时间来发掘。

但是，其他一些教训能直接看到。危机证明，不受审核的金融部门创新加上不够充分的政府监管，可能产生一个脆弱的金融体系，私人部门债务过重，资产价格膨胀，很容易导致灾难性的后果。这些教训说明，中国应该培养金融机构强大的风险管理能力，建立足够的资本准备。这方面已经取得了很多进展，尤其是银行、保险和证券业监管部门的工作。

中国还可以考虑一种新提出的银行模式的作用。在这个模式中，一部分银行体系被隔离起来并受到严格监管。这些银行提供有限类型的服务，例如存款和储蓄账户等，保留有限类型的安全资产。它们专注于金融部门的几个重要功能，包括支付体系以及一定范围内的信贷中介（将存款转化为贷款）等，但不参与自营交易，不得动用自己的资金进行投机。

这个模式的目的是，让信贷中介免受市场完全崩溃的风险冲击。在本次危机中，发达国家只是凭借迅速的非常规干预手段（主要通过中央银行），才极为艰难地避免了系统性的崩溃，是一次极其惊险的经历。新提议的银行模式将一部分银行体系排除在大多数财务损失风险之外，给金融体系建造了防波堤，保证在金融体系的其他部分出现问题之后，至少还有某些信贷渠道仍保持畅通。在某些方面，中国目前的政策实践与这个建议的模式有相似之处。但中国的商业银行还缺乏正式的存款保险机制，随着经济的发展，或许需要政府来填补这个缺口。

资产证券化在金融危机的总结中广受诟病。危机揭示了复杂的证券化资产的危险，它们对风险的评估很不准确，缺乏监管控制，美国和欧洲对“影子银行系统”（shadow banking system）的监管措施都很少。但中国不应该就此认为所有的证券化都不好。实际上，有严格监管的资产证券化是银行贷款的有效替代工具，应该按可控的步骤加以鼓励，与监管能力的培养保持平行或者稍有超前。对中国而言，这可能意味着目前应该把证券化产品限制在普通掉期交易的范围内。

衍生工具可以发挥分散和重新配置风险的作用，但也是金融部门各机构的资产状况相互联系如此紧密的一个原因。我们认为，客观地说，在衍生工具的监管方面目前还没有设计较为完善、得到一致认可的模式，只能期待未来。在此之前，中国的最好策略应该是谨慎前行，主要关注在有监管的交易所中买卖和结算的简单合同。

与此相关的一个主题是系统性风险和审慎监管。本次危机暴露了传统的审慎监管思路的局限，它主要关注个别银行和中介机构所出现的问题征兆，并且逐个分别进行处理。不幸的是，在看似个体状况不错的金融机构的相互作用中，也可能突然产生危险。为了检测和预防这些系统性风险，许多国家如今设立了宏观经济或系统性监管机构。中国也应该采纳这种做法。可以创建一个专门负责的机构，或指派现有的监管机构之一（或中国人民银行）作为系统性监管人，或创立一个包含所有相关监管机构的综合委员会。但不管责任如何安排，不同监管机构之间的合作都是必需的。

就像银行和资本市场逐渐扩张到全球范围一样，金融监管也应该完美地覆盖所有国家。否则，金融机构会将业务转移到监管最为宽松的国家，这被称为监管套利行为。但实际上，各个国家必须建立符合自身条件的金融体系。例如，发达国家的监管主要考虑资本标准问题，而许多发展中国家则还需要建立必要的法律和会计规范，能够让资本标准发挥作用。

即使在发达国家中，监管原则和实际操作也存在很大的差异。中国的监管者可以从它们的不同中比较、学习。特别是，最近可以关注加拿大金融业（在近年来运转良好）和美国金融业（表现相当糟糕）的差异。

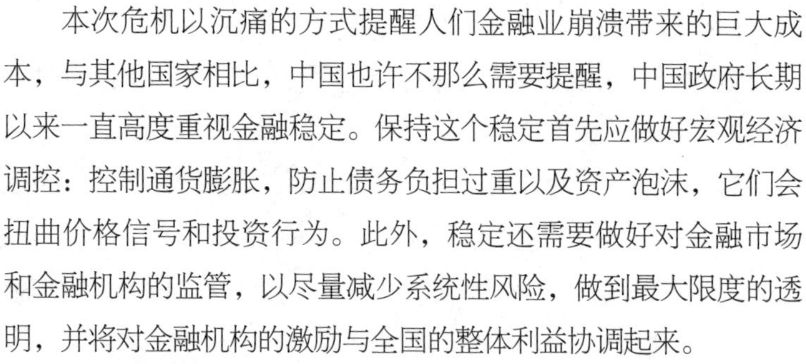

本次危机以沉痛的方式提醒人们金融业崩溃带来的巨大成本，与其他国家相比，中国也许不那么需要提醒，中国政府长期以来一直高度重视金融稳定。保持这个稳定首先应做好宏观经济调控：控制通货膨胀，防止债务负担过重以及资产泡沫，它们会扭曲价格信号和投资行为。此外，稳定还需要做好对金融市场和金融机构的监管，以尽量减少系统性风险，做到最大限度的透明，并将对金融机构的激励与全国的整体利益协调起来。

尽管金融稳定是中国发展的必要条件，却不是充分条件。特别是，稳定不代表僵化。对于一个追求快速增长并在转变增长模式的国家而言，必须允许金融部门开展创新，找到更好的办法来引导储蓄，充分利用各种活跃的投资机会。原则上说，一个有效运转的金融市场可以帮助达到理想的储蓄水平，实现最佳的投资分配。随着经济复杂程度的提高，政府的资源配置能力将不足以应对，金融市场的功能就显得越来越重要。

全球金融危机使西方国家金融中心的监管者们陷入了质疑和混乱，而中国的发展方向却相当清晰。一个急迫的任务仍然是促进金融体系的继续发展和谨慎的自由化，使其成为动员储蓄、分散风险、为越来越多样化的企业配置资本的主要工具。

第三章　城市和地区发展*

中国取得的巨大经济进步在很大程度上应归功于成功打破了国内对劳动力、资本和商品流动的各种限制。由于这些流动的扩大，中国最近的发展显示出一个特有的空间模式。简单地说，人员和投资向城市和沿海转移，而且这个增长模式仍有很大空间。2008年，城市常住人口还只占全国人口的46%，而收入水平接近的国家一般为55%，发达国家则是70%~85%。[1]经济学理论和国际经验都肯定，城市化对经济增长具有极为重要的意义，因为制造业和服务业生产在城市进行更有效率，同时城市还是促进创新和发展复杂技能的主要基地。

因此，一个很重要的启示是，政府要鼓励实现快速而健康的城市化。城市发展必须基于对基础设施和公共服务的投资，中国的城市建设已经达到相当高的水平，还需要进一步提高。中国必须采取措施改善治理水平，包括公共财政、发展统一的国内市场（视其为全国性的公共品），并培育城市之间的良性竞争。同样重要的还有禁止保护主义和地方优惠等不利于竞争的行为。

* 本章主要参考了背景论文十一：弗农·亨德森，《中国的城市化：面临的问题及政策选择》；背景论文十：樊胜根、拉维·坎布尔和张晓波，《中国的地区差距：经验和政策》。

❶ 背景论文十一：弗农·亨德森，《中国的城市化：面临的问题及政策选择》。

为做到这些，并确保城市化的高效完成，政府还需要解决目前在地区发展过程中出现的若干问题，包括：

- 城乡收入差距太大，并远高于其他处于类似发展阶段的国家。
- 中国城市的规模和经济结构缺乏效率：中等规模的城市不够多，城市经济缺乏专业化分工。
- 城市的土地利用缺乏效率，城区边缘的开发过于碎片化。
- 城市的财政和管理能力不足。
- 地区之间的收入和发展水平差异大。

缩小城乡之间的收入差距

在过去 30 年中，中国各地的居民家庭收入都有所提高，但城市和沿海地区的涨幅最为显著。目前，城乡之间的收入差距很大：2008 年，城市的人均收入相当于农村的 3.3 倍，如果把对城市居民更有利的政府补贴考虑进来，差距会更大。这个数字远高于其他亚洲国家。理论和其他国家的经验表明，在目前的发展阶段，这个差距本应缩小，但实际上仍在继续扩大——1995 年的城乡收入差距是 2.8 倍。[1] 为了缩小城乡收入差距并提高总体的生产率，中国需要通过进一步整合劳动力市场，让人们可以更方便地转移到生产率最高的地方，完成从农村向城市的就业转移。中国必须增加对劳动力的投资，尤其是帮助来到城市的农民工和仍然留在农村的人，另外还必须提高农业的生产率。

---

[1] World Bank, "From Poor Areas to Poor People: China's Evolving Poverty Reduction Agenda", 2009: 35.

关键之处在于，政府要设法减少影响富余劳动力从农村向城市转移的障碍。在过去，从农村向城市移民曾受到户口制度的严格限制。近年来这一制度有所放松，转移速度也在加快。如今，每年有 500 万 ~700 万人进入城镇，总的移民人数已达 1.5 亿，其中只有 1200 万人是不参加工作的家庭成员。[1]政府最近决定进一步放宽中小城市的永久居住限制，这是正确的改革方向，尤其有利于城市化率较低、中小城市比例较高的地区。为鼓励更多移民，政府现在应该考虑将这一改革推广到较大的城市，甚至包括直辖市。中央政府、省级政府以及城市管理者都需要认识到，中国正在发生的移民几乎都是永久性的，而且很多人希望与家庭成员一起迁移，迫切需要正确的激励机制鼓励城市增加永久居民的人数，并给他们提供必要的公共服务。

增加对农村劳动者、农民工及其子女的教育和培训投入会获得很高的回报。与处于类似发展阶段的其他国家相比，中国的劳动力教育水平较高。来自农村的大多数移民都接受过初中及以上水平的学校教育，这是中国的优势之一，其他发展中国家很少能够做到。中国需要继续保持和提高在教育方面的良好纪录，并给农民工提供更多的职业培训，让他们的子女能进入城市中条件较好的学校。中国还需要将农民工家庭纳入医疗和社保体制，社保体制应该在范围上更多实现全国性覆盖，保证城乡居民的福利都能转移携带。农民工还应该得到《劳动合同法》和其他劳动法规的公平对待。

中国和其他国家共同面临的一个挑战是如何防止贫民区的蔓

[1] World Bank，"From Poor Areas to Poor People：China's Evolving Poverty Reduction Agenda"，2009。其中的第五章第e小节有更多关于农村向城市移民的规模估计。

延，在改善农民工和其他贫困家庭的生活条件的同时，不用给移民提供间接补贴。政府有责任帮助移民摆脱困难和贫穷，但改变移民处境的措施也会产生负面效果——吸引更多的移民到来。解决这个矛盾并不轻松，例如，中国香港和新加坡通过公共住房防止了贫民区的出现，但两个地方都对外来移民有严格限制。

对中国来说，政府应该慎重考虑是否直接卷入提供公共住房事务，而更多依靠其他政策。[1]例如，可以设法振兴大多数农民工目前居住的城中村，将其纳入城市的行政管理体系，鼓励建筑翻新，给这些区域的企业提供税收优惠，改善那里的公共服务质量等。政府需要小心，不要破坏这些城中村现有的住房市场。这些市场的运转状况不错，让许多农民工以能够负担的价格租到了合适的房屋。将城中村纳入城市的行政管理体系能够加强业主和租户的产权，给他们更多的安全感。通过这些措施就足以促进当地住房市场的发展，甚至不需要政府做更多努力。政府另外应该考虑鼓励在现有城区修建廉租住房，例如将土地出让给容积率较高的小区开发商。

另一个思路是针对人群而非针对地区。例如，政府可以给那些拥有土地、希望改善住房条件的家庭提供小额住房贷款（shelter microfinance）。还有，通过住房补贴或住房券鼓励农民工从城中村转移到租金更昂贵的城区。当然这样的改革必须和其他措施配套，以鼓励城区正规租房市场的发展。政府需要仔细甄别政策对象，以免部分较富裕的农民工占有太多福利。户口制度的放松本身就很有可能刺激对城中村以外的廉价住房的需求。当然，针对地区的政策和针对人群的政策并不相互排斥，可以结合起来

❶ 本节参考了背景论文二十：伊夫·泽诺，《中国的住房政策：面临的问题和选择》。

实施。政府还需要重视试点，在实践中研究分析私人部门能否满足市场需求的明显增加，有哪些障碍，然后采取措施来解决障碍。

调整城市的规模和经济结构

中国的城市化模式效率不高，包括城市规模分布不够合理和城市专业分工不足。通常来说，在城市化的早期阶段，最大的城市往往是引领者，成为新技术引进、消化和改进的中心。随着发展的深入，制造业技术逐渐标准化，使工业生产能分散到劳动力和土地成本较低的中小城市。由此会逐渐形成一个城市梯级体系。中小规模的城市会高度专注于特定产业的生产，例如钢铁、纺织和服装、木制品、保险、医疗乃至娱乐行业等。这样的专业分工可以让它们充分利用当地的规模经济效应并收获其他很多好处。例如，当地可以汇聚大量有经验的员工和专业化的供应商，可以从一家企业或一个产业对其他企业和产业发挥外溢效应。规模更大的城市的经济类型较为多样化，包括更高层次的服务、流通、创新和复杂制造业，那里的产业内部和产业之间的规模经济非常重要。在发达国家，规模最大的城市（纽约、伦敦、东京等）几乎没有制造业，它们在各国的金融和商业服务中占据举足轻重的地位。

中国的城市化模式与上述国际经验有所不同。经济改革初期，移民现象主要是在本地发生（离土不离乡）。近年来，更多的移民是跨省流动，从中部和西南部的省市流向沿海城市。中国目前人口规模在 100 万~1200 万的城市的数量不够多，许多地级市的人口规模仅为有效规模的一半（见图 3-1）。有研究表明，地级市的人口规模如果翻番，有望使单位员工的实际产出增加

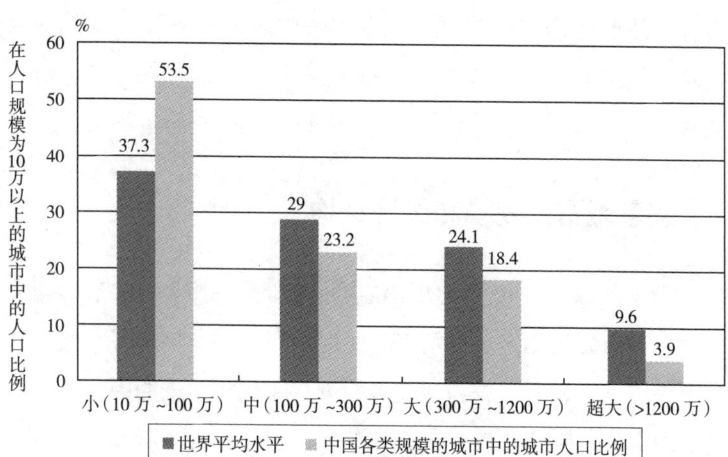

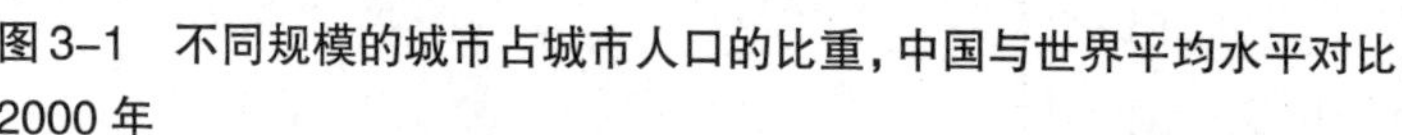

图 3–1　不同规模的城市占城市人口的比重，中国与世界平均水平对比，2000 年

资料来源：背景论文十一：弗农·亨德森，（中国的城市化：面临的问题及政策选择》，包含 10 万人口以上的城市。

20%~35%。[1] 资本市场（以及更高层级政府的行政活动）也更有利于规模最大的直辖市。虽然这些城市的投资回报率不及其他城市，但人均外国投资和固定资产投资都明显高于其他城市。[2] 许多城市尽管在制造业上没有什么比较优势，当地企业的经营规模也普遍偏小，却依然对制造业倾注了大量心力，而忽略了促进服务业的繁荣。

为解决上述问题，政府需要建立公平的竞争环境，让市场力量尽可能发挥作用。避免出台偏向于特定的城市规模或特定的城市发展模式的行政措施。在政府必须进行干预的时候，应该保证

[1] 背景论文十一：弗农·亨德森，《中国的城市化：面临的问题及政策选择》。

[2] 背景论文十一：弗农·亨德森，《中国的城市化：面临的问题及政策选择》。

公平，尽量减少对城市专业分工和效率的扭曲。

应该取消那些给劳动力市场、资本市场和商品市场造成扭曲的政策，让经济力量发挥作用。中国目前的资本市场和财政政策都有利于那些规模最大的城市（见表 3–1），如果这种偏向不能得到扭转，那么上文所建议的放宽移民限制的任何措施，都可能导致人口过度流向超大城市。为了避免超大城市的人口过于拥挤，中国应该帮助那些行政层级较低的城市吸引投资和劳动力，为此需要继续开放资本市场，让所有的企业、城市和乡村能自由竞争金融资源。这样的改革还可以确保资本流向回报最好的项目，而不是政治上最受眷顾的领域，从而促进经济增长。中国还必须防止地方保护主义，禁止市政府及地方机构通过歧视性标准、收费和其他措施来维护地方利益，这样的保护主义妨碍了城市之间的专业化分工，而专业化分工对生产率的提高至关重要。

表 3–1 资本投资去向

	人均外国直接投资额(美元，户籍人口)：2002—2007 年	人均固定资产投资额（元）：2002—2007 年	第二产业占 GDP 的比重：2007 年
直辖市（4）	3850	122500	42%
省会城市（26）	2060	98900	44%
其他地级市（238）	1570	64000	56%
县级市（367）	980	24400	54%

资料来源：《城市年鉴》（Urban Year Books，China：Data Online）。地级和以上级别的城市的数据代表城区。

其他不利于城市化空间布局效率的限制也需要取消。特大城市的天然经济基础是商业服务业和金融业。然而在中国，这些产

业虽然增长迅速，但规模依旧较小。广告业等行业最近才从政府控制下解放出来，而法律和金融服务业等依然处于政府的严格管制之中。只有在这些现代服务业得到进一步发展之后，中国才能发展出可以与东京、伦敦和纽约相媲美的超级城市。

尽管大城市的天然经济基础是服务业，但中国的许多大城市却借助自己的权力和资源，在吸引制造业方面享有不平等的优势。即使这些城市已到达应更多地专注于服务业发展的阶段，它们依旧在发掘制造业方面的优势。还有，由于过去的教育训练和工作背景，很多城市的政府领导也往往倾向于发展制造业。继续挽留制造业的原因还包括制造业可以给城市带来增值税收入，即使服务业也能提供营业税收入。如果中国的城市希望实现更合适的规模和经济结构，就必须对城市的行政管理层级体制、政府官员的思维理念以及市政府的财政模式等进行变革。

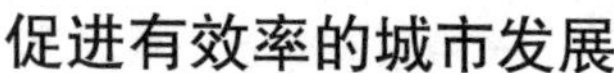

促进有效率的城市发展

城市内部联系紧密，劳动、商品、服务和信息可以迅速流通，这些交流极大地促进了城市经济的生产率的提高。历史上，中国城市的人口密度一直远高于如今的发达国家的城市。然而现在，中国新城区建设中执行的若干政策和办法对城市密度产生了消极影响。中国城市的外围区域碎片化现象越来越严重，未纳入城市行政管理的城中村四处延伸，大部分没有户口的农民工都租住在那里。城市周边的建成区又散布在农用土地中间，由于对农业用地转作其他用途有极其严格的配额限制，这些土地的开发很难顺利开展。工业企业正在从中心城区迁置到城市周边的新型工业园区，周边新开发的城镇对土地使用密度缺乏重视。限制市内的建筑密度的做法也降低了土地利用率，导致城区的平面延伸。此外，土地利用和基础设施建设之间缺乏配合，导致通勤时间和成本上升，土地消耗量超过了必要水平。这样的平面蔓延和分割开发现象一旦扎下根来，将很难逆转，由此带来的基础设施建设成本、通勤时间和污染程度的上升会逐渐吞噬城市的生产率。所以，中国需要将这个问题的解决列入紧急议程，加强产权保护，促进土地市场的竞争，并改进土地利用的规划。

城市边缘的土地定价是需要紧急处理的重要问题。目前，城市开发并没有为征用的农用土地负担真实成本，相反，市政府以很低的价格从农民和村庄手里购买土地，大幅加价后卖给开发商，从中获取了大笔利润。这样的套利机会给地方政府带来了巨大的动力，诱使各地积极征用农村土地，恶化了城市蔓延现象。中国亟须抓紧时机对此加以遏制。

目前，地方政府面临的约束主要来自上级的指示，但这些指示的效果有限。更重要的约束应该是加强农村的产权保护，让农民和村庄获得的补偿能尽可能反映土地的市场价值。2008 年 10 月作出的将土地承包期限从 30 年延长到不确定年限的决定，是中央政府决心加强农民土地保障的明确信号。不过这方面还需要更深入的措施，政府应该引进一套对农村土地按地块登记的制度，给农民提供土地权利证明。这些可以借鉴越南的经验，那里的土地制度安排与中国相似。此外还应该保证土地租赁权可以完全转让和出售，并确保任何村级土地交易不但要得到村领导的认可，还要得到地块所涉及的相关村民的同意。

城市土地市场的效率需要提高。开发商目前通过政府组织的土地出让来获得城市土地，出让方式必须保持公开、透明和公正，让开发商为项目支付包括必要的基础设施在内的真实成本，如可以采取开放式的英国式拍卖[1]的办法。另外还应该让工业、商业和住房项目的开发商能够在平等的基础上竞价。通过逐渐努力，这些变革会产生更为真实的土地定价，从而制约工业用地的过度开发。更高的土地拍卖价格还可以促使某些工业活动分散到较小的城市，政府应该考虑用税收优惠等财政刺激手段来鼓励国有企业的土地再开发。

改善城市规划至关重要。即使那些高度尊重市场规律的国家也对土地市场制定了规划法规，这些法规限制了地块的用途，规定了建筑的密度。中国目前对土地利用有总体规划（一般称为城市规划方案），但这样的规划需要获得更强的法律效力，或许可以要求通过地方人大的审批。同样重要的是，这些规划应该显示地块的容积率的许可范围，政府可以利用容积率的许可范围将城市发展引导到预定的位置，例如，靠近公共交通枢纽的地段可以允许更高的容积率，以鼓励集约化。中国还应该采取更广泛的地区规划来促进城市发展，主要是加强城市周边的规划设计，并最终将城中村纳入城市的行政管理体系。这种一体化可以通过若干途径来实现：允许对城市周边范围内的农村地块进行开发，而不需要占用土地指标；处理好交通基础设施和住房建设的次序，在干道基础设施建成后才允许周边的住房和其他建设项目的开发。各个城市还必须改进规划的设计和执行能力，包括培训城市规划和交通规划的专业人员等。

最后，城市需要新的财政收入来源。以上讨论的各项措施都能帮助改进城市的土地利用效率，但要说服当局作出这些改变

[1] 英国式拍卖或许是最常见的拍卖形式，从较低价格起拍，报价逐渐提高，直至拍卖时间结束或者没有更高报价出现为止。卖方通常会确定一个保留价格，若报价低于保留价格，则拍卖会被放弃。

却依旧困难，除非市政府能找到土地出让收入以外的其他收入来源。中国还需要开展相应的城市财政和管理制度改革，这是下节的焦点。

改革城市的财政和管理制度

没有哪个国家在处理快速城市化方面有特别出色的记录，与其他国家相比，中国迄今为止做得并不坏。然而，随着城市化进程的加速，中国必须对城市管理制度进行深入改革，包括重新安排城市财政结构、重新确定政府官员的职责，并对城市区域的行政管理层级进行改革。

中国的城市政府和基层政府必须减少对土地出让收入的依赖。中国的城市过于依赖土地出让作为收入来源，由任期相对短暂的政府官员来负责城市的长期资产（土地）出售，以此维持经常性支出（以及部分资本性支出），这样做等于剥夺了未来的市民可以从这些资产中获得的收入。这是一颗潜在的“定时炸弹”，急需排除。作为公共财政改革的一部分，土地出让收入应该仅用于资本性支出，长期资产的出售应该与资产的购置相匹配。还有，即使是资本性支出也应该减少对土地出让的依赖，开发其他来源，例如在中央政府或省级政府的严密监督下发行城市债券（若干发展中国家采用了这个办法），或者由中央划拨转移支付。

对住房和商业房产开征从价房产税（ad valorem property tax）将是一大进步。目前，中国的城市财政收入主要来自增值税和营业税以及土地出让收入，它们都鼓励城市吸引产业而不是吸引居民。对住处征收房产税不但有利于增加地方收入，还能鼓励城市接纳更多的居民。类似的还有，对商业地产征收房产税将鼓励良性的行为转变，促使企业节约使用土地和空间。此类税收将更好地反映商业地产需要的交通、排污和电力等公共服务的成本，通过支付房产税，受益于这些服务的业主会负担更多的供给成本。

房产税将会降低出让土地对潜在买房人的价值，因为房地产要负担未来的税收。因此，地方政府从土地出让中获得的收入会下降，但这个下降将带来经常性财政收入的有利转变——从资产出售收入更多地转向经常性收入。政府还可以希望将土地出让期限永久化，以此作为对引入房产税的补偿。房产税在执行时不会有太大的难度，从价房产税要求对产权进行登记，以及建立一套公正的房产评估体系，但并不意味着需要成本昂贵的土地清册系统。一个按区域计征的类似于英国的市政税（council tax）就能满足需要。

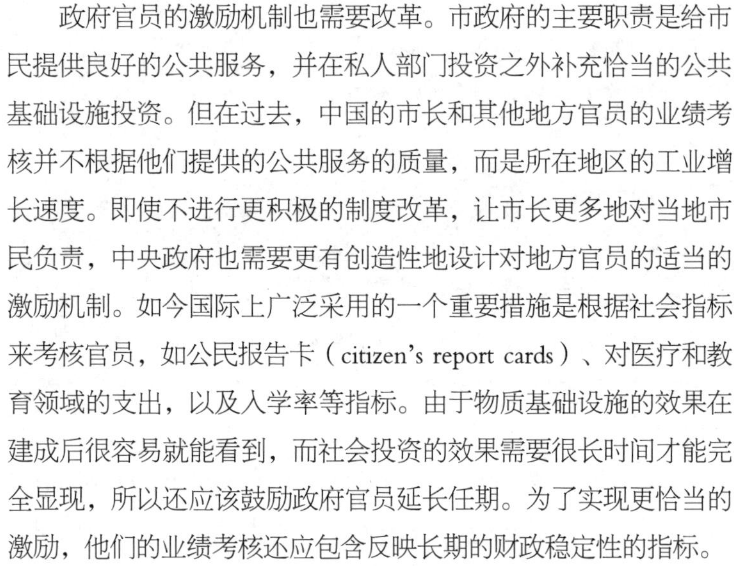

政府官员的激励机制也需要改革。市政府的主要职责是给市民提供良好的公共服务，并在私人部门投资之外补充恰当的公共基础设施投资。但在过去，中国的市长和其他地方官员的业绩考核并不根据他们提供的公共服务的质量，而是所在地区的工业增长速度。即使不进行更积极的制度改革，让市长更多地对当地市民负责，中央政府也需要更有创造性地设计对地方官员的适当的激励机制。如今国际上广泛采用的一个重要措施是根据社会指标来考核官员，如公民报告卡（citizen's report cards）、对医疗和教育领域的支出，以及入学率等指标。由于物质基础设施的效果在建成后很容易就能看到，而社会投资的效果需要很长时间才能完全显现，所以还应该鼓励政府官员延长任期。为了实现更恰当的激励，他们的业绩考核还应包含反映长期的财政稳定性的指标。

最后，很关键的一点是要允许较小的城市在更平等的基础上同大城市竞争。在目前的体制下，层级较低的城市由层级较高的城市主管。层级较高的城市在决策制定上有更大的自主权，掌握着更多的财政资源，还享有更靠近交通走廊和铁路等优势。这种层级关系应该改革。中国需要在目前的一些试点项目的基础上继续推进，使得每个城市，不论其规模大小，都应该在明确规定的若干领域内享有完全的自主权，并让所有的城镇享有相同的税基、税收工具、优惠政策，执行统一的政府间转移公式，以及承担相同的支出责任。当然，规模较小的城市需要更长的时间才能充分利用各种财政工具（如市政债券等），因此在过渡时期，可以靠政府间财政补助的公式设计，使它们能与较大的城市平等竞争。

缩小地区差异

如第二章所述，进入中等收入国家向更高阶段的转型进程后，可供中国借鉴的模式不多了。历史上只有两个规模较大的国家（日本和韩国）比较顺利地完成了这个转型，它们都是同质化程度相对很高的国家，而中国的经济发展高度多样化，各地处于非常不同的经济发展阶段。实际上，可以把中国视为三个人均收入水平差别极大的经济体的综合体：农村经济，仍然以农业为主，存在数量极多的就业不足的劳动力；低工资的出口导向型沿海经济，它引领了过去 20 年的经济增长：新兴的生产率驱动的知识经济，它将在未来数十年引领中国向高收入国家迈进。中国的宏观经济政策组合必须在这三个不同的经济体的截然不同的需要中寻求平衡，例如，对新兴的知识经济适合的汇率和工资政策可能并不适用于出口导向经济或农村经济。

中国贫困的内地农业区的持续存在，意味着追赶式增长的机遇还没有耗尽，这对中国的宏观经济前景是件好事，但差距同时也是建设和谐社会的一大障碍。从经济学理论和国际经验中可以发现，单靠经济力量似乎难以消灭这些差距。为了解决仍然存在的不平等问题，许多国家引入了各种地区发展政策，它们试图给同一个问题提供不同的答案："是应该把人迁置到有工作的地方，还是把工作转移到人们所在的地方？"这并不是一个简单的技术问题，不是简单地比较不同政策工具的成本和收益。答案还取决于地区发展政策希望具体实现的目标。例如在欧盟，地区发展政策既关注落后国家，也关注各国内部的落后地区，既承认需要放宽移民限制，让人们可以自由地寻求新的工作，但也明确肯定维持落后地区生存能力的必要性，这就要求把工作岗位转移到当地的居民手里。

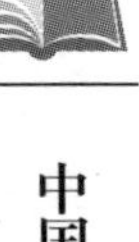

在中国，任何旨在缩小地区差异、促进从中等收入国家向高收入国家转型的战略，都应该把提高农业生产率和农村收入作为基本内容之一。由于我们团队的各国经济学家对农业领域没有深入研究，因此本报告没有对该产业进行详细讨论，但农业对中国的未来发展依旧具有基础性作用。农民工在城市的工作通常能获得比农业更大的产出，因此随着更多劳动力从农村转移到城市，总体的生产率水平必然提高（即使城市的生产率出现降低）。事实上，研究显示，农业劳动力向非农产业转移每增加 1%，全国的 GDP 就能提高 0.9%。[1]

随着劳动力离开人手太多的农村，农业生产率将会提高。人们的离开将带来机遇，将传统的小块土地的自耕农业改造成大规模农业，由受过良好教育的高技能劳动力完成。韩国是成功完成这一转变的范例。在过去 30 年中，韩国的土地所有权被集中起

[1] Au and Henderson, "How Migration Restrictions Limit Agglomeration and Productivity in China", *Journal of Development Economics*, 2006a.

来，农场主、受过良好教育的年轻农业劳动力、机械化农场和新的农业技术大量出现。2005 年，韩国的农业人口仅相当于 1975 年的 26%，农业用地减少了 16%，产量却提高了 61%。[1] 要想复制这一成果，中国需要加强农村的产权保护，对金融业进行改革，以促进更多的农业投资（近来的一些研究显示，中国城市的资本每向农村转移 1%，全国的 GDP 就能提高 0.5%[2]）。中国还需要改进教育，因为受教育程度更高的农民将更能接受新的知识，更懂得分析市场形势，有针对性地选择作物和投入。

在考虑引入任何新的特殊政策去帮助落后地区时，很重要的一点是，政府应首先取消阻碍这些地区发展的政策。关系若干重要的公共服务（如基础教育、医疗、用水和卫生等）的政策，在设计时应该打破区域界限并做到覆盖全国。

中国需要纠正土地、劳动力、资本和产品市场上的各种扭曲，这意味着一个重大改变，扭转过去执行的向沿海地区倾斜的优惠政策。这方面的改革应完成实现全国经济一体化的任务，既鼓励人们迁移到发展机遇更多的地方，也鼓励企业在最有经济效益的地方设点。其实，这些改革并不需要更多的财政投入，跨省的人员转移本身就可以成为重要的活力来源。改革还能让富裕省市引入更多处于最佳工作年龄段的年轻移民，从而抵消自然提高的抚养率，同时会给来自贫困省市的农村劳动力带来就业机会，他们可以在获得更高的收入后把钱汇回老家。

基础设施对克服距离因素至关重要。与其他很多国家一样，

---

[1] 背景论文十一：弗农·亨德森，《中国的城市化：面临的问题及政策选择》。

[2] Au and Henderson, "How Migration Restrictions Limit Agglomeration and Productivity in China", *Journal of Development Economics*, 2006a.

中国采取了加快落后地区基础设施建设的战略，并取得了一定的成功，一个特别的案例是中国的西部大开发战略，该战略尤其重视公路和铁路建设。中国的地区差异自21世纪头10年的中期以来保持稳定，甚至出现缩小迹象，西部大开发战略看来是一个重要原因。其他一些投资也取得了显著成效，例如对落后地区的农村的通信和电网投资等。对教育的投资或许有更大的回报，既能促进增长，也有助于扶贫。因此，中国显然应该继续强调对贫困地区的基础设施（以及社会项目）的投资。不过，也需要更仔细地分析在特定的地区、哪些特定类型的基础设施建设的回报最高。还有，在非常偏远的地区，基础设施投资的边际回报可能会随着成本增加快速下降，更实惠的办法可能是将那些人从偏远且往往脆弱的环境中迁置出来，安排到工作机会更多的地方。

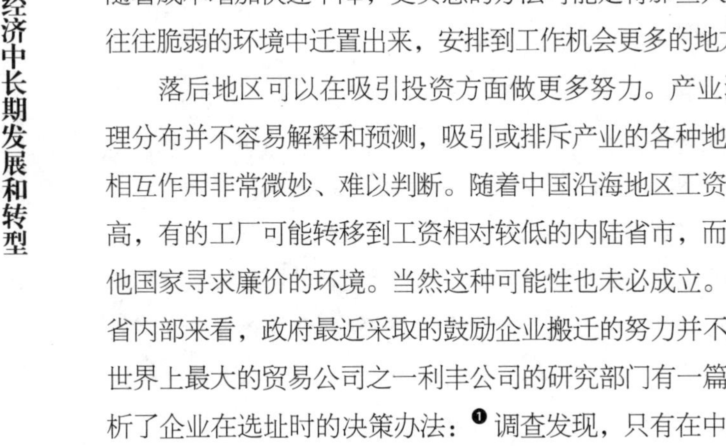

落后地区可以在吸引投资方面做更多努力。产业活动的地理分布并不容易解释和预测，吸引或排斥产业的各种地理因素的相互作用非常微妙、难以判断。随着中国沿海地区工资水平的提高，有的工厂可能转移到工资相对较低的内陆省市，而不是去其他国家寻求廉价的环境。当然这种可能性也未必成立。仅从广东省内部来看，政府最近采取的鼓励企业搬迁的努力并不算成功。世界上最大的贸易公司之一利丰公司的研究部门有一篇论文，分析了企业在选址时的决策办法：[1] 调查发现，只有在中间投入能从中国获得且海外销售所占的份额较低的情况下，沿海企业才会迁移到内地。那些大部分投入依靠进口而产品多用于出口的企业，更多会转移到其他低成本国家，而依靠当地产业集群支持的出口企业则不太容易搬迁到内地或其他国家。

[1] 背景论文十四：香港利丰集团研究中心，《中国工业生产的分散化和面向国内市场的制造业前景》。

由于这样的复杂性，中国应该慎重采用把产业吸引到内陆省市的特殊政策，更好的做法是让市场来引导经济活动的选址，充分认识到产业向落后地区转移将是一个逐步而漫长的过程。

当然，这些都不影响落后地区努力增强自身对投资者的吸引力。它们应该着手对投资环境进行全面评估，发现不足之处（例如缺乏可靠的信息、土地和税收政策造成的负担过重，以及基础设施限制等），然后采取必要的措施来克服这些缺陷。

落后地区还需要考虑定向干预，帮助那些偏远村庄和集镇的居民。例如，偏远地区的儿童往往离中学很远，许多人因此不得不住校。但住校的费用对许多贫困家庭来说是沉重的经济负担，也是学生辍学的一个普遍原因。为减轻这一负担，政府可以考虑在贫困地区实施有条件的现金补贴项目或者学校餐补项目，这些项目可以同时降低上学的成本、改善儿童的营养以及促进教育成绩的提高。为了进一步鼓励贫困地区的农村学生，政府还可以考虑减免中学学费并提供更多的奖学金。为解决这些地方的教师资源不足的问题，政府还可以考虑招聘大学毕业生去落后地区担任教师的计划，墨西哥、孟加拉国和美国都有很多类似的非常成功的案例。

第四章　增加国内消费和壮大中产阶层*

增加国内消费的政策

随着经济发展达到中等收入水平，国内需求通常会成为增长的重要发动机，对于中国这样的大国而言尤其如此。中国的巨大规模本身对出口扩张构成了天然的制约，在未来10年，受金融危机的打击和贸易保护主义的威胁，世界市场很难再像过去20年那样成功消化来自中国的巨大的出口增长。

国内需求并非国际需求的现成替代。一个国家在面向国际市场的时候可以专注于有限种类的产品，以获取规模经济效益。但在更多面向国内需求的时候，就需要生产品种更为广泛的产品，以免在任何细分的本地专门市场上迅速饱和。还必须将更多的资源投入服务和非贸易产品，这些产业不属于出口部门，但在国内需求上占据主要地位。

为转变发展方式，中国必须对本国经济的需求面进行改造，

* 本章主要参考了背景论文十二：霍米·卡拉斯，《中国向高收入国家转型：避免中等收入陷阱的因应之道》，其中包含对中国中产阶层规模估算的技术细节；背景论文七：安德鲁·克罗克特，《中国在世界经济中的角色：展望第十二个五年规划》。

这意味着将注意力从长期关注的、表现极其出色的供给面转移出来。在过去 30 年中，中国充分动员了本国劳动力，允许农村的大量失业和就业不足的人员离开家乡。中国还迅速扩充了资本存量，这得益于高投资率、信贷条件的放松，以及将土地、电力、供水和其他公用事业的价格控制在较低水平。中国的技术效率（或者说全要素生产率）也以每年 3%~4%的速度提高。

在扩大需求方面，中国的表现就逊色一些，当然这不是蓄意所为。早在全球金融危机爆发前，中国的“十一五”规划就明确要求在以出口促进增长和以内需（尤其是消费）带动增长上实现更好的平衡。但是实际的经济表现却颇为不同。20 世纪 90 年代，中国的居民消费仅相当于 GDP 的 45%，以国际标准衡量已经属于很低的水平。在过去 10 年，这个份额进一步下滑，到全球金融危机爆发前降至 36%，远低于世界平均水平（61%）以及越南（66%）、印度尼西亚（63%）、印度（54%）和泰国（51%）等的份额，也远低于中国的历史水平。自 2000 年以来，消费的增长率比 GDP 的增长率平均低 2.5 个百分点。与已经成熟的市场经济体不同，中国还没有成功培育出可以驱动经济进步的消费导向的大批居民家庭。

居民消费份额下降的主要原因是劳动收入所占份额的下跌。中国的工资收入在国民收入中的份额从 1980 年的 2/3 下跌到如今的 50%出头。考虑到这段时期人力资本的快速增长，以及劳动力从低效率的农业岗位转移到效率更高的制造业和服务业，工资份额的下跌就显得尤其突出。因为那两个变化在正常情况下会提高劳动收入在国民收入中的份额，可是都不足以抵消由于生产率的巨大进步和高水平的投资带来的利润飞涨。

一段时间以来，中国政府已在密切关注增加劳动收入在 GDP 中的份额，将其视为实现经济再平衡的目标之一。在这方面有若

干政策工具可以采纳。一个选择是直接干预工资水平，政府可以在合理限度内规定最低工资标准并强制执行。在中期，应该确保现有的劳动监管措施（如《劳动合同法》等）覆盖包括农民工在内的所有员工。除了这些以外，则应避免用强制干预手段来涨工资，因为它可能扭曲企业的技术选择，鼓励企业采用资本密集度更高的技术，而减少就业量，对于劳动收入在国民收入中份额的变化造成相反的效果。更多内容可参见第五章有关就业、教育和劳动力市场的讨论。

例如，新加坡政府曾在1979—1981年试图通过人为提高实际工资水平（涨幅约为25%）来强行完成向知识经济的转型。一段时间之后，技能和生产率水平的确有所提高，但工资的抬升也带来了意想不到的不利后果，致使1981—1986年的制造业就业量大幅减少。1985年，新加坡经济出现衰退。到1986年，为了重振对劳动力的需求，政府采取了相反的行动，用严厉的措施来削减工资成本：冻结名义工资，并将公积金缴费率从工资额的25%下调到10%。

更有前途的做法应该是减少不利于就业的政策障碍，使经济增长的劳动密集度提高。有些分析师认为，中国的私人企业不容易获得金融资源，因此会限制就业的增加。[1]这个看法得到了调查数据的证实。世界银行的《营商环境报告》（*Doing Business*）在信贷便利度指标上中国的排名是世界第61位。数据显示，只有不足一半的中小企业获得了银行贷款。经济计量研究显示，企业获取信贷的难度越大，创造的就业量就越少。如果贷款政策能

[1] Jahangir Azjz and Li Cui, "Explaining China's Low Consumption: The Neglected Role of Household Income." International Monetary Fund, July, 2007.

得到改善，就有可能在不牺牲贷款质量和增加违约风险的同时改善小企业的信贷环境。

政策制定者们还可以通过开放中国的服务业来帮助新兴的私人企业。大多数就业岗位往往是新企业创造的，如果这些企业是在服务业领域，效果就会更大。从本质上来说，服务业的劳动密集度比制造业高得多。

另一个阻碍劳动密集型增长的障碍是国有企业的继续扩张，这些企业的资本密集度比私人企业高很多。自20世纪90年代后期以来，国有企业单位员工资本占有量大幅增加，如今几乎已是私人企业的4倍。[1]在一定程度上，这是由于国有企业集中在本身就属于资本密集型的产业，但也反映了由国有机构控制的银行业在发放贷款时对国有企业的长期倾斜（参见第九章有关国有企业作用的深入讨论）。对国有企业进行改革，例如，要求它们接受更激烈的竞争或者更严格的贷款标准，或许可以扭转中国经济增长中的过度资本倾向，带来更多的就业和提高劳动收入所占的份额。另外，如果要求国有企业将更多利润上缴财政，还能让政府在不减少公共支出总水平的情况下对居民家庭和私人企业减税。

第一个应优先考虑的议题是削减对劳动力征收的许多税费。在中国员工的全部收入中，能真正到手的部分平均只占65%，其余属于政府征收的工薪类税收和各类社会保险缴费（医疗、工伤和失业保险等）。第二个优先议题是降低企业税负。有研究估计，私人企业上缴的增值税超过了利润的一半，给增长造成了巨大障碍。

[1] 参见*OECD Economic，Survey：China 2010*，第110页。该报告详细分析了国有企业相对于私人企业的表现。

居民家庭还可以从储蓄和投资中获得更多的收入。中国长期以来对银行存款执行较低的管制利率，损害了储户的收益，减少了家庭收入。提高存款利率和降低贷款利率的空间并非没有可能，这样可以适当挤压银行利润，让居民储户和借款人从中获益。

如果储蓄率下降，居民消费在GDP中的份额也有望提高。在20世纪90年代，中国的居民储蓄约占可支配收入的30%，从国际标准来看，这已是较高的水平，最近10年则进一步提高。一个可能的解释是缺乏社会安全网，有统计数据表明，在部分发展中国家，政府对社会项目的投入降低了国民储蓄率。国际货币基金组织最近的研究得到的结论是，政府增加医疗领域的支出会促进中国的居民消费。[1]

如果信贷的获取更加容易，储蓄率同样可望降低。为了在整个生命周期中实现更平稳的消费，信贷有时候是必需的，一个发达的金融体系会提供大量的借贷方式。中国当然不应该无限制地放开消费信贷，以免重复韩国在过去10年中滥发信用卡带来的教训，但谨慎地放松信贷控制将有助于居民储蓄率从不必要的高水平上降下来。

在储蓄回报较低的时候，居民家庭往往还会增加储蓄。这看似奇怪，其实是因为他们希望有更多积蓄，保证退休之后还有足够的收入水平。如果金融体系能提供更多种类的回报更高的储蓄工具，储蓄率就有可能下跌，还可以给居民家庭提供房地产之外的另外一种投资工具。

消费者的支出还反映其财富状况。对很多农村家庭来说，最

---

[1] Steve Barnett and Ray Brooks, “China: Does Government Health and Education Spending Boost Consumption?”, International Monetary Fund, January, 2010.

重要的资产是他们的土地使用权。但这个权利往往不够安全，因此改善这些权利可以增加农民的消费倾向。在中期，中国促进消费的一个直接办法是扩大政府公共服务支出。2003—2007年，中国政府的总储蓄率约为GDP的7.4%，到金融危机爆发前进一步提高到10%以上。中国的公共财政状况相当良好，完全有能力永久性地提高教育、医疗和其他急需的社会项目的支出。扩大社会支出对中国的和谐社会建设来说也是必需的，这将是后面三章要讨论的主题。

因此很显然，政府有多种政策工具来提高居民收入在国民经济中的份额。另外随着经济的增长和进步，这个提高也可以自然发生。从长期来看，就业将更多转向服务业，在高收入国家，服务业约占总就业量的70%，而中国今天仅为33%。由于服务业的劳动密集度高于农业，服务业的增长将自然地扩大劳动者所得在国民收入中的份额。随着国家向知识经济转轨，高技能劳动力的回报也将提高，或许会带来整体劳动收入的增加。

此外，政府还可以选择把过去几十年积累的部分财富转移给居民家庭，以刺激居民消费。20世纪90年代，中国以低价将公共住房卖给私人租户，就非常成功地把财富从政府转移到了民众手中。中国政府可以考虑，在中期从庞大的国有资产股权中拿出一部分进行类似的转移，以促进内需。几年前，政府曾建议将部分国有企业股权划转给社保基金，以负担强制缴费型养老金体系的历史成本，并降低在岗员工的缴费率（参见第六章）。可惜这项值得鼓励的措施还没有得到充分落实。

中产阶层

20世纪90年代后期的公房出售一举将中国转变成自有住房社会。房屋所有权经常被视为中产阶层的判定标准之一。虽然中产阶层的定义往往不够清晰，但绝对不容忽视。繁荣的中产阶层是促进消费需求、维持经济增长和摆脱中等收入陷阱的必要条件。如果中国希望将增长更多转向国内消费，就必须培育一个庞大的中产阶层。然而，尽管中国的消费市场在很多指标上号称全球“最大”，例如，全球最大的手机、汽车和住房市场，但是，中国今天的中产阶层在促进快速增长方面发挥的作用依然太小。所以，问题在于，中国的中产阶层将在什么时候才能强大到可以主导经济发展，需要什么样的政策来推动这个进程。

“中产阶层”是一个较为含糊的社会分类术语，大致反映了人们维持较为舒适的生活的能力。中产阶层通常拥有稳定的住房、医疗、给子女提供的教育机会（包括大学）、可靠的退休和工作保障，以及能用于度假和休闲的宽裕收入。这个阶层由各种职业构成，可以是政府官员、富裕农民、商人、企业员工和专业人士等。他们可以从事各种不同的管理和办公室工作，还有许多是小企业、作坊和商业化家庭农场的自雇就业者。

从经济角度看，中产阶层可以定义为，享有一定数量的宽裕收入的家庭。在应付完生活必需品之后，他们还有一些节余，可以自由地用于耐用消费品、高质量的教育和医疗、住房、度假和其他休闲活动等。与贫困家庭不同，这个群体对于消费品有更多选择。与富裕阶层不同，他们的选择更受制于预算，对价格和品质都比较敏感。

对中国的中产阶层进行定义和测算，是许多咨询公司、银行和商业机构乐意开展的项目。虽然使用的定义各不相同，但它们都认为中国的中产阶层将在未来数年显著增加。美林银行相信，到 2016 年，中国的中产阶层人数会达到 3.5 亿。麦肯锡公司采用了不同的定义，推测到 2025 年，人数将达到 5.2 亿 ~6 亿。国家统计局在 2005 年的一项研究中所采纳的城市中产阶层的定义是：

三口之家，年收入在 6 万 ~50 万元，或者说在对购买力进行调整后，按 2005 年美元价值计算，每人每天 16~132 美元。按照这个标准测算，到 2020 年，45％的中国城市人口将成为中产阶层。[1]

本报告的一个背景研究采纳了一个可以适用于世界各国的中产阶层的定义，由此能对中国大量涌现的中产阶层与目前主要集中在美国、欧洲和日本的多数中产阶层进行比较。[2] 在那些国家，中产阶层可以将收入提升到更高水平，中国也同样如此。

这个研究统一地将全球的中产阶层定义为：按购买力平价计算，每人每天的支出在 10~100 美元。区间的下限与葡萄牙和意大利的平均贫困线相当，这两个欧洲发达国家规定的贫困线标准最为严格：一个四口之家的贫困线标准是每年 14533 美元，或者说每人每天 9.95 美元（2005 年美元价值，购买力平价调整后）。区间的上限相当于最富裕的发达国家卢森堡的中位数收入的 2 倍。按照这个定义，全球中产阶层不包括最贫困的发达国家的穷人和最富裕的发达国家的富人。

中产阶层的重要性

以这个标准定义的全球中产阶层有一些共同的特征：他们的耐用消费品拥有率比较高（住房、汽车、手机和电器等）。他们的需求有较高的收入弹性，因此构筑了一个“消费者阶层”。他们不需要像传统意义上的阶层那样紧密组织起来实现自己的目标（因此有些专家认为存在若干中产阶层），但显然形成了一个非

[1] Cheng Li（ed），*China's Emerging Middle Class*，Brookings Institution Press，2010.

[2] 背景论文十二：霍米·卡拉斯，《中国向高收入国家转型：避免中等收入陷阱的因应之道》。

常重要的市场。全球中产阶层推动了世界经济；然而，北美和欧洲中产阶层脆弱的财务状况，或许将阻碍世界经济回到过去20年的健康的增长水平上。

危机提醒人们，以亚洲的生产、西方的消费和世界其他地区的资源开采为基础的世界增长模式不再能持续下去。这给中国和亚洲其他国家的中产阶层带来了更大的影响。全球经济再平衡要求亚洲国家有更多消费，但为此制定的许多政策在本质上是制度性和长期性的：建立社会安全网、医疗保险体制以及改进公共教育等。对中期来说，更有希望促进消费的途径是：让中产阶层引领增长，通过信用卡、抵押贷款和其他形式的分期付款刺激他们的购买力。因此，全球经济的可持续增长取决于亚洲国家中产阶层的崛起。

中产阶层与可持续的经济增长：国际经验

某些国家没有成功完成从中等收入向高收入国家的转型，未能培育出强大的中产阶层或许是一个解释。如果没有这样的群体，就很难创造支撑增长所需要的巨大的消费市场、对教育的投资、制度化的储蓄和社会动员力。这个问题从拉丁美洲的历史中得到了最好的说明（参见专栏4–1）。

专栏4–1

拉丁美洲的中产阶层

拉丁美洲的快速增长年代也确实创造了中产阶层的萌芽，他们本来有望使该地区动荡的政治环境稳定下来，然而长期的贫困和巨大的收入差距却持续下来，破坏了社会成长的力量。虽然就业岗位快速增加，社会流动性（social mobility，指人们改变自己的收入和身份、进入其他阶层的可能性）却很有限。增长伴随着城市化，但大城市的中心区却被条件较差的聚居区包围，那里享受不到城市的现代化设施和生活水准的同等改进。当中产阶层在城市中心区成长时，居住在快速扩张的城市外围的人依然被边缘化。他们得到的学校教育质量很差，不能让这些年轻人掌握现代经济所需要的工作技能。缺乏合适的教育训练给中产阶层的增长设置了上限。这些教训显示，人力资本的积累是促进社会流动和培养强大的中产阶层的关键。

作为该地区最大的国家，巴西在近年来已接近突破原来的模式。历经多次的失败尝试，巴西在2003年的经济复苏后成功地大幅扩大了中产阶层的规模。根据热图利奥·瓦加斯基金会（Foundation Getulio Vargas），巴西目前的中产阶层大约占巴西总人口的52%，而2003年，这一比例仅为36.5%。这个成功显然拓展了国内市场，并创造了强大的民意基础，支持政治上的稳定，以及拥护卡多佐总统和卢拉总统制定的增长战略的延续。如今，人们终于看到希望，巴西经济可以在更加持续的基础上真正起飞。与以前的危机相比，本轮金融危机给巴西的中产阶层的冲击要小得多。受影响最大的并非工业和出口产业的中产阶层，而是金融和服务业中汇聚的高收入阶层。新兴的中产阶层的适应能力增强了巴西将最终走向成熟的希望。

资料来源：感谢阿根廷中央银行前行长、国际货币基金组织前高级顾问马里奥·布雷杰博士（Mario Blejer）的贡献。

巴西的经历与韩国形成了强烈对比。韩国的人均收入在1986年达到4600美元（相当于巴西在1979年出现停滞时的水平），

此后，韩国继续保持快速增长，尽管经历了1997—1998年的亚洲金融危机、2001年的互联网泡沫破灭以及最近的大衰退的冲击，在2010年人均收入依然达到了18000美元。当然，韩国的成功要归功于对增长战略的积极调整，完成了向知识经济的转轨。但另外一部分原因也在于其庞大的中产阶层，韩国在1986年的人均收入与巴西在1979年的水平相当，但是，韩国的中产阶层占总人口的55%，是巴西的2倍。

其他保持快速增长的国家也拥有强大的中产阶层，日本的人均收入水平在1965年约为4900美元，中产阶层的比例也接近55%。今天很多快速增长的中等收入国家，如波兰、俄罗斯、泰国和马来西亚，都有相当数量的中产阶层（见表4–1）。只有印度尼西亚与中国相似，中产阶层的规模较小，但印度尼西亚的收入水平明显更低。相反，增长速度较慢的中等收入国家，如埃及、叙利亚、玻利维亚和菲律宾等，中产阶层的规模都较小，唯一的例外是墨西哥。

表4–1 2009年部分国家的中产阶层所占比重及人均收入水平

	中产阶层所占比重（%）	人均GDP（购买力平价，2005美元）	长期增长率
玻利维亚	16	4123	慢
巴西	37	9283	慢
中国	12	5991	快
埃及	18	5849	慢
印度尼西亚	12	3635	快
马来西亚	47	12418	快
墨西哥	65	12577	慢
摩洛哥	10	4161	慢

续表

	中产阶层所占比重(%)	人均 GDP(购买力平价，2005 美元)	长期增长率
菲律宾	13	3383	慢
波兰	85	16230	快
俄罗斯	69	13846	快
南非	36	9247	慢
叙利亚	16	4518	慢
泰国	32	7544	快
土耳其	45	7694	慢
乌克兰	37	6357	快

资料来源：背景论文十二：霍米·卡拉斯，《中国向高收入国家转型：避免中等收入陷阱的因应之道》。

有些学者认为，在发达国家，中产阶层的停滞和收入的加速集中甚至对近期的金融危机起了重要作用。规范的经济模型显示，如果最高收入阶层在国民收入中所占的份额不断增加，其他居民可能会需要借款来支撑消费，从而导致中产阶层及社会底层的债务负担加重。如果持续时间足够长，居民家庭的债务负担将最终达到无法承受的地步，在遭受负面打击的情况下，会导致广泛的债务拖欠和破产。[1]

对中国的中产阶层规模的估计

从某些角度看，中国已经拥有相当数量的中产阶层。由于

[1] M. Kumhof and R. Ranciere, "Inequality, Leverage and Crises", mimeo, November, 2010.

1998 年启动的住房私有化改革，城市地区的自有住房拥有率在 2007 年已达到 82%。2009 年，在校大学生人数达到 2600 万，登记轿车数量达 2600 万，销售量更是达到 1360 万辆。2008 年底，流通中的信用卡数量约为 1.5 亿张。目前的移动电话用户估计有 7 亿人。在 2007 年对 6000 位购物者的调查显示，超过 40% 将购物视为自己喜爱的活动。从这些统计看来，中国的中产阶层人数已达到相当的规模。

我们估计，中国在 2010 年约有 1.7 亿人属于中产阶层，相当于全部人口的 1/8。[1] 相比之下，美国的中产阶层拥有 2.3 亿人，占全国人口的 3/4。韩国、日本和欧盟国家的情况则与美国类似，中产阶层人数超过全部人口的 90%。

展望未来，中国的中产阶层还有大幅扩充的潜力。几十年的高速经济增长使很多中国人走出了绝对贫困，达到中产阶层的门槛。但今天仍有 26% 的中国人每天的支出水平在 5~10 美元，还有 41% 的支出水平仅为 2~5 美元。因此，随着未来几十年的经济增长的持续，将有更高比重的人口加入中产阶层的行列。

随着收入提高，越过中产阶层门槛的人数将快速增加。假定中国人的平均收入从目前到 2030 年维持 7% 的增长率，那么日均支出超过 10 美元的人口所占的比重将提高到 74%（见图 4−1），

[1] 具体计算方法介绍参见背景论文十二：霍米·卡拉斯，《中国向高收入国家转型：避免中等收入陷阱的因应之道》。中产阶级（阶层）人数的估算取决于若干假设条件。卡拉斯博士估计中国的中产阶级约占全国人口的12%，是属于偏低的估算。其他一些估算可能达到20%。考虑到中国的居民收入在GDP中的比重较低，以及收入差距较大，所以可以解释，中国目前的中产阶级所占比重显著低于韩国和巴西在同等发展水平时（也就是已达到中等收入水平，正准备向高收入国家转轨的时候）的比重。

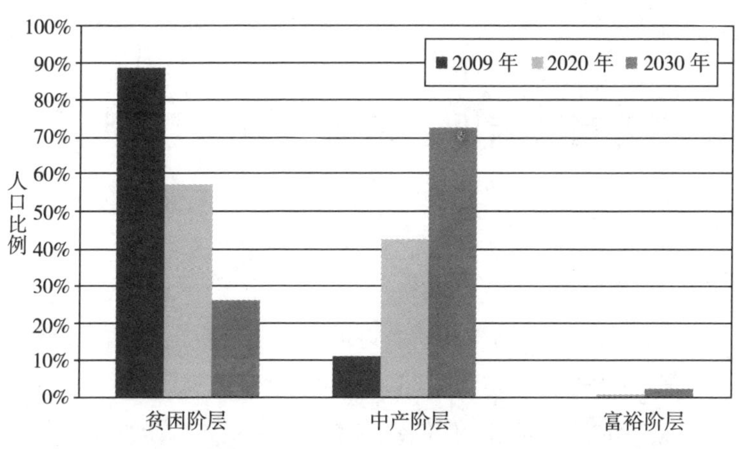

图 4–1　中国的中产阶层的壮大

大致相当于美国今天的水平。在一代人的时间里，大多数中国人可以从相对贫困的阶层进入中产阶层。当然，中国的中产阶层在未来几十年的实际成长状况，将取决于政府的政策能否成功提高居民收入在 GDP 中的份额、刺激国内消费的增长（如本章前文所述），以及接下来的三章所讨论的社会政策和社会项目的实施效果。

第五章　就业、教育与劳动力市场*

就业的水平、结构和质量将是中国和谐社会建设的关键组成部分。中国领导人经常提到就业的重要性，在2008—2009年的全球经济衰退期间，他们曾高度关注大学毕业生就业和出口企业的广大农民工下岗后的再就业问题。"十一五"规划强调了就业问题，并制定了就业方面的多项法律法规（从1994年的《劳动法》到2008年的《劳动合同法》）和劳动争议的调解机制，以及通过各种渠道来促进就业的法规。这些政策的制定参考了国际上的经验，也考虑了中国的国情。当然就中国正在和即将面对的就业问题而言，其他国家的做法仍然可以提供很多借鉴。

就业问题之所以重要，是因为它直接影响到个人和家庭的收入，包括收入的水平、收入在个人和群体中的分配以及收入的稳定性。工资薪金类就业在保证收入的稳定性和可预测性方面尤其受重视。失业则不仅会造成收入的下降，还会给人们的幸福感和精神状态带来负面影响——类似于离婚或家庭成员去世所造成的打击。不过，在市场经济中，几乎所有需要谋生的人都可以找到活路，所以问题并不仅仅在于得到一份工作，还更多地涉及收入

* 本章主要参考了背景论文六：蔡昉、理查德·弗里曼和阿德里安·伍德，《中国就业政策的国际视角》；背景论文十七：保罗·罗默，《中国新增长方式的最优化探析》。

水平和工作条件。

对于就业方面的政策目标，发达国家比发展中国家、中等收入国家比低收入国家更加重视，原因在于国家的富裕程度越高，自耕农的数量就越少，越多人的就业要受劳动法规监管。因此，随着中国经济的持续发展，就业政策的重要程度可能还会提高。这项议题在今天还主要是人力资源和社会保障部负责的内容，但财政部、中国人民银行及国家发展和改革委员会也应将其列入重要议程。

世界各国共同面对的一个就业政策的指标是工资类就业的数量，它既与失业的波动相关，又受长期趋势的影响。不过在发展中国家，由于很大一部分人是在非正规部门就业，他们的数量难以准确测算，质量则普遍不如正规部门，使该指标变得模糊不清（发达国家也越来越受到这个问题的困扰）。

就业政策的第二个关键指标是工资薪金类就业的质量，它主要取决于教育的质量以及各级教育体系对学生的技能开发。在这方面，经济学理论和其他国家的经验可以给中国提供很多参考。

各国的就业政策都会涉及一些较为具体的领域，包括工资水平和工作条件等，这是出于两方面的考虑：一是确保全国的劳动力和技能供给能比较自由地从产出贡献较低的行业、职业和地区转移到产出贡献较高的领域，从而提高经济效率；二是确保有类似技能的员工在体面的工作岗位上能获得水平相近的工资，避免女性和少数群体遭受歧视，以及防止员工在不知情的情况下承担职业健康风险，从而增进就业领域的公平。在某些情况下，效率和公平的考虑是一致的，但在其他情况下却存在冲突，这就要求政府权衡利弊得失。

就业增长、产业结构和调整

经济增长与就业

在发展中国家，经济增长的加速往往伴随着以自雇就业为主的农业所占份额的下降。劳动力由农业向非农业部门转移会带来工资薪金类就业岗位的增加，同时也会提高就业的质量，这一方面是因为非农业部门的工资水平高于农业，另一方面是因为非农业部门的就业通常没有农业劳动那么艰苦，产生的收入又更为稳定。

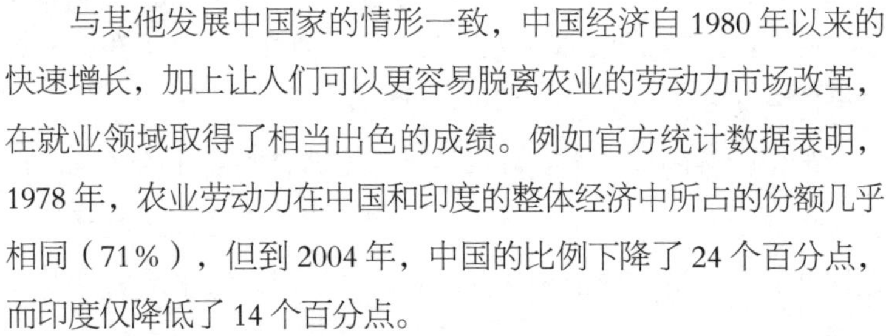

与其他发展中国家的情形一致，中国经济自 1980 年以来的快速增长，加上让人们可以更容易脱离农业的劳动力市场改革，在就业领域取得了相当出色的成绩。例如官方统计数据表明，1978 年，农业劳动力在中国和印度的整体经济中所占的份额几乎相同（71%），但到 2004 年，中国的比例下降了 24 个百分点，而印度仅降低了 14 个百分点。

不过在展望未来的时候，如果依然让有关就业的考虑来决定经济增长的快慢，将是错误的政策选择。中国农业部门的就业人数已经比较少了，许多农业劳动者的年龄偏大，劳动力由农业部门向工资类就业进一步转移的空间正变得越来越有限。还有，在不到 10 年之内，中国的劳动力总量也会停止增长。

在这样的背景下，中国的情况将变得更接近发达国家：短期的产出波动会导致就业波动（但就业波动的幅度通常要小一些，因为劳动生产率会出现顺周期变化），不过，总产出的增长率与总就业的变化趋势之间不存在太多联系。因此，中国未来的挑战在于提高非农业就业的质量，而不再是总的数量，并将劳动力由生产率较低的非农产业向较高的非农产业转移。

还需要指出的是，尽管就业从农业向非农产业的结构性转移在中国进行得非常迅速，过程也比较顺利，但正如本报告第三章所述，与此相关的从农村就业向城市就业的转轨却较为缓慢，困难更多。在接下来的大约 20 年中，顺利完成从农村到城市就业的转轨将是中国建设和谐社会所面临的最艰巨的挑战之一。

宏观经济再平衡和就业

国内外经济学家都认为，中国需要从多个方面实现经济的再平衡：压缩投资，降低储蓄，增加居民家庭消费，扩大政府支出，以及减少外贸盈余。所有这些调整都会影响对劳动力的需求。从中长期来看，没有哪项调整会对总就业水平产生较大影响（包括自雇就业、非正规就业以及正规的工资类就业）。然而，再平衡会影响就业的结构、工资水平和工作条件，需要妥善处理，以尽量缩小员工和雇主的调整成本。

与此相关的一个问题是，再平衡对正规的工资类就业在总就业中的比重会造成何种影响。从这个角度看，各方提交给中国的两套主要的再平衡方案存在较大差别。第一套方案是调整国内的支出结构，从投资更多地转向家庭消费，这会减少工资类就业的比重，特别是对正规部门，因为大多数投资都与此类就业有关（机械制造业或者建筑业），相反，大量的家庭支出是用于购买自雇或非正规就业生产的农业、轻工业和服务业产品。相比之下，从投资更多地转向政府支出则不会影响工资类就业的比重，还可能增加正规部门的份额，因为政府提供的就业岗位几乎都属于正规就业。

另外一套再平衡方案是削减贸易盈余，同时增加国内支出，这会导致总产出的结构变化，从可贸易的产品和服务转向非贸易品（建筑或服务）。这个变化对于工资类就业的影响尚不确定，因为可贸易品的产出减少既包括农业（进口增加）也包括制造业（出口减少），非贸易品的生产也包含工资类就业和自雇就业。不过总体而言，贸易盈余的减少很可能降低工资类就业的比重，因为此类就业在服务业中所占的比重低于出口导向的制造业。还有，替代出口导向的制造业的就业岗位（不管是在服务业还是在面向国内市场的制造业）将主要位于内陆省市，那里的收入水平相对较低。

尽管通过这些途径来减少贸易顺差可能导致就业质量降低，但非农产业的总就业人数却可能增加，这是因为贸易顺差是中国的服务业比重低于其他国家的主要原因之一，同时中国目前的服务业每单位产值所创造的就业岗位是制造业的 2 倍以上。据测算，完全消除贸易顺差将使服务业在中国的总就业中所占的比重提高 3~4 个百分点。

如果实施速度过快又缺乏辅助性政策，那么劳动力需求结构的变化可能会给员工们造成巨大的调整成本，迫使他们转而从事质量更低的工作甚至失业。从萎缩产业中释放出来的员工可能缺乏扩张产业所要求的劳动技能。这方面的政策建议是，调整应该逐步进行，最好让就业结构的调整主要通过不同产业活动的不同增长率来实现，而不是在某些产业扩张的同时让其他一些产业出现绝对下滑。政府还可以通过其他措施来降低员工们的调整成本，特别是改善劳动力市场的信息传递。

吸纳不断增加的大学毕业生就业

近年来，中国高等教育的学生人数大幅增加，毕业生人数从 2002 年的 110 万 ~150 万猛增到 2009 年的 630 万。这些毕业生进入就业市场的时候，他们的职业预期很难得到满足，其就业前景也成为政府关注的重要议题。这一情况在未来会得到缓解，随着大学毕业生供给的增加，他们在就业市场所要求的待遇会降低，对他们的需求则会相应增加。这是一种沿着现有需求曲线发生的移动，更为重要的是，随着中国经济向技能更熟练、技术更复杂的产业转轨，整个需求曲线可能发生移动。

中国的大学教育在近年来的快速和大规模扩张，与韩国之前的经历最为相似。从 20 世纪 80 年代中期到整个 90 年代，韩国的大学毕业生人数也出现了超速增长，而韩国的劳动力市场则非常顺利地接纳了大量的毕业生，部分原因是毕业生的相对收入（也就是雇主支付的劳动力成本）大幅降低，另一部分原因则是经济产业结构的变化。服装和鞋类等劳动密集型的出口产业萎缩，而化工和半导体等技术密集度更高的产业出现扩张，相比受教育程度较低的员工而言，对拥有大学文化的工程师和其他雇员的需求显著增加。

中国也将遇到类似的情况。教育水平的提高将使技术工人变得相对廉价，使整个国家的比较优势转向技术密集度更高的制造业和服务业，从而吸收一部分增加的技能供应。当然，韩国的经验也提供了另一个启发，尽管高技术产业增长迅猛，但大部分新增的大学毕业生所找到的工作还是一些传统上由较低学历的员工从事的岗位，全社会各个职业和产业的员工的教育水平普遍提升。

教育和技能开发

教育对经济增长的重要性

许多国家都非常重视物质财富的积累：工厂、设备、公路和港口等。然而，经济学家们却已证明，物质资本存量的规模差异只能很有限地影响不同国家的生产率，最大的影响因素是人力资本，也就是国民的技能。

诺贝尔经济学奖得主詹姆斯·赫克曼（James Heckman）在2004年开展的一项研究[1]表明，中国的人力资本投资回报远高于物质资本的投资回报（后来的几项研究也进一步证实了这个结论）。还有，较贫困地区的投资回报高于较富裕地区。这意味着与人力资本的投资相比，中国对物质资本的投资过多了。事实上，有关中国近期经济增长的研究得出的一个明确的结论是，中国应该进行更多的人力资本投资，尤其是针对在目前的教育支出模式下投资不足的青少年。仅从经济角度考虑，这个建议就非常有说服力，何况它还完全符合中国建设和谐社会的战略目标。

人力资本投资不足的部分原因是价格水平的误导：高技能员工获得的工资水平不能充分反映他们对经济的贡献，这会降低人们提高技能的动力。解决此问题的办法之一是给培训和技能开发提供更多的补贴。特别是中央政府给教育和培训不足的地区提供更大的投入，这既符合公平原则，也有助于改进效率，因为贫困地区的教育投入的回报更高。

办法之二是纠正高技能员工的工资偏低的现象，这要求进一步开放劳动力市场。例如，增强劳动力市场的流动性可以帮助不同地区和城乡之间的人力资本回报率趋于平等。在更加自由的劳动力市场中，人们凭借技能可以获得更多回报，从而鼓励他们提

[1] James J. Heckman, “China’s Human Capital Investment”，载于*China Economic Review* 16（2005），第50~70页。该文的中文版见《比较》第22辑，北京：中信出版社，2006年1月。

高自己的人力资本。此外，还应该发展助学贷款市场，让学生可以靠未来的收入借到资金，否则，如果只有富裕家庭才能把子女送进大学，收入不平等的现象可能代代相传。

提高员工的技能

中国必须设法提高许多目前教育水平较低（或者在未来显得较低）的员工和年轻人的技能。美国、英国和其他发达国家的经验表明，教育水平较低的这部分群体在现代经济中既是人力资源的巨大浪费，又是收入不平等和社会两极化的一个重要原因。中国应该积极努力避免类似问题的发生，并且立即着手预防，因为在下一个 10 年接受教育的孩童将是今后半个世纪的劳动力。

目前最突出的一个问题是广大农村地区的教育水平低下，加上第三章所讨论的大量农民工面临不理想的环境，情况进一步恶化。农民工的子女难以在父母工作的城市获得教育，不得不留在农村老家。这些儿童的受教育前景令人担心，一方面许多农村学校的教育质量不高，另一方面他们往往与教育水平较低的祖父母一起生活，还可能因为与父母分离产生情感问题。因此，改进基础教育的质量，尤其是帮助那些教育水平较低的学校和儿童，必须列入中国最急迫的议事日程。

至于和职业有关的教育与培训，国际经验更为复杂。如果是以毕业生的工资水平为标准进行测算，那么职业教育的经济回报往往低于普通教育。由政府主导的特定培训项目的回报往往也较低，即使瑞典等在这方面投入了大量资源的国家同样如此。职业培训如果采取学徒工的形式，或者由雇主而非政府或学校来举办，效率是最高的。中国在发展与职业有关的教育和培训的时候，可以借鉴这些经验。

改革高等教育

近年来，中国正确地强调了扩大高等教育的必要性，结果使大学入学率显著提高。中央政府和省级政府对高等教育的投入也在近年来大幅增加。然而，有关中国高等教育的质量及其能否满足经济和社会发展的要求的问题，现在却越来越引人关注。尤其需要注意，中国的高等教育体系是改革触动最少的领域之一，还保留着很多计划经济的特征。政府部门对大学的学术和行政事务干预太多，影响了学校的工作效率和生产率。大学内部目前实行的“党委领导下的校长负责制”缺乏清晰的领导和责任机制。还有，对设立私立大学的限制太多。需要制定有关政策，让私立大学能通过简单的程序进行注册、获得学术资质，并对私立学校获得的财务捐助提供税收减免。

有关的国际经验还给中国提供了若干重要启发：

首先，大学之间的竞争是有益的，当然质量保障是关键。竞争环境会给大学创造激励，让它们更积极地应对雇主和学生两方面的要求。大多数学生已经掌握了（或将会掌握）充分的信息，他们最有能力作出既符合自身利益又符合经济发展需要的适当选择。对中国而言，这意味着现有的大学应该获得比目前大得多的自主权，包括学生录取、课程表和学习环境的安排以及校内人力资源和财务资源的动员和配置等方面。政府研究经费的发放方式也可以鼓励大学之间的健康竞争，例如，允许教授们在获得中央政府部委的项目经费之后，将其带到任何一所国内大学。此外还应该鼓励创办私立大学。

其次，大学的经费来源应该既有政府的支持也有其他收费。高等教育带来的收益不限于接受教育的个人，因此需要政府提供补贴。不过，毕业生也会得到明显的个人收益——更理想的工作岗位和更高的收入水平，所以让学生们负担部分教育成本既有助于提高效率也符合公平原则。当然，学生们可以在自己有支付能力以后（也就是毕业之后）再负担成本，而不是在上学的时候，因此建立助学贷款体系非常关键。

最后，高等教育的普及要求引入一系列政府政策的作用，其中许多应该在较早期的教育阶段实施。一些国家（主要是澳大利亚、新西兰和英国）的经验表明，如果助学贷款按照收入比例偿还，就不会给来自贫困家庭的学生接受高等教育造成不利影响。不过，帮助贫困家庭的学生上大学的许多措施需要在更早的教育阶段开展，其中最主要的是提高这些学生的高中毕业成绩。

提高教育支出的效率

更普遍地说，各方面的经验都强调，中国应该大力加强激励和竞争的作用，以推动各级教育水平的提高和教育支出效率的改善。对于那些教育方法更好的中小学和大学，应该给予更多的资源作为奖励，让它们可以招收更多的学生。政府可以考虑如下几方面的措施：例如对教育效果（学生获得的技能和这些技能的市场价值）进行良好测评，以衡量哪些学校对资源的使用最有效率；政府还可以要求大学向报考学生提供有关毕业生的工资水平和工作安排的信息。强制性的信息披露有助于加强竞争，也符合全社会的整体利益。

目前对于教育效果的测评办法是，大多数中小学和大学会在期末对学生进行考试，如果学生的成绩良好，所在的学校就会获得好评。但这个制度会鼓励学校对生源进行激励竞争，而未必能更好地对学生们进行教育。政府对此应该作出调整，至少在两个时点上考察学生的知识水平：在开始学习某个课程之前以及完成课程之后。由此获得的测评才能反映学校提供的附加价值。表现最好的教育机构不见得是那些生源最好的学校，而是那些让自己的学生获得最大进步的学校。

为鼓励学校之间的竞争，还应该给予学生们更大的择校自主权。给学术竞赛的优胜者发放奖学金，可以鼓励学生们追求卓越，让优等生自己选择大学。政府下属的教育机构还需要更多地面对私立教育机构的竞争，包括商学院和技术研究机构等。再辅以对学生表现的严格测评，这些措施有望显著提高中国的教育生产率。

竞争还可以帮助中小学提高教育质量。随着中国城市化进程的推进，许多新的学校需要建设，特别是小学和中学。学校的硬件建设应该对那些表现最好的学校倾斜。除了给学校提供补贴外，政府还可以向目标人群（如农民工的子女等）发放教育券，让他们在择校的时候把这种证券“消费”出去。

通过激励机制和竞争市场来促进人力资本的培养，政府甚至可以在不增加财政投入的前提下，大力改善全国的教育基础设施。国际经验表明，改善基础教育（尤其是针对贫困地区）的一个有效办法是，由中央政府承担资金投入的责任，由基层政府继续负责学校管理。这样，基层政府将有更多动力改进所在地方的教育质量，并吸引更多的学生，包括农民工的子女（参见第九章的“改革政府间财政体制”部分）。

劳动力市场的制度和监管

制度和市场的平衡

任何一个市场经济都需要劳动力市场制度和监管框架来保护员工的工作权利，允许他们组成集体与雇主谈判，处理员工与管理层的冲突。良好的劳动关系体制可以在单个企业和全社会给员工提供集体的话语权，鼓励参与集体谈判的雇员同雇主达成最有效率的契约（像理想的竞争市场那样获得最大限度的产出），同时对产出的分配又不同于没有此类制度的市场。有效率的谈判会使共同利益最大化，这往往是通过劳资合作、防止罢工和充分的信息分享来实现，有时还需要中立的调停方或仲裁机构的协助。

根据工资水平和工作条件在多大程度上由制度因素（集体谈判或监管）而非市场力量决定，研究人员划分了不同的劳动体制类型。更多地依赖制度将使可观测的同类员工（即教育水平、年龄和性别接近的员工）的工资差异缩小，并减少普通员工同管理层的收入差距。发达国家平均来说比发展中国家更多地依赖制度，但无论是发达国家还是发展中国家，各国对于制度的依赖程度又不尽相同。

国际经济组织对于什么是制度和市场的最佳组合有不同看法。国际劳工组织提倡“社会对话型”的制度，因为它能带来更大的公平。经合组织、国际货币基金组织和世界银行则更推崇市场的作用，因为它能增强工资的灵活性，给管理层更大的安排就业岗位和工作细节的权力。20 世纪 90 年代，这三个组织都更支持美国的劳动力市场模式，流动率高、监管少、工会势力较弱，它们更看重美国的高就业率，而不太关心其较大的收入差距和较高的贫困率。但某些发达国家（特别是东亚和北欧国家）有着与美国模式大不相同的劳动力市场，也能保证较高的就业率。近年来美国金融市场出现动荡，失业率飙升，使人们的认识有了很大转变，对于由市场而非制度来决定产出的优点出现了更多怀疑。事实上，最近在发达国家进行的劳动力市场制度调查以及在发展中国家进行的工会、监管和社会保障调查都表明，唯一没有争议的结论是制度安排缩小了收入不平等现象。

因此对中国而言，没有什么完美的劳动力市场制度和监管体系可以照搬。经合组织、国际货币基金组织和世界银行所倡导的对劳动力的市场导向政策本身没有导致经济灾难（不同于金融市场上的自由放任政策），但也没有证据表明，这套政策优于让政府或集体谈判在劳动力市场上发挥更大作用的方案。现有的经验教训并不偏向于哪套政策方案或制度选择，而是突出了它们各自的利弊得失：劳动力市场制度有助于缩小收入差距和提供社会安全网，但同时会约束劳动力流动，并将失业现象集中在弱势群体。

了解世界其他国家如何处理劳动力市场的问题，能帮助中国掌握各种政策的选择区间及其在不同环境下的潜在后果，但不能保证，在某一时段、某一环境能发挥作用的政策，到了其他时段、其他环境能同样有效。劳动力市场是高度差异化的，因此，中国应该建立符合自身特色的制度和监管框架。具体的选择既要根据国家所面临的问题，也取决于不同目标之间的权衡以及政策制定和实施的政治决策过程。在过去30年中，一个较为灵活的劳动力市场帮助中国扩大了就业。展望未来，严重的收入分配不平等可能威胁到和谐社会的建设目标，这表明应该增强劳动力市场制度的作用。

工会的作用

各国的劳动法规的特性和劳工们的工会化程度差异很大。例如，欧盟和美国的工会化比例就相差悬殊，集体谈判所覆盖的员工的比例差别更大。各国工会的运转模式也存在不同，有的国家的工会谈判是高度分散的，在各个企业单独进行，常见于美国和部分东亚经济体（如日本、韩国、马来西亚和中国香港等），它们的劳资关系体系以单个企业为基础。相反，许多欧洲国家的谈判是在统一的产业工会和整个产业的雇主联盟之间展开。由全国性工会联盟进行的跨行业工资谈判已经在全球式微。

工会会员制度和运转模式的差别主要是由各国的政策和制度发展历史造成的，而非员工们的偏好不同。从美国到德国到韩国的针对员工需要的调查（甚至包括在中国进行的小型调查）都反映了惊人的相似性，员工们希望从企业内部产生较为独立的工会代表，希望与重视自身意见和利益的管理层合作。

中国 2008 年推出的《劳动合同法》（其中要求企业与包括农民工在内的全体雇员签订书面的劳动合同，要求减少工资拖欠，加强全国总工会对私人产业部门的员工的组织领导）以及近年来对有关仲裁的其他劳动法规的修改都符合国际惯例。此外，中国的工会的作用和影响已经和其他国家的组织在性质上较为接近，这表现在：有工会组织的企业工资水平稍高，福利条件更好等。未来的关键议题应该是劳动法规的有效实施以及全国总工会对这些法规的有力支持，包括督促企业遵守国家的劳动法规，作为制衡力量抵消富裕的工商业阶层对（涉及员工利益的）政策制定施加更大影响，以及帮助农民工保护自身权益等。

最低工资政策

世界各国政府几乎都制定了最低工资标准，当然，具体做法差别极大。有些国家针对全国的所有员工执行同一套最低工资标准，有些则对不同地域的员工或者年轻人等执行不同标准。中国是在 1993 年开始首次实施对最低工资的监管，2004 年，劳动和社会保障部要求各省、市、自治区制定当地的最低工资标准，结果使较为发达的地区制定了较高的标准。许多地方是采取月工资标准而非小时工资标准，没有充分考虑农民工每月的劳动时间过长的问题。有人担心，让各地自行制定最低工资标准会鼓励竞相压价来吸引投资，但实际上，最低工资标准较低的地区的员工往往会要求上调标准。例如，美国有全国性的最低小时工资标准，同时各州和各城市也可以制定自己的标准。到2008年，很多地方都采纳了自己的标准，大部分美国劳动者所在地区的最低标准都显著高于联邦的统一标准。

有关最低工资标准的讨论集中在对就业的负面影响上。大多数研究都发现存在一定的影响，最低工资标准每提高10个百分点，就业总量会下降1个百分点。但也有研究发现没有任何影响。有的经济学家对于没有影响的发现感到吃惊，但完全可以在理论上得到恰当解释，例如，对劳动力的需求弹性可能较低，政府在选择最低工资标准的时候已经考虑了对就业的负面影响，还有企业在工资成本略有提高的情况下会调整劳动用工细节、维持原有的雇员人数等。最低工资标准如果过高有可能造成较多的失业，或者难以实施，但世界各国大多会谨慎地选择最低标准，事实上并没有对就业造成显著的不利影响，还给很多员工带来了好处，因为如果没有最低工资标准，某些雇主可能有权力将工资压低到市场水平以下。

最低工资标准（以及政府对劳动收入的其他直接监管措施）的关键问题依然是执行。工会和员工们自己可以在实施过程中发挥核心作用，他们可以向政府举报工资过低、工作时间和工作条件违法等现象。然而，多数员工只有在相信诉诸法律不会导致自己失业的时候才会举报。当员工们或工会组织认为，严格遵守法律规定，雇主就不会维持现有的就业量，那法律将很难得到执行（在下文有关非正规部门的劳动关系议题时还将讨论）。

失业保险

失业保险是另一个争议颇多的议题：它可以让失业员工维持合理的生活水平，但往往也会延长他们失业的时间。研究发现，失业保险金的发放期限给失业率造成的负面影响更大，而非保险金与正常工资水平的比例（替代率）。因此可以考虑借鉴美国的做法，在经济繁荣期缩短员工们可以领取失业保险金的期限，而在严重的萧条期则延长领取期限。最好的政策组合也许是制定可变的期限、辅以较高的替代率。

中国在失业保险领域的一个重要任务是扩大覆盖面，目前的失业保险仅覆盖城市，未涉及乡镇企业的大量员工。即使在城市地区，大多数农民工也没有被覆盖。这些遗漏严重制约了失业保险对员工的保护作用，并影响了保险体制的经济效率。在2008年，失业保险仅覆盖了41%的城市户口的员工和不到4%的在城市居住6个月或以上的农民工。自2002年以来，失业保险金的收支盈余持续扩大，到2008年已达1300亿元。盈余的增加对于这类保险项目来说没有任何意义，或许可以用这些盈余来扩大覆盖面。

非正规部门

很难对非正规就业进行准确的定义和测算，但人们普遍认为，非正规就业在大多数国家都有很大规模，其中包括那些没有在政府机构登记的企业提供的工资类就业、没有正规的劳动合同或者没有纳入社会保障项目的就业等。这个术语有时候还泛指那些偶然性、临时性、家庭劳动式或者自雇性质的就业。世界各国对于非正规就业的定义各有不同，这取决于各国的国情以及家庭和机构调查所能收集到的信息。

但无论是采取哪种定义，中国目前都有大量非正规就业存在。劳动力调查显示：超过 1/2 的城市就业未列入官方统计数据，农村地区的比例可能更高；大约有 1/2 的被调查员工没有签订劳动合同或者没有加入社会保障。自 20 世纪 90 年代中期以来，中国政府将“灵活”就业视为吸纳效益不佳、冗员太多的国有企业下岗员工的一个有效办法。当然在同一时期，政府也制定了较为完善的就业法规，并在城市地区建立与市场经济体制相适应的社会保障体系。

以国际标准衡量，非正规就业在中国所占的比重并不算特别大，全世界有超过一半的非农业就业可以归入非正规性质。在发展中国家，该比重从 1/2~3/4 不等，其中有 30%~40%（在亚洲超过 50%）是工资类就业岗位，其余是自雇性质。与中国一样，在过去二三十年间，非正规就业的比重在大多数国家都有所提高或保持稳定，其中包括发达国家和韩国等高速增长的发展中国家。从全球范围来看，没有数据表明发展中国家的非正规就业所占的比重在可以预见的将来会出现下降。

有关非正规就业的政策涉及某些棘手的问题，因为非正规就业的原因既包含自愿性质的决定也包含非自愿决定，其结果也包含利弊两个方面。某些未注册的企业逃避政府税收，拖欠员工的工资福利，或者让员工承担不合理的职业健康风险。但有的逃避注册和税收的企业以及它们提供的就业岗位，在正规渠道难以获得生存。类似的情况是，有的员工之所以肯接受不签合同、不提供社会保障、需要承担健康风险或者低于法定工资标准的工作，是因为另外的选择更差，甚至会完全找不到工作。还有一些人发现，与正规部门相比，非正规部门可以给他们提供更好的创业或者增加收入（通过逃避税收）的机会。中国的许多非正规就业的质量是不错的，还在劳动力从计划体制到市场配置的转轨过程中发挥了积极作用。

国际上的一个共识是，恰当的政策选择应该介于两个破坏性极端的中间。没有必要实施过于严厉的法律和监管手段来禁止非正规就业，即使有这样的法律和监管手段也有可能是不可实施的。这样的政策会伤害许多贫困家庭，剥夺他们的工作机会，同时还伴随着很高的行政执法成本。但对这个领域完全放任不管也是错误的，放任可能导致非正规就业问题恶化，不利于改善就业质量，不利于实现建设公平而有效的法治社会的基本目标。因为有些类型的非正规就业会给贫困人群造成伤害，有必要在劳动力市场监管领域努力寻求政策上的平衡点，这是一个战略性的议题，从而避免放任带来的损失，包括违法行为造成的税收流失，以及在健康、养老金和扶贫项目的支出等。

除了将社会福利延伸到非正规部门的员工以外（这在第七章中讨论），劳动力市场更突出的急迫任务就是解决非正规企业严重违反职业健康和安全监管的问题，这导致了很多生产事故。从全世界来看，职业伤害和死亡在小企业发生的比例都更大。在某些情况下，员工会出于经济方面的考虑自愿承担政府不能完全控制的某些职业健康和安全风险。但是，政府依然可以通过对这些风险的性质和程度的宣传，把信息传递给那些在承担风险时往往不了解情况的员工，从而改善结果。与此相似的是，劳动力市场的信息改善对于那些依然选择在非正规部门工作的员工也有帮助，这会使他们有机会寻求更好的岗位和更高的收入。

另一个与非正规就业有关的战略性议题是，非正规就业的存在对于正规部门的工资水平和工作条件所采纳法律和监管标准，会带来怎样的影响。大量非正规就业的存在或许意味着，正规部门的法律监管标准的设置应该低于理想状态，以减少规避的动力（规避法规将导致非正规部门继续膨胀）。另外，近来的研究得到的一个惊人发现是，政府的政策即使不能对非正规部门强制执行，也会对其运行结果产生影响（例如，可以改善员工的福利）。在某些方面，非正规部门的员工和企业会自觉遵循正规部门执行的政策规定（例如，最低工资标准或者法定周工作时间限制等），并将这些政策视为社会的统一规范。这个发现能够推动中国劳动法规的制定和实施。

第六章　加强养老金体系建设*

在过去20年中，中国对养老金体系从根本上进行了改造。城市里建立了一个包含基本养老金和个人账户的强制性养老体系，对公共部门雇员则另有一个独立体系。另外还制定了有关自愿养老金计划的条款。低保制度可以给城乡地区的部分老年贫困人口提供补助。此外，政府正在农村地区进行养老金体系试点，也包含基本养老金和自愿性质的个人账户两部分。

然而，中国的养老金体系依然被若干问题困扰。强制性养老金体系呈高度碎片化状态，大多数城市的养老金入不敷出。强制性缴费的执行情况参差不齐；对城市的覆盖并不全面，大多数非正规部门的企业没有参与；也没有覆盖农民工和农村地区的劳动力。个人账户体系同样存在缺陷，没有如当初设计的那样实现资金积累，导致了所谓"空账"现象，也没有机构帮助员工选择投资组合、对不同资产进行直接投资。公共部门雇员的养老金体系设计有待改进。此外，农村养老金体系建设还面临几个方面的重大选择：一是基本养老金的发放是否应该与缴费挂钩；二是这样的养老金是应该仅限于农村地区，还是扩大到全国。

作为中国的社会政策和社会项目建设的重要组成部分，国家养老金体系的进一步改革依然是需要优先考虑的议题。

---

* 本章主要参考背景论文四：尼古拉斯·巴尔和彼得·戴蒙德，《中国的养老金改革：问题、选择和政策建议》的摘要。

经济学理论和国际经验的启发

养老金体系的核心目标

世界各国的养老金体系的核心目标包括：熨平消费、提供保险、进行收入再分配和扶贫。

熨平消费。养老金体制让人们能够将年富力强时期的部分消费转移到退休以后使用，使他们在退出劳动力市场、不再有收入来源后仍然能维持生活。[1]

提供保险。人们并不知道自己的确切寿命有多长，养老金体系能够以年金形式提供保险，在退休者的余生中按周或按月向其支付退休金。这样的年金是一种风险分担办法，使退休者避免过早耗尽养老金储蓄的风险。遇到有的员工在退休前去世，养老金体系还能够给其配偶和年幼的子女提供保障。

收入再分配。养老金体系可以在同代人中间进行收入再分配，例如，与高收入者相比，低收入者得到的养老金的替代率（即养老金占他们以前收入的比例）较高。养老金体系还能进行跨代的收入再分配，例如，对当代人执行较高的缴费率，可以使后代人得到较高的养老金或者降低后代人的缴费水平。类似的情况还包括，养老金体系可以给退休人员提供超出他们过去缴费标准的更高的待遇，从而把收入从未来的纳税人转移到当前的退休人员手里。

扶贫。面向全体国民的普惠式扶贫制度可能超出承受能力，还可能打击人们的工作积极性。然而就老年人而言，社会本来就

[1] 本章中所提到的养老金体系参与者可能是男性，也可能是女性。

不期望他们参与太多劳动，因此是很合适的特定扶贫对象，这样的特定扶贫计划比惠及所有年龄群体的计划效果更好。

在以上四个目标中，有的很明确应该是政府的责任，有的则适合交给市场来实现。熨平消费和提供保险可以通过政府和市场两种渠道进行，各国的安排不尽相同，理论上也没有定论。

世界各国的养老金体系

国际经验和经济学理论都表明，没有哪种养老金体系能适应所有国家的情况（参见专栏 6–1），不同的体系都能实现良好的运行。这些体系包含如下一些要素，其重要性和规模则不尽相同。

非缴费型养老金、最低收入保障和最低退休金保障（公民养老金）。在很多方面，最简单的选择是向所有达到一定年龄的人提供养老金，以税收作为资金来源，荷兰和新西兰就是采取这一做法。这种体制通常被称为公民养老金（citizen’s pension）。作为变种，公民养老金可以采取财富门槛，也就是不向少数最高收入阶层的人发放，澳大利亚、加拿大、智利（自 2008 年 7 月开始）和南非属于此列。或者像很多国家那样，给所有未达到一定收入标准的较为贫困的老年人提供最低收入保障。

专栏 6–1

没有一套能适应所有国家的最佳养老金体系

养老金体系有多重目标，包括烫平消费、提供保险、扶贫和进行收入再分配等，这些体系也都面临一系列约束：

- 政府财力：政府财力越强，就越容易为养老金体系提供更多的资金。

- 组织能力：组织能力越强，养老金体系设计中可行的选择就越多。
- 行为参数：包括劳动力供给对养老金体系设计的敏感度，养老金对私人储蓄的影响等。
- 转移支付发生前的收入分配状况：低收入者比重越大，扶贫的任务就越重。

之所以没有一套能适应所有国家的最佳养老金体系，是源于如下几方面的理由：

- 政策制定者对各个目标的重视程度不同，例如对扶贫的重要性、风险的代内及代际分担方式等都可能有不同看法。
- 各国面临的约束条件、关键的行为参数值等可能不同。
- 政治影响：在某些国家可行的选择，在其他国家可能在政治上通不过。
- 从历史上沿袭的各种制度会影响今天的政策选择，这些制度遗产可能值得尊重，至少不容易被彻底改造。

总而言之，目标和约束条件的不同会导致不同的最优方案，因此：

- 不同国家采纳了不同的养老金体系来实现多重目标。
- 尽管没有哪个国家的体系是完美的，但很多体系都能实现良好的运转。

待遇确定型养老金计划（Defined-benefit plans，DB）。在全国性的待遇确定型养老金体系中，参保人获得的养老金取决于个人的缴费历史和开始领取的年龄，保险金水平的计算可以基于最后几年的工资水平，或者更长时期乃至整个职业生涯的平均数。此类保险可以从一般性财政收入中获得补贴。有的国家的待遇确定型养老保险带有部分积累的性质，也就是说将部分金融资产划入专门的信托基金，作为未来的养老金的支付来源。但大多数此类计划属于现收现付性质，用当期的缴费收入抵扣当期的支出，几乎没有预先积累。

基金积累制缴费确定型养老金计划（基金积累型个人账户，Funded defined-contribution plans，FDC）。此类养老金设有个人账户积累，将参保人的累计缴费投资到证券和其他资产上，形成一笔基金，以此来支付未来的养老金。缴费率是固定的，到退休的时候，参保人将获得年金，年金的水平取决于他一生的养老金积累、预期寿命和利率等因素。采用此类制度的国家可以通过公共组织来进行投资（如新加坡），也可以交给受到严格监管的私人金融中介机构来进行（如智利）。

记账式缴费确定型养老金体系（记账式个人账户[1]，Notional defined-contribution systems，NDC）。这是一项最近才出现的创新，纯粹记账式缴费确定型养老金体系（有时也称为“非金

---

[1] 记账式个人账户有时又译为名义个人账户。在基金积累制个人账户体系下，每年的养老金缴费都被用来购买不同的资产——股票、债券、共同基金和银行存款。这样，完全积累制的个人账户就类似于一个私有的投资账户。而记账式个人账户则类似于一个银行账户，其资金的收益率由政府根据所持有资产的收益率和预期新缴费的现金流来确定。因此，对于工作者来说，记账式个人账户和基金积累制个人账户的唯一区别在于：前者的收益率是根据总体资金状况预先规定的（就如银行存款账户一样），而后者的收益率则取决于账户中所持有资产的未来收益率。相比较而言，工作者对于退休时可以获得养老金的信心并非依赖于其个人账户中是否有资产，而是依赖于其对政府的信心。这类似于银行账户，存款人只关心其存款银行的实力和决定收益水平的规则的可持续性，而不关心自己的存款是如何被运用的。在基金积累制个人账户体系下，工作者面临着更大的市场不确定性、收益不确定性，在分散投资管理的情况下，还要面临着自己的投资经理是否称职和可信的不确定性。

融积累制的缴费确定型养老金体系”，non–financial defined–contribution systems）是一种结合了缴费确定和待遇确定特点的混合体系。它给参保人建立个人账户，记录每个人的缴费情况。该体系也会让养老金领取人分担一部分风险，因为福利水平有可能涨落。但与缴费确定型个人账户体系类似的是，记账式个人账户体系并不进行完全积累，参保人的缴费大部分进入国库，而不是单独投资于金融产品。养老金的支出主要来自当期收入，这与现收现付体系相似。养老金水平的计算用公式给定，但不与市场回报率和预期死亡率挂钩，而是更多地取决于预期寿命的长短和薪资税基的增长速度。

公共雇员养老金体系。许多国家的政府给公共部门雇员建立了养老金体系，大多数是待遇确定型体系，也有一些是缴费确定型，或者将缴费确定作为一种选择。某些国家的公共雇员养老纳入全国性的强制性保险体系，政府以雇主的身份另外再提供一份补充养老金，这与有的大公司给员工提供的福利类似。其他国家则将部分或全部公共雇员排除在强制性的全国养老保险体系之外。

自愿性质的养老金。此类保险独立于强制保险体系，包含两种类型。即便政府没有要求，有些雇主也会选择自行建立养老基金，这样的养老金体系对雇主来说是自愿性质的，当然雇主可以要求全体员工都参加，以此作为受雇的条件之一。对于已纳入强制性全国养老体系的员工而言，这类自愿养老金可以视为补充养老（中国的企业年金就属于此类）。另外，许多国家的员工还可以向自愿性质的个人养老计划缴费。以上两类自愿养老金一般都能享受税收优惠，例如，缴费可以从个人的应税收入中抵扣。各国的强制性保险体系差别巨大，也就给自愿养老保险的安排提供了很大空间。

国际经验的启发

从世界各国的经验中得到的一个主要结论是，养老金体系的设计有各种类型，不存在某种占绝对优势的制度安排。有许多办法可以设计出良好的养老金体系，不同国家的不同制度选择都可能实现良好运转。本节将讨论其他一些重要的启发。

劳动力市场的效率。养老金体系设计应该关注的重点之一是要避免过度限制劳动力的流动，顺畅的流动是提高劳动力市场效率和生产率的关键所在。养老金应该可以灵活转移，至少能应付员工发生如下四种工作变动的情况：从一家企业转到另一家企业，从一个地区转到另一个地区，从政府部门转到私人部门（包括自雇就业），以及从没有保险覆盖的就业部门（如农村）转到有覆盖的就业部门等。如果一个国家的养老体系有了统一的、跨地区和跨部门的结构设计（当然各地执行的参数可以不同），这样的转移就能轻易实现。

养老金体系应可以覆盖自雇就业和间歇性就业。即便是那些养老金覆盖率很高的国家也担心有的员工没有完整的受雇履历，特别是女性和非正规部门的员工。各国往往都难以将这些群体纳入为正规企业的雇员设计的养老金体系。解决办法之一是给达到某个年龄的全体国民提供养老金，给终身居住在国内的公民提供同样水平的福利，给部分时间曾居住在国外的公民按比例提供福利。

性别和家庭问题。基本养老金是应该发给个人还是发给其家庭？这一问题的决策会导致不同的结果。养老金体系可以将保障重点放在员工身上，让他们自己去决定如何在本人和家庭成员之间分配福利，也可以通过强制保障规定将重点放在家庭上面，特别是保护仍然在世的配偶（主要是遗孀）以及年幼的子女。养老

金的制度设计可能对不同性别的人产生不同后果，例如，非缴费型养老金比缴费型养老金对女性更有利，因为女性的受雇史往往更加不连续。

基金积累型个人账户会带来交易成本问题，并且对资本市场所起的作用也不确定。基金积累型个人账户让人们可以选择投资组合或基金管理者，这会带来显著的交易成本。如果由政府来选择投资组合或者限制投资的范围，这些成本可以降低，然而，如果政府的选择不佳，或者政府还要追求退休资产积累以外的其他目标，投资回报率就难以保证。需要指出，基金积累型个人账户有可能促进资本市场的发展，但实际情况未必如此，没有理论上的必然性。政策制定者需要考虑：现有的资本市场和金融中介能否满足基金积累型个人账户的要求？如果不能，基金积累型个人账户对于金融工具和中介服务的需求能否有效促进资本市场的发展？

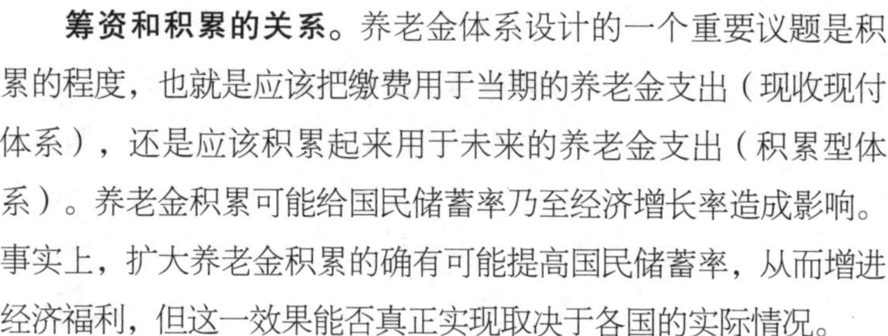

筹资和积累的关系。养老金体系设计的一个重要议题是积累的程度，也就是应该把缴费用于当期的养老金支出（现收现付体系），还是应该积累起来用于未来的养老金支出（积累型体系）。养老金积累可能给国民储蓄率乃至经济增长率造成影响。事实上，扩大养老金积累的确有可能提高国民储蓄率，从而增进经济福利，但这一效果能否真正实现取决于各国的实际情况。

实施的重要性。强制性养老金体系的规模和复杂性说明，制度设计必须考虑财力和技术能力的约束。很显然，一个国家的养老金体系必须是有能力支付的，政府管理的强制性养老金还要求公共部门有较强的行政能力。政府必须能够有效地征集缴费，并给那些在企业和地区之间转换工作的员工建立多年的连续记录；政府还必须进行精算，以便准确和及时地支付养老金；如果中央、省级和基层各级政府都要参与养老金管理，它们之间就需要密切合作。由于现收现付制度通常也包含部分积累，投资组合就必须得到妥善的管理（如果不限于购买政府债券的话）。大多数国家有这方面的能力，但同样重要的一点是要开展良好的审计和监督。完全基金积累型个人账户制度所要求的技术能力更高。

政府的重要作用。不只是强制性养老金体系高度依赖政府的有效运作，自愿性质的养老金也需要政府制定规则并保证其实施。政府必须有能力执行缴费规定和保护资产积累，还必须维持宏观经济的稳定（否则居民家庭不可能进行长期金融资产投资），确保对金融市场的有效监管等。如果离开政府的监管，包括保险和年金市场在内的金融市场就不可能实现良好的运转。这是一些高度复杂的市场领域，单靠个人难以保护自己，监管的作用至关重要。

能力培养。随着收入的增加、改革的推进以及政府行政水平的提高，养老金体系也需要逐步培养自身的管理能力。这项原则对中国来说尤其重要，因为中国正处在广泛的变革中，劳动者正在从农村转移到城市、从国有部门转移到私人部门，人口的年龄结构在快速改变，劳动力市场和金融市场也正在经历深刻的改革。

中国养老金体系下一步改革的政策选择

中国现行养老金体系的三个支柱——基本养老金、个人账户和自愿养老金——给下一步的改革打下了良好的基础，改革既需要关注覆盖面的扩大，也应关注设计的改进。

非缴费型基本养老金（公民养老金）

即使对一个现代经济体来说，缴费型养老金体系还是会有所遗漏。为了填补遗漏和扶贫，一些国家（包括某些中等收入国家）的政府提供了普惠式的公民养老金。这些养老金的资金来源是税收，不需要领取人缴费，覆盖全体国民（包括城乡、正式就业和非正规就业、男性和女性），通常对满足一定年龄和居住条件的任何人执行统一的发放标准。与缴费型养老金不同，此类养老金在推广到非正规部门的时候不会遇到太多执行上的困难。公民养老金不但可以帮助退休人员，还能惠及其家庭，包括孙辈的儿童。

在中国，政府也在考虑扩大覆盖率，并从最近开始在农村引入了养老金计划试点，这是非常受欢迎的一大进步。作为建立覆盖全国且可转移的福利体系改革的一个组成部分，这项试点应该尽可能迅速地制度化。政府还可以考虑对其进行部分改善，例如，可以将非缴费部分与缴费部分分开，以便让农村地区的所有老年人都能够领取非缴费型的基本养老金。把两个部分捆绑起来虽然有利于增加缴费总额，却会使养老体制的管理复杂化，并可能把许多人排除在外。另外，政府可以考虑将非缴费型的基本养老金扩展到城市居民，形成公民养老金体系。这样可以结束城市、农村和农民工三种养老金体系并存的情况，以实现全国养老体系的统一。

该制度显然要满足支付能力的要求，从这个角度看，政策制定者应该仔细考虑养老金的水平、首次领取的年龄限制，以及有充裕的其他收入来源的较富裕老年人的领取资格等。足额的养老金应该足够高，切实起到扶贫的作用，与发放的管理成本相称。例如，荷兰的发放标准相当于最低工资净额的70%；新西兰的标准相当于一对夫妇平均工资净额的72.5%，给独居老人发放的标准更高。为了保证中国各地的老人达到统一的生活标准，养老金水平应该有所变化，以反映领取人居住地的生活费用。地方政府还可以自行决定用本地财力提供补充福利，以更好地反映当地的生活标准。非缴费型养老金福利标准应该与物价或工资指数挂钩，这同缴费型养老金的做法一样。

此类非缴费型养老金应该覆盖所有满足一定年龄和居住时间要求的国民，领取年龄完全可以参照缴费型养老金中有关全额领取的年龄规定。从长期来看，随着预期寿命的延长，领取年龄应该随之自动向上调整，当然不一定保持严格的比例。中国应该认真考虑福利水平和领取年龄资格之间的权衡关系，可能有必要推迟领取年龄，以保证有能力支付足够高的养老金，增强这个制度的吸引。这一权衡显然取决于投入养老金体系的财力。中国还需要考虑，是否应该降低那些曾经在国外居住的老年人（作为学生或员工等）的福利水平，这些人中有很多在老年阶段可能不那么需要资金补助，应该是个可行的政策选择。

公民养老金的发放水平是否应该同个人收入挂钩？这里有几种选择。仅考虑年龄和居住时间、与其他因素无关的统一发放标准有着简单易行的优点（荷兰和新西兰的案例），但也是费用最昂贵的选择（因为福利水平和退休年龄都不变）。如果希望减少乃至取消给富裕阶层的福利，那可以通过收入门槛的测算来实现，测算指标可以是个人的总收入或者强制性养老金收入，或者是二者之和。

如果暂不考虑这些细节，合适的做法是在非缴费型养老金体系能实现有效运转之前，先提供较低水平的福利。待制度成形后则应提高支付水平，与缴费型养老金一样，同物价和工资的上涨挂钩。该制度应该尽快引入，并保证在“十二五”规划期间完成。

强制性缴费型养老金

强制性缴费型养老金体系也应该逐步扩展，首先应保证覆盖所有城市地区的大企业（指正规部门），然后扩大到农村地区的正规部门。这将是建立统一的养老金体系、实现全国劳动力市场一体化的巨大进步。最后，该体系还应该把小企业和自雇就业（即非正规部门）包括进来，不过与其他所有国家一样，这项任务对中国而言也同样极其艰巨，在短期内将政府部门的主要精力放在这里并不合适。

过渡时期存在一个危险，强制性缴费型养老金可能会影响某些企业从非正规部门向正规部门转变的积极性。为避免这种影响，养老金的净成本（缴费成本减去未来的福利）一定不能过大。中国应该小心，不要重蹈某些南美国家的覆辙。这些国家的社会保障制度与工资类就业的捆绑过于紧密，被雇主和员工双方都视为极不受欢迎的一种税收，[1]不利于生产率提高，并阻碍了非正规企业加入正规经济的行列。

缴费基础也需要改变。目前的养老金缴费是基于标准工资，这促使员工和企业转向标准工资外的其他收入，从而使缴费基数变得不真实。因此，缴费基数的测算方式应该改变，使其接近总体的报酬水平。养老保险缴费和所得税应该采取同样的收入测算数据，让税务部门和养老金管理部门的征收动力协调起来。类似的，计算基本养老金水平所参考的各地平均收入，也应该采取与缴费基础相同的定义。各地的福利水平可以不同，但应该采用中央制定的统一公式。

---

[1] 这一问题的详细讨论参见背景论文十三：圣蒂亚戈·莱维，《对拉丁美洲社会政策的有关评论》。

个人账户

个人账户体系的运行同样可以得到改善，中国是在 1997 年作为养老金体系改革的一部分引入个人账户的，最初的设计是进行完全积累，但实际上并没有如标准模式那样运转起来。目前还没有合适的机构帮助参保人选择个人投资组合或者对不同资产进行直接投资，此外，由于需要支付当期的养老金，该体系没有财力如最初设计那样去购买投资资产，严重影响其信誉。

中国可以借鉴其他一些国家（如瑞典）的做法，建立记账式缴费确定型个人账户。此类养老金体系是最近才出现的创新，采用的国家希望既能保持缴费确定型体系的优点，又不需要实现完全积累。这种体系给每个员工建立一个账户，记录其长年的累计缴费。缴费可以获得利息，由养老金管理机构按照法定利率逐年计入账户。于是，记录的缴费积累每年都会增值，既包括新缴纳的保费，又包括名义利率与上年年末累计余额相乘得到的利息。然而，这些缴费事实上并不投资于金融资产。每名员工在退休的时候得到的养老金水平基于其个人账户积累的精算结果，但实际上是由当期缴费来支付。

如果适应中国未来的发展形势需要，这一制度安排并不排除最终转向完全积累。记账式积累和完全积累两种制度安排也可以并存，例如，瑞典的养老金缴费率为 18.5%，其中 16%计入记账式个人账户，2.5%计入完全积累账户。但即使中国最终转向完全积累，也不应该是“十二五”时期的目标。采取完全积累制度的条件今天尚不具备。积累制的另一个好处是可以导致国民储蓄率的提高，但中国的储蓄率已足够高并超出了当前的投资水平的需要。积累制的好处还包括改善资本市场的效率，但中国的金融市场目前仍处在较初级的发展阶段，在近期内，完全积累型个人账户可能面临低收益、高风险的不利局面。此外，由个人选择投资组合的强制性积累账户对管理有着很严格的要求，中国现在也难以具备。

相比之下，更为急迫而重要的一个目标是为个人账户提供透明的报告。目前，很多员工的缴费没有得到准确记录，管理机构的记录既不公开也不接受查询。为解决此问题，中国需要建立更为严格的管理制度，保证所有个人账户的缴费有明确记录并能查询。决定养老金积累的回报率的规则也需要公开，让参保人知道每年能获得多少回报。还应该向参保人保证，现有的账户并非真正的“空账”，而是政府或养老金管理机构的负债。他们应该收到自己的个人账户的年报，并清楚从基本养老金和个人账户中能获得的收入替代率（占以前收入的比例）。

公共雇员养老金

公共雇员（包括公务员和教师等提供公共服务的其他人员）享受的养老金水平在世界各国普遍偏高。包括中国在内，大多数国家的此类养老金都是待遇确定型的，养老金水平根据职业生涯末期的较短时期的收入水平来计算。这样的制度设计不合理，会鼓励人们钻体制的空子，并影响劳动力在公共部门和私人部门之间的就业选择和退休安排，以及两个部门之间的人员流动。

中国目前正在尝试将政府公务员以外的公共部门雇员纳入强制性缴费型养老体制，这是值得鼓励的做法，该决定应该贯彻实施并推广到政府公务员。改革并不一定要降低公务员享受的养老金待遇，因为他们在纳入全国性的养老体系后，还可以由政府提供补充养老金，这种做法与鼓励私人企业提供补充养老金一样。当然任何补偿型养老体系都应该努力控制管理成本，美国对联邦政府雇员制定的“节约储蓄计划”（Thrift Savings Plan）就是个成功范例。

自愿养老金

在许多国家，人们都通过自愿养老计划为强制性养老保险提供补充，由雇主或员工本人通过获得批准的专门机构进行。在中国，这两类自愿退休计划都有望在未来数年获得增长和发展，也应该加以鼓励。不过中国还需要改善监管，为个人和企业退休计划提供保护。对于任何提供年金式养老福利的保险公司，都应该加强监管。国际经验明确表明，自愿养老计划应该采取完全积累型的缴费确定模式，应明确执行与强制性保险一致的所得税优惠办法。

中国养老金体系的整体管理

上文讨论的改革要求对中国养老金体系的整体管理也进行重大变革。其中一项关键议题是考虑提高退休年龄，另一项议题是需要加强和扩大对该体系的整体管理，使其成为覆盖全国的体系。

提高退休年龄

全世界的人类寿命都在延长，这是件很好的事情，但也意味着如果人们的退休年龄保持不变，维持养老金福利的成本就会增加。对于中国来说，预期寿命的延长目前还伴随着大规模的提前退休现象，这主要是因为困难企业鼓励员工提前退休，以便把支付责任转移到养老金管理机构，从而给养老金带来了更大的财务压力。

为应对这一挑战，有些国家提高了部分或全额领取养老金的最低年龄限制，更多国家也在当前的财政压力下正考虑推行改革。例如，美国在 1982 年就通过立法，分阶段地缓慢提高全额领取养老金的年龄，1982 年的规定是 65 岁，现在已提高到 66 岁，到 2022 年将达到 67 岁。在英国，最近的立法规定将分阶段提高政府养老金的领取年龄，从目前的 65 岁提高到 2024 年的 66 岁，然后每 10 年提高 1 岁（目前还有加快这一进程的讨论）。日本也正在将官方规定的领取年龄从 60 岁慢慢提高到 65 岁。此外，许多国家对男性和女性的退休年龄有不同规定，它们正在立法，将女性的退休年龄提高到与男性相同的水平。

虽然中国的劳动力市场运转效率还不算很高，但养老金体系的建设需要从长远着手。在这个背景下，中国的确需要提高退休年龄，目前对国有企业的男性员工的规定是 60 岁，对女性是 50 岁或 55 岁。中国还需要避免鼓励甚至强制员工提前退休的现象。当然，提高退休年龄在操作时要非常谨慎，应遵循以下几条基本原则，包括确保规则的制定应该与员工的出生日期而非退休日期挂钩；调整应年年进行；只要合理，涉及福利改变的规则都应公开执行等（这些原则的详细解释参见专栏 6–2）。

专栏 6–2

调整退休年龄的基本原则

提高退休年龄应遵循如下三项原则。

● 规则应与员工的出生日期（这是个人无法改变的），而不是退休日期（个人可以根据情况改变）挂钩。否则，任何改变福利的措施在实施前都会引发退休潮，以此来鼓励人们退休是缺乏效率的。仅考虑提高退休年龄可能会促使员工提前退休，因为他们担心尚未退休的人的退休年龄会发生变化。

- 调整应年年进行，以避免在年龄相近的人群中间出现福利水平的大幅变化。过大的差距不但不公平，在政治上也难以实现。原因在于：在相邻年份出生的人群，哪怕有时仅相隔几天，待遇水平也有可能出现巨大差别。福利水平的较大差异、加上按退休日期来制定规则，这二者结合起来将会进一步鼓励员工无效率地提前退休。

- 只要合理，涉及福利改变的规则都应公开执行。公众完全可以理解随着预期寿命的变化，调整养老金待遇水平是有必要的。根据明确的规则进行自动调整可以让人们更好地进行预测，并减少政治上的压力。如果自动调整是基于实际死亡率（而不是估测值），运作效果会更好。当然，无论自动调整规则的运行效果如何，都可以通过立法去修正。

中国的许多人担心，提高退休年龄会加重失业。这种担心的根据是，员工们在其工作岗位上滞留的时间越长，提供给新增劳动力的工作机会就越少。除了临时性的短期影响外，这一观点是完全错误的。正如专栏 6–3 所述，在一个市场经济体中，工作岗位的数量并非一成不变，经济中的就业岗位数量会对劳动力的供给作出反应。

专栏 6–3

没有根据的担心：提前退休与失业的关系

提前退休。如果一个经济体中的工作岗位数量是固定的，那么让一位年长的员工退休自然会给其他人创造一个新岗位，在这种情况下，提前退休可以帮助解决失业问题。然而这个观点一般来说是错误的，因为一个经济体中的工作岗位并非固定不变。发达国家的经验表明，平均退休年龄在过去几十年显著下降，并没有带来失业率的相应降低。对部分发达国家10年期以上的实证研究发现，鼓励提前退休与降低失业率之间没有系统性的联系。也没有理由认为发展中国家的情况会有什么不同。

认为市场经济中的工作岗位数量固定不变，这样的观点错在如下几个方面：第一，新加入市场的员工会给工资带来向下调整的压力，并使企业更容易找到合适的员工，从而鼓励创造更多的工作岗位。因此工作岗位的数量不是固定的，而是会受到劳动者数量的影响。第二，提前领取养老金通常并不会使员工退出劳动力市场，某些员工会一边从前任雇主那里领取养老金，一边在新雇主那里继续工作。第三，大量的农村劳动力才是最大的潜在失业来源。

因此，无论鼓励提前退休还是强制退休来解决失业问题都是错误的。退休往往会导致员工彻底退出劳动力市场，所产生的毕竟是长期影响，而失业总体而言是种短期现象。指望退休政策能有效解决失业问题，而人为地扭曲劳动力市场是徒劳无益的，与其如此，还不如更多地关注失业保险的待遇，以及如何促进经济的长期增长。同样，给予残疾人的福利待遇也应该以他们的残疾情况为基础，而不是当成失业问题来处理。

提高退休年龄。由此得出的一个必然结论是，缓慢地提高中国的退休年龄不会给失业问题带来显著影响。

养老金体系的管理

对养老金体系的管理，政府还需要在如下几个关键领域进行改革。

建立全国性的养老金管理机构。如果没有统一的全国体系，养老金福利就难以转移，从而制约劳动力流动。强制性缴费型养老金应该遵循一套简单的监管规则，同时让各个地方对福利水平有一定的调整空间。所有的养老金缴费，包括基本养老金和个人账户部分，都应该汇入一个总的统筹账户，一个全国性的信托基金。养老金的记录和发放应该由这个统一的全国性养老金管理机构负责。该机构还需要管理全国的数据库，包含每名员工的账户信息，并建立唯一的一套记录系统。这样一个全国性养老金管理机构应该有能力对强制性养老保险的财务前景进行准确预测，并开展更广泛的研究。为了增强社会对养老金体系的信心，体系的任何变化都应该在决策制定后及时通报公众。

缴费型养老金体系与政府预算分离。缴费型养老金体系应该继续与政府财政分离，这些养老金应该有专门的收入来源，盈余应该转移到全国社保基金（National Social Security Fund，NSSF），赤字则由该基金的资产收益（或者在必要的时候出售资产）来弥补。养老保险缴费应该由税务部门征收，然后迅速转移给养老金管理机构。在目前的并行体制下，劳动和社保部门以及税务部门都在负责征收，这增加了征收成本，结果也更加不准确。

历史成本的处理。在 1998 年推行养老制度改革的时候，中国需要处理好两方面的历史成本：给 1998 年以前退休的员工支付养老金，以及承认在岗员工在 1998 年前所累积的领取养老金的权利。认识到这些历史成本后，政府在 2003 年决定把部分国有企业的股权划拨给全国社保基金。然而划拨进程较为缓慢，只有较少数量的股份完成了转移。鉴于历史成本的巨大规模，继续向全国社保基金转移国有股权有两方面的潜在好处：一方面，把企业分红转移到养老金体系可以改善养老金的财务状况，减少财政补贴的需要；另一方面，全国社保基金作为长期投资者有助于改进国有企业的公司治理。

非缴费型基本养老金的管理。这一任务可以在短期和长期内通过不同的机构来执行。从长期来看，非缴费型基本养老金的管理机构与缴费型养老金的管理机构有着同样的任务：准确而及时地发放养老金。随着缴费型养老保险的普及，两个体制所覆盖的人群将变得越来越接近。那时，缴费型养老金的管理机构就可以自然而然地成为非缴费型养老金的管理者，因为所服务的对象越来越相似。但是，就目前而言，缴费型养老金并不是对全国发放，因此在近期，非缴费型养老金的发放任务让负责全国扶贫工作的低保管理机构来完成或许更合适。

结论

以上介绍的改革策略的目标是：给每个国民提供养老金，解决现有体系的问题，最终实现养老体系的合并。

这个策略具有内在一致性，符合中国今天的经济社会发展需要。有的建议与下一个五年规划有着直接的联系：为全国性养老保险体系建立统一的规则；建立有关的管理机制负责管理公民养老金并开始进行发放；通过引入公开的记账式个人账户体系来解决“空账”问题；将强制性城市养老保险体系扩展到农村地区的大企业，以及公共部门雇员；改进对自愿养老保险及其投资的资本市场的监管；以及改进管理水平，以支持全国性保险体制的建设等。

这一策略也能够适应长期的经济和社会发展需要。启动的改革最终会覆盖所有产业部门和所有地区的员工，避免分类建立的保险体制的各种问题（例如，界限划分不合理，有些人未能纳入任何一种类别，有些人的类别属性会在不同时期改变，有些分类已经过时等）。这一改革策略有利于保证劳动力的有效流动，也可以帮助在未来的适当时机做实强制性缴费体系中的个人账户。

总而言之，这一改革策略符合中国向高收入国家迈进的要求。

第七章　社会政策*

应对收入不平等的问题

中国在过去30年的经济改革帮助了5亿多人口摆脱了贫困。除了收入提高以外，在更广泛的“人类发展”指标上，中国也取得了长足的进步。然而，贫困依旧是中国面临的一个重要问题，国家实施的各个社会项目的范围和质量还有待提高，许多群体（例如农民工）基本上被排除在外。此外，最近10年，城乡之间以及城市和农村内部的收入不平等状况都有所恶化，中国的总体基尼系数大约从0.3攀升到0.45，城市内部和农村内部的基尼系数也都在上升（见图7–1）。贫富分化现象如果不能得到妥善解决，有可能导致更大的社会矛盾和社会动荡。

决策者应该如何应对收入不平等的问题？一个选择是从收

---

* 本章主要参考了如下背景论文：背景论文十五：李实，《中国社会保障改革：争论与选择》；背景论文五：尼古拉斯·巴尔和霍华德·格伦纳斯特，《社会政策：中国发展中的一项中心内容》；背景论文二：A.B.阿特金森，《中国社会政策改革中的问题》；背景论文三：朱迪思·巴尼斯特、大卫·布卢姆和拉里·罗森伯格，《中国的人口老龄化与经济增长》；背景论文十九：黄佩华，《为中国和谐社会建设而进行的公共部门改革》；以及背景论文十三：圣蒂亚戈·莱维，《对拉丁美洲社会政策的有关评论》。

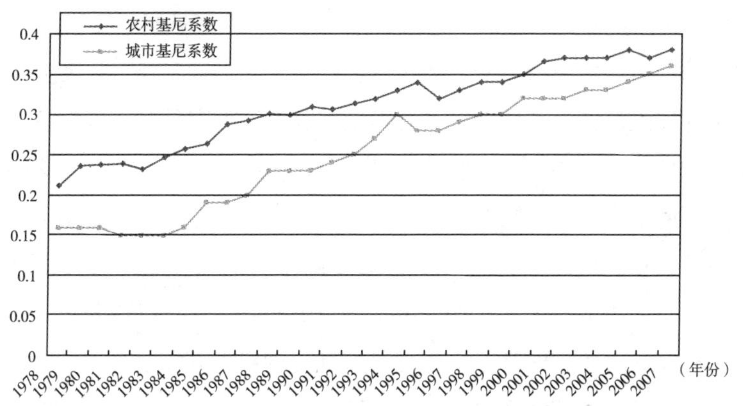

图 7-1　1978—2007 年中国的城市和农村的收入不平等状况

资料来源：张东生主编，《中国居民收入分配年度报告（2008）》，北京：经济科学出版社，2008 年 12 月。

入来源上采取行动，政府可以干预市场，调整市场的分配结果，例如大幅度提高最低工资标准等，但是这样的措施有可能给资源配置带来破坏性的扭曲。虽然加强劳动力市场监管的某些措施通常能发挥作用，但其他国家的经验表明，缩小收入差距的最佳办法还是应通过全方位的社会政策来实现。在英国，通过教育和医疗领域的现金补贴和实物福利，以基尼系数测算的不平等程度从 0.52 下降到了 0.31。[1] 瑞典和丹麦通过现金补贴也取得了类似的结果。美国利用各种社会项目把收入不平等程度缩小了 20%。在公平方面取得的这些进步并不需要以效率的巨大损失来换取，事实上，设计良好的社会政策完全可以促进生产率和增长速度的提高。

中国显然非常关注这方面的议题。“十一五”规划明确阐述了政府要缩小收入分配差距和改进社会项目的目标。作为和谐社

[1] 参见背景论文五：尼古拉斯·巴尔和霍华德·格伦纳斯特，《社会政策：中国发展中的一项中心内容》。

会建设的内容之一，政府在最近几年启动了几项重要的新政策和新项目，包括农村免费义务教育、农村合作医疗保险以及为困难家庭提供最低生活保障等。当然，与高收入国家乃至许多中等收入国家相比，中国的社会项目支出与 GDP 的比值还很低。这些项目还受到范围有限、覆盖面较为零散、福利分配非常不均以及不方便转移等问题的困扰，有的社会项目实际上对收入差距会产生利弊兼有的影响。例如，由于城市中的福利水平高于农村，富裕地区又高于贫困地区，虽然这些社会项目可以缩小当地的收入差距，却扩大了地区之间的不平等。

社会政策是政府实现缩小收入差距目标的强有力的工具。但为了切实发挥作用，现有的社会项目需要在多个方面进行改革，包括设计、规模、筹资办法，以及中央和地方政府的责任划分等。

改革的一般原则[1]

没有哪套社会制度能适合所有国家。人们无法从理论推理或者其他国家的经验中得出一套最优的社会模式，即使存在这样的模式，也不能从一个国家照搬到另一个国家。每个国家都需要根据历史背景和发展目标建设自己的制度，不过参与本报告和相关背景论文写作的各国学者们都一致认为，中国在对社会项目进行改进的时候，需要记住以下几项基本原则。

社会政策的制定必须与经济政策的制定紧密联系起来。社会政策和经济政策既可以实现互补，也可能发生冲突。应该预先认识和考虑这些可能的协同作用或相互摩擦，其目标是让社会项目

[1] 这些原则详见背景论文二：A.B.阿特金森，《中国社会政策改革中的问题》。

最大限度地发挥对经济的积极影响。近来的世界金融危机凸显了协同作用的效果，在危机来临时，许多国家的经济得到了社会安全网的缓冲，加速了复苏步伐。

在市场与政府之间寻求恰当的平衡。政府与市场之间的分工应根据谨慎的分析来决策，在政府采取干预措施前，应该准确查明希望纠正的市场失灵所在。政府在作出是否干预的决定之后，还必须考虑如何干预的问题：是直接提供相应的服务、购买所需要的服务、对相关服务进行监管，还是尊重服务对象的需要、发放补贴让人们自己购买服务？对这些问题的回答有时可以借鉴其他国家的经验和理论上的看法，例如，食品的生产和分配就可以在有监管之下或多或少交给市场去处理。相反，离开政府的积极介入，市场自身难以在扶贫、失业保险和初等教育等领域提供可靠的服务。在养老和医疗等其他一些领域，政府与市场实现恰当分工的界限较为模糊，各国必须根据自己的国情来制定决策。

社会项目尽可能地确保全国性的普遍覆盖。普遍覆盖可以帮助缩小贫富差距，促进社会融合，还能有助于效率的提高。政府的社会项目如果通过覆盖全国范围的体系来实施，就能顺利实现福利权益的转移。这反过来会加强劳动力市场的灵活性，方便人们在其他地方寻求工作的时候携带自己的福利和权益。

尽量避免制度性的缺陷，因为历史问题很难纠正。制度一旦成型，社会就会形成维持其存在的既得利益。美国的医疗体制清楚地表明，有缺陷的制度对改革可能产生令人震惊的巨大阻挠作用。中国的社会项目在设计时，尤其需要关注正规部门与非正规部门的二元结构问题。

在资源允许的情况下，社会项目应该能够比较容易地推广。社会项目的规模当然要与能动用的财力相匹配，但项目设计应容易实现“升级”：在资源投入增加以后，可以在不对原有体制进行根本改造的情况下推广扩大。能投入的资源取决于国家的财力，财力又取决于国家的经济实力和政治形势。比较崇尚个人主义和冒险精神的国家（如美国）往往倾向于福利水平较低的制度，而更加关注社会团结和风险规避的国家（如瑞典）则会选择更广泛和深入的福利政策。

在中央政府、地方政府和个人之间公平地分配服务成本。社会服务的管理应该根据其特性以及对地方需求作出及时响应的重要性，寻求最理想的分权安排。向服务对象收取一定的费用（即使是很小的金额）也可能有助于实现更合理的利用。然而，许多社会项目（包括初等教育、基本医疗和扶贫等）会对更大范围的经济发展和社会团结产生外溢效应，符合全国性公共品的定义。根据这一认识，许多发达国家的中央政府近年来越来越多地参与这些项目的制度设计、筹资安排和监管事务，制定服务的最低标准，为满足这些标准提供必要的资金支持，并由中央来推动项目的强制执行。

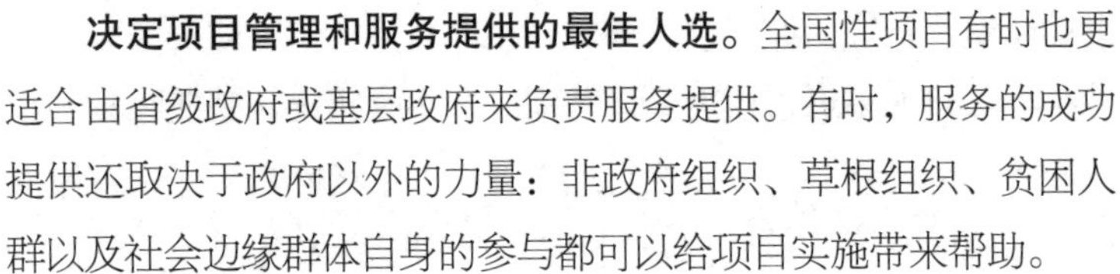

决定项目管理和服务提供的最佳人选。全国性项目有时也更适合由省级政府或基层政府来负责服务提供。有时，服务的成功提供还取决于政府以外的力量：非政府组织、草根组织、贫困人群以及社会边缘群体自身的参与都可以给项目实施带来帮助。

确保项目能够得到有效的监督、测算和评估。很多时候，政府并不清楚它们的社会项目究竟有没有取得成功。因此在项目设计的时候就应该考虑对成果的测算，政府必须确定合适的指标、收集必要的数据并长期坚持不懈地进行监督，还需要提高合格的研究和评估能力。

这些基本原则适用于各种类型的社会政策和社会项目。有些项目已经在前文进行了讨论（如第五章涉及的失业保险和教育领域的某些方面，第六章涉及的养老保险等）。本章将重点放在其他关键的社会政策和社会项目上，首先是进一步分析教育对社会公平和经济发展的重要性。

教育

在很大程度上，中国的贫富差距源于教育。富人和穷人的受教育状况相差很大，他们从教育中获得的投资回报也不同。对政府来说，减轻穷人的教育负担、增加受教育机会应该是一项首要任务。中国已经成功地将小学教育扩大到几乎所有的儿童（包括最贫困地区在内），也扩大了中学教育。贫困家庭的子女能享受书本费减免，另外还得到了一笔生活补助，补偿儿童入学的机会成本。

假如不是每个人都能得到良好的教育，经济增长最终会减慢，经济会形成二元特征，导致生产率低下的非熟练生产与现代化的高技术生产并存。拉丁美洲国家的历史突出反映了这一危险，非洲国家在某些程度上同样如此。在那些国家，很多没有受过良好教育的人难以在经济现代化进程找到合适的工作，可以说，这些人是被抛弃了。随着社会中的富裕人群逐渐接近发达国家的收入水平，经济增长率最终会下降，而贫困现象却依然持续。中国还没有凸显这一问题，国民的识字率高于几乎所有其他发展中国家，然而绝不能忽视教育普及的困难和教育质量下滑的风险。

中国对教育经费支出作了分权化的安排，各个学校依靠当地政府提供资金。结果导致，各地在经济发展水平上的巨大差距也反映到学校质量的巨大差距上来。按照经济学的原理，基础教育总体上应该由政府负担，但理论并没有明确指出，支出责任是应该交给地方政府还是中央政府。不过在发达国家，中央政府正越来越关心提高学生的成绩，并缩小他们之间的差距。教育标准的提高越来越被视为全国性的公共产品，它的实现必须依靠中央政府向教育投入很大的资源，并正确调动起学校的积极性。

这些国家的实践对中国有哪些启发呢？它们表明，如果中央政府希望提高教育水平、缩小学生之间的差距，就必须将更多的资源用于支持教育和发展学校。具体做法可以有很多，例如，中央政府可以根据各地的经济发展水平和人口数量给地方提供专门拨款，但为改进教育质量，这笔资金必须有附加条件，以促使地方政府或学校致力于改进教育水平和提高学生成绩。

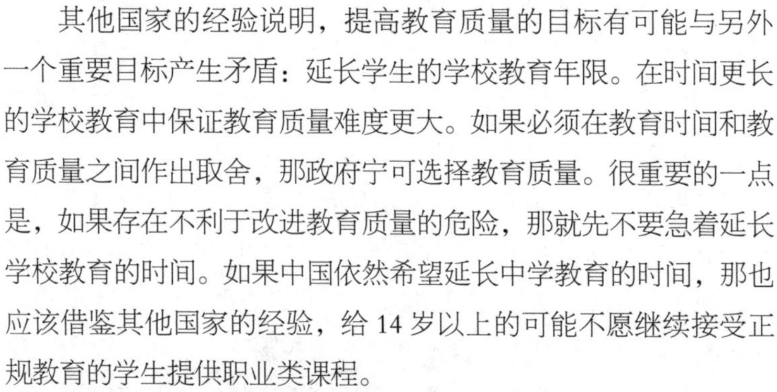

其他国家的经验说明，提高教育质量的目标有可能与另外一个重要目标产生矛盾：延长学生的学校教育年限。在时间更长的学校教育中保证教育质量难度更大。如果必须在教育时间和教育质量之间作出取舍，那政府宁可选择教育质量。很重要的一点是，如果存在不利于改进教育质量的危险，那就先不要急着延长学校教育的时间。如果中国依然希望延长中学教育的时间，那也应该借鉴其他国家的经验，给 14 岁以上的可能不愿继续接受正规教育的学生提供职业类课程。

更多地关注学龄前教育以及婴幼儿的营养和看护，对中国也是大为有益的。最新的研究发现，一个人的智力、社交和情感开发的基础基本上是在 5 岁以前成型的，因此，早期教育开发至关重要。很多国家采取的相应措施包括：通过立法要求雇主给男女雇员提供产假，积极发展学龄前教育机构，延长在校时间，加强学校与日托机构及其他看护机构的联系以满足工作时间各不相同的父母的要求等。许多国家目前都通过家庭帮助中心提供健康检查和育儿经验，有的国家还给带子女接种疫苗和上学的父母提供现金补助。

人力资本对中国的经济发展战略至关重要。保证儿童的福利水平和智力开发是最佳的人力资本投资，因此，在资源允许的范围内逐步扩大学龄前教育机构应该是合理的选择。在中长期，中国还可以效仿一些国家的做法，引入儿童福利制度：无论家庭收入状况如何，给每名儿童都按周发放补贴，通常是交给孩子的母亲。

医疗卫生

中国的医疗卫生体制曾经是实现全面覆盖的典范，尤其是相对于当初的经济发展阶段而言。但目前的情况已不复如此。在医疗领域，中国给市场的空间或许过大了。医疗服务的责任被下放给资源极其有限的基层政府，旧体制中的初级卫生所以及疾病预防体系大部分崩溃。医院成为主要的医疗服务提供方，费用上升很快。结果导致医疗方面的进步减慢，个人的医疗费用急剧提高（包括参与了医疗保险的人），收入不平等也传递到医疗卫生的不平等上面。

中国政府没有忽视这些问题，从 1998 年开始就引入了各项改革，包括对城镇职工实行的强制性医疗保险，给其他城市居民提供的基本医疗保险，以及给农村居民提供的新型合作医疗保险计划等。这些措施是值得欢迎的，但仍然存在令人担忧的方面：医疗服务的便利性依然不平等，随地区、工作岗位和年龄有很大差异；许多人依旧面临收入水平难以承担巨额的医疗费用；成本较低并能惠及全社会的初级医疗服务和疾病预防没有得到充分重视；医院的财务安排较复杂，太关注投入而非效果；农村的医疗保障创新方向虽然正确，但如果参保人罹患重病，仍需负担相对收入水平而言太重的个人支出。

有关医疗体制的任何讨论都必须首先把费用问题和服务提供问题区分开来。几乎所有发达国家都采取了某种形式的集体负担医疗费用的做法，医疗费用越来越多地来自税收，而非雇主。许多国家还引入和提高了共同负担的比例，或者用户付费制度，但其目标主要是防止过度医疗服务，控制成本，而非以此作为主要筹资手段。

这些国家的经验同经济学理论是一致的，理论上认为，医疗服务的费用应主要来自公共机构，对医疗保险体制来说尤其如此。其理由是，每个人在不同时期面临的健康风险不尽相同，完全依赖私人保险最后总会导致市场按照风险类别进行区别对待（这是保险业的利润来源），结果使得那些先天或后天（如在罹患癌症以后）面临较高风险的人难以负担高昂的保险费用，也就无法获得其覆盖的医疗服务。更糟糕的是，如果像美国那样，把医疗保障与就业紧密挂钩，健康风险较高的人在离开某位雇主或失业之后会同时失去医疗保险及医疗服务，由于健康风险高，他们也更难找到工作。

但是，公共筹资并不必然代表服务也要由公共机构提供。在英国和北欧国家，医疗服务主要是由公立机构负责，加拿大主要依靠私立机构，法国和德国则是二者的混合。无论是采取哪种服务提供方式，一个广泛的共识是，良好的初级医疗服务是改进健康、预防疾病和控制医疗成本的最佳办法。

中国应该抓住机会在医疗卫生领域显示出更坚定的决心。国际经验表明，中国应该考虑建立一个更加统一、普遍覆盖和主要由税收收入支持的医疗体制。中国需要改进医院管理以控制成本，并通过测算诊疗效果、等候时间以及质量标准执行情况等措施，来激发医疗机构从业者提供优质服务的动力。政府在医疗卫生领域的目标需要提高，支出也应增加。虽然近年来医疗费用在持续上升，但以国际标准来看还较低。此外，还需要考虑在医疗服务中引入更多的私人机构，以加强竞争和丰富消费者的选择。

低保制度

医疗和教育的改善可以帮助缓解中国依然存在的贫困问题（当然自 20 世纪 70 年代末以来贫困率已大幅降低），但政府并不只是依靠这些项目，90 年代后期中国政府引入了低保制度（即最低生活保障制度，简称低保制度），给符合条件的人提供最低生活标准保障，到 2005 年扩大到农村，如今已经惠及约 7000 万对象（见表 7–1）。

表 7–1　2000—2008 年低保制度所帮助的城市和农村人口（百万）

年份	2000	2001	2002	2003	2004	2005	2006	2007	2008
城市	4.0	11.7	20.6	22.5	22.1	22.3	22.4	22.7	23.3
农村	3.0	3.0	4.1	3.7	4.9	8.3	15.9	35.7	43.1

资料来源：民政部，《2008 年全国民政事业发展统计报告》。

扶贫既有助于改善社会公平，也能帮助提高经济效率。例如，如果有学生挨饿，那么对学校的投入就会被浪费。还有，中东欧国家的政策制定者在经济自由化过程中发现，如果受到不利影响的人没有社会安全网的保护，经济发展将会面临更大的阻碍。财政联邦制理论得出的一个有力的结论是，穷人的社会福利支出不应该让地方政府来负担，部分原因是贫困地区的财力更为有限，还有部分原因是地方更容易受到常见的经济冲击，例如一家大型企业关闭可能波及所有当地居民。

这表明，如果要把低保制度作为中国未来的社会扶助项目的基石，有几个方面还需要加以改进。该制度的覆盖面应该扩大到所有符合条件的人，包括农民工和非正规部门的员工。资格的判定应该更为严格，福利发放则应简化，执行中的偏差现象要消除。低保标准的设计还必须更加系统，根据更准确的贫困测评结果，需要与生活成本的变化挂钩。为了使该制度对各地保持公平，中央政府应该考虑在支出义务方面承担更大的责任。当然，制度的执行需要各级政府、基层管理单位以及社区的共同努力。此外还应建立一套监督体系，以追踪项目的执行情况并评估实施效果。

人口政策

中国的人口在迅速老龄化，15~64 岁的人口所占的比重在过去几十年曾快速上升，但已经越过峰值，并将在未来数十年中快速下滑。人口趋势预测显示，到 2050 年，60 岁以上的人口所占的比重将超过 30%。[1]中国人口老龄化的根本原因与其他国家相似：生育率下降，预期寿命延长，以及过去的出生率和死亡率的变化造成的长期影响等。另外一个关键的影响因素是中国的独生子女政策。

中国目前存在一个普遍担心：未来的人口结构会影响经济增长，并给那时的劳动群体造成巨大的赡养负担。这样的困难并不罕见，其他老龄化国家也遇到了类似的困扰。中国或许可以考虑借鉴其他国家已采取的某些政策措施，包括提高退休年龄，帮助需要照看小孩的家长兼顾工作，提高女性的劳动参与率，以及改进在岗员工的生产率等。这些措施的落实有望在相当程度上抵消社会老龄化对经济的消极影响。

适当放松独生子女政策对维持中国的经济增长率来说并非关键因素，但这一调整可以让工作年龄段的人口所占的比重逐步回

[1] 参见背景论文三：朱迪思·巴尼斯特、大卫·布卢姆和拉里·罗森伯格，《中国的人口老龄化和经济增长》的综述部分。

升。更重要的是，该政策的放松或许有助于扭转人口中男女比例严重失衡的状况。男女比例失衡是有选择的人工流产以及轻视女孩的结果，它可能导致上千万男性难以找到结婚对象，并使他们在晚年也得不到配偶和子孙的关怀。

社会政策的总体规划和管理

中国政府在“十一五”规划期间的创新措施符合各国专家们为本报告总结的若干原则，但很明显，在社会政策领域，要想建立一个有着良好设计、管理和监督的体系，以有效应对贫富差距问题、促进经济增长，还有大量工作要做，也有可能完成。

社会政策应该更好地与经济政策相协调。中国在“十一五”规划和“十二五”规划建议中突出了社会政策的重要性，已经在社会目标上取得的显著进步也值得肯定。但规划本身还不是一个能充分实现社会政策与经济政策相互协调的机制。规划虽然列举了指导原则和发展目标，但这些列举并没有详尽的政策内容提供支持。规划的法律地位也不明确，对于负责政策执行的部委和省市没有足够的影响力。还有，中国面临的实际情况正处于迅速变化中，这要求更频繁地开展监督工作。为了在未来的中长期发展中更好地协调社会政策和经济政策，中国应该考虑采取另外的机制，这些机制能够有效地把宽泛的目标转化成中央、省级和基层各级的具体行动计划，通过清晰的指标来监督执行。

考虑到中国的巨大规模以及各地在经济社会发展方面的差异，欧盟的“社会融合进程”在这方面可以给中国带来有益的启发。欧盟的“社会融合进程”试图解决若干领域的社会排斥现象，而不是仅仅将关注点放在贫困问题上。由于社会政策主要是各成员国的内部事务，社会融合进程负责制定共同的政策目标，然后将其转化成各国的行动计划。目标的完成情况根据预先同意的一套社会指标来进行监督，并通过各国间的同行评估和比较政策分析来推进，鼓励各成员国的相互借鉴。项目的进展根据共同的社会指标来追踪，并可以进行跨国的数据比较，以便对各国的成绩作出对比评估。中国可以通过类似的程序来监督各省市和地区的社会政策的效果。

中国的各个社会项目还较为零碎和分散。尽管覆盖面有所扩大，但多数项目主要还是服务于城市的正规部门的就业人员，而非其他群体。许多项目忽略了广大农村人口，以及越来越多的农民工和非正规部门的其他员工（他们约占城市劳动力总数的一半）。政府在扩大社会项目的时候，往往采取修修补补的做法，增加一些社会项目来覆盖需要帮助的特定群体，如失地农民或者农民工等。从风险汇聚的角度来看，这样的做法效率不高，更重要的是，它会限制福利的转移，从而制约劳动力的流动和灵活性。更好的政策选择应该是将更多的群体纳入现有的体制。

中国有能力扩大社会项目的支出。与其他国家相比，中国政府目前对该领域的投入明显偏低。例如，政府预算中的教育经费仅占 GDP 的 3.2%，远低于越南以及下中等收入国家的平均值，更无法同经合组织的国家相比（参见图 7–2）。中国在医疗领域的公共支出仅占 GDP 的 1.8%，也显著低于大多数下中等收入国家（见表 7–2）。[1] 从国际标准来看，中国政府的财政状况良好，完全可以向医疗、教育以及其他紧要的社会项目投入更多的资金。

❶ 教育和医疗支出的数据来自背景论文十九：黄佩华，《为中国和谐社会建设而进行的公共部门改革》。

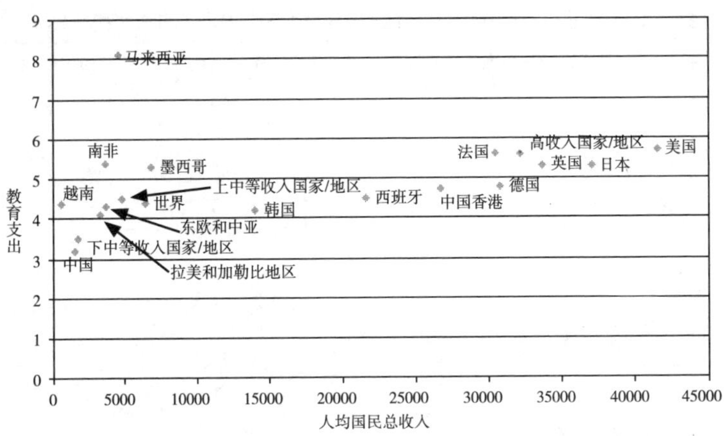

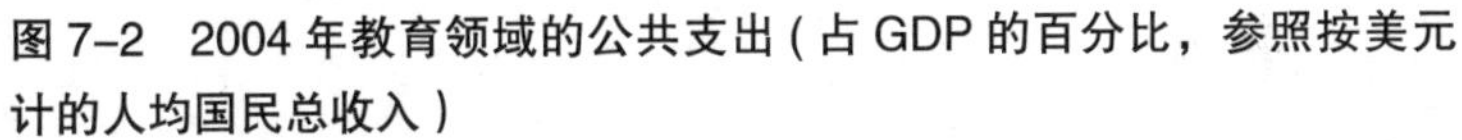

图 7-2　2004 年教育领域的公共支出（占 GDP 的百分比，参照按美元计的人均国民总收入）

资料来源：Dahlman、Zeng and Wang，“The Challenge of Life Long Learning for Education Finance in China”，为中国财政部和世界银行在 2006 年组织的研讨会提供的论文。

中国将大多数基本公共服务的责任下放给了较低层级的政府，对于一个规模如此巨大、中央政府的机构编制相对很小的国家来说，这样的做法可以理解。然而，受各地自力更生的传统原则的影响，中国在这方面的分权化程度超过了任何一个发达国家和大多数发展中国家。结果导致贫困地区，尤其是农村地区能用于社会项目的资金太少。事实上，尽管城市人口还少于农村人口，中国政府对城市的社会福利的投入却几乎相当于农村的社会福利投入的 4 倍。因此，如果中国希望在教育和医疗等公共服务领域确保全国性的最低保障水平，中央政府就必须大幅增加资金投入，制定标准并激励地方政府达标。

表 7-2 中国和不同国家或地区的公共医疗支出占 GDP 之比（%）

国家 / 经济体 / 地区	1990—1998 年 *	2005 年
中国	2.0	1.8
高收入国家	6.2	7.0
中等收入国家	3.1	2.9
下中等收入国家		2.2
低收入国家	1.3	1.2
位于不同地区的低收入和中等收入国家		
东亚和太平洋地区	1.7	1.8
欧洲和中亚地区	4.0	4.1
拉美和加勒比地区	3.3	3.3
中东和北非地区	2.4	3.0
南亚地区	0.8	0.9
撒哈拉以南非洲地区	1.5	2.6

* 数据来自这个时间段中最近的能获得数据的年份。

资料来源：世界银行的《世界发展报告》（1998—2006 年）以及 2008 年的世界发展指数。

中央政府应该在社会项目的设计、筹资和监管方面发挥更大的作用，但首先必须强化相关的行政能力。如果没有培养出足够的行政管理能力，中国就不可能过渡到全国性体制。随着中央政府作用的扩大，其他层级的政府的责任也必须相应调整，也要培养履行新职责所需要的能力。

在政府机构培养出执行社会项目的能力之后，还必须让官员们有意愿来推动体制的运转，对他们的激励也要与正在实施的社会项目的总目标挂钩。这就要求更好地收集和公布有关项目执行和效果的信息，还包括广泛征求公众的意见，因为他们才是社会项目的目标受益者。通常来说，一项政策是否做到了“以人为本”，最好是让人民自己来判断。

第八章　中国在世界经济中的角色*

与二战以后其他国家出现的追赶式增长一样，中国最近取得的经济成就也是全球化的成果，包括关税的下调、运输成本的降低以及通信交流的顺畅。开放的全球经济给中国的增长提供了两个关键要素：知识和市场。中国从世界其他国家获取了大量的技术、诀窍和观念，将其消化吸收并在很多地方加以改进。这样的学习促进了生产率的快速提高，扩大了经济的供给能力。供给能力的发挥离不开需求，而中国也充分利用了国际市场深化扩大的机遇，给工业革命的成果创造了可靠的出路。中国在受益于全球化的同时，也为这一进程作出了极大贡献。中国的对外开放在2001年12月加入世界贸易组织时达到高潮，成为全球化历史中值得专门书写的一个篇章。

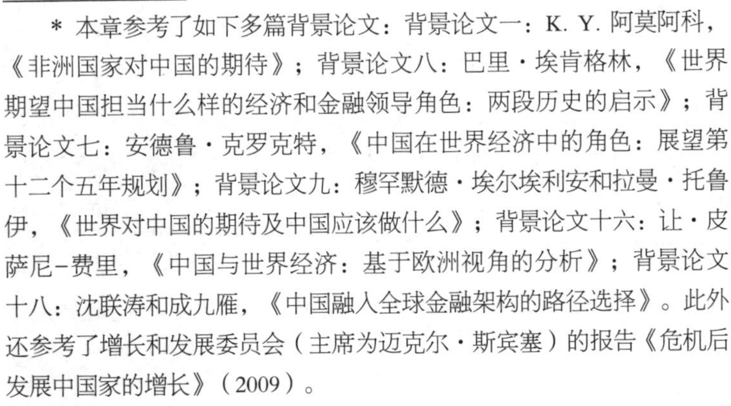

* 本章参考了如下多篇背景论文：背景论文一：K. Y. 阿莫阿科，《非洲国家对中国的期待》；背景论文八：巴里·埃肯格林，《世界期望中国担当什么样的经济和金融领导角色：两段历史的启示》；背景论文七：安德鲁·克罗克特，《中国在世界经济中的角色：展望第十二个五年规划》；背景论文九：穆罕默德·埃尔埃利安和拉曼·托鲁伊，《世界对中国的期待及中国应该做什么》；背景论文十六：让·皮萨尼-费里，《中国与世界经济：基于欧洲视角的分析》；背景论文十八：沈联涛和成九雁，《中国融入全球金融架构的路径选择》。此外还参考了增长和发展委员会（主席为迈克尔·斯宾塞）的报告《危机后发展中国家的增长》（2009）。

中国经济总量已在近期超越日本，成为全球第二大经济体，具有了可以影响全局的地位。对全球市场上从大宗商品到制造品的各类产品的相对价格而言，中国的经济增长具有显著的影响力。中国的外汇储备全球领先，高达 2.85 万亿美元，对全球金融市场举足轻重。此外，中国还在若干发展中国家发挥着越来越显著的重要作用，购买当地产品、投资于当地资产尤其是自然资源。发展中国家在本次金融危机之后的强劲复苏很大程度上也是由于中国的增长反弹和持续开放。

金融危机的后果

世界经济给中国的成功带来了巨大支持，但近年来却遭受自大萧条以来最严重的打击。债务刺激下的资产价格膨胀、消费过度、储蓄不足以及持续的经常账户赤字，在 2008 年秋无以为继，最终演变成金融危机，给美国经济健康造成全面破坏，也波及世界很多地区。随之而来的消费、投资、就业和国际贸易额迅速下滑，使危机蔓延至实体经济。危机的策源地是美国的金融业，但其辐射范围却远超过美国，全球没有哪个国家能独善其身。

美国居民和银行的财务状况仍处于修复中，而美国政府的负债却在迅速增加。美国金融市场的信贷利差的确已经缩小，增长率有所恢复。但即使联邦基金利率已降低到接近零利率的水平，产出却没有如许多人期望的那样强势反弹，而且增长所创造的就业机会少得可怜。美国目前的失业率仍高达 9%，如果把那些原本希望找一份全职工作，却因形势所迫而不得不做临时工或彻底放弃找工作的人考虑进来，总失业率可能高达 16%。随着高失业率持续时间的延长，更多分析师开始担心增长率和就业率的背离是否有更深层的结构性原因，反映了几个新兴经济大国在全球供应链中的竞争力的增强。

欧元区则受到部分成员国主权债务危机带来的多次市场冲击的影响。欧盟已经着手帮助这些国家解决近期的资金需要，但被迫以某种形式进行债务重组的威胁依然存在。这一结果导致，欧元面临的不稳定风险仍未消失。这些问题需要欧盟就如何在成员国中分担成本达成艰难的政治决定，才可能解决。

占全球 GDP 总额 2/3（按市场汇率测算）的发达国家可能会面临更长时间的低速增长，很多国家的高失业率将很难改善。相比之下，发展中国家却非常顺利地度过了本次风暴的洗礼，这要归功于它们采取的谨慎的宏观经济政策，还有受到严格监管的相对稳健的金融业避免了有毒资产的侵害。

不过，尽管新兴经济体实现了强劲复苏，世界经济不太可能也不必回到危机前的增长率水平。在 2007—2008 年看似是“常态”的增长条件实际上是不可持续的，尤其是在美国。美国的经济增长过度依赖居民家庭资产的膨胀，而世界经济又过度依赖美国的居民需求。本次危机不仅仅是这些趋势的中断，在很多方面，还是趋势发展到极限的必然结果。

所以，全球经济需要转向新的常态模式，但问题是将会走向什么样的常态模式？这很难预测，因为它在很大程度上还处于变化过程中。新的模式将取决于各国政府在退出危机时作出的政策选择，如重振需求、改革金融体系、抵制贸易保守主义、解决汇率和贸易失衡问题，以及克服危机前的体制中潜伏的制约增长的结构性障碍等。因此，新的常态模式不只是预测的问题，还要考虑如何建设。中国通过转变增长方式和在国际决策中发挥影响力，将为新的常态模式作出重要贡献。

世界经济的重新调整

发达国家的危机爆发和新兴市场的反弹加快了世界经济的重组。美国在忙于摆脱债务危机的时候，会更加关注内部问题，在需要合作与妥协的国际事务上投入的精力会减少，包括世界贸易谈判和国际金融体系改革等。如果幸运，在国内经济复苏后，美国对这些国际议题的关注将随之提升。欧盟是全球治理议题的天然拥护者，但目前它面临太多的内部经济挑战，在全球经济中的地位也在下降。日本在全球经济中的相对重要性同样在减弱，此外，日本通常不情愿在世界经济和全球金融体系的管理上发挥主导性的作用。

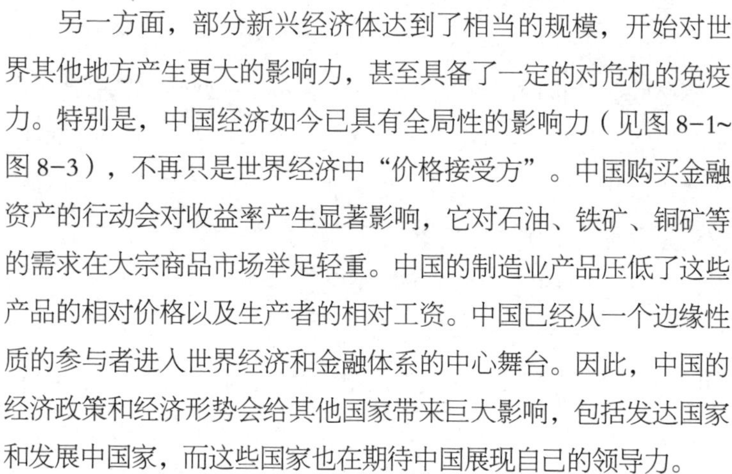

另一方面，部分新兴经济体达到了相当的规模，开始对世界其他地方产生更大的影响力，甚至具备了一定的对危机的免疫力。特别是，中国经济如今已具有全局性的影响力（见图 8-1~图 8-3），不再只是世界经济中“价格接受方”。中国购买金融资产的行动会对收益率产生显著影响，它对石油、铁矿、铜矿等的需求在大宗商品市场举足轻重。中国的制造业产品压低了这些产品的相对价格以及生产者的相对工资。中国已经从一个边缘性质的参与者进入世界经济和金融体系的中心舞台。因此，中国的经济政策和经济形势会给其他国家带来巨大影响，包括发达国家和发展中国家，而这些国家也在期待中国展现自己的领导力。

在发达国家的复苏步伐缓慢且依旧不稳定的情况下，新兴经济体在已获得足够的分量后，看来能够依然保持稳健的增长。部分原因是它们自身规模的扩大，另外也是由于这些经济体的需求结构发生了改变。随着收入水平的提升，某些新兴经济体已成长为足够庞大的、颇具吸引力的市场。一个与此有关的因素是新兴

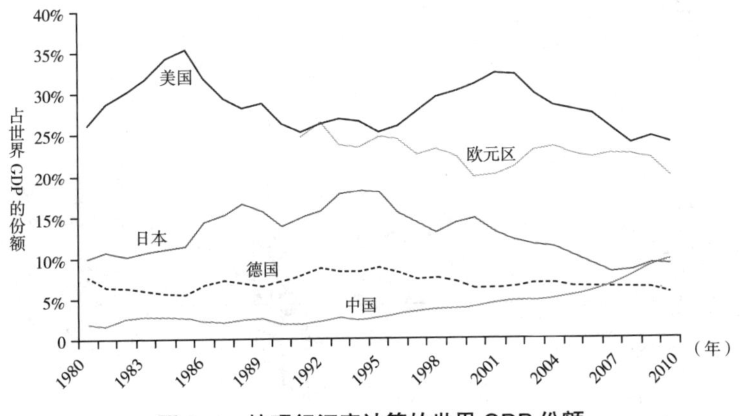

图 8–1　按现行汇率计算的世界 GDP 份额

资料来源：IMF。

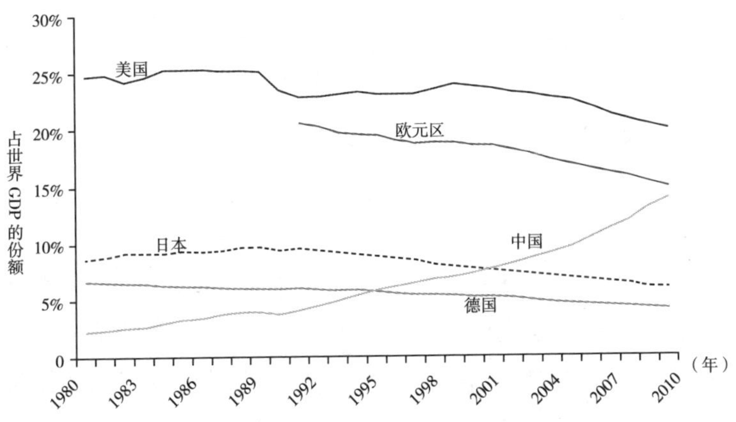

图 8–2　按购买力平价计算的世界 GDP 份额

资料来源：IMF。

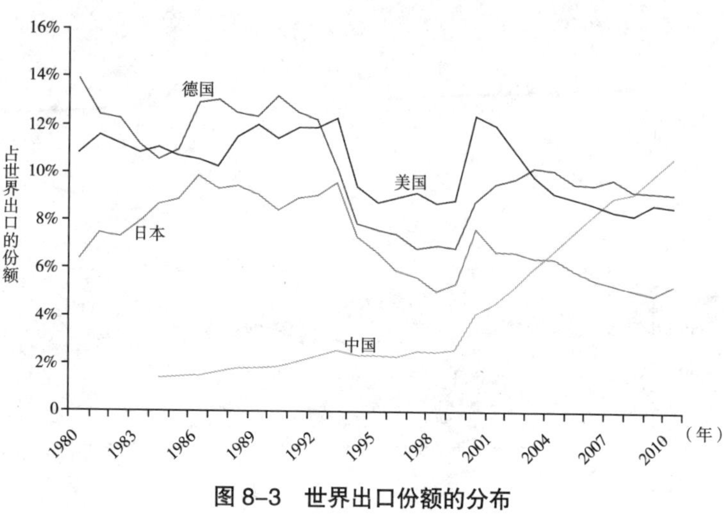

图 8–3　世界出口份额的分布

资料来源：IMF。

经济体之间的贸易额的增长，如今，对于韩国和印度等一系列国家而言，中国都是一个规模巨大的贸易伙伴，甚至是很多国家最大的贸易伙伴。

这个在 10 年前还不存在的新形势增强了新兴经济体的复原力和经济上的独立性，但并不代表与发达国家的完全脱钩。发达国家依然是它们外需的重要组成部分，其影响力不难想象，假设发达国家再遭受一次经济衰退的打击（这种情况不容易发生，但可能性也不能排除），新兴经济体要想完好无损是不可能的。

随着新兴经济体对发达国家经济依赖程度的下降，它们对中国的经济依赖程度会相应提高。如果中国的增长速度快速下滑，其他发展中国家将立刻有所感受，例如，拉丁美洲国家经济增长迅速复苏的一个关键因素是与中国的贸易，这已不是什么秘密。

显然，世界经济将继续呈现更加多极化的特征，新兴经济体尤其是中国将成为更加重要的角色。这样的经济实力重组将造成紧张关系，会削弱其他国家长期拥有的地位，要求采取新的程序和新的思考方式，并使某些政策的效力下降。这种变化有可能促发严重的政策失误和市场事故。

这些紧张关系将由于世界经济复苏的不平衡而加剧，增长速度不同的国家可能会有不同的政策诉求。复苏滞后的经济体可能采用非常规的政策（如量化宽松的货币政策）来刺激增长，增长速度更快的国家则可能以非常规的政策来回应，包括宏观上的审慎监管和资本管制等。复苏的不平衡还会加剧贸易保护主义抬头的危险，一些失业率很高的国家的政治风向可能会转向敌视对外贸易。

自二战以来，美国作为世界经济领头羊的地位给它带来了一系列特权和义务，世界其他国家一直希望美国负责提供若干服务。这些服务通常被视为全球公共品，其中包括：扮演终极消费者的角色；在某些情况下，通过《广场协议》等约定来帮助协调宏观经济政策；提供储备货币；在金融危机中扮演终极贷款人的角色，给美元短缺的新兴市场补充资金；引领全球贸易谈判，支持世界贸易组织等多边机构的运转。

美国经济在世界经济中的份额正在下降，履行上述责任的能力因为本次金融危机受到严重削弱，例如，美国已很难重新担任终极消费者的角色。随着美国支配地位的下降，人们很不清楚美国是否仍能继续提供以上那些关键的全球性公共产品。担当若干重要的全球事务，包括世界总需求的再平衡和重振、促进国际贸易和跨国投资，以及应对气候变化等，迫切要求得到各国的集体关注时，今天的世界却面临一个全球治理缺乏领导的时期。

有些人希望中国承担起与其经济实力匹配的全球责任，然而，尽管中国经济的规模已十分庞大，其人均收入却仍处于较低水平，数以百万计的中国人还需要从农村转移出来，加入经济现代化进程。由于中国依然是个相对贫穷的国家，它会很自然地认为尚不足以承担起国际上的各种责任。中国仍专注于国内问题，希望在达到更高收入水平后再负担国际体系的各种义务。一个经济体在早期的发展阶段就产生了如此全局性的影响力，这在世界历史上恐怕还没有先例。

全球需求的再平衡

在美国现今很难继续承担的国际责任中，最显著的一个就是终极消费者的角色。二十国集团（G20）就中期的全球需求再平衡和重振进行了大量讨论，但还没有真正行动起来。

随着美国储蓄率的提高，全球总需求将出现不足。美国方面相信，如果不增加净出口就不能实现充分就业。重振美国的出口产业将伴随着供给方面的一些艰难调整，让资源离开建筑业，进入可贸易部门。在进行这些调整的时候，美国或许可以借鉴德国的思路，通过对工资水平的严格控制和出色的生产率改进来刺激出口繁荣。不过供给方面的调整只是问题的一个方面，这是道简单的算术题，单靠美国自身是无法提高净出口水平的，除非世界其他国家能扩大总体的需求。

欧洲和日本的人口老龄化严重，难以在重振世界需求方面扮演重要角色（当然，缩小德国的巨额经常项目盈余会有所帮助）。因此，世界普遍希望巴西、俄罗斯、印度和中国（所谓的“金砖四国”，BRICs）能发挥作用。责任尤其落到中国身上，希望它能进一步刺激消费者支出，减少经常项目盈余。这与中国自身正积极推进的新的增长方式是一致的，在目标上不存在根本冲突。分歧主要在于调整的方式和速度上，批评者们敦促中国更快地缩小贸易盈余。但很重要的一点是应该注意到，如果太急于减少中国的过度储蓄，使经济稳定和增长受到影响，对任何人其实都没有好处。国际舆论经常忽略了这一点。

有些批评中国经常项目盈余的人似乎相信，贸易是个零和游戏，一个国家的所得就是另一个国家的损失。这种思路没有认识到中国的增长带来了显著的外部收益。尽管这样的批评是片面的，却能够极大地影响政界。各种抱怨可能会破坏有关国际贸易和外国投资（包括跨国并购和技术转移等）的政治决策。然而，一旦在讨论中摒弃零和游戏的错误观念，就能认识到，中国和世界其他国家的利益在很大程度上是一致的。中国应该缩小贸易盈余的规模，这既对本国的经济有益，也能惠及更广泛的世界经济。

中国的再平衡

中国的经常账户盈余加上巨大的外国直接投资和其他形式的不那么受欢迎的资本流入，造成了外汇储备的高速增长。对于一个处于现有发展阶段的国家而言，连续数年将多达相当于GDP10%的资金用于积累外国资产，显然是个浪费。这些外汇储备大多用于购买美国国债。考虑到美国的财政状况和未来走势，这些资产很容易受通货膨胀和美元进一步贬值的冲击，属于高风险、低回报的类型。也就是说，对人民币实行有管理的升值政策可以带来一个副产品，让中国的外汇储备能获得超过美国国债利率水平的更高收益。

中国的贸易盈余是高储蓄率和巨额出口的反映。但随着中国在发达国家的传统产品市场出现一段时期的停滞，未来出口对经济增长的促进作用会减小。当然，一个国家的出口可以比市场总体增长得更快，但这也意味着会进一步扩大中国市场的份额，从而会与发达国家和发展中国家的贸易伙伴形成紧张关系。所以，即便巨额贸易盈余符合中国自身的利益，但如果可能引发破坏性的贸易战，还是应该放弃。

中国也应该减少对发达国家市场的依赖，更多转向新兴经济体，特别是本国市场。除了为应对危机采取的财政刺激以外，中国还应该最大限度地利用国内市场来刺激增长，这并不代表排斥出口产业的继续进步，而是二者的叠加。在目前阶段，谨慎的做法是尽可能在各个市场上分散份额，刺激经济转型，减少增长面临的风险。

事实上，减少经常账户盈余也是中国“十一五”规划的一个目标，关键的问题在于如何做到？有一派意见认为，中国的贸易盈余和汇率机制有着密切联系，这个观点很常见，反映在众多知名分析师和记者近期发表的大量评论中。他们认为汇率是贸易盈余的主要原因，也是解决问题的主要政策工具，在他们看来，人民币汇率的升值足以消除贸易盈余。

要想恢复外部平衡而不影响经济增长，的确会涉及汇率，但仅关注汇率是不够的，汇率实际上甚至不能算贸易盈余的主要原因。中国的上一轮汇率升值发生在2005—2008年，那段时期却伴随着经常账户盈余的剧增，而非减少。国外的许多评论家简单地归结说，汇率升值还不够，但他们显然低估了中国如果保持过度储蓄不变而必须经历的结构调整幅度。中国的过度储蓄有着深刻的原因（美国的储蓄不足同样有着深刻的原因），并不仅仅是汇率的问题。

单靠汇率的进一步升值未必能发挥作用，除非中国的政策能改变收入、消费和储蓄领域的结构性参数。有一个很好的观点是，把汇率升值作为促进消费、推动产业结构升级和实现内部平衡的一种手段。较为强势的人民币会给贸易部门带来有益的压力，促进管理改善和结构调整，还可以减缓外汇储备的增长，以及帮助抑制国内经济过热。

准确测算的人民币的真实汇率的升值速度比名义汇率快得多，因为某些出口产业的工资增长速度高于生产率的提高。这是个积极的变化，工资的提高有助于促进消费、减轻经济对投资和出口的依赖。在经济的供给方面，更高的工资将刺激生产率的相应提高，让经济结构转向附加价值更高的生产活动。

中国有人担心，出口导向型制造业的竞争力下降会阻碍创造就业机会，不利于人口从农村向城市转移。其他国家特别是拉丁美洲的经验显示，这种担心有一定道理，不能采取把大量人口排除在现代化进程之外的增长和发展方式。不过，无论是国内还是国外，都没有人认为从长期来看中国依旧应该发展低附加值的制造业。随着收入水平的提升，这样的产业将转移到内地（假定基础设施的条件许可）并出现下滑。韩国等国家已经成功走完了从中等收入国家向高收入国家的路程，随着购买力的提升，国内市场的重要性逐步增加。随着出口产业的就业增速减缓，面向国内市场的产业将在工作岗位创造上贡献更大的份额。

正如前文的章节所言，中国需要首先关注以下几个领域：（1）国内经济的拓展和一体化；（2）提高教育的数量和质量。通过培育国内市场，中国将创造对劳动力的新需求。通过改善教育的数量和质量，将使国民获得从事更高附加价值产业的技能。这些措施有利于同时减轻汇率机制的负担，不需要过分保护劳动密集型的出口产业。

促进全球贸易和投资

同意减少贸易盈余还可以给中国带来间接的好处，这可以为重振世界经济的需求作出贡献，从而有利于自由贸易和多边合

作的事业。从长远来看，这一事业符合中国和其他所有国家的利益。保持开放的国际贸易和投资环境对所有国家都有好处，对中国而言尤其重要。

中国在2001年获得世界贸易组织成员国的身份前进行了很长时间的努力，如今，维护世界贸易组织作为开放贸易体系的监护人的信誉，对中国来说很有价值。因此，十分重要的一点是，中国乃至世界贸易组织的所有成员国都应该遵守该组织的规则和争端解决机制。很多人普遍相信（或许也是正确的感觉），如果前进的动力不能维持，多边贸易自由化进程将可能迅速逆转。鉴于对外开放在中国发展战略中的重要性，很少有国家能像中国这样需要坚定地抗击贸易保护主义。

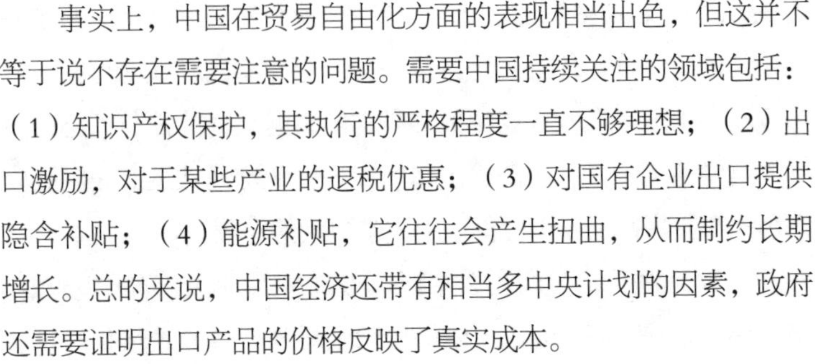

事实上，中国在贸易自由化方面的表现相当出色，但这并不等于说不存在需要注意的问题。需要中国持续关注的领域包括：（1）知识产权保护，其执行的严格程度一直不够理想；（2）出口激励，对于某些产业的退税优惠；（3）对国有企业出口提供隐含补贴；（4）能源补贴，它往往会产生扭曲，从而制约长期增长。总的来说，中国经济还带有相当多中央计划的因素，政府还需要证明出口产品的价格反映了真实成本。

对于规范国际投资的规则和政策，中国也需要做更详细的审视。中国应该尽可能允许市场力量来决定投资的选址，无论是国内还是跨国。资本的自由流动不但可以让储蓄跨越边界，也能够促进管理手段和技术诀窍的交流。

从长期来看，中国应该考虑逐渐取消直接投资和证券投资方面的障碍。当然作为对价，中国也应该获得其他国家的互惠的自由化待遇。只要中国的市场能得到妥善监管，更加自由的资本流动就可以带来更有效率的资源配置。海外投资除了引进资金以外，还往往能带来健康的竞争和知识交流。例如，外国投资者可以帮助中国鉴别和促进适应未来发展阶段的高级产业。

不过在目前的环境下，资本流入可能过多，并带来不稳定因素。2010 年，进入新兴经济体的外国证券投资出现高峰，这是西方国家的危机应对措施导致的一种扭曲：投资者希望摆脱本国的低回报，在海外寻找更好的机会。在这样的形势下，政府完全有理由进行干预，为控制通货膨胀和资产价格上涨限制资本的流入。当然，确立一个渐进的自由化目标，并辅以这个方向上的恰当改革步骤，可以给国内产业和国外贸易伙伴发出有价值的信号。

中国不只是本国投资的唯一目的地，也正在成为越来越大的对外投资输出国。巨大的贸易盈余加上证券投资资金的大量涌入，给了中国足够的财力开展大型海外投资。到目前为止，大部分投资还是采取政府债务的形式（尤其是美国国债）。出于可以理解的原因，中国正在为自己的外汇资产寻求更高的收益。但不幸的是，为促进投资多元化而购买长期股权资产的尝试引发了投资对象国的保护主义反应，这些反应多数是没有理由的，但对中国的投资政策而言，很重要的一点是，不要为投资合法性的忧虑提供根据。如果人们认为，外国投资是出于政治或战略目的而非商业考虑，此类问题就容易出现。国有企业开展的海外并购容易遇到这样的阻挠，因为它们的股权受中国政府的控制。在未来，中国可以设法减轻这方面的担忧，确保投资决策是基于商业上的标准，给予明确陈述并且通告投资对象国。新加坡的很多股权投资也是通过主权财富基金进行的，但并未引起太多争议，表明这个办法依旧可行。

另外，在外国投资引起企业管理控制权转手的时候，也需要特别小心。中国应该做好充分准备，证明获得控制权有清晰的商业理由。中国对新兴经济体和发展中国家的原材料领域的投资也需要考虑策略，这样的投资是一个国家多余储蓄的恰当出口，但不应该导致对自然资源的控制特权，而损坏其他国家利益。换句话说，对原材料资源的控制不要破坏大宗商品在国际市场出售的原则，即以大致相同的价格标准向所有的顾客供应。这是一条重要的原则，应该得到二十国集团的集体支持。

国际货币基金组织如今正在组织主权财富基金与投资对象国之间的对话。中国可以也应该利用这个渠道，推动各国更多接受基于商业目的的跨国投资，减少对象国方面的过度担心。中国还可以加强与投资对象国的金融机构合作，寻找对双方国家都有利的投资机会。

向低碳经济转轨

在“十二五”规划及之后的一段时期，世界经济面临的一个最优先的议题将是减缓气候变化速度，转向能源效率更高的低碳经济。气候变化的影响正在世界各地显现，中国也不例外，极端天气现象（洪水、干旱等）正变得越来越频繁，威胁到社会进步和经济发展。因此，中国也必须在制定增长战略的时候给予气候变化足够的重视，否则将使中国陷入陈旧的产业结构和城市模式，这些将会在低碳世界中成为显著的不利条件。

中国已经开始了向低碳经济转轨的积极行动，前面章节所讨论的发展方式转变以及最近的规划文件中表述的能源效率目标，都显示出减排方面的巨大努力，在世界各国中是最突出的之一。不过，“十二五”规划还需要进一步充实如何实现这些目标的具体政策，特别是需要制定战略，将发电厂使用的煤炭转向低碳燃料。

在现有的人均收入水平上，中国的人均排放量相当高。例如，巴西的人均收入按市场汇率计算约为 8100 美元，而中国是 3800 美元，但巴西的人均排放量仅为 1.9 吨，远低于中国目前的 4.9 吨。当然这也意味着，中国还有很大的空间逐渐提高能源效率和减少相对于收入水平而言的二氧化碳排放量，同时又不至于影响经济增长。

世界各国期待中国将在减缓气候变化方面取得显著成绩。来自国外的监督可能会让人感觉不舒服，但中国应该能够在不损害增长战略的前提下满足国际社会的期望，原因有以下几条：

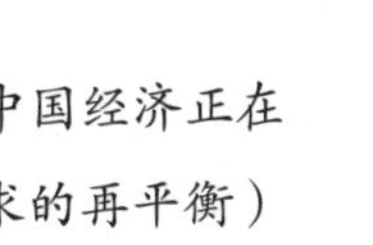

- 减少温室气体排放和提高能源利用效率，与中国经济正在努力实现的更广泛的统筹平衡（以及全球经济所要求的再平衡）是一致的。从中期来看，这一转变对于到 21 世纪中期实现可持续的经济发展将是有益的，甚至是必要的。
- 中国在很多方面比其他处于类似发展阶段的国家更有条件应对气候变化。中国有强大的政府机构，可以落实和强制实施政府规定的目标。中国的财政状况良好，可以负担必要的公共投资。
- 减少碳排放会给中国增加转轨负担，但如果政府能肯定明确的方向，作出可信的减排承诺，这些转轨成本可以最小化。政府的态度会给企业正确的信号和充裕的时间，为提高排放成本做好准备。相反，拖延的时间越长，转轨成本反而会越大。因为在耽误期间，企业依然会忙于工厂和设备投资，这些投资可能不适应未来的低碳要求。
- 这个转变不会危及中国的能源安全，甚至可以促进能源安全。

这几点可以进行进一步阐述。例如经济再平衡的问题，从全球角度看，这意味着美国的进口（包括进口的工业产品）会减少，同时中国更多由出口（主要是工业产品）转向内需（很大一部分是服务业）。这样的再平衡将降低世界经济的碳排放强度。

当然，减排并不容易。如上文所述，中国经济相对于自己的发展阶段而言碳排放水平较高，这主要是因为工业占中国 GDP 的很大一部分，能源是工业的重要投入，而煤炭在中国的能源生产中又占据主要地位。结果导致，中国仅靠改进当前产业的能源效率还是不够的，还必须改变产业的构成，转向能源密集度更低的产业。

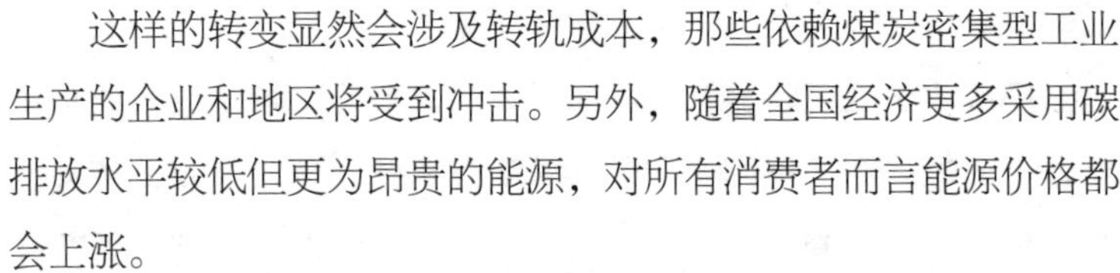

这样的转变显然会涉及转轨成本，那些依赖煤炭密集型工业生产的企业和地区将受到冲击。另外，随着全国经济更多采用碳排放水平较低但更为昂贵的能源，对所有消费者而言能源价格都会上涨。

经济增长的构成会发生变化，但增长率并不一定减慢。服务业和附加价值更高的工业生产的加速扩张可以抵消碳排放水平更高的工业生产的放缓。只要可以在增加产量的同时能足够快地降低能源消耗强度即可，甚至以煤炭为基础的工业产出也可以继续增长，但速度比过去更慢。

虽然“十一五”规划曾明确将转变增长方式作为目标，但没有取得彻底成功。中国在促进增长方面表现得更出色，而非实现再平衡上。2008 年的刺激政策确实增加了社会支出，但并不代表对中国过去的增长方式的突破。因此，如果中国希望转向低碳经济，就有必要宣布一条新的路线，并以一系列新的政策目标和措施来保证。

为实现这样的转变，仅有能源消耗密度的目标是不够的。中国还需要创造激励，鼓励在经济活动中使用低碳能源和发展低碳产业。中国可以引入以市场为基础的政策工具，如碳排放税或碳排放交易制度（cap-and-trade scheme），或者二者结合使用。它们可以尽可能经济而便利地鼓励企业和居民降低碳排放，以及给创新带来刺激。

碳排放税相当于给能源的外部成本定价，以此消除经济扭曲，让能源使用者承担经济决策的所有成本。这样的逻辑使碳排放税在理论上很受欢迎。这个措施还是全面覆盖的，对经济中所有涉及碳排放的用户一视同仁。在实施中，碳排放税却存在一个严重缺陷，因为碳排放税不可避免地会导致大量的人普遍受损，包括所有的电力用户。当然这个缺陷可以完全弥补：

- 这个税种可以从低水平开征，逐渐提高；或者从有限范围开征，逐渐扩大。只要存在可信的加税或者扩大范围的政策承诺，就可以在一开始明智地采取小步走的策略，使税收的短期成本最小化，又能带来对投资的长期激励。
- 碳排放税可以带来一系列降低成本的创新反应，例如，刺激非常规能源的开发以及改进能源效率的努力。
- 碳排放税产生的税收收入可以用以解决各种转轨问题，例如，可以给低收入的消费者提供补偿，缓解电费涨价的压力，还可以给隔热材料和其他节约能源的措施提供补贴等。

另一个可以采用的政策工具是碳排放交易制度，它可以单独实施，也可以和碳排放税结合。该制度允许企业买卖温室气体的排放权利，既可以给总排放量设置硬指标，又可以有非常灵活的具体实现方式。中国加入《京都议定书》的碳信用评级机制为排放交易制度的有效运转奠定了必要的制度基础。根据交易制度的具体建立方式，还可以通过排放配额的拍卖增加政府收入。在中长期，中国采用的碳排放交易制度或许还能与其他国家的碳排放市场联系起来，加速中国向低碳经济的过渡速度。

除了给碳排放定价以外，中国还应该考虑某些更具体的措施，例如汽车动力效率标准和建筑规范，以及通过规划法规限制城市的蔓延，规划建设吸收碳排放的公园或其他绿地等。

这些减排政策不需要牺牲中国的能源安全，原因如下：

- 这些政策可以提高运输产业和其他产业的价格和效率，减少中国对进口矿物燃料（如石油等）的需求，由此减轻中国对生产这些燃料的不够安全地区的依赖。
- 中国国内的煤炭产业在数十年来为国家能源安全作出了巨大贡献，但这个产业已经面临一定的压力（如在近来的某些年份出现了进口需求），或许也不能跟上中国经济腾飞的步伐。因此，中国需要寻求更广泛的能源种类并提高利用效率。
- 对生产替代能源和改进能源效率的激励，会增强能源产业的弹性和多样性。
- 更多利用可再生能源将加强中国的能源安全，因为可再生能源能够在国内生产。核能也不会给供给安全带来太多担忧，至少在必要的时候，核能原料容易预先做好储备。
- 减排会要求一系列的支持措施，例如引进智能电网等。许多补充措施也有助于改善能源安全、提高国家的能源效率、促进发达经济所需要的现代化基础设施的建设。

因此，中国可以在减少碳排放的同时确保能源安全。事实上，对于碳排放的持续依赖不但在环境方面有害，还可能是危险的选择。到21世纪中期，世界经济或许将已经完成向低碳模式转轨。不适应这一模式的产品和服务会被摒弃，而低碳产品将获得重视。中国已经证明，它完全可以将传统的制造业技术转向风能和太阳能等绿色产业的开发，因此也可以在符合低碳经济要求

的技术和产业方面扮演先锋的角色，如碳捕获和电动汽车等。但如果国内市场依然是以高碳排放模式为主体，中国企业要想在这些产业取得进步就会更为困难。

全球治理

平衡世界需求结构、促进国际贸易和投资、应对气候变化以及改革汇率体制，这些是发达国家和发展中国家需要共同应对的众多国际议题中的四个案例。全球议题，无论是涉及经济、社会、生态还是更广泛的安全事务，相互关联程度都在显著提高。可是处理这些议题的现有的国际组织依然显得凌乱而松散。政策制定者们必须通过这些组织或特别委员会的松散的联合体来开展工作，在代表发展中国家的利益上面缺乏统一的设计和一致的规则。这些国际组织不灵活的结构是为响应各种历史事件和危机而逐渐形成的，如今则急需加以改革。如果中国能积极参与如何开展改革的讨论，世界将受益良多。

最明显需要改革的国际领域是国际金融体系。该体系的某些主要原则在过去 3 年的金融危机中饱受质疑。市场的混乱证明，放任自流的金融市场不能做好自我监管，其动荡会破坏整个世界经济。虽然金融市场也具有实现自我稳定的机制，但如果风险的感受和测算出现失误，这些机制就不能发挥作用，导致灾难性的后果。因此，国际和国内都在积极讨论金融市场是否可以通过对现行体制的增量改革来实现稳定，还是必须进行大规模的变革。

中国这样的新兴经济体有充分的理由参与这一讨论：一方面，新兴经济体经常受到全球金融动荡的消极影响（虽然本次危机的打击要小得多）；另一方面，新兴经济体也是资本市场开放和自由投资的主要受益方之一。它们的看法值得重视，新的体系需要保持恰当的平衡，既要为国际金融体系设计可靠的监控框架，又要继续维护全球化带来的收益。

另一个与中国直接相关的问题是如何扩大对国际经济决策的参与，同时又不至于让讨论过程过于烦琐和缺乏效率。随着新兴经济体比重的急剧提高，欧洲在国际货币基金组织及世界银行的代表份额过大的问题变得越来越不正常，已促使国际货币基金组织对表决权和发言权进行了小幅调整。同样重要的是，发展中国家总体上还需要在巴塞尔银行监管委员会（Basel Committee on Banking Supervision）和国际会计准则委员会（International Accounting Standards Board）上获得充分的代表权，它们如今在全球治理上发挥着比过去远为显著的作用。新兴的二十国集团（也召开了金融稳定理事会）是一个促进国际合作的有力组织，它更好地反映了各国当前的实力对比。但目前还难以断言，这个扩充的大国组成的集团能否在确定国际优先议题和协调政策方面发挥有效的作用。

那么，二十国集团和其他国际组织对中国会有哪些要求？世界对这个崛起中的强国有怎样的期待？总的来说，它们希望中国能认识到自己的国内政策选择会产生超出国境的影响，并在决策过程中把这些影响考虑进去。另外，它们还希望中国与其他国家合作，推动对大家共同有益的调整，这些调整如果单独进行未必能取得良好效果。它们期待中国帮助加强国际货币基金组织等负责国际合作的国际机构的地位，当然这些机构本身也需要采取步骤来适应新的形势。最重要的一点是，世界其他国家都希望中国等金砖四国清楚地描绘未来的前景，让世界能适应它们的崛起。如果没有这样的描绘，其他国家就不能采取相应的措施。

除了这些普遍的共同期待以外，各国还对中国有各自的期待。在发达国家中，美国特别关心对中国的巨额贸易逆差，尤其

是在目前受高失业率困扰的时候。与美国不同，欧洲是全球治理的天然拥护者。虽然新兴经济体的崛起将削弱欧洲在布雷顿森林体系的国际组织中的影响力，但多极化世界的逐渐出现不会让欧洲感受到更大的威胁。欧洲容易接受中国的建议，支持包括欧元、人民币和美元的多货币储备体系。欧洲和中国还会对区域一体化议题有共同的兴趣，包括中日韩在内的东盟加三集团，可以从欧盟的发展中借鉴很多经验。在接下来的10年，中国经济的崛起既会带来与欧盟的摩擦，也蕴含着富有成果的合作机遇。双方的政策制定者面对的问题都是如何避免被零和博弈的思维控制和主导。这需要高质量的对话，既承认摩擦的可能，又更强调成功合作的潜力。

发展中国家对中国积极参与全球治理有不同的利益考虑，它们急于借鉴中国发展过程的成功经验，还欣赏中国反对干预其他国家的内部事务以及愿意在没有责难和条件的前提下提供投资和援助的态度。它们受益于中国的外贸、投资和援助的增长，并希望中国不会重复某些更富裕国家曾犯的错误。

从这个角度出发，发展中国家应该会鼓励中国考虑：（1）加强中国市场对发展中国家制造品的开放，在一定程度上，随着中国国内市场的扩大和中国企业逐步退出全球供应链中属于最劳动密集的部分，这自然会发生；（2）鼓励中国企业和本国企业的合资项目，以便学习技术和诀窍；（3）放松援助，提供更灵活的融资；（4）通过区域性组织和次区域性组织提供援助。非洲国家希望中国提供的更具体的内容参见阿莫阿科的背景论文《非洲对中国的期待》。

尽管各国对中国的期待不尽相同，但几乎所有国家都非常关心中国的国内政策，因为这会给它们带来影响。因此，这些国家会在“十二五”规划中寻求有关中国发展目标和宗旨的线索。

中国不需要对这样的外部审视感到反感，事实上这是一种恭维，因为它今天所吸引的注意力正是一个有着全局性影响力的崛起的大国所应有的。中国政府没有必要将国际社会对自己政策的支持视为很大的义务，但应该把自己的经济目标清晰地传达给伙伴国（并保证实际政策与这些目标相符）。

然而国际经验表明，让中国扮演国际社会所期待的角色并不轻松。美国和欧盟（尤其是英国）还主导着有关国际金融及其他事务的国际讨论，这是基于它们在国际政策制定方面的长期经验，以及由此积累的技能，不仅仅是在政府机构，还包括它们的立法部门及众多智库的人才。相比之下，日本的表现就弱于其经济实力，这是由一系列原因导致的。在国际谈判中，日本采取的协调政策的方法一开始就给负责谈判的人太少的发挥空间。日本的职员轮换太快，不容易熟悉合同框架，难以赶上其他国家的对手长期积累的制度经验。此外，日本还相对缺乏能支持国际政策制定的高水平智库和大学。最后，日本还受制于语言障碍，国际的交流高度依赖英语的语言技能。

为了加强对国际事务的参与，中国必须加强人力投资：需要经过高水平训练的、不但对中国现实还对其他国家情况有深入而细致的了解的谈判人和对话人。这些协调人应该代表中国面对世界其他国家，也代表其他国家面对中国：需要做到双向传达。他们应该能够有理有据和令人信服地陈述中国的立场，同时也能传递国际上的感受，将国际上的立场清晰、高效和客观地告诉中国的民众。

中国必须建设国际性的智库，作为与世界其他国家交流的界面。这些智库应该安排外国学者和政策分析师来中国工作，安排中国学者去海外。与国际组织和区域性组织的人员交流项目也将非常重要。中国还需要扩大其交流圈，与其他新兴市场国家进

行更多对话，还需要认识到与全球的许多利益相关方互动的重要性，包括各国政府、私人部门、民间团体和社区组织等在全球治理上都有发言权的角色。

到未来的某个时间，中国乃至印度将发挥与如今的美国和欧洲相似的全球性作用。在那个阶段到来之前，世界经济将如何进步取决于这两个经济巨人如何利用好它们的资源和影响力。中国在未来 5 年的进步是向这个目标前进的漫长旅程的一部分。在实现转型的过程中，中国必须与其他国家和国际组织谈判、合作，偶尔也需要妥协。在此期间获得的宝贵经验，将会有助于中国承担起未来应尽的国际责任。

第九章　体制改革 *

本报告从国际视角讨论了中国从中等收入国家向高收入的繁荣国家演进的时候将面临的各种挑战。在未来10年，中国经济必须应对至少五个方面的转变：（1）随着劳动力成本的提高，改变经济增长方式；（2）调整需求结构，从过度依靠投资和出口更多地转向消费；（3）妥善安置迅速增长的城市人口；（4）完善和谐社会所必需的社会基础设施；（5）随着规模和国际影响的增大，承担起相称的国际责任，包括引导世界经济增长和应对气候变化等。历史上很少有国家能一帆风顺地完成这一转变过程，更不用说有着中国这样的规模和多样性的国家。

中国人自己早就认识到了这些挑战，"九五"规划已承认了寻求新的增长方式的必要性，随后的几个五年规划也对此反复重申。本报告前面各章所讨论的所有议题，几乎都在"十一五"规划中有所论述，并出现在国家领导人和党代会近期的政策文件中。当然认识到这些问题距离妥善解决还很远，事实也表明，过去的规划已强调的许多结构性调整，实现起来相当艰难。目前，中国的经济增长依然主要依靠投资和出口拉动，服务业发展滞后，最重要的一点是，城乡之间以及沿海和内陆之间的收入、教育及医疗服务的差距仍然巨大。

---

* 本章有关财政体制改革的部分参考了背景论文十九：黄佩华，《为中国和谐社会建设而进行的公共部门改革》。

在中国开始实施新的五年规划之际，我们需要研究如何才能缩小规划目标和实施效果之间的差距。本章将讨论的议题是：为了引导中国经济迈向更高收入的阶段，顺利完成复杂的转轨任务，政府自身需要进行的改革。

这些改革要求中央政府和地方政府重新思考自身的角色并改进行政能力。改革还要拓展到国有企业，让它们更多地分配红利，在目前占据统治地位的市场上迎接更激烈的竞争，加强税后巨大的红利分配。中国还需要改革财政体制，特别是中央、省级和县级政府之间的收入和责任划分。如果没有这三个领域的改革，政府将很难实现发展规划所确立的远大目标。

增进政府的效率和应负的责任

国际经验表明，中国在未来数年或许必须重新平衡政府干预和市场的关系。为了实现中长期发展目标，政府需要借助更多类型的基于市场的工具，并高度重视省级和县级政府的激励问题，因为它们是中长期发展规划能否成功实施的最终决定环节。更广泛地争取民众参与也是有益的，还有，确保政府能获得高质量的数据和信息，以准确监督规划的进展和评估自身的表现。

统一的政策规划

在传统的中央计划经济中，政府负责制定一系列的目标、配额、责任和权利，直接引导企业和居民家庭的行为。而现在，中国经历了30多年改革，已经成为复杂的混合经济体，政策制定者必须通过其他途径来发挥影响，规划获得成功实施的关键在于“政策规划”（policy planning），其含义是，将规划目标转换成一系列直接或间接引导国家发展的政策，这些政策又利用各种各样的工具来影响市场参与者的决策，通过对他们的激励来最终实现规划目标。

要想取得成功，这些政策不能各自为战，而是需要形成有内在统一性的政策组合。政府并非铁板一块，各个部委以及中央和地方政府对规划目标的认识都可能有差异，因此，政策规划需要政府内部的广泛合作。

此外，由于许多政策未必能很快见效，政策规划必须有 3~5 年的时间跨度。政策可能需要随着时间推移分阶段设计；可能要随着成果的显现和环境的变化进行调整和改进。中国和世界其他国家在这方面遇到过大量的案例，某些经济政策在开头几年实施情况良好，但最后却不再有效。过去的成功还经常会给未来的改革造成障碍。

许多国家的经验表明，如果能更多地依靠价格及其他基于市场的机制，规划的实施效果会最好。借助市场激励的作用，规划制定者可以取得更为持久、可持续的成效，同时也能获得更高的效率。例如，“十二五”规划的目标之一是降低单位 GDP 的能源消耗，如果能对能源的定价和税收办法进行改革，则成功实现这个目标的可能性将会增加（参见专栏 9–1）。

专栏 9–1

能源效率规划

中国的能源效率规划是“十一五”规划的首要目标之一，规划的范围和细节都令人称道。它包含五个主要部分，从关闭小型发电厂和设备陈旧的工厂到工业锅炉的更新换代等。但在实践中，政府官员们却经常发现，他们不得不通过行政手段来达成目标，例如，为了减少能源消耗量而随意中断对重工业的电力供应，或者临时关闭某些工厂等。这些措施有可能在短期发挥作用，但既没有效率也不可持续，不免让人联想起传统的中央计划经济的控制手段。

为了实现提高能源效率的目标，政府需要更多地借助政策规划的作用。首要的一点应该是对能源定价机制进行改革，使价格能充分地反映全部供给成本，包括能源资源的稀缺价值和环境外部性造成的影响。例如，中国目前的电力价格还处在严格管控之下，远低于发电成本，从而给企业和消费者带来了错误的信号。从长远来看，合理的市场价格可以打击浪费、促进能源节约型技术的创新。此外，政府还可以更多地借助税收和补贴来促进能源利用效率较高的产品的开发和普及。

此类政策规划需要以精确的分析为基础。规划中的政策必须进行准确陈述、对比研究、监控和评估。本报告所涉及的所有议题都不可能仅靠单一工具解决，或者在短时期内一蹴而就。另外，解决这些问题的方案可能不止一个，各有其成本和收益。在不同方案间进行选择的时候，政策制定者要有能力在不同的场景下对各种政策建议的优缺点进行全面的分析。

随着中国在世界经济中的崛起，其政策选择还会给其他国家带来影响。中国的领导人在充分了解政策制定内容的时候，也需要对外溢影响的性质和程度加以认识。

对于特定领域的经济政策的研究，中国已比过去加强了很多，但政府目前缺乏一个有足够广泛的研究视野的专门机构来开展政策规划工作。政府需要这样一个内部“智库”，能够将不同条块的政策研究汇集起来，使所有与某项议题有关的机构能够共同分享材料和分析成果，以此为基础来制定决策。其他国家有过这方面的成功经验，让这些有着专业技能、影响力和自主权的

"改革团队"发挥作用（参见专栏 9–2）。国际经验还表明，要想让此类机构充分发挥作用，应该让它们能够直通最高层的决策制定者，而不是负责具体的行政事务。

专栏 9–2

改革团队

在一些高速增长的经济体，"摸着石头过河"的任务经常是交给由高水平的技术官员组成的小型专业化"改革团队"，例如新加坡的经济发展局、韩国的经济企划院和日本的通产省等。这些改革团队不承担行政方面的具体责任，而与政府的最高层有直接联系渠道。马来西亚的经济计划署就直接向总理报告。甚至有数位后来的政府首脑也来自这些机构。

改革团队有着独特的定位——既居于政府内部，又远离日常的行政事务和现实的政治压力，因此有助于协调政府的各种力量，并克服官僚机构容易产生的惯性和阻力。

当然，这些政治压力较小的技术官员在思考经济政策时可能不太注重政治和社会影响，但反过来说，不依靠专业分析、完全屈从于政治压力也可能带来破坏性的后果。

资料来源：International Commission on Growth and Development（Chairman：Michael Spence），"Strategies for Sustained Growth and Inclusive Development". 见 *The Growth Report*. 第 28 页。

对地方政府结构和角色进行改革

要想在下一个 10 年中保持经济繁荣，除了中央政府的强力引导之外，中国还需要地方各级政府的良好运作。目前，实行的

"以县为主"的行政体制改革有助于简化地方政府的层级，缩短国家政策与地方实施之间的"摩擦距离"。

然而这些改革也带来了省级政府和县级政府负担过重的问题。省级政府可能要将太多的县级单位编入预算，而县级政府可能有太多的学校和医疗机构需要监管。中国的各省在人口规模和辖县数量上相差悬殊，各县的规模差距也极大，从 3.1 万人到 215 万人不等。鉴于这个原因，采取一刀切式地对学校、医院和其他地方服务的管理办法恐怕难以成功。政府或许可以考虑对某些地区的行政区划边界重新进行调整，使区划符合更容易管理的规模；还可以考虑按照不同的地理界限来组织某些公共服务，使功能区的规模更符合这些服务的性质，而不是仅在现有的行政区划边界内行动。

中国还应该考虑对城市的行政层级制度进行改革，使规模不等的各个城市可以在平等的基础上开展竞争。在目前的体制下，层级较低的城市由层级较高的城市主管。层级较高的城市在决策制定上有更大的自主权，掌握着更多的财政资源，还享有更靠近交通走廊和铁路等优势。为取代这种层级关系，每个城市，不论其规模大小，都应该在明确规定的若干领域内享有完全的自主权。所有的城镇都应该享有相同的税基，承担相同的支出责任。当然，规模较小的城市需要更长的时间才能充分利用所有可以获得的财政资源，在过渡时期，它们可能需要较高层级的政府划拨更多资金，才能与较大的城市平等竞争。

中国还需要确保各级政府的角色得到清晰界定，并且与国家政策的方向保持一致。目前的情况并不总是这样，例如，国家制定了经济增长要更多依赖内需的目标，却经常遇到地方政府的阻碍，包括干预国内贸易、保护当地产业、限制商品的跨省甚至省内流动等。在过去，中央政府的作用没有到达省级之下，许多政策的实施交给各省来执行，并由基层政府来提供大多数公共服务。然而，地方各级政府可能缺乏相应的责任和动力来完成这些任务，导致实施效果参差不齐。

因此，中央政府、省级政府和基层政府的关系应该是改革的焦点之一。解决办法之一是要求省级政府负责，保证基层政府严格执行国家政策。另一个办法是让中国借鉴其他许多国家的做法，让中央政府承担更多责任，由中央政府驻扎在地方的职员直接监督公共服务的提供情况。

对政府官员和公共服务机构的激励

确保政府官员和事业单位得到正确激励，与国家政策的目标保持一致，同样至关重要。例如，对市长的考评不应该仅仅以所在城市的工业产量和 GDP 为基准，也要依据其他指标，包括向城市居民提供的交通和其他公共服务的质量等。政府还可以不断征集公众和有关方面对政府官员表现的反馈，要求公众来评判政府官员在某些确定目标上的完成情况。

事业单位则应该对它们提供的公共服务负责，而不是关注它们创造的利润。国际经验表明，只有在得到了明确的责任委派、掌握了提供服务所必需的资源，并需要承担相应责任的时候，事业单位的运营效率才最高，反应才最快。而在目前的中国，事业单位有太多收费空间，既不接受监督，也不对效果负责，它们的行为更多的是源于利润导向而非服务导向。

事业单位的改革同时要求对其薪酬体系进行改革，以切断单位的收入和雇员的报酬之间的联系。用户付费和其他类型的收入应该有充足的理由，并得到妥善管理。事业单位还需要接受私人机构提供的类似服务的竞争。管理的改善和竞争的加剧都有助于让事业单位更专注地为公众服务。

更多的公众参与

其他国家的经验表明，在政策设计、社会指标选择和执行监督等方面向公众广泛征求意见，对政策效果是有益的。通过“公民报告卡”（citizen’s report cards）之类的工具，这些国家的民众可以帮助政府改进公共服务的质量，减少腐败发生。欧盟就高度肯定了在社会政策的设计和实施中走向公众、邀请他们参与的做法（参见专栏 9-3），当然事实也证明在实践操作时未必容易。在中国，“十二五”规划也已在准备过程中广泛征求了各省、市、自治区公众的意见。政府今天应该认真考虑如何将这样的公众参与办法延伸到规划的实施阶段。

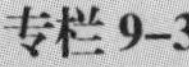

专栏 9-3

欧盟的“社会融合进程”

欧盟在过去几十年的经验表明，仅依靠政府自身难以保证社会融合计划（social inclusion）的推进，这项事业还必须得到包括草根组织和社会边缘群体（socially excluded）等民间势力的支持。为了争取这些支持，政府必须尊重民族传统和社区现实，与其他势力结成伙伴关系。公众的积极参与有助于确保政府的行动保持透明、目标广为人知。所以，社会融合事业的所有工作都应该尽可能地欢迎地方和基层政府机构、致力于扶贫和消除社会排斥的非政府组织，以及低收入阶层和社会边缘群体的积极参与。欧盟的经验表明，广泛的参与对政策的成功至关重要，但另一方面又不容易做到。特别是民间势力的群体难以跨越地方和国家边界提供服务或倡导变革。

资料来源：背景论文二：A. B. 阿特金森，《中国社会政策改革中的问题》。

对测算、信息和监督的改进

问责制度离不开信息收集，中国的统计数据的质量需要得到改进。中国虽然已经能经常性地获得大量信息报告，却缺乏相关的审核与协调机制，以便对不同部委和机构提供的可能彼此差异巨大的数据进行加工。要妥善管理迈向高收入经济体的转型期，中国还需要引入若干新的评价指标，以真实反映国家的发展战略、目标和成绩。可靠而及时的数据还有助于政府对国家政策的落实、公共服务提供方和政府官员的表现进行准确评估。

改革国有企业的范围和功能

中国在过去 30 年的快速增长在很大程度上要归功于非国有经济部门的活力。经合组织最近的一项研究比较了中国的国有企业和非国有企业的表现，发现由于“公司治理的改善和其他领域的改革，国有企业的经营在某些方面更接近私人公司”。然而，国有企业的业绩仍然不及私人企业。经合组织的研究在排除了各企业的资本密集度、规模、所在地及行业等因素之后，测算了全要素生产率，结果发现私人企业的生产效率最高。这个结果与以前用各种不同方法进行的很多研究的结论一致，它们都普遍认为中国的国有企业的效率明显低于其他所有制形式的企业。“鉴于资本积累是中国 GDP 增长的主要推动力，而国有企业又在全部投资中占据相当大的比重，这些企业的资本生产率低下严重影响了中国的经济增长率”。[1]

[1] *OECD Economic Survey*：*China*，2010：109~118.

国有企业改革在多年以来一直是中国改革进程的关键环节。在改革开放前，国有企业完全主导着城市经济，其范围和功能自那时以来已发生了深刻的变化，但在今天依然是一股不可忽视的经济力量。工业普查结果显示，非金融部门的国有企业的固定资产净值在 2008 年达 7.593 万亿元，比 2001 年翻了一番，超过私人企业和外资企业固定资产净值的总和（见表 9–1）。国有企业的利润总和也更高，达 9060 亿元。此外，政府近期推出的经济刺激计划集中在国有企业主导的建筑和基础设施领域，它们从中获得了更大的好处，这意味着国有企业今天在经济中的比重可能比 2008 年的时候更高。

表 9–1 2001—2008 年部分工业统计数据（亿元）

	2001 年	2005 年	2008 年
工业企业固定资产净值			
国有企业及控股公司	38638	49140	75927
私人企业	2039	9587	23945
外资企业（a）	11112	21419	36871
利润总额			
国有企业及控股公司	2389	6520	9064
私人企业	313	2121	8302
外资企业（a）	1443	4141	8243

（a）包括来自香港、澳门和台湾的投资。

资料来源：CEIC，工业企业调查（Industrial Enterprise Survey）。

国有企业在今天的中国经济中继续维持统治地位，这在很大程度上应归功于政府的政策——尽管政府也强调不同所有制企业之间的公平竞争。2006 年 12 月，国有资产监督管理委员会宣布，将维持对七大“战略”行业的绝对控制（国防、电力电网、石油化工、电信、煤炭、民航和航运等），以及保持对基础性和支柱产业领域的较强控制力，包括机械、汽车、信息技术、建筑、钢铁、冶金和化工等。

这样长的产业清单是否有必要？在如此多的工业和服务业领域赋予国有企业垄断或寡头地位，将难以改进经济效率、维持稳定增长。中国应该考虑重新检视，到底哪些行业或活动真正需要国有制。归根结底，政府未必需要在某个产业领域（哪怕是战略产业）掌握很大的所有权，才能引导该产业的发展。经济学理论和广泛的国际经验都表明，通过监管、竞争政策和市场激励等手段，政府往往能更有效地引导战略产业和重点企业的发展。

在中国改革开放的早期阶段，国有制是维持稳定的堡垒，东欧和苏联国家的私有化进程造成了巨大混乱，中国很小心地没有选择这种方式，从而避免了混乱。不过，今天中国面临的形势已全然不同，有序地缩小国有企业的规模和范围已成为可行。政府在国有企业的股份可以通过国内外的资本市场向公众转移。对于某些国有企业，政府可以将全部股份出售，将其改造成公众公司；对于其他一些企业，则可以逐渐减持股份，不用完全放手。

在很多产业部门，所有制因素可能不如竞争重要。政府可以取消产业进入壁垒和其他竞争障碍（包括国有企业享有的信贷资源方面的优势），来削弱国有企业的垄断地位。服务业向私人开放尤其重要。这些改革可以在困难的转型时期创造急需的经济活力。

对于留存的国有企业，则需要改善公司治理。与金融企业不同，国有工业企业的公司化进程还很不彻底，改革往往局限于二级公司，而没有推广到集团公司或母公司。这造成了极不正常的情况，二级企业已完成了公司化改革，负责控股和监督它们的母公司的治理却处于较次的水平。

国有部门理应对其终极所有者——全体国民——负责，这要求对包括集团公司在内的所有国有企业进行公司化改革，并改善其内部治理结构。当然，不可能让全体国民都扮演“积极所有者”的角色，代表国民行使所有权的任何机构（无论是国资委还是其他机构）有责任维护人民的权益，要求国有企业对其负责。

公司的所有者享有对利润的剩余索取权，但中国的国有企业事实上并没有通过分红或其他形式向政府上缴净利润，这是非常不正常的情况，其他国家也没有这方面的先例。许多已经上市的二级企业在分红，但这些红利是分配给它们的母公司或集团公司，并没有再转移给政府。允许国有企业留存全部利润是 20 世纪 90 年代中期引进的临时措施，当时许多国有企业的财务状况不佳。今天的国有企业利润非常丰厚，这个措施却沿用了下来。

根据经济学原理和国际惯例，国有企业的所有净利润都属于政府。在大多数国家，这些利润直接划归政府财政，有的国家则是间接汇入一笔基金，而政府依然是最终受益者。在中国，最近的讨论也认为国有企业可以将更多的利润上缴给政府，但建议的上缴比例仍然太低，从 0%~15%。

从逻辑上说，有关国企利润的上缴比例的讨论出发点应是百分之百上缴，不上缴应该视为例外。合理的前提是，国有企业的绝大部分净利润都应该上缴财政，企业可以申请部分留存，如用于支付特殊的历史成本等。国有企业还可以申请留存部分利润用于扩大投资，但政府应该通盘考虑国有部门的所有投资需求以及其他预算需求，包括教育和医疗支出等。国际上有很多类似的教训，某些企业留存的利润太多，最后导致缺乏效率的投资。提高分红比例还有助于通过消除过度投资倾向来改善国有企业的公司治理，特别是对大型工业企业。

改革财政体制

加强公共财政

在市场经济中，财政体制（即政府征税能力和支出能力）是实现收入和机会再分配的最有效的工具之一。中国目前的财政规模从国际标准上说是较低的。近年来，财政收入仅占 GDP 的 20%左右，加上预算外收入也仅占 25%，仍然低于公共支出比例相对较低的美国（联邦财政收入约占 GDP 的 20%，州财政收入约占 10%，总计为 30%左右）。欧洲国家对公共服务的支出较多，财政收入相当于 GDP 的 40%甚至更高。

为建设和谐社会和促进经济繁荣，中国政府的财政规模需要扩大。尽管已经在“十一五”规划期间取得了显著进展，但中国仍需增加对社会保障、医疗和教育等方面的政府投入，这些领域的公共支出仍明显低于下中等收入国家的平均水平。政府在教育、医疗和社会保障等项目上承担更大份额的支出，将有助于减轻居民家庭的压力，增加他们的可支配收入。新增的公共支出还将有助于贫困家庭和贫困地区享受到更好的服务。

中国各地的人均公共支出水平相差悬殊，造成基本医疗、教育和最低生活保障等公共服务标准的地区差异太大。中央政府在“十一五”规划期间增大了对地方政府的转移支付，试图缩小地区差距。但以国际标准衡量差距依然过大，也不符合建设和谐社会的目标。

因此，财政收入应该在近期提高到 GDP 的至少 30%，这相当于美国目前的水平，低于大多数发达国家。财政收入的增长及其来源应该尽可能不加重居民家庭的负担（除了极少数高收入阶

层以外），避免与提高家庭收入占 GDP 的比重的目标相冲突。如果遵循世界上绝大多数国家的惯例，要求中国的国有企业将净利润全部上交给财政，那么财政收入占 GDP 的比重将立刻提高到 30%以上。

在增加财政总收入的同时，中国还应该尝试调整税负分配。目前的财政体制对制造业和投资过于有利，消除这一扭曲将有助于经济的重新平衡，这在中国已获得广泛认同。其他有意义的变革还包括将增值税扩展到服务业，征收消费型而非生产型的增值税等。

各级政府的预算编制机制也急需要加强。在全国层面，中央政府需要提高政策设计和分析能力，以制定更符合实际的预算并严格监督项目的执行。在美国，这一任务主要委派给两家机构完成：行政系统的行政管理和预算局（Office of Management and Budget，OMB）和立法系统的国会预算办公室（Congressional Budget Office，CBO），这两家机构的雇员分别达到 500 人和 250 人，大多数是拥有高学位的经济学家和公共政策分析师（参见专栏 9-4）。对于中国的地方各级政府而言，这方面的管理和分析人才就更加缺乏，它们迫切需要与其重要地位相称的技术能力来制定和实施财政政策。

改革政府间财政体制

前文的章节中提到，如果中国希望缩小地区差异、鼓励更平衡的增长，政府就需要将更多的社会支出投入贫困地区。在现有的分权化体制下，改善教育、扩大医疗保险覆盖面和强化社会安全网等社会项目的许多内容都需要基层政府来实施。对于大多数中国人来说，这些服务是由县、乡（镇）两级的农村基层政府提供的。因而，改善这些服务的希望就取决于基层政府的愿望和能力。但在目前的政府间财政体制下，基层政府往往既没有资源也没有动力来履行社会支出方面的责任。为了有效实施发展规划中列入的社会服务项目，中国还需要将更多的中央财力投入社会事业支出，缩小地区之间的差异，并启动政府间财政体制的深刻改革。

专栏 9-4

美国的预算编制与评估

行政管理和预算局是美国总统办事机构（Executive Office of the President of the United States，EOP）中最大的部门，拥有 500 名雇员，年度预算达 7090 万美元（2008 年），局长为内阁阁员。该机构的主要使命是帮助总统进行联邦预算的编制并且监督其在行政机构中的执行。行政管理和预算局在协助总统编制支出计划的时候会对各类计划、政策和程序的有效性进行评估，就各类机构对资金的需求进行比较分析，并且确定支出的优先顺序。该机构要确保各机构的报告、规则、陈述和法律提议同总统的预算方案及政府的政策保持一致。此外，行政管理和预算局还负责对行政机构的办事程序、财务管理、信息系统及监管政策进行监督和协调。

行政管理和预算局还负责改善政府内部的管理标准，包括信息技术、财务管理、办事规程和职员表现等。联邦政府各机构的表现按照行政管理和预算局设计的记分卡进行评级（绿、黄、红三级）。行政管理和预算局还负责督促政府各机构对项目进行评估，衡量其成败，总结经验教训等。

行政管理和预算局的全部雇员中约有一半的编制是在四个资

源管理办公室（Resource Management Offices），大部分是担任项目核查员（program examiners）。这些核查员可以受命监督一家或多家联邦机构，或者负责某个专门领域，例如审核与美国海军军舰有关的支出项目等。这些雇员担负着管理和预算两方面的责任，并且有责任提供专业建议。

这些核查员每年会对联邦政府各机构的预算需求进行审核，帮助决定把哪些资金要求纳入总统的预算方案并提交国会。他们要进行深入的评估工作，审核有关的规则、机构的陈述，对提交讨论的议案进行分析。他们还经常会受命为总统办公室的职员提供分析信息。

资料来源：背景论文十九：黄佩华，《为中国和谐社会建设而进行的公共部门改革》。

表 9–2　地方各级政府在政府总收支中所占的比重（%）

	发展中国家	经合组织国家	转轨国家	中国（2008）
地方政府在政府税收收入中所占比重	9	19	17	47
地方政府在政府总支出中所占比重	14	32	26	79

注：其他国家的数据来自各不同年份。

资料来源：World Bank（2006）、CSY（2009），转引自背景论文十九：黄佩华，《为中国和谐社会建设而进行的公共部门改革》。

如表 9–2 所示，中国的地方政府在全部公共支出中所占的比重接近 80%，但在税收收入中所占的份额却不到 50%，在大国中间，这个现象不同寻常。对于一个地区差异较大的大国来说，中央政府的确需要掌握较多的收入，以便用资金补贴贫困地区。

可是对中国而言，地方政府支出对转移支付的依赖程度在国际上达到了前所未有的高度。如此大规模的转移支付给中央政府造成了沉重的行政管理负担，必须为规模高达万亿元的转移支付编制预算计划和监督执行情况。这个问题应该作为政府间财政体制下一步改革的关键且重要的部分认真研究。

当前的首要任务之一是明确和合理划分各级政府的支出责任，现有的责任分配格局在很大程度上来自旧有的计划经济体制，不再适应目前的高度分权化的混合经济体。随着中国的人口流动的增加，许多地方性的公共品产生了显著的跨地区甚至全国范围的溢出效应。这方面的一个例子是公共健康，传染病可能随着高速铁路在国内迅速蔓延；另一个例子是农民工的子女教育，他们可能被各自为政的地方教育体制忽视。在如今中国的发展阶段，将教育和公共健康等责任完全下放给基层政府已不再适合。与此类似的是，将养老保险和失业保险下放给基层政府同样会制约人口的有效流动。

经济学原理和国际经验给政府间财政体制改革提供了如下三种思路：

中央政府应该接管需要全国统筹的社会事业筹资和管理。一个典型案例是基础养老金领域，将现有的分散化的地方体制整合成一个全国养老金体系，这对效率和公平两方面都有好处，既能鼓励国内的劳动力流动（从而提高经济效率），又能在考虑各地的生活成本差异之后，让养老金标准趋于平等（从而改善公平）（参见之前章节有关养老金改革的内容）。这个思路对于失业保险体制同样适用。

对其他一些项目而言，更好的办法是将筹资责任与服务提供责任相分离，由基层政府负责提供公共服务，由更高层级的政府提供资金。在大多数发达国家，目前对基础教育就是采取此种体制：学校由最基层的政府负责管理，以便让决策制定者尽可能地了解学生及其家庭的需求；公共教育的成本则由较高层级的政府负担，以确保国内的公平标准。中国现有的情况与此相反，基础教育的大部分支出是由县级政府负担，由于各县掌握的财政资源相差悬殊，各地的教育质量必然存在巨大差异。为了缩小这些差距，中央政府必须更多地承担基础教育支出，服务提供则可以继续由县级政府负责。对于基本医疗、低保等其他社会项目同样如此，国家的目标应该是制定平等标准、实施普遍覆盖。前文曾介绍过，对最贫困地区的人力资本投资是中国促进增长和改善公平的最佳途径。

在大多数国家，中央政府对地方政府的转移支付与特定类型的收入挂钩。例如，中央政府可以承诺将固定比例的某种税费按照事先约定的公式进行分配，这样做可以给地方政府创造一个稳定的收入源，让它们有更大的把握开展预算编制和管理。中国已经有相当大规模的转移支付是属于此种公式化类型，但许多地方政府认为，它们在全部转移支付中所占的比例还是太小。如果根据上面的建议，免除地方政府的部分支出责任，那么基于公式计算的转移支付在剩下的转移支付中所占的比例有望大幅提高。

同样值得研究的是，是否应该借鉴其他许多国家的做法，给地方政府正式赋予收入征收方面的一定的自主权，这有助于强化地方政府对当地居民负责，加快反应速度。经济学原理认为，地方税应该主要来自房地产和自然资源，这些不动产的价值在很大程度上取决于地方政府所创造的治理环境。自然资源税对于那些矿产资源丰富的欠发达地区尤其有利。

总的来说，财政体制改革应该给所有层级的政府提供相匹配的资源和动力，以促进国家的进一步发展。

结束语

本章的主要议题是研究如何才能缩小规划目标和实施效果之间的差距。在过去 30 年，经济体制改革和对外开放是中国取得巨大成就的关键因素，同样，在未来数十年实现中国的发展目标，也需要深化改革和坚持开放。这对任何国家而言都是极其复杂而艰巨的任务，本章只是开启了对这个议题的思考而非最后的结论。

第二篇

2

背景论文

（按作者姓氏首字母排序）

背景论文一　非洲国家对中国的期待

K.Y. 阿莫阿科

背景论文二　中国社会政策改革中的问题

A.B. 阿特金森

背景论文三　中国的人口老龄化与经济增长

朱迪思·巴尼斯特　大卫·布卢姆

拉里·罗森伯格

背景论文四　中国的养老金改革：问题、选择和政策建议

尼古拉斯·巴尔　彼得·戴蒙德

背景论文五　社会政策：中国发展中的一项中心内容

尼古拉斯·巴尔　霍华德·格伦纳斯特

背景论文六　中国就业政策的国际视角

蔡　昉　理查德·弗里曼　阿德里安·伍德

背景论文七　中国在世界经济中的角色：展望第十二个五年规划

安德鲁·克罗克特

背景论文八　世界期望中国担当什么样的经济和金融领导角色：两段历史的启示

巴里·埃肯格林

背景论文九　世界对中国的期待及中国应该做什么

穆罕默德·埃尔埃利安　拉曼·托鲁伊

背景论文十　中国的地区差距：经验和政策

樊胜根　拉维·坎布尔　张晓波

背景论文十一　中国的城市化：面临的问题及政策选择

弗农·亨德森

背景论文十二　中国向高收入国家转型：避免中等收入陷阱的因应之道

霍米·卡拉斯

背景论文十三　对拉丁美洲社会政策的有关评论

圣蒂亚戈·莱维

背景论文十四　中国工业生产的分散化和面向国内市场的制造业前景

香港利丰集团研究中心

背景论文十五　中国社会保障改革：争论与选择

李　实

背景论文十六　中国与世界经济：基于欧洲视角的分析

让·皮萨尼－费里

背景论文十七　中国新增长方式的最优化探析

保罗·罗默

背景论文十八　中国融入全球金融架构的路径选择

沈联涛　成九雁

背景论文十九　为中国和谐社会建设而进行的公共部门改革

黄佩华

背景论文二十　中国的住房政策：面临的问题和选择

伊夫·泽诺

作者介绍

K. Y. 阿莫阿科（K. Y. Amoako），非洲经济转型研究中心的创办者和负责人。1974 年曾就职于世界银行，他是第一个升上高级职位的非洲人。他先后担任世界银行非洲地区项目处长、拉丁美洲和加勒比地区项目处长，以及教育和社会政策部主任。1995—2005 年，阿莫阿科担任联合国非洲经济委员会执行秘书。2006 年作为一名杰出的非洲学者进入了华盛顿智库伍德罗·威尔逊国际学者中心。阿莫阿科拥有加纳大学经济学学士学位以及美国加州大学伯克利分校经济学博士学位。

A.B. 阿特金森（A.B. Atkinson），牛津大学纳菲尔德学院研究员，1994—2005 年担任过纳菲尔德学院院长。目前任伦敦经济学院终身教授。他曾经担任过皇家经济学会、计量经济学会、欧洲经济学会以及国际经济学会的主席。曾在英国皇家收入财富分配委员会、养老金法律审查委员会、社会公平委员会就职。他曾是法国经济分析委员会的成员暨法国总理的经济顾问。2001 年，因对经济学的贡献被封为爵士。最新著作为《经合组织国家收入分配的变化》（*The Changing Distribution of Earnings in OECD Countries*）。

朱迪思·巴尼斯特（Judith Banister），资深人口统计学专家，专门研究中国人口学。她的研究主要集中在人口以及相关的社会经济学发展趋势上。巴尼斯特博士正在进行的研究项目包括：中国人口老龄化与经济增长、中国健康与死亡率趋势、中国制造业雇用与劳动报酬、中国女性状况研究。她拥有斯坦福大学博士学位。她的职业生涯横跨公共部门——美国国家统计局国际项目主任，私营部门——美国经济咨商局全球人口所所长，学术部门——香港科技大学教授。她还出任加利福尼亚硅谷以及北京金戈投资公司顾问。

尼古拉斯·巴尔（Nicholas Barr），伦敦经济学院公共经济学教授。他著述颇丰，包括《福利国家经济学》《养老金改革：原则和政策选择》（与 Peter Diamond 合著）等。他是《国际社会保障评论》编委会成员，以及《*CESifo* 经济研究》和《澳大利亚经济评论》副主编。除了学术研究外，他还有两段在世界银行的工作史，主要负责医疗保健制度的设计等。

大卫·布卢姆（David E. Bloom），哈佛大学经济学和人口学 Clarence James Gamble 讲座教授。哈佛大学公共卫生学院全球卫生和人口统计系主任，以及哈佛大学全球人口老龄化项目负责人。他是美国国民经济研究局助理研究员，美国艺术与科学学院研究员。1981年获得普林斯顿大学经济学与人口学博士

学位。他撰写了大量有关卫生、劳动力、经济学发展以及人口学领域的文章。

蔡昉（Cai Fang），先后毕业于中国人民大学、中国社会科学院研究生院，经济学博士。现任中国社会科学院人口与劳动经济研究所所长，第十一届全国人大常委会委员；兼任中国人口学会副会长、国家规划专家委员会委员。主要研究领域包括：农村经济理论与政策、劳动经济学、人口经济学、中国经济改革、经济增长、收入分配和贫困等领域。著有《中国经济》《中国劳动力市场的发育与转型》等，主编《中国人口与劳动问题报告》系列专著等。获第二届张培刚发展经济学优秀成果奖；第四届中国发展百人奖。

安德鲁·克罗克特（Andrew Crockett），摩根大通公司主席的特别顾问以及执行委员会委员，同时也是中国银行业监督管理委员会国际咨询理事会以及国家开发银行国际理事会委员。在加入摩根大通公司之前，1993—2003年，曾担任过国际清算银行总裁，并在1999—2003年担任金融稳定论坛（现为金融稳定委员会）第一任主席。在他的职业生涯早期，曾在英格兰银行以及国际货币基金组织担任高级职位。

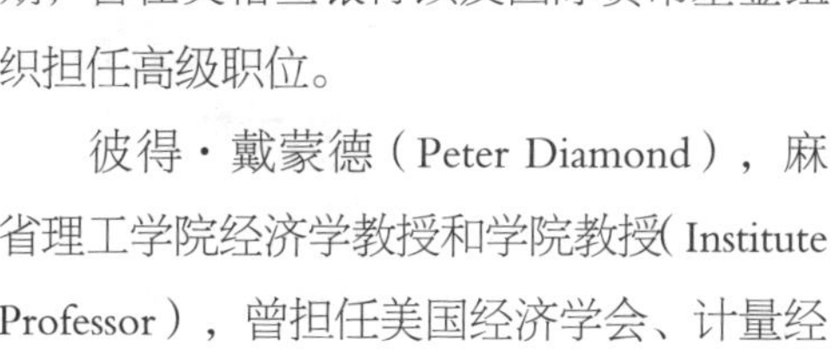

彼得·戴蒙德（Peter Diamond），麻省理工学院经济学教授和学院教授(Institute Professor)，曾担任美国经济学会、计量经济学学会主席以及国家社会保险科学院院

长。2010 年获诺贝尔经济学奖。自 1974 年首次担任美国国会有关社会保障制度改革的顾问后，一直积极从事这项课题研究。在 2004—2005 年度及 2009—2010 年度，他两度撰写过有关中国养老金改革的报告。近期著作有《改革养老金：原则和政策选择》（与 Nicholas Barr 合著）等。

巴里·埃肯格林（Barry Eichengreen），加州大学伯克利分校 George C. Pardee 和 Helen N. Pardee 经济学和政治学讲座教授。同时兼任美国艺术科学学院院士、美国国民经济研究局（NBER）研究员、经济政策研究中心研究员、德国基尔世界经济研究所研究员及彼得森国际经济研究所学术咨询委员会主席等。1997—1998 年，他担任过国际货币基金组织高级政策顾问。

埃肯格林教授于 2002 年荣获美国经济史学会 Jonathan R. T. Hughes 优秀教学奖，2004 年荣获美国加州大学伯克利分校社会科学系杰出教学奖。2010 年荣获国际熊彼特协会颁发的熊彼特奖。2010—2011 学年美国经济史学会主席。最新著作包括《嚣张的特权：美元的兴衰与国际货币体系的未来》（*Exorbitant Privilege: The Rise and Fall of the Dollar and the Future of the International Monetary System*）。

穆罕默德·埃尔埃利安（Mohamed A. EL-Erian），太平洋投资管理公司首席执行官兼联席首席信息官，该公司是全球性的投资管理公司，管理的资产逾 13 万亿美元（截至 2010 年 12 月）。埃尔埃利安于 2007 年底再次加入太平洋投资管理公司之

前，曾是哈佛管理公司的董事长兼首席执行官（从2006年2月起），该公司管理哈佛大学的捐赠基金和有关资产。埃尔埃利安也曾担任过哈佛商学院教员。他拥有剑桥大学经济学学士和硕士学位，以及牛津大学经济学硕士和博士学位。在美国学术杂志《外交政策》评选的“全球思想家100强”中，他位列第16名。

樊胜根（Shenggen Fan），国际粮食政策研究所所长。在1995年加入国际粮食政策研究所后，负责公共投资项目，主持了大量有关非洲、亚洲和中东等发展中国家扶贫发展策略的研究。在加入国际粮食政策研究所之前，他曾在荷兰国家农业研究国际服务中心以及阿肯色大学农业经济学和农业社会学系任职。他拥有明尼苏达大学应用经济学博士学位及中国南京农业大学学士和硕士学位。

理查德·弗里曼（Richard B. Freeman），哈佛大学经济学Herbert Ascherman讲座教授，目前他在哈佛法学院担任劳动和职业生涯项目的主任。他指导NBER / Sloan Science Engineering劳动研究项目，并在伦敦经济学院任高级研究员。他还是美国艺术与科学学院研究员。2006年获得劳动经济学会颁发的明塞尔终身成就奖。2007年他被授予IZA劳动经济学奖。

霍华德·格伦纳斯特（Howard Glennerster），伦敦经济学院名誉教授，多年来在该校教授社会政策、卫生经济学、教育以及社会保障等学科。他发表了大量相关

文章，并担任英国卫生部和财政部顾问。

弗农·亨德森（J. Vernon Henderson），芝加哥大学经济学博士，布朗大学 Eastman 政治经济学讲座教授以及经济学与城市研究教授，美国国民经济研究局助理研究员。他主要从事关于美国、巴西、加拿大、印度、中国、韩国和印度尼西亚的城市化和地方政府财政及监管等方面的研究。目前从事有关城市系统、工业选址、城市生产力、环境监管、城市副中心（sub-center）发展，以及城市之间税收和公共服务竞争的研究。

霍米·卡拉斯（Homi Kharas），布鲁金斯学会全球经济与发展高级研究员，经合组织发展中心客座研究员，马来西亚首相的国家经济顾问委员会成员。他还曾是由迈克尔·斯宾塞教授主持的增长与发展委员会工作小组成员。此前，曾担任世界银行东亚和太平洋地区首席经济学家，以及减贫和经济管理、金融与私营部门发展部主任，负责经济结构和经济政策、财政问题、债务、贸易、治理和金融市场等方面的研究。他的研究领域主要包括全球贸易、东亚经济增长与发展，以及对最贫困国家的国际援助。他获得了哈佛大学经济学博士学位。

拉维·坎布尔（Ravi Kanbur），康奈尔大学世界事务部 T. H. Lee 讲座教授、应用经济学教授。康奈尔大学农业和生命科学学院应用经济学与管理学系 Charles H. Dyson 讲座教授以及文理学院经济学系终

身教授。曾在世界银行就职，担任过经济顾问、高级经济顾问、驻加纳代表、世界银行非洲局首席经济学家以及世界银行首席经济学家主管顾问、世界银行《世界发展报告》负责人。获得牛津大学经济学博士学位。主要研究领域为公共经济学和发展经济学。

圣蒂亚戈·莱维（Santiago Levy），泛美开发银行副行长。2007 年 8 月—2008 年 2 月，担任泛美开发银行研究部门总经理和首席经济学家。2000 年 12 月—2005 年 10 月担任过墨西哥社会保障局局长。1994—2000 年，担任墨西哥财政和公共信贷部副部长。获得波士顿大学的政治经济学硕士学位和经济学博士学位，曾在剑桥大学做过博士后研究员。他的最新著作包括《没有平等就没有增长？墨西哥的不平等、利益和竞争力》（*No Growth without Equity? Inequality, Interests and Competition in Mexico*，和 Michael Walton 共同编著）等。

李实，北京师范大学教授，博士生导师，收入分配与贫困研究中心主任。多次担任世界银行、亚洲开发银行、联合国开发署、国家发改委、国务院扶贫办等机构的研究项目专家。主要研究领域：发展经济学与劳动经济学。近年来的研究重点包括：收入分配、公共政策、贫困、劳动力市场。1994 年获孙冶方经济科学奖；1996 年、2000 年、2002 年获中国社会科学院优秀成果奖；1999 年获国务院政府津贴；2007 年获联合国人类发展奖；2009 年获教育部人文社科优秀成果奖；2010 年获张培刚发展经济学奖。

林重庚（Edwin R.Lim），前世界银行官员，1980—1990年，任世界银行中国事务首席经济学家。1985—1990年，组建世界银行驻华代表处并任首任首席代表。先后参与世界银行在加纳、尼日利亚、印度尼西亚、泰国、越南、印度等国的管理事务，曾任世界银行西非局局长、印度局局长等职。1994—1996年，林先生从世界银行外调，领导组建了中国国际金融有限公司（CICC），并任首任总裁。自2003年始，组建并主持由中国和世界著名经济学家团队组成的中国经济研究和咨询项目。林先生拥有普林斯顿大学学士学位和哈佛大学博士学位。

让·皮萨尼－费里（Jean Pisani–Ferry），自2005年1月担任欧洲智库Bruegel（欧洲布鲁塞尔和全球经济实验室）主任，同时兼任巴黎第九大学经济学教授。主要从事政策制定与学术研究。在法国研究部门和政府部门任职后，1989年他加入了欧洲委员会，成为欧盟经济及金融事务总司总干事的经济顾问。1992—1997年，任法国国际经济研究所（法国主要国际经济研究中心）主任。1997年，任法国财政部长高级经济顾问，不久即被任命为法国总理经济分析委员会执行总监（2001—2002年）。2002—2004年，任法国国库署署长的高级顾问。

伊恩·波特（Ian Porter），前世界银行官员，曾任东南亚局局长、董事会政策支持负责人、西非局人口与人力资源处长、驻坦桑尼亚首席代表，早年从事于中国、泰国和越南的经济和部门改革的研究事务。现着重于东亚和东南亚地区，与亚洲开

发银行、世界银行、联合国等机构和组织密切合作，从事国际发展问题的咨询工作，并参与了中国经济研究和咨询项目的课题。他拥有牛津大学哲学、政治学和经济学学士学位，苏赛克斯大学（Sussex University）发展经济学硕士学位。

保罗·罗默（Paul Romer），非营利研究组织Charter Cities主席，从事于规则、城市化和发展问题之间的互动研究。他是斯坦福大学经济政策研究所高级研究员，在斯坦福大学商学院任教期间，为鼓励学生参与，曾创建一家教育技术公司，该公司开发的软件为经济学及其他课程的作业解决了大量问题。他的主要研究领域为经济增长，1986年建立了内生经济增长模型。他还是全球发展中心（华盛顿）的客座研究员，卡内基基金会理事会成员，纽约大学斯特恩商学院Henry Kaufman访问教授。

沈联涛（Andrew L. T. Sheng），中国银行业监督管理委员会高级顾问、卡塔尔金融中心监管局董事、马来西亚森那美有限公司和国库控股公司董事。他还是清华大学经济管理学院和马来亚大学的兼职教授。1998年10月1日至2005年9月30日，任香港证监会主席。1993—1998年出任香港金融管理局副主席。1989—1993年在世界银行任职，出任金融部门发展部高级经理。1976—1989年间，出任马来西亚中央

银行不同职位，包括首席经济学家及主管银行与保险业监管工作的行长助理。

迈克尔·斯宾塞（Michael Spence），2001 年诺贝尔经济学奖获得者，曾任 2006—2010 年间存续的增长与发展独立委员会主席、斯坦福大学商学院院长、哈佛大学艺术与科学学院院长。他是斯坦福大学商学院研究生院管理学名誉教授，斯坦福大学胡佛研究所高级研究员，纽约大学斯特恩商学院经济学教授，还任多家私人公司及斯坦福管理公司董事会成员，多家投资管理和咨询公司高级顾问及咨询专家。斯宾塞教授拥有普林斯顿大学哲学学士学位，并获罗氏奖学金；牛津大学数学学士和硕士学位及哈佛大学经济学博士学位。

拉曼·托鲁伊（Ramin Toloui），太平洋投资管理公司新港海滩办事处执行副总裁和新兴市场组合投资经理。在 2006 年加入太平洋投资管理公司之前，曾在美国财政部国际司工作了 7 年，最近作为西半球办公室主任，领导一支由经济学家组成的团队，给美国高级政府官员提供在拉美投资的政策建议。2001—2003 年，阿根廷、巴西、乌拉圭和土耳其危机期间他曾担任过美国国际事务副国务卿的高级顾问。

黄佩华（Christine Wong），牛津大学跨学科领域研究院和赛德商学院中国研究中心高级研究员和主任。曾担任过世界银行、亚洲开发银行、经合组织、联合国开发计划署、联合国儿童基金会和英国国际发展部有关中国财政改革和权力下放问题的顾

问。此前她曾在华盛顿大学的亨利·M. 杰克逊国际研究学院任国际研究教授（2000—2007 年）。她也曾在加州大学圣克鲁斯分校、加州大学伯克利分校和霍利奥克山学院的经济系任教。她撰写了大量关于中国公共财政和公共部门改革的文章。她与一些中国研究组织密切合作，同时也是清华大学中国财政税收研究所学术咨询委员会成员以及清华大学产业发展和环境治理中心名誉理事。

阿德里安·伍德（Adrian Wood），牛津大学国际发展学院教授及沃尔夫森学院研究员。曾就读于剑桥大学和哈佛大学。1969—1977 年，任剑桥大学国王学院研究员及经济系讲师。1977—1985 年，任世界银行高级经济学家，从事有关中国、土耳其方面的研究，参与撰写《1980 年世界发展报告》。1985—2000 年，他在英国萨塞克斯大学发展研究所担任专职研究员。2000—2005 年，任英国国际发展部首席经济学家。

伊夫·泽诺（Yves Zenou），斯德哥尔摩大学经济学教授，并在瑞典工业经济研究所担任高级研究员。他的研究领域包括：社会互动及网络理论、城市经济学、对少数族裔的隔离及歧视问题、犯罪行为和教育。伊夫·泽诺还担任过英国南安普顿大学经济学教授，以及加州大学伯克利分校、欧洲大学学院和特拉维夫大学客座教授。现任《区域科学和城市经济学》编辑、《公共经济理论》杂志、《城市经济学》杂志、《城市管理》杂志、斯堪的纳维亚《经济学》杂志以及《经济与统计年刊》副主编。

张晓波，国际粮食政策研究所发展策略和管理部门高级研究员，《中国经济评论》联合主编。他获得南开大学数学学士学位，天津财经大学经济学硕士学位，以及康奈尔大学应用经济学和管理学的硕士与博士学位。2005—2006年他被推选为中国留美经济学会会长。他著述颇丰，其所著涉及区域发展、公共投资、中国农村工业化对人口变化的影响等主题。

利丰集团及利丰研究中心　利丰于1906年在广州创办时，是一家由家族经营的传统出口贸易公司。1937年到香港注册成立利丰（1937）有限公司，以私人全资拥有，现已成为利丰集团的控股股东。

经过多年的努力经营及业务拓展，利丰集团已发展成为一家跨国商贸集团，以香港为基地，经营出口贸易、经销批发和零售三大核心业务，分别通过利丰有限公司经营出口业务；利和经营经销批发；利亚零售经营连锁便利店及饼店；利邦控股有限公司经营高级男士服装零售；玩具反斗城经营玩具及儿童用品零售等。至2009年，利丰在全球70多个城市拥有35000多名员工，总营业额超过160亿美元。哈佛大学、斯坦福大学及沃顿商学院等曾对利丰的供应链管理、网络经营及价值链业务模式进行多个个案研究。

利丰研究中心于2000年成立，致力于为利丰集团管理层及客户提供宏观经济及中国商贸研究分析，作为决策参考。

Medium and Long Term Development and Transformation of the Chinese Economy

—An International Perspective

A Synthesis Report

Edwin Lim, Ian Porter, Paul Romer and Michael Spence

Preface

It is my honor that Mr. Edwin Lim invited me to write a Preface for this research report. This research on China's medium and long term development strategy was initiated by the Beijing Cairncross Economic Research Foundation at the invitation of the Office of the Central Leading Group on Finance and Economies and the National Development and Reform Commission (NDRC). Mr. Lim and Nobel Laureate Professor Michael Spence were responsible for the overall study. To this end, they invited more than 20 eminent economists from different institutions around the world to participate, each drafting a background paper in their areas of expertise.

The international team included prominent economists with diverse backgrounds and experiences, including, for example, Professor Peter Diamond, the winner of the 2010 Nobel Prize in Economies, Professor Paul Romer, the father of the "New Growth Theory" , and Mr. Mohamed EL–Erian, CEO of PIMCO, one of the largest asset management companies in the world. Our objective on the Chinese side in requesting this study was to have the opinions of the international experts on the formulation of China's 12thFive–Year Plan (FYP).

This study began in early 2009 and was completed just before the

Spring Festival of 2010. In the intervening period, the participating experts met with us many times to exchange views on the scope as well as the substance of the study.

I believe this research report is of a high quality. It is compulsory reading for anyone interested in understanding China in the context of global structural changes and in understanding the key development trends in China. Because of the broad perspectives and deep knowledge of the top experts, the report accurately analyzes the trends, key areas and priorities in China's development and reform. It is an important and valuable reference for policy making.

At the completion of the study, in accordance with our suggestion, Professor Spence, Professor Paul Romer, Mr. Ian Porter (former Director of the World Bank) and Mr. Lim summarized and integrated the key findings in a synthesis report entitled "Thoughts and Suggestions for China's 12th Five–Year Plan from an International Perspective." When we received this report, we discovered it was full of insights on China's development over the coming five years.

The report was soon distributed to every member of the team drafting the Chinese Government's "Proposal" for the 12th Five–Year Plan. This was a high level and large team led by Premier Wen Jiabao and Vice Premier Li Keqiang. More than 70 ministers, experts and scholars participated in this important assignment. Without doubt, the research report submitted by the team of international experts played an important role in the formulation of the "Proposal" for the 12th Five–Year Plan.

China's 12th Five–Year Plan presents the future Chinese economic and social development strategy. Coming after the global financial crisis and at a time when China is beginning its evolution into a high income country, it is an important strategy at a critical junction in history. The strategy not only defines the direction for the building of a "Xiao Kang" society in China but will also greatly influence the global economic balance and the welfare of humankind. It was a fortunate and rare opportunity for any one able to participate in the formulation of the 12th Five-Year Plan, given its significance. These participants should also be thanked.

Let me use this opportunity, on behalf of the Chinese agencies involved, to express our sincere appreciation to the international team of experts headed by Professor Spence and Mr. Lim. I would also propose that China should establish a special award for those international experts who have made important contributions to China's reform and openness. Because of them, China was able to acquire advanced development concepts and "valuable (stepping) stones from distant mountains."

It is unprecedented in China for official government agencies to invite international experts without official affiliations to conduct a study of China's development strategy. We now see that this is a unique method of cooperation that assures high quality and high efficiency. I hope we can continue to cooperate in this way in the future.

Liu He

March 10, 2011

Foreword

This study was conducted in 2009—2010 by an international team headed by Michael Spence, Nobel Laureate, and Edwin Lim, the first Chief Representative of the World Bank in China. Undertaken at the request of the Office of Central Leading Group on Financial and Economic Affairs (Zhong Cai Ban) and the National Development and Reform Commission (NDRC) of the People's Republic of China, the purpose of the study was to provide some thoughts and suggestions on China's medium and long term development and the 12th Five-Year Plan (2011—2015) from an international perspective.

The international team comprised prominent economists and experts from universities, businesses and public institutions from around the world. Members of the team were:

K. Y. Amoako, former Executive Secretary of the UN Economic Commission for Africa

A. B. Atkinson, Research Professor, Oxford University

Judith Banister, Director of Global Demographics at the Conference Board (USA)

Nicholas Barr, Professor of Public Economics, London School of Economics

David Bloom, Professor of Economics and Demography, Harvard

University

Cai Fang, Director of the Institute of Population and Labor Economics, CASS

Andrew Crockett, President of J. P. Morgan Chase International; former General Manager of the Bank for International Settlements

Peter Diamond, Nobel Laureate in 2010, Institute Professor of Economics, MIT

Barry Eichengreen, Professor of Economics and Political Science, University of California, Berkeley

Mohamed EL–Erian, CEO of PIMCO

Shenggen Fan, Director–General, International Food Policy Research Institute

Richard Freeman, Professor of Economics, Harvard University

Howard Glennerster, Professor Emeritus of Social Policy, London School of Economics

J. Vernon Henderson, Professor of Economics and Urban Studies, Brown University, and NBER

Ravi Kanbur, International Professor of Applied Economies and Management, Cornell University

Homi Kharas, former Chief Economist, East Asia Region, World Bank

Santiago Levy, Vice President for Sector and Knowledge, Inter–America Development Bank; former Deputy Minister of Finance, Mexico

Li Shi, Professor, Beijing Normal University

Edwin Lim, first Chief Representative of the World Bank in China; founding CEO of China International Capital Corporation

Jean Pisani-Ferry, Director of the Bruegel Institute

Ian Porter, former Director, the World Bank

Paul Romer, Professor of Economics, Stanford University

Andrew Sheng, Chief Advisor to the China Banking Regulatory Commission; former Chairman of Hong Kong Securities and Futures Commission

Michael Spence, Nobel Laureate, Professor in Economics, New York University; Professor Emeritus of Management, Stanford University

Christine Wong, Senior Research Fellow, Oxford University

Adrian Wood, Professor of International Development, Oxford University

Yves Zenou, Professor of Economics, Stockholm University

Xiaobo Zhang, Senior Research Fellow, International Food Policy Research Institute

Li & Fung Research Center (Hong Kong)

Mario Blejer, former Governor of the Central Bank of Argentina; William Hsiao, Professor of Economics at the School of Public Health, Harvard University and Martin Wolf, Chief Economics Commentator of the Financial Times also made important contributions to this study.

The study was guided by an Advisory Committee that included: Liu Zhongli, Xiang Huaicheng, Wu Jinglian, Zhou Xiaochuan, Lou Jiwei, Guo Shuqing, Li Jiange, Liu He, Victor Fung (Hong Kong) and Teh Kok-Peng (Singapore).

In the course of study, the international team maintained close contacts with the relevant departments of Zhong Cai Ban and NDRC. The international team met with Vice Minister Liu He of

Zhong Cai Ban and Secretary General Yang Weimin of NDRC on numerous occasions to exchange views that played an important role in the preparation and completion of the study. Invaluable support was received from Deputy Director–General Han Wenxiu, Deputy Director–General Wang Zhijun, Deputy Director–General Meng Jian of Zhong Cai Ban, and Deputy Director–General Tian Jinchen and Director Zhang Gengtian of the Planning Department, NDRC, in the execution of the study. The NDRC also provided a grant for this study.

The study was mainly funded and supported by Beijing Cairncross Economic Research Foundation. Professor Zhao Renwei, President of the Foundation, participated fully in the study's preparation, implementation and dissemination and also provided comprehensive advice. Comprehensive organization, and logistical coordination support was received from the Foundation's Programme Director, Dr.Cyril Lin, and the Secretary–General, Susan Su.

Financial and administrative support was also provided by the East Asian Institute (EAI) of the National University of Singapore. Since 2004, the EAI has supported a number of research studies on Chinese policy issues directed by Professor. Michael Spence and Mr. Edwin Lim, beginning with a study on social security reform and most recently a study on urbanization. Findings from these studies have contributed significantly to the present study. Within EAI, Professor Zheng Yongnian, Director, and Lian Wee Li, Senior Associate Director, in particular provided valuable support.

Simon Cox edited the earlier shorter version of the synthesis report as well as the current expanded version. He brought both clarity

and consistency to the various chapters of the report that were prepared by different authors.

The study benefited from discussions with leading Chinese economists and officials who provided invaluable comments on the synthesis report. They included: Bai Chong-en, Ding Ningning, Fu Jun, He Di, Lai Desheng, Long Guoqiang, Lu Feng, Ma Xiaohe, Qian Yingyi, Wang Xiaolu, Wu Xiaoling, Xu Shanda, Yi Gang, Yu Yongding, Zhang Weiying and Zhang Xiulan.

The People's Bank of China, the Institute of Population and Labor Economics (CASS), China International Capital Corporation Ltd (CICC) and the China Development Research Foundation kindly organized discussions and seminars for the international and Chinese experts in the course of the study. The participants included: Chen Jiagui, Chen Yulu, Cui Zhiyuan, Du Yang, Gao Shiji, Ge Yanfeng, Ha Jiming, Han Jun, He Ping, He Yupeng, Jing Tiankui, Li Daokui, Li Shantong, Li Yang, Liu Guo-en, Liu Guohong, Lu Mai, Lu Xueyi, Lu Ying, Shan Jingjing, Shen Bing, Si Jinsong, Song Li, Song Xiaowu, Su Ming, Tang Min, Wang Dewen, Wang Jianlun, Wang Yanzhong, Wang Youqiang, Wang Zhenyao, Xie Duo, You Jun, Yu Faming, Zeng Xiangquan, Zhang Li, Zhang Xiulan, Zhang Zhenzhong, Zhao Dianguo, Zheng Bingwen, Zheng Gongcheng, Zheng Yongnian, Zhu Ling, Zhu Min, Louis Kuijs, Philip O'Keefe and Yvonne Sin.

The heads of the study's international team would like to express their deep gratitude to all those who contributed and provided support to the study. The findings, interpretations, and conclusions expressed in each of the background papers are the responsibilities of the author (s) alone.

Contents

Preface *177*

Foreword *180*

Chapter 1 Introduction: International Growth Experience *189*

History of Economic Growth *189*

Middle–income Transition *193*

Implications for China's Medium Term Development *196*

Outline of this Report *198*

Chapter 2 Changing the Growth Model *204*

A New Pattern of Growth *204*

Industrial and Technological Upgrading *208*

Investment System *212*

Financial Sector Development *216*

Chapter 3 Urban and Regional Development *226*

Reducing Urban–Rural Income Disparities *227*

Changing the Size and Structure of Cities *231*

Promoting Efficient Cities *236*

Reforming Urban Financing and Management *239*

Reducing Regional Disparities as Part of the Middle–Income Transition *242*

Chapter 4 Strengthening Domestic Consumption and the Middle Class 249

Policies to Strengthen Domestic Consumption 249

The Middle Class 256

The Significance of the Middle Class 259

The Middle Class and Sustaining Economic Growth: International Experience 260

Estimating the Size of China's Middle Class 264

Chapter 5 Employment, Education and the Labor Market 267

Employment Growth, Sectoral Structure and Adjustment 269

Education and Skills Development 274

Labor Market Institutions and Regulations 281

Chapter 6 Strengthening the Pension System 292

Lessons from Economic Theory and International Experience 293

Options for Further Reform of China's Pension System 303

Overall Management of China's Pension System 311

Concluding Remarks 317

Chapter 7 Social Policy 319

Tackling Income Inequality 319

Common Principles of Reform 322

Education 325

Health 328

The Dibao Program 330

Population Policy 332

Overall Planning and Governance of Social Policy 333

Chapter 8 China's Role in the Global Economy *339*

The aftermath of the Financial Crisis *340*

The Realignment of the World Economy *343*

Rebalancing Global Demand *348*

Rebalancing China *349*

Promoting G1obal Trade and Investment *353*

Shifting to a Low–Carbon Economy *356*

Global Governance *362*

Chapter 9 System Reform *369*

Enhancing the Effectiveness and Accountability of the Government *370*

Changes in the Scope and Functioning of the SOEs *379*

Reform of the Fiscal System *384*

Concluding Remarks *392*

Background Papers

1. K. Y. Amoako: What African Countries Expect from China

2. A. B. Atkinson: Issues in the Reform of Social Policy in China

3. Judith Bannister, David Bloom and Larry Rosenberg: Population Ageing and Economic Growth in China

4. Nicholas Barr and Peter Diamond: Pension Reform in China: Issues, Options and Recommendations

5. Nicholas Barr and Howard Glennerster: Social Policy: A Central Element in China's Development

6. Cai Fang. Richard Freeman and Adrian Wood: China's Employment Policies in International Perspective

7. Andrew Crockett: China's Role in the World Economy:

Looking Forward to the 12th Five-Year Plan

8. Barry Eichengreen: What Kind of Economic and Financial Leadership does the World Expect of China? —Lessons from Two Historical Episodes

9. Mohamed EL-Erian and Ramin Toloui: What Does the World Expect from China, and What Should China Provide?

10. Shenggen Fan, Ravi Kanbur and Xiaobo Zhang: China's Regional Disparities: Experience and Policy

11. J. Vernon Henderson: Urbanization in China: Policy Issues and Options

12. Homi Kharas: China's Transition to a High Income Economy: Escaping the Middle Income Trap

13. Santiago Levy: Some Remarks on Social Policy of Latin America

14. Li and Fung Research Center: Notes on Decentralization of Industrial Production in China and Prospects for Manufacturing for the Domestic Market

15. Li Shi: Issues and Options for Social Security Reform in China

16. Jean Pisani-Ferry: China and the World Economy: A European Perspective

17. Paul Romer: Notes on Optimizing China's New Pattern of Growth

18. Andrew Sheng: China's Approach to Networked Globalization—an Institutional Response

19. Christine Wong: Public Sector Reforms toward Building the Harmonious Society in China

20. Yves Zenou: Housing Policies in China: Issues and Options

Introduction to Authors *393*

Chapter 1 Introduction:International Growth Experience*

History of Economic Growth

Economic growth is a recent phenomenon in human history. It began with the industrial revolution in Britain at the end of the 18th century. This progress spread to Europe and North America in the 19th century, accelerating as it traveled. In the 20th century, particularly in the second half, it spread and accelerated again (See Figure1).

As its economy grows, a society becomes more tightly organized, more densely interwoven. A growing economy is one in which

* In 2006 a group of the world's leading development practitioners—including former Prime Ministers, Ministers, planners and businessmen, plus two Nobel Laureates in Economics—were brought together to form the Commission on Growth and Development. Governor Zhou Xiaochuan of China was a Commissioner and Professor Michael Spence, who is one of the authors of this report, was the Chairman. This chapter is based on "The Growth Report: Strategies for Sustained Growth and Inclusive Development" issued in 2008 by the Commission. The report, background papers and more information on the Commission are available at www. growthcommission, org.

energies are better directed; resources better deployed; techniques mastered, then advanced. It is not just about making money.

Today's economists explain growth with the triple formula of technology, capital, and human capital. But these are only the proximate causes of growth. Its deeper roots draw on advances in science, finance, trade, education, medicine, public health, and government, to name but a few of the factors in play. Over the past two centuries, what we now call the global economy has expanded in fits and starts. Interrupted by the slump of the 1930s, it was rebuilt in the 1940s, when the institutional foundations of today's world economy were laid. Globalization has since proceeded apace, aided by legislation (the lowering of tariffs and quotas and the relaxation of capital controls) and innovation (the declining cost of transport and communication).

This renaissance of globalization helps to explain the acceleration in world growth since the latter half of the 20th century. As the world economy has opened and integrated, technology and know–how have flowed more easily to developing countries. Late–comers can assimilate new techniques much more quickly than the pioneering economies can invent them. That is why poorer countries can "catch up" with richer ones.

The lessons that countries import are not only technological. Both China and then India reformed their closed, heavily regulated economies, motivated in part by the force of international example. Reform and openness in China brought about not only dramatic changes in China but also the global economy. This accelerating growth has created new challenges. The first is a clear divergence in

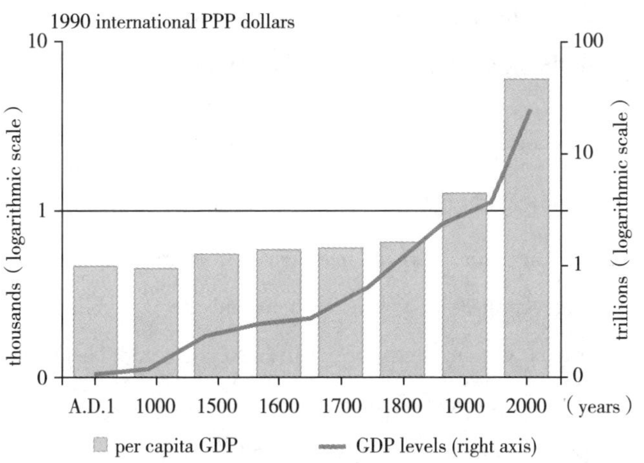

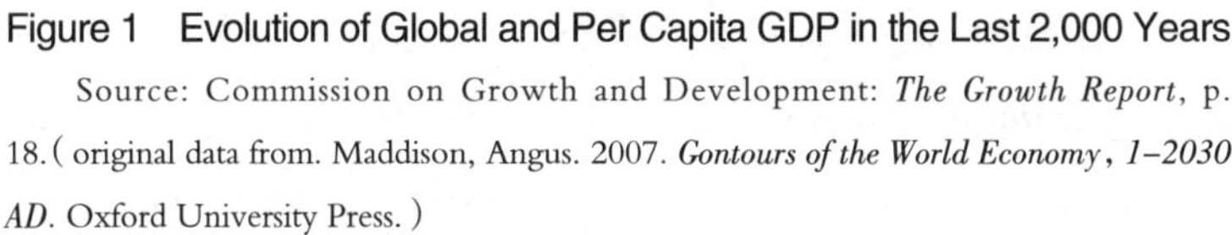

Figure 1 Evolution of Global and Per Capita GDP in the Last 2,000 Years

Source: Commission on Growth and Development: *The Growth Report*, p. 18. (original data from. Maddison, Angus. 2007. *Gontours of the World Economy, 1–2030 AD*. Oxford University Press.)

incomes within and between countries. Of the roughly 6 billion people on the planet, about 65 percent live in high–income or high–growth economies, up from less than a fifth 30 years ago. The remaining 2 billion people live in countries with stagnating, or even declining, incomes. The world population is projected to increase by 3 billion people by 2050. Unfortunately, 2 billion of this extra population will live in countries that are currently enjoying little or no growth. Thus, if these trends persist, the proportion of the world population living in low–growth environments might increase.

The second challenge is environmental. The quickened growth of world GDP has put new pressure on the planet's ecology and climate. This strain may ultimately threaten the growth environment of the last 200 years. If an economy fails to grow, man's efforts to better himself

become a scramble for a bigger share of a fixed amount of resources. Ecological stress quickly becomes social and political.

Since the end of the Second World War, many countries and regions have experienced at least brief periods of rapid growth, but only thirteen have enjoyed sustained growth of 7 percent a year or more, on average, for 25 years or longer. These are: Botswana; Brazil; China; Hong Kong, China; Indonesia; Japan; the Republic of Korea; Malaysia; Malta; Oman; Singapore; Taiwan, China; and Thailand. Two other countries, India and Vietnam, may be on their way to joining this group. It is to be hoped other countries will emerge soon.

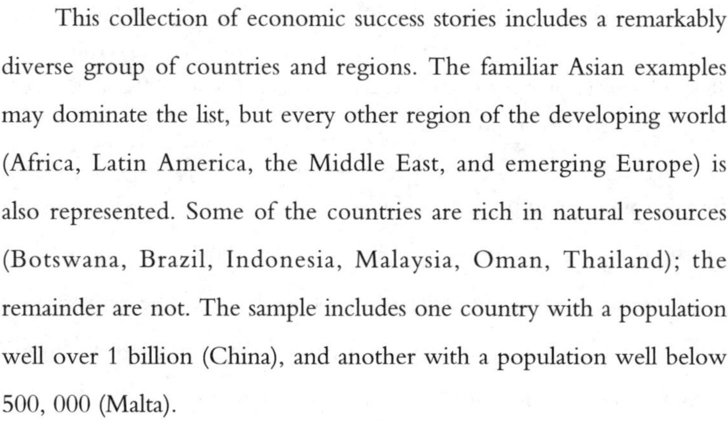

This collection of economic success stories includes a remarkably diverse group of countries and regions. The familiar Asian examples may dominate the list, but every other region of the developing world (Africa, Latin America, the Middle East, and emerging Europe) is also represented. Some of the countries are rich in natural resources (Botswana, Brazil, Indonesia, Malaysia, Oman, Thailand); the remainder are not. The sample includes one country with a population well over 1 billion (China), and another with a population well below 500, 000 (Malta).

The 13 economies each, then, have their idiosyncrasies. But it would be wrong to conclude that they defy generalization, or that there is no point in learning about their growth paths because the lessons cannot be applied at home. A close look at the 13 cases reveals five striking points of resemblance:

1. They fully exploited the world economy
2. They maintained macroeconomic stability

3. They mustered high rates of saving and investment

4. They let markets allocate resources

5. They had committed, credible, and capable governments

Middle–Income Transition

These stories all, then, share some common themes. But it is intriguing how their experiences in sustaining growth after reaching middle income status and attempting to reach high income have differed. Six of the economies (Hong Kong, China; Japan; Korea; Malta; Singapore; and Taiwan, China) continued to grow all the way to high–income levels. But several of the others lost some or all of their growth momentum long before catching the leading economies. The failure to evolve from middle to high income is not an uncommon phenomenon. In a large group of countries, including many in Latin America, growth has slowed markedly at the middle–income level. The reasons are complex. If anything, this second stage of growth, from middle to high income, is less understood, and certainly less studied, than the first stage.

No one can identify all the reasons why some economies lose momentum, and others don't. But there are common patterns across countries that are suggestive. As a country evolves successfully from middle to high income, its economy branches out into more skill–intensive industries. The service sector grows. The domestic economy with its increased size and wealth becomes a more important engine of growth.

The supply of labor in middle–income countries, which once

seemed infinitely elastic, ceases to be so. As surplus labor disappears, the opportunity cost of employing a worker in one sector rather than another, rises. Firms compete for workers and wages increase. These higher wages slow the growth of the labor–intensive sectors. Indeed, the export industries that once drove growth decline and eventually disappear.

Shortages of high–skilled labor emerge. As a result, policies shift toward promoting human capital and technology. The policy maker's role must also change. When a country is far behind the leading economies, it is very clear what it has to do, so policy makers can run things like an army. But as an economy catches up with the leaders, it becomes less obvious what it should make and where its future prosperity lies. More must be left to the bets of private investors and the collective judgment of the market.

The first priority for policy makers is to anticipate this transition and the new demands it will make of them. Many governments have a planning unit, which focuses on the future evolution of the economy and anticipates the public policies and outlays needed to support it. Korea, for example, changed its policies and public investments in the 1980s and 1990s to help the economy's evolution from labor–intensive manufacturing to a more knowledge–and capital–intensive economy. It opened the door to foreign–direct investment, privatized the national steel company, joined the OECD, and watched labor–intensive manufacturing move to new destinations.

A government's second task—not easy—is to let go of some of its earlier policies, even the successful ones. To cite some specific examples: special export zones, heavily managed exchange rates, and

other forms of industrial policy can be pursued for too long. The problems these policies address decline over time, so they are not needed forever. Resisting such forces will delay the structural change of the economy. It will divert investment away from new export industries and from industries that serve the domestic market.

Latin America provides many examples of countries that failed to sustain growth beyond the middle income level. All of the major economies in the region—particularly Argentina, Brazil, Chile, Colombia, and Mexico—experienced periods of rapid growth. But none enjoyed the prolonged, robust expansion required to "graduate" once and for all as a high-income country. Their progress has instead been spasmodic: vigorous growth punctuated by serious macroeconomic crises, followed by strong recoveries and renewed growth.

What explains this unstable pattern? The underlying cause may be the region's longstanding inequality and the failure of its social policies to tackle it. To this day, Latin America's income distribution is one of the worst in the world ; even several decades of fitful growth has failed to overcome it. Because of its inequality, Latin America suffers from a profound lack of political consensus, and because it lacks consensus, it is prone to chronic political turmoil. That instability weighs on long-term expectations, undermines investment, and makes it harder to build a solid institutional framework. Without those things, it is impossible to sustain growth.[1]

[1] See also Box 2 in Chapter 4 on "The Middle Class in Latin America" —a contribution from Mario Blejer, former Governor of the Central Bank of Argentina and Senior Advisor in the IMF.

Implications for China's Medium Term Development

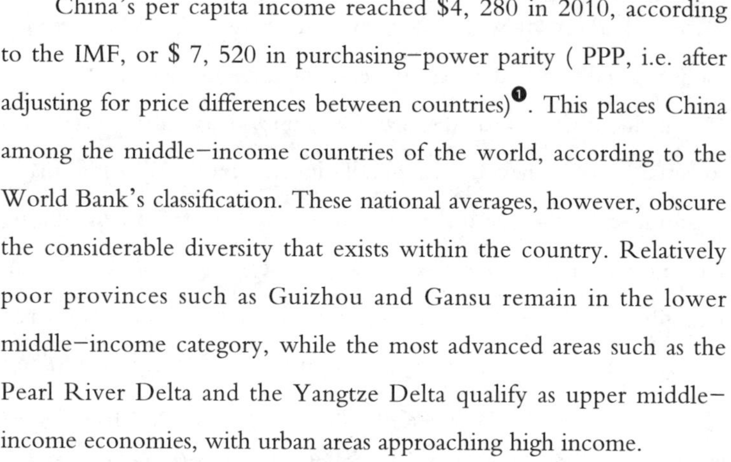

China's per capita income reached $4, 280 in 2010, according to the IMF, or $ 7, 520 in purchasing–power parity (PPP, i.e. after adjusting for price differences between countries)[1]. This places China among the middle–income countries of the world, according to the World Bank's classification. These national averages, however, obscure the considerable diversity that exists within the country. Relatively poor provinces such as Guizhou and Gansu remain in the lower middle–income category, while the most advanced areas such as the Pearl River Delta and the Yangtze Delta qualify as upper middle–income economies, with urban areas approaching high income.

These regional disparities should not be forgotten. Nonetheless, despite its lagging regions, China can still legitimately aspire to become a high–income country in the foreseeable future, and it should plan for the challenges that entails. The government has set the worthy goal of becoming a "Xiao Kang" society by 2020. But that should not be the summit of China's ambitions or define the limit of its planners' horizons. Policy makers should also look beyond that goal to the ultimate aim of becoming a high–income country.

That challenge has been recognized by Chinese policy makers and economists for some time. They often discuss the need for

[1] On February 28, 2011 the State Statistical Bureau estimates China's GDP in 2010 as RMB 39, 783 billion, and the population at the end of 2010 as 1, 341 million. With the exchange rate of RMB 6.57 per US $, China's GDP per capita in 2010 comes to US $ 4, 517.

a "Transformation of the Development Pattern". This usually comprises three elements: first, a transition from input–driven growth, based on the accumulation of capital and labor, to growth based on productivity gains; second, a shift in the mix of output, from industry to services; and third, a change in the source of demand, from foreign to domestic spending. A second set of challenges relates to building a "harmonious society" and ensuring that China's development is "putting people first." These Chinese priorities are entirely consistent with the lessons of international experience.

Two characteristics of China, however, make its development challenges unique. One is the disparity noted above, between different regions of the country and between rural and urban areas. These wide disparities must be taken into account when designing the new growth model and formulating the social programs required to achieve a harmonious society.

The other distinguishing characteristic is the sheer size of the country itself. China's size colors its interaction with the rest of the global economy. Although its growth pattern over the past two decades is not dissimilar to that of the Asian Tigers that preceded it, China's trade surplus and exchange rate have drawn far greater attention. Although still at a relatively low level of development, China consumes roughly half of the world's cement, a third of its steel and a quarter of its aluminum.

China's size means that it can never emulate the pattern of development pursued by today's advanced countries: the world simply does not contain enough natural resources to sustain that kind of growth. An obvious and controversial example is carbon emissions, which pose the risk of catastrophic climate change. Although emissions per capita in China are only about a quarter of those in the United States, China's total emissions are now the largest in the world — a fact the rest of the world cannot fail to notice. More generally, China has achieved a measure of dominance and power in the global economy at a relatively low level of per capita income and development (See Figure 2). Unlike any other country in history, China has to manage its difficult transformation into an advanced and rich country while assuming the responsibilities and obligations of an economic super power.

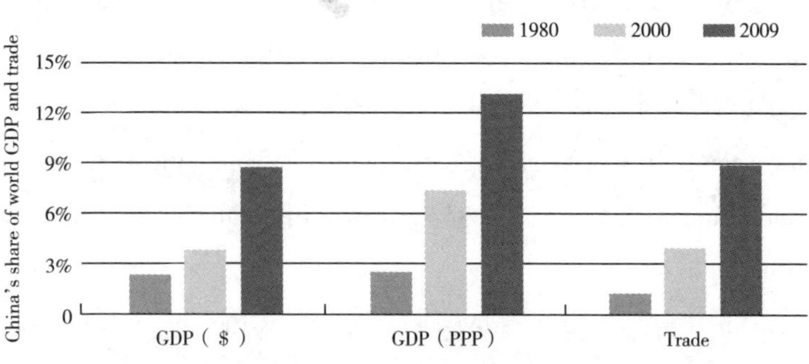

Figure 2 China's Rising Share

Source: International Monetary Fund, Arora and Vamvakids, "Gauging China's Influence", *Finance & Development*, December 2010, p.12, chart 1.

Outline of this Report

As China began the process of transition to high income status, we offer some thoughts and suggestions for China's medium term development, drawing on modern economic theory and the lessons of international experience. For this purpose we invited more than 20 prominent economists—from universities, businesses and public institutions around the world—to prepare papers in their respective areas of expertise. We also organized a number of seminars, from which we learned an enormous amount from Chinese economists and officials.

This volume collects all of the papers prepared for this initiative. The table of contents lists the papers and their authors, and also offers a short introduction to the team of international economists. A synthesis of the main findings and conclusions of the papers and discussions can be found in the following eight chapters of this report.

Chapters 2 to 4 detail the necessary transformation of China's development pattern.

Chapter 2 discusses China's growth model. In the past, China could grow quickly simply by moving people out of agriculture and into manufacturing. That process is not yet over. But in the future, China's growth will depend less on expanding manufacturing employment and more on improving productivity. That will require some creative destruction, as established firms give way to new, more productive enterprises. The government could help this process along, through judicious policies that favor new activities or techniques, without supplanting the role of the market in finding the best investments. Indeed, China will have to give market forces freer rein in capital allocation, because too much of its investment is currently financed by routine bank loans to safe state-owned enterprises (SOEs), or by the SOEs themselves, reinvesting the excess profits they are allowed to retain. China's future growth will depend, to a large extent, on a financial system that can mobilize saving, spread risk, and allocate capital to a growing variety of enterprises.

Chapter 3 looks at the geographical implications of China's growth strategy. China, it points out, is not as urbanized as many other countries at its stage of development. Many of its cities are of inefficient size (it needs more cities in the population range of 1–12 million) and economic scope, clinging too long to manufacturing. China's cities are also prone to the twin problems of sprawl and fragmentation of land–use on their outer fringes. The chapter argues that China's cities should be free to compete with one another for people and investment, but not at the expense of a seamless domestic market unimpeded by local protectionism. Greater urbanization should help narrow the stark income disparities between different regions of China. The government should remove policies that discriminate against lagging regions, before it embarks on expensive regional policies that discriminate in favor of them.

Chapter 4 turns from the supply side of China's economy, which has grown prodigiously, to the demand side, which has lagged behind. Over the next decade, China should rely more on domestic consumption as an engine of growth. Consumption, however, has fallen as a percentage of GDP, because wage–earners have received a shrinking share of the national income. The chapter discusses a number of measures the government could take to lift consumption, including cutting taxes on labor, easing consumer credit, and transferring some state assets to the public. To sustain growth, China must foster a strong middle class, secure and confident enough about the future to spend more freely on discretionary items.The chapter compares the size of China's middle class to that of other countries, some of whom succeeded in sustaining growth and some of whom failed.

Chapters 5 to 7 cover topics related to the government's objective of "putting people first" and building a "harmonious society".

Chapter 5 on employment, education and labor market observes that China's labor market is fast approaching a turning point: China's total labor force will probably cease to grow in less than ten years. In the past, China's challenge was to reallocate labor from agriculture to industry. In the future, the challenge will be to reallocate workers outside agriculture from lower to higher productivity activities. In this connection, it should be recognized that productivity differences among countries attributable to physical capital are limited. Human capital, i. e. the skills and competence of the population is much more important. Sustaining growth to high income level will require improvements in the skills of many workers and young people who lack the education required to prosper in an increasingly sophisticated economy. Investing more in human capital in the poorer regions would contribute to both efficiency and equity.

Chapter 6 points out that pension serve multiple purposes—consumption smoothing, insurance, poverty relief and redistribution. Since countries rank these objectives differently, no single pension system best serves all countries. The three elements of China's recently reformed system—the basic pension, individual accounts, and voluntary pensions—provide a good basic structure. China now needs to focus on extending coverage and improving the administration of the system. It should turn the basic pension into a universal state pension, payable to every resident above a certain age, thus removing the tripartite distinction between rural, urban and migrant. It should strengthen the overall management of the pension system. China should learn from other countries' mistakes as well as their example. To further reform

the individual accounts, it could consider the "notional" defined–contribution accounts pioneered in Sweden and elsewhere.

Chapter 7 on social policy reviews the sharp rise in inequality that has accompanied China's rapid growth from a comparative perspective. Governments elsewhere have succeeded in offsetting inequality through social policy. But in China social spending is low as a percentage of GDP, the coverage of its social programs is patchy and benefits are not portable from place to place and job to job, impeding the mobility of labor. Income disparity should be reduced to avoid social tension and instability. Successful social policies should cover the nation as a whole, even if that means a low level of benefits. Their delivery should be as localized and decentralized as possible, but their funding should come largely from the central government so as to permit redistribution from rich areas to poor.

The last two chapters of this synthesis report discusses China's role in the world economy and the further reform of the economic system needed to meet future challenges.

Chapter 8 notes that globalization has provided China with two critical ingredients for catch–up growth: knowledge and deep markets for its goods. As a result of its success, China's economy is systemically significant: it influences world prices and attracts global scrutiny. Other countries now expect China to shoulder some international responsibilities, such as rebalancing global demand and curbing carbon emissions. However China has just reached middle income. Its vast global influence and power at a relatively low level of development is unprecedented in world's history. The chapter argues that there is no insurmountable conflict between the rest of the world's expectations

of China and China's objectives for itself. But there is ample scope for disagreement about the manner and speed with which China fulfils these objectives. It is therefore important that China plays an active role in the miscellaneous international fora that steer the world economy.

Chapter 9 on system reform explores some of the institutional reforms China needs if it is to implement its Five–Year Plan successfully. Both the central government and the sub–national administrations will have to rethink their roles and strengthen their capacities. Institutional reform should not stop there. It should also encompass the SOEs, which face too little competition and give too little back to the state in the form of dividends. China will also have to reform its fiscal arrangements, particularly the division of revenue and expenditure responsibilities between the central government, the provinces and the counties. This chapter's over–riding question is how to reduce the gap between the ambition of China's plans and their uneven implementation. This is an extremely complex and challenging question for any country, and this last chapter should be seen as the beginning of the thinking on this topic rather than the end.

In making its transition to a "Xiao Kang" society and beyond, China faces a daunting list of challenges. However, China is also in a strong position to meet them. We find no insurmountable trade–off between China's long–and short–term goals, no great conflict between sustained growth and a harmonious society, and indeed no contradiction between China's aspirations and the rest of the world's interests. The country's accomplishments over the past three decades inspire a great deal of confidence that its present challenges will be met and its future opportunities realized.

Chapter 2 Changing the Growth Model*

A New Pattern of Growth

Many countries have enjoyed spurts of rapid growth. But as the previous chapter pointed out, few have sustained it for three decades, as China has done.Indeed, rapid growth of 5%–10% a year became possible only in the second half of the 20th century. Development at that pace required an open world economy, knitted together by trade liberalization and technological advances in transport and communications. This global integration made it possible for less developed countries to import ideas and knowhow from the leading economies. It also offered them entry to a vast world market, which allowed economies of scale and specialization their domestic markets alone could not support. As production expanded briskly, they could draw on an abundant supply of labor previously trapped in agriculture.

Once countries reach middle–income status, decisions about where best to use their labor and capital become more complex. A

* This chapter draws on Background paper No.17 by Paul Romer: "Notes·on Optimizing China's New Pattern of Growth" and No.7 by Andrew Crockett: "China's Role in the World Economy: Looking Forward to the 12th Five–Year Plan."

country's broad characteristics and endowments may provide some clues, suggesting a future in more skill–intensive services or more capital–intensive manufacturing, for example. But what line of manufacturing, exactly, using what technology? A great deal is left open. Economies that saw export success as the true test of a product or firm's worth must rely increasingly on the verdict of their domestic marketplace. Having assimilated technologies from abroad, they must also rely increasingly on local entrepreneurs as a source of new ideas and innovations.

In the early stages of development, the best indicator of progress is an increase in employment, particularly in the formal sector and in urban areas. Once a country reaches middle–income status, the best indicator of success is an increase in the average wage. This is for two reasons. As development proceeds, competition increases for workers of a given skill level, driving up their wages. In addition, workers become more skilled, allowing them to shift to more challenging and more rewarding jobs. Firms that rely on low–wage workers shift to higher value–added components of global supply chains, go out of business or move offshore, taking the less rewarding jobs to workers in poorer countries.

As nations go through this process of creative destruction, firms complain that they can no longer afford to hire workers. At this point, the nation must choose. Does it want to protect the existing firms or to see continued growth in the wages of its workers? Nations that protect their firms stop growing, and productivity stagnates. Nations that strive for higher wages keep growing. It is clear then that continued growth requires substantial structural change in the supply side of the economy, in the tradable sector and specifically in the export sector.

If a country's wages are to keep growing, then its productivity must keep pace. Some existing firms will develop new lines of business that require higher skills and justify higher–wage workers. But some incumbent firms will not be able to keep up. In high–income economies, many of the new, higher paying jobs come from new firms. These new entrepreneurial ventures start out small. Many of them fail. But the ones that succeed grow rapidly and drive improvements in productivity.

If this transition is to succeed, investment must be quick to switch to the most productive firms and activities. And as the economy relies increasingly on ideas, knowledge, and entrepreneurship, investment (including public–sector investment) must shift its emphasis from physical capital to human capital.

Box 1

On Changing China's Growth Model: An Analogy

In his 1890 classic, "Principles of Economics", Alfred Marshall compared the upheaval of economic progress with the growth of a forest. A similar analogy can also shed light on China's development. Before reform China was like a forest of pine planted long ago. All the trees had stopped growing. The reforms made it possible to plant seedlings for new redwood trees, which grow much taller than pines. The redwoods brought new vigor to the forest, just as China's new firms brought new vigor to its economy.

In the next stage, sustaining growth is more difficult. One part of the challenge is to find better seeds each year, so that each generation of redwoods grows taller still. Fortunately, China can still benefit from a large stock of ideas tested and developed in other economies, as well as developing its own capacity for innovation at the technological frontier.

The second challenge is to make room for these new, more productive seedlings. This requires the removal of some existing trees, which will otherwise block the light of their younger rivals. When everyone wants a tall forest, it is easy to persuade people to cut down a short pine tree that has stopped growing. It is more difficult to persuade them to cut down some tall redwoods to make room for younger trees that might eventually grow even taller. And it is more difficult still to cut down redwoods that are still growing. But if each generation of seedlings is much better than the last, the economy must find a way to keep planting many new ones each year. This is what economists call creative destruction.

Nations and firms do embrace the necessary reforms when their circumstances become desperate. But after a first round of reforms is rewarded with a burst of growth, it is easy to become complacent. People fail to appreciate that making room for new ideas requires a constant process of renewal.

As part of a commitment to sustained productivity growth in the next Five-Year Plan, China will have to encourage not just the entry of new organizations, but also the shrinkage and even the closure of organizations that were once very successful but which are starting to fall behind. The competition between new entrants and older firms ensures that a society's most valuable resource, its people, are working

in organizations that become steadily more productive on average from one year to the next.

Source: Background Paper No.17 by Paul Romer: "Notes on Optimizing China's New Pattern of Growth" .

Industrial and Technological Upgrading

Some economists would argue that China does not yet need a new development pattern. Its comparative advantage, they would suggest, remains in labor–intensive pro duction. Parts of China, after all, have barely moved out of the low–income stage of development, and a large amount of surplus labor still exists in the rural areas. Some economists therefore argue that China's comparative advantage remains in labor–intensive manufacturing.

There is scope for China's manufacturing to expand further and also to migrate to poorer parts of China, where labor is cheaper. But to sustain steady improvements in wages, China will need a new growth model at some point—and that point may have already arrived in its coastal cities. Moreover, a new growth model based on knowledge accumulation and productivity gains will require new institutions and rules that take time to develop. China should therefore start this process as soon as it can.

Other economists would agree that China needs to upgrade its industry, but argue that the government is the wrong entity to do it. Industrial policies can easily backfire; governments cannot pick winners. However, the experience of many East Asian economies, including China itself, suggests otherwise. Japan, Taiwan, China; South Korea and Singapore all intervened in the market to shepherd their economies successfully through the middle-income stage to advanced levels of development. Policies that encourage this transition need not pick particular firms, or even particular industries, to favor. Industrial policies should apply across the board, favoring new technologies or new entrants across the board, irrespective of the industry or sector they are in. Such policies can encourage both the birth of new firms and innovation in existing firms, while still allowing the market to decide which specific firms or industries take off.

This is not to deny that industrial policy is difficult to formulate and implement. There are no universal blueprints. Each country must develop its own institutional model, based on its own circumstances. Nonetheless, the experience of Asian and Latin American countries suggests a number of guidelines.

As a general principle, the government should seek not to replace market forces but merely to supplement market incentives, when they fall short in some way. The market may, for example, under invest in non-traditional industries because of the uncertainty that shrouds them. A useful rule would be to provide incentives and subsidies only for new activities, and to withdraw support from failing projects, so that resources do not get bottled up in unproductive activities. To this end, it will be necessary to:

- specify monitorable criteria for success and failure and build in an automatic sunset clause for subsidies

• target economic activities or directions of technological change (e.g.low–carbon technology), not industrial sectors or firms

• subsidize only activities that can potentially provide spillovers and demonstration effects

• maintain competition between firms at all stages in the process, by subsidizing buyers, for example, and letting many firms compete for their business

• promote activities that can potentially sustain and renew themselves, so that the government–backed venture is only the first turn in an ongoing cycle of innovation

The agencies responsible for implementing industrial policy, such as the NDRC, should stay as close as possible to the market, building channels of communication and feedback with private investors and customers.

In this way, the government may help firms to adopt and apply new ideas and techniques. But the government also has a key role further upstream, in encouraging the research that produces new ideas in the first place. Some principles gleaned from international experience may help guide its technology and research policy.

A key question is how to allocate research grants to reward the best researchers. One way to do this is to allow researchers to take their grants with them to any university in China. These grants should offer a net financial benefit to the institution that hosts the researcher. This arrangement would encourage healthy competition between institutions for the best researchers, and this competition would ensure that productive researchers are better compensated than their less productive peers.

The government should also allow several agencies to commission their own outside research. Experience suggests that agencies can learn a lot by funding university research on topics of interest to them. This outside research is often more productive than research produced by their own in–house labs. A variant of this model is to allow competition between their in–house research and the external research they sponsor.

The government should not, however, make research grants directly to firms. The pitfalls of this approach are well illustrated by the Clean Car initiative in the United States. The US government spent hundreds of millions of dollars in an ultimately futile attempt to get American auto–makers to introduce hybrid cars. Unfortunately, the US firms did not perceive it to be in their interest to develop fuel–efficient cars. They saw profits primarily in large vehicles, and the research funds did nothing to change this strategic commitment. If a government wants to encourage a specific outcome it should create an incentive for the behavior it wants to induce. It may be more effective to give a subsidy to consumers of the new technology rather than to the producers. An alternative is to tax (or at least avoid subsidizing) the consumption of rival products that do not employ the new technology. Research grants for firms inevitably end up helping the firms but not the research or technology goals they were intended to promote.

The government thus has a key role to play in steering a new pattern of growth. The main responsibility for allocating resources should, however, lie with the financial sector, to which we shall return later in this chapter.

Investment System

Without strong rates of investment, China could not have grown at such rapid rates over the past three decades. By sacrificing consumption in favor of investment, China made a choice in favor of the future over the present. This difficult choice has brought great benefits; it should be admired and imitated.

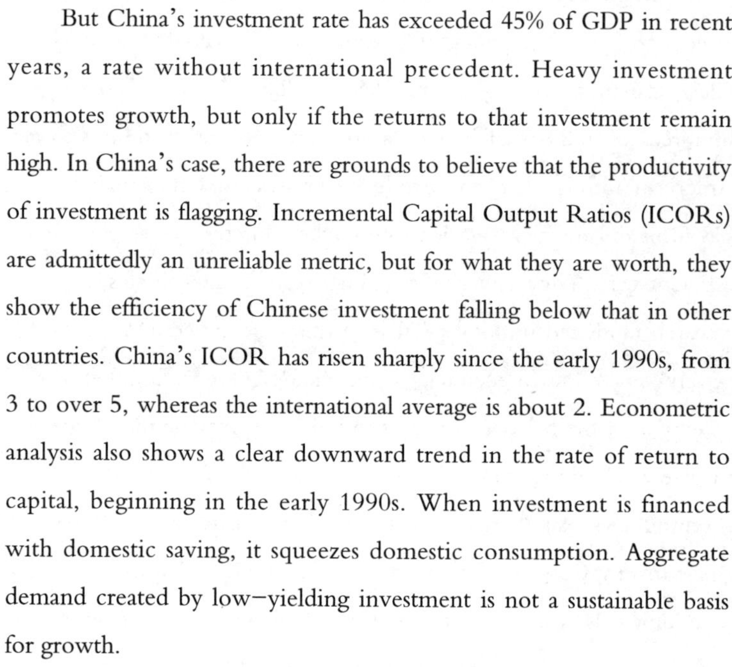

But China's investment rate has exceeded 45% of GDP in recent years, a rate without international precedent. Heavy investment promotes growth, but only if the returns to that investment remain high. In China's case, there are grounds to believe that the productivity of investment is flagging. Incremental Capital Output Ratios (ICORs) are admittedly an unreliable metric, but for what they are worth, they show the efficiency of Chinese investment falling below that in other countries. China's ICOR has risen sharply since the early 1990s, from 3 to over 5, whereas the international average is about 2. Econometric analysis also shows a clear downward trend in the rate of return to capital, beginning in the early 1990s. When investment is financed with domestic saving, it squeezes domestic consumption. Aggregate demand created by low–yielding investment is not a sustainable basis for growth.

Three decades of economic reform have given the forces of supply and demand wide reign in China's labor and product markets. By contrast, market forces play a relatively small role in the allocation of capital[1]. Half of the fixed–asset investment in China is financed from the internal funds of enterprises. Manufacturing investment is also strongly correlated with liquidity, which largely reflects retained earnings. This would matter less if companies were closely policed by their boards or their shareholders. But the heavy reliance on self–financing, combined with weak enterprise governance, contributes to an investment boom that feeds on itself. Managers reinvest earnings to expand their assets and their market share, rather than concentrating on innovation or productivity.

(Foreign investment probably pays greater heed to market forces. It was likely responsible for the higher return to investment in the earlier years of reform. Its share has, however, declined over the last decade and is now less than 5% of total investment.)

The problem arises in part because of a surprising side effect of creative destruction. Firms that are very profitable may, paradoxically, have few good investment opportunities. This is particularly true of firms that are well established in mature or declining industries. Conversely, firms that are rich in opportunity, may be short of cash or capital. This is particularly true of start–up firms in new industries. If the financial system encourages the reinvestment of profits, the first type of firm will make large investments in projects that pay little return. The new startups will not be able to exploit the opportunities that they have uncovered.

---

❶ IMF Working Paper: Barnett and Brooks, "What's Driving Investment in China?" November, 2006. See also OECD Economic Surveys: China 2010, Chapters 3 and 4.

The traditional central planning system sustained very high rates of investment at the expense of consumption. Three decades of reform have erased many aspects of what was known as the "shortage economy" . But the so-called "investment hunger" seems to persist. This hunger combines a disregard for risk (abetted by soft budget constraints) with an appetite for size, which adds to the status of the enterprise, its supervising agency and its manager.

In China this hunger is felt not only by enterprises, but also by local governments and their managers. Such is the enthusiasm of local authorities for investment that they circumvent controls on their borrowing, by doing their infrastructure spending through State-Owned Enterprises (SOEs), funded by bank loans, instead. The sheer scale of investment, coupled with these shortcomings, has contributed to some wasteful spending. There is plentiful anecdotal evidence of "white elephant" projects that duplicate infrastructure or contribute to excess capacity. Thus, despite the efforts of the government and party leadership to increase the share of household consumption in GDP, investment has claimed a large and growing share of national resources over the past decade, even in the face of diminishing returns.

The role of SOEs in the investment system deserves special attention. The weight of SOEs in the economy has diminished, as private and foreign-invested enterprises have grown in importance. Nonetheless they remain a significant force, which may prove to be a significant drag on the economy's effort to transform its development model. (See Chapter 9 for a fuller discussion of the role of the SOEs.)

These shortcomings in capital allocation may assume greater significance as China's development pattern evolves. In the early stages of development, a country's production structure is relatively simple and it can draw plenty of guidance from the many countries above it on the development ladder. Governments thus find it relatively easy to spot opportunities to improve productivity, and to guide resources accordingly. But as China's economy grows in complexity, the government will find it harder to guide resources to their best uses. Deciding to invest in manufacturing instead of agriculture is much easier than deciding to invest in one manufacturing firm instead of another.

As long as investable funds are administered by government officials and high–level managers, they will favor firms and divisions that are large, established and influential, regardless of their productivity. It is not only a question of ownership. International experience shows that even big private firms have succumbed to the same malaise. The US automobile companies, for example, reinvested a large share of their profits in a bid to keep market share, while resisting innovation. The industry would have fared better if GM had paid out more of its profits as dividends and if new entrants had carried out more of the industry's investment, using funds raised from outside. The key is to make sure that managers are not able to reinvest profits solely to build "empires."

The transformation of the development pattern will require a very different system of investment. An independent financial sector should be encouraged to play a bigger role in the allocation of funds between non–SOE firms, and even between SOEs and private firms. Investment should be guided by risk–adjusted returns, and not primarily by which entities have the funds. Government can and should intervene to shift

investment incentives when there are important social objectives that are not captured in the private returns. Beyond that, the goal should be to have the investment process increasingly guided by market evaluation and discipline.

When it works as it should, market–based finance allows financial intermediaries to allocate both fresh household saving and the profits of existing firms to the most promising investment opportunities. Because financial intermediaries seek the highest–possible returns, they search diligently for the firms with the best ideas. If capital is guided by realistic evaluations of potential returns in new ventures, then firms rich in cash, but bereft of good investment opportunities, should no longer be able to invest indiscriminately in lackluster projects. Instead, their funds should be allocated to new firms that can make better use of the money, or to new lines of business with higher returns.

Markets can also flounder, of course, as the global financial crisis amply demonstrates. Although we believe China should let markets, including financial markets, play a bigger role in allocating capital, we also believe those markets should be regulated. Or to put it another way: China should leave more investment to market forces, but it should not leave those markets to themselves. The kind of regulation and supervision required is the subject of the next section.

Financial Sector Development

The financial sector acts as the main control center in a market economy: through asset prices, interest rates and institutional norms, it guides the allocation of resources across competing uses. If the financial system is working well, the whole economy benefits, enjoying higher productivity, growth, and employment. By the same token, if it misfires, or ceases to function at all, it inflicts pervasive damage on the broader economy.

A fully developed financial system has many parts. It deserves a separate study in itself. What follows is a brief summary of the key financial–sector improvements China needs to support its changing growth pattern. We also reflect on the experience of the crisis and the lessons that can be drawn from it.

The financial sector remains a relatively underdeveloped part of China's economy, even in comparison with other middle–income countries in Latin America and South Asia. Most of China's prodigious savings are mobilized and allocated through the banking system. But banks are not the most appropriate source of long–term funds for industrial investment. More must be done to foster equity markets and other channels for allocating equity capital, such as private equity. China also needs an expanded set of fixed–income markets, which would allow companies to leverage equity capital prudently. Despite recent initiatives, credit is still hard to come by for small and medium–sized enterprises and rural businesses. The corporate bond market has expanded, but issuance remains relatively light.

If China's "real" economy is to evolve towards a productivity–driven, knowledge–based growth model, it must allow the financial system to evolve in tandem. The experience of other countries shows that the financial sector helps an economy branch out into a more sophisticated and diversified mix of activities.

China's financial system must keep pace with changes not only

in China, but also in the world. In a recent study, the McKinsey Global Institute argued that the era of cheap capital around the world is coming to an end. Investment rates are rising in the emerging economies, it pointed out, and as these economies grow larger, their capital spending will offset declining investment rates in the advanced economies. That will be enough to raise the cost of capital around the world. Put bluntly, there will be more competition for savings. China, of course, is a net capital exporter, partly insulated from global capital markets by regulatory controls. Nonetheless, as the global cost of capital rises, it will, if nothing else, raise the opportunity cost of investments at home. As a consequence, it will become more important to allocate capital efficiently. The financial sector must therefore be a priority in the 12th Five–Year Plan.

Saving

If China's financial system is to help change its growth pattern, it needs to rapidly develop several key functions. They include providing a rich menu of saving vehicles that offer an appropriate risk–adjusted return, rewarding the thrifty for investing prudently. China's savers would benefit from a wider array of mutual funds, which would give them an alternative to deposits or property. If households could hold better–diversified portfolios of equity and fixed–income instruments, it would help them spread the risks they face.

Increasing the return to savers might have the welcome, if paradoxical, side–effect of reducing excess savings. If they received a higher income on their savings and investments, people would not need to set quite as much aside in order to meet their savings goals, such as providing for retirement or the costs of medical care. A higher return to savers might also have the second side–effect of reducing imprudent investment behavior. Under the present financial regime, many frustrated savers pursue higher returns, for instance, in speculative investment in properties, at the cost of excessive risks.

Corporate Finance

In addition to providing a variety of savings vehicles, the financial system must do a better job of channeling capital to new and growing enterprises of all sizes and in a variety of sectors. In the early stages of development, banks are traditionally the main sources of finance and debt is the principal instrument. That needs to change as the economy moves to higher value–added activity, expands services, and generates more of its own technology.

China is now at the stage where it would benefit greatly from the kind of capital and expertise associated with private equity. Private equity includes venture capital for startups, but also a host of other types of investment that allow businesses to grow, family firms to transfer ownership, and new services to be created. Private–equity institutions require in–depth knowledge of particular industries and sectors to play their assigned role. This expertise inevitably takes time to build. But policy makers should seek to encourage this sector with appropriate regulations and reporting requirements, drawing on the lessons of international experience.

To help this process along, China should encourage the entry of foreign investment firms, just as it has historically welcomed FDI. Of course, China does not need to attract foreign capital for the sake of the money: its domestic savings are more than enough to finance its own investment. But venture capital and private equity typically come packaged with a various kinds of expertise, which can help businesses in a wide range of industries, from agriculture to biomedical technologies and environmental startups. Apple, Sun, Cisco, Google, Intel, Oracle and many other successful companies, including several technology firms in China (like Baidu), were financed by venture capital. It is possible to "reinvent the wheel" so to speak, but it is more efficient to learn selectively from past successes and failures in other settings.

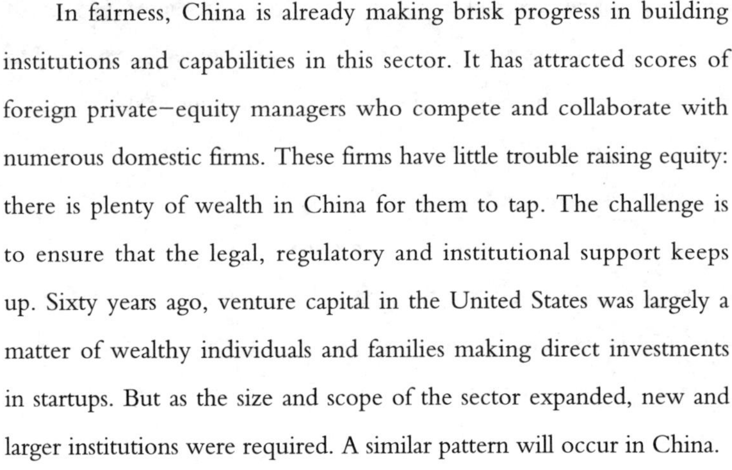

In fairness, China is already making brisk progress in building institutions and capabilities in this sector. It has attracted scores of foreign private–equity managers who compete and collaborate with numerous domestic firms. These firms have little trouble raising equity: there is plenty of wealth in China for them to tap. The challenge is to ensure that the legal, regulatory and institutional support keeps up. Sixty years ago, venture capital in the United States was largely a matter of wealthy individuals and families making direct investments in startups. But as the size and scope of the sector expanded, new and larger institutions were required. A similar pattern will occur in China.

To support China's economic transformation, other financial developments are also needed. China will require bigger, more liquid bond markets, including a market for municipal bonds issued by local governments to finance the rapid growth of cities. Land sales may serve as a transitional device for financing urban infrastructure, but they clearly do not provide long–term financing on a sustainable basis. As in other areas, legal and regulatory institutions are required to support this development.

China's banking regulator has made progress in fostering a "credit culture" among banks and their customers. But the government and other public institutions, particularly at the local level, still exert an influence over lending decisions. In its reforms, China should aim to free bank lending decisions from non–financial considerations. China's banking supervisors would also have an easier task if the country's capital markets were better developed. The market could then complement the supervisors in their job of policing and scrutinizing banks, expressing their suspicions through the sale of a bank's shares, or the purchase of credit–default swaps on their bonds.

These are all formidable tasks. In tackling them, China can undoubtedly benefit from foreign expertise and experience, embodied either in foreign–owned operations, or in joint ventures with Chinese institutions. But ultimately China will have to solve these challenges in its own way.

Lessons of the Crisis

The recent global financial crisis, which originated in the advanced countries (particularly the United States), has exposed fallacies and flaws in their approach to regulation. Before the crisis, many regulators believed that financial institutions could accurately perceive most of the risks they were taking, and that the system therefore had self–regulatory properties. That approach is now being rejected in favor of more intrusive regulation. The new systems being put in place are untested and we will not know for some time how they will perform. Thus some lessons from the crisis will require time to discover.

But other lessons are more immediate. The crisis demonstrated

that unchecked financial sector innovation, coupled with inadequate official regulation, can produce a fragile financial system with excess levels of private sector debt and inflated asset prices, liable to shatter with catastrophic results. Given this experience, China should foster strong risk management and robust capital cushions in its financial institutions. Much has already been achieved in this regard, particularly by the Banking, Insurance and Securities regulatory commissions.

China may also wish to consider the merits of a banking model in which, a portion of the banking system is segregated and heavily regulated. These banks offer a limited range of services, such as deposit and savings accounts, and hold a restricted range of safe assets. These banks concentrate on performing the vital functions of the financial sector, including a payments system and, under some definitions, credit intermediation, i. e. turning deposits into loans. They do not engage in proprietary trading, that is, making speculative bets with their own money.

This approach aims to insulate credit intermediation from any danger of complete collapse. Such a collapse was only narrowly averted in the advanced countries during the crisis, thanks to quick and unconventional intervention, mainly by central banks. It was a dangerous episode. The proposed banking model isolates a subset of the banking system from most of the risks of balance-sheet damage. This creates a bulwark in the financial system, ensuring that at least some channels of credit remain open, even if the rest of the system goes under. In some ways, current practice in China already resembles the proposed banking model. But commercial banks lack a formal system of deposit insurance, a gap the government may need to fill as China develops.

Securitization has been much criticized in the wake of the financial crisis. The turmoil starkly revealed the dangers of complex securitized asset, created with poorly assessed risks and lax regulatory oversight (the shadow banking system in the United States and Europe was very lightly regulated). But China should not draw the conclusion that all securitization is unwise. In fact, properly regulated securitization is a cost–effective alternative to bank credit. It should be encouraged at a measured pace, evolving in parallel with, and not too far ahead of, the regulators' capabilities. For China, this may mean limiting the products on offer to plain–vanilla securitizations.

Derivatives can serve the useful purpose of spreading and reallocating risk. But they are also one reason why financial–sector balance sheets are so tightly interconnected. We think it is fair to say that there is not yet a well worked–out and agreed–on model for derivative regulation. That will come in the future. In the meantime, the best policy for China is to proceed with caution, focusing on simple contracts traded on, and cleared through, regulated exchanges.

A related subject is systemic risk and prudential regulation. The crisis has exposed the limits of conventional prudential regulation, which looked for signs of trouble in individual banks and other intermediaries, institution by institution. Unfortunately, financial dangers can also emerge out of the interaction between institutions that might each seem individually sound. To spot and prevent these "systemic" hazards, many countries are now appointing a "macro–prudential" or "systemic" regulator. China should do the same. It could create a new body specifically for the task. It could designate one of the existing regulators (or the People's Bank) as the systemic regulator. Or it could create a "council" of all the relevant regulatory authorities. Regardless of how responsibility is assigned, strong cooperation will be required among all the various regulatory bodies.

Just as banks and capital markets increasingly span the world, financial regulation should ideally converge across countries. Otherwise financial firms can simply shift their operations to the least regulated countries, a process known as regulatory arbitrage. In practice, however, countries must develop a financial system that reflects their own circumstances. Regulation in the advanced countries, for example, has revolved around capital standards. But many developing countries have yet to build the necessary legal and accounting frameworks to make capital standards fully effective.

Even among the advanced countries, considerable diversity remains in regulatory principles and practices. China's regulators can learn from these differences. In particular, they may want to pay attention to the differences between the Canadian financial sector, which has performed very well in recent years, and the US financial sector, which has performed badly.

If nothing else, the crisis served as a painful reminder of the costs of financial breakdown. China perhaps needed that reminder less than many other countries. Its government has long appreciated the importance of financial stability. Safeguarding that stability begins with sound macroeconomic management—keeping a lid on inflation, excessive debt and asset bubbles, which distort price signals and investment behavior. In addition, stability entails regulating

financial markets and institutions to minimize systemic risk, maximize transparency, and reconcile the incentives of financial institutions with the collective interests of the country.

But although financial stability is a necessary condition for China's development, it is not sufficient. Stability should not, in particular, mean immobility. In an economy seeking to expand rapidly and make the transition from one growth model to another, the financial sector must be allowed to innovate. It must find better ways to intermediate savings and exploit the flurry of investment opportunities that arise. In principle, well–functioning financial markets can help achieve both the optimal level of savings and the best pattern of investment. This function assumes greater importance as the economy grows in complexity, outstripping the ability of the state to allocate resources well.

The global financial crisis has plunged regulators in Western financial centers into doubt and confusion. But the necessary direction of development for China is quite clear. There remains a compelling case for further development and careful liberalization of the financial system as the principal vehicle for mobilizing saving, spreading risk, and allocating capital to a growing variety of enterprises.

Chapter 3 Urban and Regional Development*

China's remarkable economic progress owes much to its success in breaking the gridlock that once impeded the movement of labor, capital and goods across the country. Thanks to this increased mobility, China's recent development has followed a distinctive spatial pattern. Put simply, people and investment have migrated to the cities and the coasts. China still has room to grow in this way. Only 46% of China's population lived in cities in 2008, compared with 55% in a typical country with its per capita income, and 70%–85% in developed countries[1]. Economic theory and international experience also confirm that urbanization, in particular, is critical to economic growth because manufacturing and service production is more efficient when undertaken in urbanized areas and cities are the places where innovations are incubated and sophisticated skills are developed.

---

* This chapter draws mainly on the Background paper No.11 by J. Vernon Henderson: "Urbanization in China: Policy Issues and Options" and the Background paper No.10 by Shenggen Fan, Ravi Kanbur and Xiaobo Zhang: "China's Regional Disparities: Experience and Policy" .

[1] See Background paper No.11 by J. Vernon Henderson: "Urbanization in China: Policy Issues and Options" , page 6.

It is important, therefore, that the government encourage rapid as well as healthy urbanization. Investment in urban infrastructure and services must be a foundation: urban construction is already at an exceptionally high level, but it may need to rise even higher. China must also take steps to promote good governance, including in finance, develop an integrated domestic market as a national "public good" and foster healthy competition among cities. It will also be important to ban bad non–competitive practices such as protectionism and local preferences.

But to do all of this and ensure that urbanization is efficient and is accompanied by even development for the people of China the government needs to address a number of problems with the current process of spatial development. These include:

- The income disparity between urban and rural areas, which is far larger than other countries at a comparable stage of development
- The inefficient size and economic scope of China's cities: China does not have enough mid–sized cities and its urban economies lack specialization
- Land is used inefficiently within cities and it is excessively fragmented on the fringes of urban areas
- The weakness of urban finance and management
- The disparities in income and development between regions

Reducing Urban–Rural Income Disparities

Over the past three decades, household incomes have increased throughout China. But they have risen most dramatically in the cities and along the coast. The gap between urban and rural incomes is now enormous: per capita income was 3.3 times higher in the cities than in the rural areas in 2008 (and the gap is even larger if government subsidies, which disproportionately favor urban residents, are taken into account).This ratio far exceeds that observed in other Asian countries. It has also widened—up from 2.8 times in 1995—at a point in China's overall development when, international evidence and theory suggests, it ought to be narrowing[1]. To reduce this disparity and increase overall productivity, China will need to complete the rural–urban employment transition by further integrating the labor market, so that people can move to wherever they are most productive. It must invest more in its labor force, particularly migrant workers in the cities and the people they leave behind in the villages. It will also have to raise the productivity of agriculture.

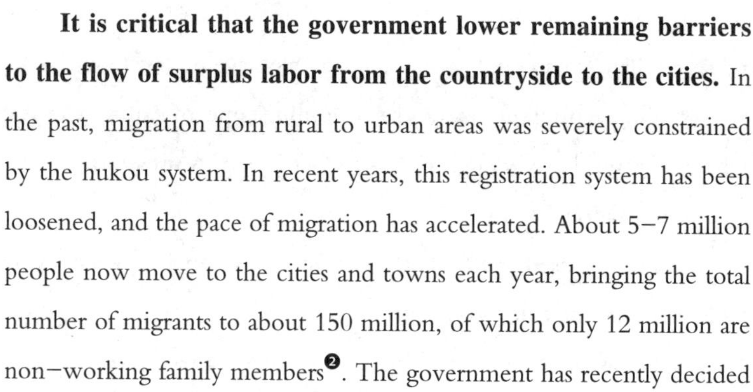

It is critical that the government lower remaining barriers to the flow of surplus labor from the countryside to the cities. In the past, migration from rural to urban areas was severely constrained by the hukou system. In recent years, this registration system has been loosened, and the pace of migration has accelerated. About 5–7 million people now move to the cities and towns each year, bringing the total number of migrants to about 150 million, of which only 12 million are non–working family members[2]. The government has recently decided

---

[1] World Bank "From Poor Areas to Poor People: China's Evolving Poverty Reduction Agenda" , 2009, page 35.

[2] World Bank, 2009 Chapter 5 section e provides further information on estimated levels of rural–urban migration.

to further relax controls on permanent-residence permits in small and medium-sized cities. This is a step in the right direction, which will be of particular benefit to regions with low rates of urbanization and a high proportion of small and medium-sized cities. To encourage more migration, the government should now consider extending the reform to larger cities and certainly to prefecture-level cities. Central and provincial governments as well as city administrations also need to recognize that the migration China is experiencing is almost all permanent, that migrants will want to move with their families, and that the appropriate incentives need to be in place for cities to increase their permanent population and provide them with the necessary services.

More investment in educating and training rural workers, migrants and their children will also have a very high pay-off. Compared with other countries at a similar stage of development, China's labor force is well educated. Most migrants from the countryside have enjoyed a junior secondary school education or more. This is one of China's great strengths, which few other developing countries can match. China needs to maintain and improve upon this good educational record by providing more job training for migrants and allowing their children to attend good schools in urban areas. It also needs to include migrant families in health and social security systems, which should become increasingly national in scope, providing portable benefits to both urban and rural residents.Migrant workers should also benefit from equal treatment under China's Employment Contracts Law and other labor laws.

A challenge for China, as for other countries, is how

to prevent the development of slums and improve the living conditions of of migrants (and other poor households), without indirectly subsidizing migration. Governments have a duty to spare migrants from hardship and squalor. But efforts to improve the lot of migrants can have the perverse effect of attracting more migrants. It is not easy to resolve this dilemma. Hong Kong and Singapore, for example, have both prevented the emergence of slums by providing public housing. But in both places migration was strictly controlled.

In China's case, the government should be cautious about getting directly involved in provision of public housing and rely more on alternative policies[1]. It could, for example, revitalize the urban villages where most migrants currently live by bringing them under city administration, encouraging the renovation of buildings, offering tax breaks to firms that set up in these villages, and improving the quality of public services. But care needs to be taken to avoid damaging existing housing markets in these villages. These markets appear to be working quite well, allowing many migrants to rent the space they want at prices they can afford. Bringing urban villages under city administration should strengthen the property rights of owners and tenants, making them feel more secure. If so, this alone will stimulate the housing market, without the government having to do anything more. The government could also consider measures to support the construction of low-cost rental housing in existing urban areas, for example by leasing land to developers for the building of high-density

[1] This section draws on the Background paper No.20 by Yves Zenou: "Housing Policies in China: Issues and Options".

apartments.

An alternative approach is to target people rather than places. The government could, for example, provide small housing loans ("shelter microfinance") to households with land who wish to improve their structures. It could also encourage migrants to move from urban villages to more expensive parts of the city by providing housing subsidies or vouchers. But such a reform would need to be accompanied by other reforms to encourage a formal sector rental market in urban areas. The government should also target such policies carefully, lest richer migrants capture the bulk of the benefits. It is also very likely that the easing of hukou rules will, on its own, stimulate demand for low–income housing outside the urban villages. Of course, place–targeted policies and people–targeted policies are not mutually exclusive and can be implemented together. The government will also have to be somewhat experimental, discovering along the way what impediments there are to the private sector supplying the evident and growing demand and introducing measures to address those impediments.

Changing the Size and Structure of Cities

China's pattern of urbanization is inefficient, both in the size distribution of its cities and their lack of specialization. Typically, in the early stages of industrialization, the largest cities take the lead, becoming focal points for the introduction, assimilation and refinement of new technologies. As development proceeds, manufacturing technologies become standardized. This allows the decentralization of industrial

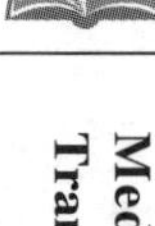

production to small and medium–sized cities with lower labor and land costs. Over time an urban hierarchy emerges. Small and medium–sized cities become highly specialized in industries such as steel, textiles and apparel, wood products, insurance, health care and even entertainment. This specialization allows them to exploit local economies of scale and to capture many of the benefits, such as trained workers or specialized suppliers that can spill over from one firm in an industry to another. Larger cities have more diverse economies, including higher order services, distribution, innovation and sophisticated manufacturing, where economies of scale between industries, as well as within them, are important. The very largest cities in developed countries (e. g. New York, Tokyo, London) have little manufacturing but provide a huge share of the country's financial services and business services.

China's pattern of urbanization does not conform to this international experience. In the initial period of economic reform, migration was highly localized ("leave the land but not the village"). In more recent years, more migration has been inter–provincial, from the central provinces and the southwest to coastal cities. But China still lacks cities in the population range of 1–12 million, and many prefecture–level cities are about half their efficient size(See Figure 3). Indeed, estimates suggest that a doubling of the population in prefecture–level cities would lead to a 20%–35% increase in real output per worker[1]. The capital market (as well as administrative actions by higher levels of government) also appears to have favored

[1] See Background paper No.11 by J. Vernon Henderson: "Urbanization in China: Policy Issues and Options" , page 8.

the very largest provincial-level cities. Such cities enjoy much more foreign investment per capita and fixed-asset investment per capita than other urban areas, even though rates of return have been higher elsewhere[1]. Many cities have also clung to their manufacturing industry instead of nurturing a flourishing services sector, even though they have little comparative advantage in manufacturing and their local firms frequently operate at too small a scale.

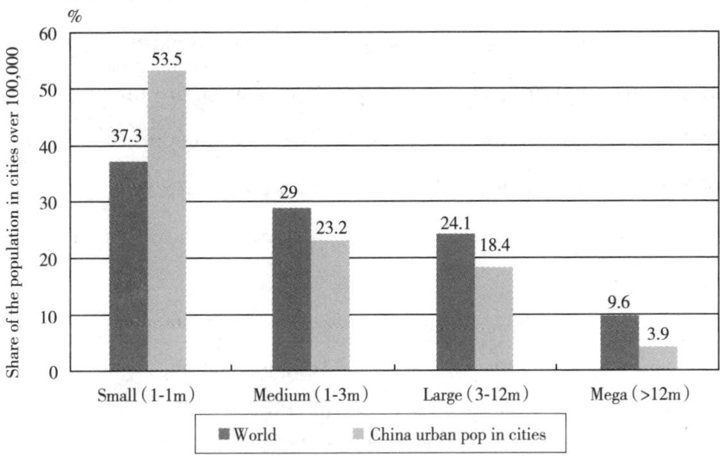

Figure 3 Share in Urban Population of Each City Size Category: World vs. China, 2000

Source: Background paper No.11 by J. Vernon Henderson: "Urbanization in China: Policy Issues and Options".

To resolve such problems, the government needs to create a level playing field, allowing market forces to work as well as possible and avoiding administrative actions that favor a particular size of city or

---

❶ See Background paper No.11 by J. Vernon Henderson: "Urbanization in China: Policy Issues and Options", page 12.

pattern of urban development. Where the government must intervene, it should do so even–handedly, minimizing any distortions to the specialization and efficiency of cities.

Policies that distort the labor, capital and goods markets need to be repealed, allowing economic forces to evolve. China's capital markets and fiscal policies currently favor the biggest cities (See Table1). If this favoritism is not curbed, then any relaxation of the constraints on migration, as recommended above, could result in excessive flows of people to the biggest cities. To avoid the emergence of unduly over–populated mega–cities, China should help those further down the administrative hierarchy attract investment and workers. To do so, it needs to open up the capital market so that all firms, cities and villages can compete freely for finance. Such a reform

Table 1 Where Capital Investment Goes

	Total FDI (US $) Per capita (hukou population): 2002—2007	Total investment in fixed assets (~) per capita: 2002—2007	Share of second sector in GDP 2007
Provincial level cities (4)	3850	122500	42%
Provincial capital (26)	2060	98900	44%
Other prefecture level cities (238)	1570	64000	56%
County–level cities (367)	980	24400	54%

Source: Urban Year Books (China: Data Online). Numbers for prefecture and above level cities are for urban districts.

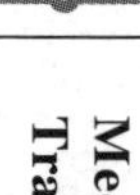

would also boost growth by ensuring that capital goes to the best ventures, not just the politically favored ones. China must also curb local protectionism, whereby cities and other local jurisdictions favor local interests through discriminatory standards, charges and other measures. This protectionism inhibits the specialization across cities, which is so important for productivity growth.

Other constraints to an efficient spatial pattern of urbanization need to be lifted. The natural economic base of the very largest cities is business services and the financial sector. In China, however, these sectors are small, albeit fast growing. Some, such as advertising, were only recently freed from government control, and others, such as legal and financial services, remain under strict state supervision. Once these modern services develop further, China should begin to develop mega–cities, comparable to Tokyo, London or New York.

Although services are the natural economic base of large cities, big cities in China also enjoy an unfair advantage in attracting manufacturing, thanks to their greater power and resources. They continue to exploit this advantage at a time when they might otherwise focus more on promoting services. Moreover, city leaders often display a bias towards manufacturing, rooted in their training and work experience. They may also wish to retain manufacturing because it generates value–added taxes for the city, even though services generate business taxes. If China's cities are to achieve the right size and scope, changes will therefore be required in the administrative hierarchy of urban areas and the attitudes of government officials, as well as in the financing of urban governments.

Promoting Efficient Cities

Because they are tightly packed, cities permit the rapid exchange of labor, goods, services and information. These exchanges contribute greatly to the productivity of urban economies. Historically, the population density of Chinese cities has been much higher than that of cities in the now developed countries. But a number of policies and practices are negatively impacting on the intensity with which Chinese cities are now increasing their built up areas. The fringes of Chinese cities are suffering from increasing fragmentation as urban villages spring up outside the city administration, housing mostly migrant workers without urban hukou. Built–up areas on the perimeter of Chinese cities are also interspersed with enclaves of agricultural land. This land is extremely difficult to develop, because of strict quotas imposed on the conversion of agricultural land to other uses. Industries are being re–located from central urban areas to new industrial estates in peri-urban areas and new towns are being developed at the periphery with little regard for the intensity of land use. Municipal practices of limiting building intensity within cities are also lowering land use efficiency and extending spatial spread. In addition, the lack of coordination between land use and infrastructure development is increasing travel times and costs and contributing to consumption of more land than necessary. Once this type of urban sprawl and fragmentation takes hold, it is difficult if not impossible to reverse, and it will sap urban productivity as well as increase infrastructure costs, travel times and pollution. China therefore needs to address this issue as a matter of urgency. This will

require strengthened property rights and a more competitive land market, as well as better regulation of land usage.

The pricing of land on the fringe of cities is a major problem that needs to be solved urgently. Currently, cities do not pay the true cost of the agricultural land they encroach upon. On the contrary, city governments make huge profits buying land from farmers and villages at low prices and selling it to developers at much higher prices. This arbitrage opportunity gives local governments a strong incentive to requisition rural land aggressively, adding to urban sprawl when China should be striving to reduce it.

At present, local governments are restrained mainly by directives from above, but these directives have only limited effect. A more important constraint would be to strengthen rural property rights so that the compensation paid to farmers and villages reflects the market value of their land as closely as possible. The decision in October 2008 to extend the length of agricultural leaseholds from 30 years to an open-ended term sent a clear signal of the central government's determination to strengthen farmers' land security. But further measures would also be worthwhile. The government should introduce a system for registering rural land at the plot level. It should grant land-rights certificates to farmers, following the example of Vietnam, where the land-rights arrangements are similar to China's. It should ensure that leaseholds are fully transferable and saleable. It should also ensure that any village-land transactions are approved not just by the village head but by all villagers who are effective shareholders in that land.

The efficiency of the urban land market needs to be improved. Developers now acquire urban land through leasehold sales. The method of sale must, therefore be open, transparent and fair, so that developers pay the true cost of their projects, including the cost of necessary infrastructure. Leaseholds could, for example, be sold through English auctions[1] with open entry. Developers of industrial, commercial and residential areas should also be able to bid competitively for land on an equal basis. Over time, such changes should result in more realistic pricing and should curb the over-consumption of industrial land. Higher prices should also spur the decentralization of some industrial activities to smaller cities. The government should also consider fiscal incentives, such as tax breaks, to encourage state enterprises to redevelop land.

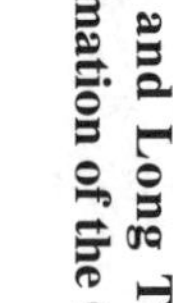

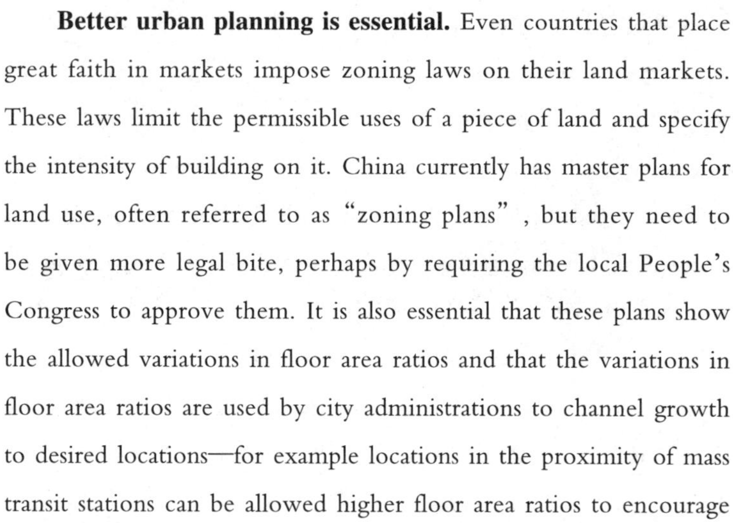

Better urban planning is essential. Even countries that place great faith in markets impose zoning laws on their land markets. These laws limit the permissible uses of a piece of land and specify the intensity of building on it. China currently has master plans for land use, often referred to as "zoning plans" , but they need to be given more legal bite, perhaps by requiring the local People's Congress to approve them. It is also essential that these plans show the allowed variations in floor area ratios and that the variations in floor area ratios are used by city administrations to channel growth to desired locations—for example locations in the proximity of mass transit stations can be allowed higher floor area ratios to encourage

---

[1] English auction is perhaps the most common form of auction in which bidding starts with a low price and is raised incrementally as progressively higher bids are solicited, until either the auction is closed or no higher bids are received. Often the seller sets a reserve price below which the item is not sold and the auction is aborted.

densification. China should also consider a broader regional approach to city development, focusing on the design of the urban perimeter and the eventual integration of "urban villages" into city administration. It could promote this integration in a number of ways. It could allow agricultural enclaves within the urban perimeter to be developed without using conversion quotas. It should also allow for the proper sequencing of transport infrastructure and housing, so that house-building and other development at the periphery are not permitted until trunk infrastructure is in place. Cities must also improve their capacity to prepare and implement such plans, by, among other things, training professionals in city and transport planning.

Finally, cities need new sources of revenue. The above-mentioned measures should all help to promote efficient land use within cities. But unless city governments find an alternative source of revenue beyond leasehold sales, it will be very difficult if not impossible to persuade city administrations to make such changes. Accordingly China also needs further reforms of urban financing and management, which is the focus of the following section.

Reforming Urban Financing and Management

No country has a particularly enviable record of managing rapid urbanization. Compared to other countries, China has not done a bad job to date. However as the pace of urbanization accelerates, China must carry out further reforms of urban management, including restructuring urban finances, redefining the role of government officials, and reforming the administrative hierarchy of urban areas.

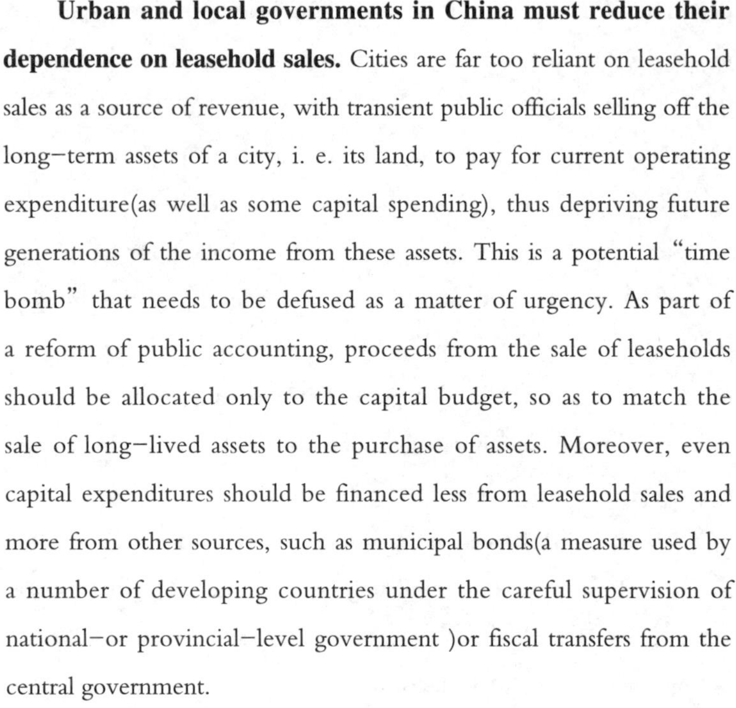

Urban and local governments in China must reduce their dependence on leasehold sales. Cities are far too reliant on leasehold sales as a source of revenue, with transient public officials selling off the long–term assets of a city, i. e. its land, to pay for current operating expenditure(as well as some capital spending), thus depriving future generations of the income from these assets. This is a potential "time bomb" that needs to be defused as a matter of urgency. As part of a reform of public accounting, proceeds from the sale of leaseholds should be allocated only to the capital budget, so as to match the sale of long–lived assets to the purchase of assets. Moreover, even capital expenditures should be financed less from leasehold sales and more from other sources, such as municipal bonds(a measure used by a number of developing countries under the careful supervision of national–or provincial–level government)or fiscal transfers from the central government.

The introduction of an ad valorem property tax on residential and business property would be a big step forward. Currently, municipal revenues in China are generated by the VAT (value added tax)and business taxes, as well as land sales, all of which encourage cities to attract business but not residents. An ad valorem tax on residences would not only help raise revenues but also encourage cities to accept new residents. Likewise, a tax on business property would encourage a welcome change in behavior, prompting firms to economize on land and the use of space. Such a tax would better reflect the cost of providing public services, such as transport, sewerage and electricity connections, to commercial property. In paying the tax, the property owners who benefit from these services would meet more of the cost of providing them.

Property taxes would reduce the value of leaseholds to potential buyers, because of the future tax obligations the real estate would entail.Local governments would, therefore, raise less money from their property sales. But this drop in value would help bring about a welcome shift in the funding of operating budgets—a shift away from asset sales towards an on–going revenue source. The government may also wish to consider making leaseholds permanent as compensation for the introduction of property taxes. Such taxes need not be too difficult to administer. An ad valorem property tax does require registration of ownership as well as a non–corrupt property assessment system, but it need not imply investing in a costly cadastre system. An area property tax, similar to the council tax in the UK, may suffice.

The incentives facing urban government officials need to be reformed. The principal roles of urban government are to provide residents with good public services, and to complement private–sector investment with appropriate public infrastructure. But in the past, the performance of mayors and other local government officials has been judged not by the quality of the public services they deliver, but by the industrial growth they oversee. In the absence of aggressive institutional reform to make mayors more accountable to city residents, the central government needs to be more creative in devising appropriate incentives for local officials. One important measure now being explored is to evaluate local officials on the basis of social indicators, such as citizen report cards, spending on health and education and enrollment rates. Because the impact of physical infrastructure is easily observed right after it is built, while it takes much longer to see the

full impact of social investments, government officials should also be encouraged to stay in their posts for longer terms; and to get incentives further in line, their performance could be judged with respect to indicators of long term financing sustainability.

Finally, it is critical that small cities be allowed to compete on a more equal footing with large cities. Currently, higher–level cities in China "oversee" the governance of lower–order cities and enjoy greater autonomy in decision–making, more fiscal resources, and greater access to transport corridors, rail capacity and so on. This hierarchy needs to be reformed. China should build on some of the on–going pilots and move in the direction of giving each city, regardless of size, a well–defined administrative area over which it has full autonomy and allowing all cities and towns access to the same set of tax bases, revenue instruments, exemptions, and formulae for inter–governmental transfers, as well as the same expenditure responsibilities. It will, of course, take longer for smaller cities to get into a position where they can utilize financing instruments such as municipal bonds so in the interim, inter–governmental financial support formulae that put them on an equal footing with larger cities will be helpful.

Reducing Regional Disparities as Part of the Middle–Income Transition

As it embarks on the middle–income transition discussed in the last chapter, China has few models to follow. Only two large countries, Japan and Korea, have successfully managed it. They are both relatively homogeneous countries, whereas China is a highly diverse economy with regions at very different stages of economic development. Indeed China can be seen as comprising three different economies with vastly different levels of per capita income between them: the rural economy, which is still dominated by agriculture and saddled with significant amounts of underemployed labor; the low–wage export–oriented coastal economy, which has led the growth of the last two decades ;and the emerging productivity–driven, knowledge–based economy that should lead the transition to high income over the coming decades. China's macroeconomic policy mix must balance the disparate needs of these different economies. The right exchange rate or wage policy for the emerging knowledge–based economy may not be right for the export–dominated economy, or for the rural economy.

The persistence of China's poor, rural hinterland suggests the country has not yet exhausted the opportunities for catch–up growth. That is good news for China's macroeconomic prospects. But these disparities are nonetheless a big obstacle to a harmonious society. If economic theory and international experience is any guide, economic forces are unlikely on their own to eliminate such disparities. To address the inequalities that remain, most countries have introduced regional policies of various kinds. These policies offer different answers to the question, "should we move people to the jobs, or move jobs to the people?" This is not simply a technical question; not a matter of simply weighing the costs and benefits of different policy instruments. The answer also depends on what exactly the regional policy hopes to achieve. In the European Union, for example, regional policy focuses on both lagging countries and lagging regions within countries. It recognizes the need to ease migration so that people can move to

new jobs away from home. But it also explicitly acknowledges the imperative to preserve regions as viable entities, which requires moving jobs to the people.

In China's case a fundamental part of any strategy for reducing regional disparities and supporting its transition from a middle to a high income country must be raising agricultural productivity and rural incomes. Because our team of international economists did not have much expertise in agriculture, the sector has not been addressed in detail in this report. But the sector remains of fundamental importance to China's future development. Migrant workers are typically more productive in their urban jobs than they were in agriculture. Therefore, as more labor flows from rural to urban areas, the economy's overall productivity increases (even though urban productivity may fall). In fact, it has been shown that reallocating even 1% of the agricultural labor force to non-agricultural activities could increase national GDP by 0.9%[1].

As workers leave overmanned farms, agricultural productivity should rise. Their departure provides an opportunity to transform traditional peasant farming on small plots into modern farming on much larger tracts of land by highly skilled, educated people.Korea provides a good example of such a transformation. Over three decades, landholdings were consolidated, farmers and rural youth educated, farms mechanized and new technologies introduced. By 2005 the

❶ Au and Henderson "How Migration Restrictions Limit Agglomeration and Productivity in China" , Journal of Development Economics, 2006a.

country's farm population was just 26% of its 1975 level and it was using 16% less agricultural land, even as grain output was up by 61%[1]. To replicate this success, China will need to strengthen rural property rights, reform the financial sector to allow more agricultural investment (some recent studies have shown that reallocating 1% of capital from urban to rural areas in China could increase national GDP by 0.5%[2]) and improve education, because more educated farmers are better equipped to adopt new technologies, understand market conditions, and choose their crops and inputs accordingly.

Before considering any additional and specific policies to help lagging regions, it is also critical that the government first remove policies that hinder lagging regions. Policies on provision of essential services—such as basic education, health care, water and sanitation—should be spatially blind in their design and national in their coverage.

Distortions in the markets for land, labor, capital and goods should also be corrected. This would represent a major change from past government policies that gave preferential treatment to the coastal region. Such reforms can shoulder much of the task of economic integration by encouraging people to migrate to places that are rich in opportunity, as well as encouraging firms to set up shop in the most cost–effective locations. Moreover, such reforms involve no additional fiscal costs. The inter–provincial movement of people can

---

❶ See Background paper No.11 by J.Vernon Henderson: "Urbanization in China: Policy Issues and Options" , page 4.

❷ Au and Henderson "How Migration Restrictions Limit Agglomeration and Productivity in China" .

be an especially important source of dynamism for China. It will allow the richer provinces to offset the natural increase in their dependency ratio by bringing in younger migrants at peak working age. And it will provide employment opportunities for rural migrants from poor provinces who can remit money back home thanks to the higher incomes they earn in rich provinces.

Infrastructure is critical to overcoming distance. Like many other countries, China has pursued a strategy of building up infrastructure in lagging regions. This strategy has had some success. One specific example is China's western development strategy, with its particular focus on roads and railways. This policy appears to be one reason why overall regional inequality has leveled off, and even declined slightly, since the mid–2000s. Other investments have also had a substantial impact, such as outlays on rural telecommunications and electricity in lagging regions. Investment in education probably has an even bigger payoff, contributing both to growth and poverty reduction. It certainly appears, therefore, that China should maintain its emphasis on infrastructure(as well as social sector)investment in poorer regions. However, it would be useful to look more closely at what specific types of infrastructure have the highest returns in which specific regions. Moreover, in very remote regions, the marginal returns to infrastructure may fall quickly as costs increase. It may be more economical to move people out of remote, and often fragile, land into areas with more jobs.

Lagging regions can do more to attract investment. The spatial pattern of industrial activity is not easy to explain or predict. The geographical forces that push and pull industry interact in subtle and unforeseeable ways. As wages rise in China's coastal regions, it is possible that factories may relocate to China's interior provinces where wages are still relatively low, instead of migrating to cheaper locations overseas. However this possibility cannot be taken for granted. The government's recent efforts to encourage industries to relocate have not been successful even within Guangdong Province for example. The kind calculations businesses make in choosing where to locate were illuminated by a paper from the research department of Li & Fung, one of the world's largest trading companies. [1]Surveys found that firms are likely to relocate within China only if their intermediate inputs are readily available elsewhere in China and their overseas sales are a relatively small share of their business. Firms that import most of their inputs and export most of their products will mainly relocate to other low–cost countries, while export firms that depend on local industrial clusters are unlikely to relocate either in China or abroad.

Because of this complexity, China should be cautious about introducing specific policies to attract industry to lagging regions. It should instead let the market guide the location of economic activity, recognizing that the spread of industry to lagging regions is likely to be a gradual, protracted process.

There is, however, nothing to stop lagging regions trying to become more attractive to investors. They should begin with a thorough assessment of their investment climate, identifying any

❶ See Background paper No.14 by Li and Fung Research Center: "Notes on Decentralization of Industrial Production in China and Prospects for Manufacturing for the Domestic Market."

shortcomings, such as a shortage of reliable information, burdensome land and tax policies, or infrastructure constraints. They should then highlight the steps required to overcome these limitations.

Lagging regions should also consider targeted interventions to help people in remote rural villages and townships. Children in remote areas often live far away from any secondary schools, for example. Many therefore need to stay at a boarding school. But the cost of boarding is a heavy financial burden for many poor families and a common reason why students drop out. To ease this burden, governments should consider a conditional cash transfer program or a school feeding program in poorer regions. This could simultaneously reduce the cost of schooling, improve child nutrition and promote education. To provide further encouragement to rural students in poorer regions, the government could consider waiving tuition fees and providing more scholarships. To redress the lack of dedicated teachers in such localities, the government could also consider a program to employ college graduates as teachers in underserved regions. There are excellent examples of such programs in countries such as Mexico, Bangladesh and the United States.

Chapter 4 Strengthening Domestic Consumption and the Middle Class*

Policies to Strengthen Domestic Consumption

As an economy reaches middle–income status, domestic demand typically becomes a more important engine of growth. This is particularly true for a country as large as China. Its size puts a natural limit on the expansion of its exports. The world market, diminished by the financial crisis and marked by increasing protectionism, will struggle to digest the kind of growth in Chinese exports over the next decade that it absorbed over the last two.

Domestic demand is not a perfect substitute for global demand. In serving world markets, a country can specialize in a narrow range of products, reaping economies of scale. But if a country must cater

* This chapter draws mainly on Background paper No.12 by Homi Kharas: "China's Transition to a High Income Economy: Escaping the Middle Income Trap" which contains details of the methodology and calculations in estimating the size of the middle class and on Background paper No.7 by Andrew Crockett : "China's Role in the World Economy: Looking Forward to the 12th Five–Year Plan."

more to domestic demand, it will need to produce a broader range of products, so as not to saturate any particular local market niche. It must also devote more of its resources to services and non-tradable items that are missing from a country's export basket, but which figure prominently in domestic demand.

To transform its development pattern, China must reform the demand side of its economy. This represents something of a departure from its longstanding focus on the supply side, where it has performed exceptionally well. Over the past 30 years, it has mobilized its labor force, by permitting migration from the pool of unemployed and underemployed workers in the countryside. It has added rapidly to its capital stock, thanks to high investment rates, fuelled by easy access to credit and low, controlled prices for land, electricity, water and other utilities. Technical efficiency(or total factor productivity)has expanded by 3–4 percent per year.

Where China has done less well is in expanding demand. This has not been deliberate. Even before the global crisis, China's 11th Five-Year Plan called for a better balance between growth led by exports and growth led by domestic demand, especially consumption. But the economy has turned out quite differently. In the 1990's personal consumption was about 45% of GDP, already very low by international standards. Over the past decade, the share has fallen even further, reaching 36% immediately before the global financial crisis. This is far below the global average (61%)and the share in economies such as Vietnam (66%), Indonesia(63%), India(54%)and Thailand(51%). It is also much lower than China's historical share. Since 2000, consumption growth has averaged 2.5 percentage points

less than GDP growth. Unlike successful market economies, China has not yet succeeded in developing large numbers of consumer–oriented households that can drive the economy forward.

The main reason for the falling share of personal consumption is the declining share of labor income. The share of wages in national income has fallen from two–thirds in 1980 to just over one half of GDP today. This fall in the wage share is all the more remarkable considering the rapid growth of human capital over the period and the reallocation of labor from low productivity rural occupations to higher productivity occupations in manufacturing and services. Both of these trends would normally raise the share of labor in national income, but neither has been strong enough to offset the rapid growth in profits resulting from strong productivity gains and high investment levels.

For some time, the government has aimed to raise the labor share in GDP, as part of its objective of rebalancing the economy. There are a number of policy instruments to do this. One option is to intervene directly in wage setting. The government could set the minimum wage at a reasonable level and see that it is enforced. In the medium term, it could ensure that existing regulations, such as the labor contract law, are applied to all workers, including migrant workers. Other than this, forceful intervention to increase wages should be avoided, however.It is likely to distort the choice of technology by industries, encouraging more capital–intensive techniques, and reduce employment. That would have the opposite of the intended effect on labor's share of national income.(See also Chapter 5 on Employment, Education and the Labor Market.)

In Singapore, for example, the government tried to force a

transition to the knowledge economy by artificially raising real wages(by about 25%)in 1979—1981. Over time, skills and productivity did increase. But the wage hike also had unintended and undesirable effects, contributing to a surprisingly steep fall in manufacturing employment throughout the period from 1981 to 1986. In 1985, the Singapore economy slumped. In 1986, to revive labor demand, the government reversed course, taking draconian action to cut wage costs by freezing nominal wages and reducing the contribution to the Provident Fund from 25% of wages to 10%.

A more promising approach is to make growth more labor-intensive by reducing policy biases against employment. Some analysts argue that China's private-sector firms have limited access to finance and so tend to limit employment[1]. This is corroborated by survey evidence.The World Bank's *Doing Business* survey ranked China 61st in the world in terms of ease of access to credit. The data suggest that less than half of small and medium enterprises have a bank loan. Econometric results indicate that firms facing greater difficulties in accessing credit create fewer jobs. With better lending policies, it should be possible to improve access to credit for smaller firms without sacrificing loan quality and risking default.

Policymakers could also help new private ventures by opening up China's service sectors. In advanced economies, it is new firms that tend to create most jobs. If these firms are in the services sector,

---

[1] International Monetary Fund, July, 2007, Jahangir Aziz and Li Cui, "Explaining China's Low Consumption: The Neglected Role of Household income."

the effect is amplified. Services, by their very nature, tend to be much more labor intensive than manufacturing.

Another impediment to labor–intensive growth is the continued expansion of a state sector that tends to be much more capital intensive than the private sector. Since the late 1990s, capital per worker in the SOEs has increased enormously and is now almost four times greater than in the private sector[1]. To some extent, this may be because SOEs are concentrated in sectors that are intrinsically capital intensive. But it may also reflect a lingering lending bias in favor of SOEs by the predominantly state–owned banking sector. (See Chapter 9 for a fuller discussion of the role of SOEs.) Reforming the SOEs, by subjecting them to stiffer competition or tougher lending standards for example, would probably reduce the capital bias in China's growth, leading to higher employment and a greater income share for labor. And if SOEs were to pay more of their profits to the treasury, it would allow the government to reduce taxes on households and private businesses without reducing the overall level of public revenues.

One priority is to cut the many fees and taxes imposed on labor. The average take–home pay of a Chinese worker is only 65% of total compensation, with the remainder lost to government–mandated labor taxes, and a variety of insurance provisions (health, occupational safety, unemployment and the like). A second priority is to cut business taxes. Some estimates suggest that over half of private–enterprise profits are

[1] See OECD "Economic Survey China 2010" p.110. The report contains a detailed analysis of the performance of the SOEs relative to the private sector.

payable in the form of value–added taxes, a big impediment to growth.

Households should also earn more personal income from their savings and investments. Low administered interest rates on bank deposits have traditionally depressed returns to savers, hurting household incomes. Scope may well exist to raise deposit rates and lower lending rates, squeezing banks' interest margins to the benefit of household depositors and borrowers.

The share of personal consumption in GDP would also rise if the saving rate fell. Personal saving averaged about 30% of disposable income during the1990s, a relatively high rate by international standards. It has risen even higher over the last decade. One possible explanation is the lack of a social safety net. Some statistical evidence suggests that government transfers to social programs have lowered the saving rate in a number of developing countries. A recent IMF study concludes that personal consumption in China goes up when government expenditure on health increases[1].

The saving rate might also fall if consumer credit were easier to obtain. Credit is sometimes necessary to smooth consumption over the life–cycle, and a more sophisticated financial system would provide plenty of ways to borrow. China should not liberalize consumer credit indiscriminately, of course, lest it repeat Korea's unhappy experience with the spread of credit cards over the last decade. But the careful relaxation of credit constraints would help to limit unnecessarily high

---

❶ International Monetary Fund, January, 2010: Steve Barnett and Ray Brooks, "China: Does Government Health and Education Spending Boost Consumption?"

household saving.

Households also tend to save more, paradoxically, when the return to saving is low. This is because they need to set aside more money to reach their desired level of retirement income. The saving rate might therefore fall if the financial system offered a greater variety of saving instruments with better returns. This would also give households an alternative to property as a vehicle for investment.

A consumer's spending will also reflect his wealth. For many rural households, the most important asset is their right to use their land. But their rights are generally insecure. Strengthening those rights would increase the farmers' propensity to consume. Over the medium term, one direct way to raise consumption in China is to increase government consumption. From 2003 to 2007, the gross domestic saving of the government averaged 7.4% of GDP, rising to more than 10% on the eve of the financial crisis. China's public finances are remarkably strong and could readily accommodate a permanently higher level of government spending on education, health and other sorely needed social programs. This higher level of social spending is essential to the building of a harmonious society in China and is the subject of discussion in the following three chapters.

Thus, it is clear there is a wide range of policy instruments available to the government to raise the share of household income in the national economy. Such a rise should also occur naturally as the economy grows and evolves. Over the long run, employment will eventually shift more to services, which account for about 70% of total employment in high-income countries, compared with 33% in China today. Since services are even more labor-intensive than agriculture,

the growth of services will naturally increase workers' slice of the national cake. With the transition to a knowledge–based economy, the returns to skilled labor should also increase, possibly resulting in an increase in aggregate labor income.

In addition the government has the further option of transferring some of the wealth it has accumulated over the past few decades to households in order to stimulate personal consumption. The sale of public housing, at low prices, to tenants in the 1990s was very successful in transferring wealth from the state to the public. The government could consider a similar distribution of part of its vast SOE shareholdings to boost domestic demand in the medium term. Some years ago the government proposed to transfer some of its SOE shares to the social security fund in order to finance the legacy obligations of the mandatory pension system and reduce the contribution rate of current workers(See Chapter 6: "Strengthening the Pension System"). Unfortunately that welcome measure has yet to be implemented.

The Middle Class

The sale of public housing in the late 1990s turned China into a home–owning society almost at a stroke. Homeownership is often cited as one of the defining attributes of the middle class, a social category that is hard to define yet impossible to ignore. A prosperous middle class is a necessary condition for strengthening consumer demand, sustaining growth and escaping the middle–income trap. If China is to rebalance its growth towards domestic consumption, therefore, it needs to foster a large middle class. But although the Chinese consumer market can claim to be the "largest" in many dimensions—it is the largest market for cell phones, automobiles, and housing, for example—the middle class in China today is probably still too small to serve as an engine of rapid growth. The question, then, is when will China's middle class become large enough to power its economy, and what policies can speed up this process.

The term "middle class" is an ambiguous social classification, broadly reflecting the ability to lead a comfortable life. The middle class usually enjoy stable housing, healthcare, educational opportunities(including college)for their children, reasonable retirement and job security, and discretionary income that can be spent on vacations and leisure pursuits. The middle class come from a range of occupations: they can be government officials, rich farmers, traders, business people and professionals. They can be found in various management and clerical jobs. Many are self-employed in small businesses, crafts and commercialized family farms.

From an economic perspective, the middle class can be defined as those households that enjoy a certain amount of discretionary income. After paying for the necessities of life, they have some money left over which they are free to spend on consumer durables, quality education and health care, housing, vacations and other leisure pursuits. Unlike the poor, this group have choices over what they consume. Unlike the rich, their choices are constrained by their budget; they are price and quality sensitive.

Defining and measuring China's middle class is a favorite pursuit of consulting companies, banks and business houses. Although they

use different definitions of the middle class, they all agree that it will grow significantly in the coming years. Merrill Lynch believes China's middle class will number 350 million by 2016; McKinsey, adopting a different definition, projects a middle class of 520–600 million by 2025. A 2005 study by China's National Bureau of Statistics defined the urban middle class as three–person households with annual incomes in the range of 60, 000 to 500, 000 yuan, or about US \$16 to US \$132 per person per day in 2005 dollars, adjusted for purchasing power. By this measure, the study suggested, 45% of China's urban population will be middle class by 2020[1].

A background study for this book adopts a definition of the middle class that can be applied globally, so as to permit a comparison between China's emerging middle class and the large middle class currently concentrated in the United States, Europe and Japan[2].In these countries, the middle class was able to drive income levels to new highs. It could do the same in China.

The study somewhat arbitrarily defines the global middle class as those households with daily expenditures between \$10 and \$100 per person in purchasing–power parity terms (PPP). The lower bound is comparable to the average poverty line in Portugal and Italy, the two advanced European countries with the strictest definition of poverty. In these countries, the poverty line for a family of four is \$14, 533, or

---

❶ Referenced in Cheng Li(ed.)*China's Emerging Middle Class*, Brookings Institution Press, 2010.

❷ See Background paper No.12 by Homi Kharas: "China's Transition to a High Income Economy: Escaping the Middle Income Trap" .

$ 9.95 per day per capita(in constant 2005 international dollars, adjusted for PPP). The upper bound represents twice the median income of Luxembourg, the richest advanced country. Defined in this way, the global middle class excludes those who are considered poor in the poorest advanced countries and those who are considered rich in the richest advanced country.

The Significance of the Middle Class

Global middle–class households, defined in this way, share some common characteristics. They tend to have high rates of ownership of consumer durables(housing, cars, cell phones, electronics). They tend to have high income elasticities of demand. They therefore constitute a "consumer class" . They are not necessarily a class in the traditional sense of being organized to further their own goals (and therefore some analysts prefer to think of several middle classes) but they do constitute a significant market. It is the global middle class that has powered the world economy and it is the financial weakness of the middle class in North America and Europe that may prevent the global economy reverting to the healthy rates of growth of the past twenty years.

In the wake of the crisis, the global growth model based on Asian production, Western consumption and resource extraction from the rest of the world is no longer sustainable. That gives the middle class in China and the rest of Asia added significance. Global rebalancing requires that Asia consume more, but many of the policies prescribed to achieve this are institutional and long–term in nature: creation of a social safety net, medical insurance schemes, and improved public education. A better hope for increasing consumption in the medium term is for a middle class to lead the way, with its purchasing power leveraged by credit cards, mortgages and other forms of hire purchase. Thus, sustained global growth depends on the emergence of an Asian middle class.

The Middle Class and Sustaining Economic Growth: International Experience

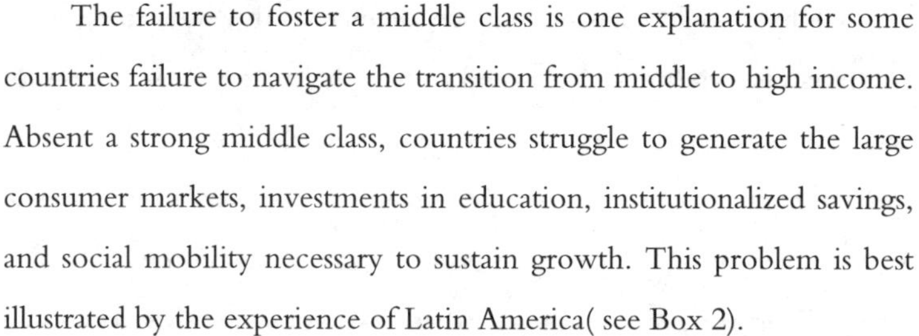
The failure to foster a middle class is one explanation for some countries failure to navigate the transition from middle to high income. Absent a strong middle class, countries struggle to generate the large consumer markets, investments in education, institutionalized savings, and social mobility necessary to sustain growth. This problem is best illustrated by the experience of Latin America(see Box 2).

Box 2

The Middle Class in Latin America

Decades of rapid growth in Latin America did create an embryonic middle class, which might have stabilized the region's tumultuous politics. But chronic poverty and glaring inequality persisted, undermining social strength. Despite fast growth of employment, social mobility was limited. Growth was accompanied by urbanization. But the large urban centers were surrounded by secondary agglomerations, which did not enjoy the modernity of cities or the same improvement in living standards. While the middle class developed in the core urban areas, those who lived on the fast-growing periphery remained permanently marginalized. They were poorly served by the school system, which failed to equip young people with the skills required to work in the modern economy. The lack of appropriate training placed a ceiling on the growth of the middle class. This experience shows that human-capital accumulation is the passport to social mobility and a stronger middle class.

Brazil, the largest country in the region, may have broken this pattern in recent years. After many frustrated attempts to strengthen its middle segments, it managed to powerfully develop its middle class after the 2003 recovery. According to Foundation Getulio Vargas, today the middle class represents about 52% of the population against 36.5% in 2003. This has, of course, fortified the internal market and created a strong constituency in favor of political stability and the continuation of the growth strategy developed by Presidents Cardoso and Lula. There is hope today that Brazil may be really taking off on a more sustained basis. In the current financial turmoil, Brazil's middle class suffered much less than in previous crises. The biggest blow was felt not by the middle class, who work in industry and exports, but by the high-earners concentrated in the financial and service sectors. The resilience of this emerging middle class raises the hope that Brazil may finally be "coming of age".

Source: Contribution by Dr. Mario Blejer, former Governor of the Central Bank of Argentina and Senior Advisor to the International Monetary Fund.

The Brazilian experience stands in sharp contrast to that of the Republic of Korea. Korea reached an income level of $ 4, 600(the level at which Brazil stalled in 1979)in 1986. Since then, it has continued to grow rapidly, reaching an income level of over $18, 000 in 2010, despite the shocks of the 1997/98 Asian crisis, the 2001 dot. com crash, and the recent Great Recession. Of course, Korea changed its growth strategy significantly, making the transition to a knowledge economy. But it was able to do so successfully in part because of the country's sizeable middle class. In 1986, with the same per capita income as Brazil in 1979, Korea's middle class was 55% of its population, over twice the proportion in Brazil.

Large middle classes could also be found in other fast growing economies. Japan's middle class in 1965, when its income level was $ 4, 900, was also 55%. The rapidly growing middle–income economies today, like Poland, Russia, Thailand and Malaysia, have large middle–class populations (See Table 2). Only Indonesia has as small a middle class as China (and Indonesia is significantly poorer). Conversely, slow growing middle–income economies, like Egypt, Syria, Bolivia, and the Philippines, tend to have a small middle class. The one exception is Mexico.

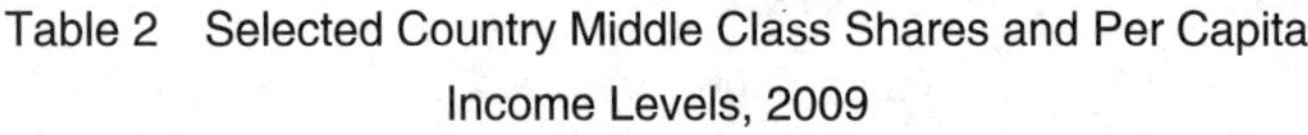

Table 2 Selected Country Middle Class Shares and Per Capita Income Levels, 2009

	Percent Middle Class	Per Capita GDP (PPP 2005 dollars)	Long–term growth
Bolivia	16	4123	slow
Brazil	37	9283	slow
China	12	5991	fast
Egypt	18	5849	slow

Continuation table

	Percent Middle Class	Per Capita GDP (PPP 2005 dollars)	Long–term growth
Indonesia	12	3635	fast
Malaysia	47	12418	fast
Mexico	65	12577	slow
Morocco	10	4161	slow
Philippines	13	3383	slow
Poland	85	16230	fast
Russia	69	13846	fast
South Africa	36	9247	slow
Syria	16	4518	slow
Thailand	32	7544	fast
Turkey	45	7694	slow
Ukraine	37	6357	fast

Source: Background paper No.12 by Homi Kharas: "China's Transition to a High Income Economy: Escaping the Middle Income Trap."

Even in advanced economies, some scholars feel, the stagnation of the middle class and the growing concentration of income might have contributed to the recent financial crisis. Formal economic models suggest that if the highest earners capture an increasing share of the national income, less fortunate households may seek to shore up their consumption by borrowing. This results in a growing debt burden for the middle and lower classes. If this continues for long enough, households eventually accumulate intolerable levels of debt, leading to widespread default and financial bankruptcies in the event of an adverse shock[1].

[1] "Inequality, Leverage and Crises" , M. Kumhof and R. Ranciere, mimeo, November 2010.

Estimating the Size of China's Middle Class

From some perspectives, China already has a substantial middle class. Home ownership in urban areas reached 82% by 2007 thanks to the privatization of housing started in 1998. College enrollment has increased to 26 million students in 2009. Some 26 million automobiles were registered in 2009, with sales of 13.6 million units in that year alone. About 150 million credit cards were in circulation by the end of 2008. There are an estimated 700 million cell phone subscribers. In fact, in a 2007 survey of 6, 000 shoppers, more than 40% said shopping was a favorite activity. Based on these statistics, it would appear that the Chinese middle class is already substantial in size.

By our estimates, China may have had 170 million people living in middle-class households in 2010, or about one-eighth of the population[1]. That can be compared to 230 million people in middle-class households in the USA, or three-quarters of the population.

---

[1] For the detailed methodology behind this calculation, see the Background paper No.12 by Homi Kharas: "China's Transition to a High Income Economy: Escaping the Middle Income Trap" . The calculation of the size of the middle class depends on many assumptions. Dr. Kharas' estimate of 12% for the share of the middle class in China's population is on the low side. Other estimates are as high as 20%. There seems no question however that because of the low share of household income in GDP and the highly unequal distribution of income among the population, the share of the middle class in China today is much lower than Korea and even Brazil at the same level of development, i. e. when these countries had achieved middle income status and were attempting to transition into higher income level.

What is more, the average US middle class household is richer and spends more than the average Chinese middle–class household. The same is true in countries like Korea, Japan, and the European Union countries. There, the middle class is over 90% of the population.

Looking into the future, China's middle class has the potential to expand exponentially. Several decades of fast economic growth have brought many Chinese out of dire, absolute poverty and up to the threshold of the middle class. Today 26% of the population lives on between $ 5 and $10 a day, and a further 41% lives on between $ 2 and $ 5 a day. A significant share of the population is therefore poised to become China's new middle class as growth continues in the decades ahead.

As incomes rise, the number of people crossing the middle–class threshold will rise rapidly. Assuming average income growth of 7% between now and 2030, the proportion of China's population with expenditures surpassing $10 per day would increase to 74%(See Figure 4), a share that is comparable with that in the United States

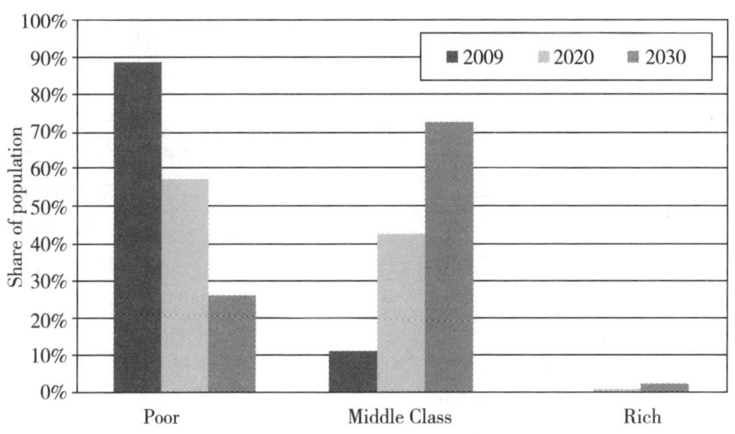

Figure 4 China's Expanding Middle Class

today. Within one generation the majority of Chinese could go from being poor to being middle class. The actual growth of China's middle class over the coming decades will depend on the success of the government's policy to increase the share of personal income in GDP and strengthen domestic consumption—as discussed in the earlier sections of this chapter—and its social policies and programs reviewed in the next three chapters.

Chapter 5 Employment, Education and the Labor Market*

The level, composition and quality of employment will be key ingredients of China's "harmonious society" . China's leaders often speak about the importance of employment. During the 2008—2009 global recession they expressed great concern about the employment of college graduates and of the millions of laid-off migrant workers in export industries. Employment issues were addressed in the 11th Five-Year Plan. China has also created a framework of employment law(from the Labor Law of 1994 to the Employment Contract Law of 2008)and a system to mediate labor disputes, as well as legislation to promote employment in various ways. These policies have drawn on international experience, adapted to China's circumstances, but there is still much to be learned from other countries which have tried to resolve employment problems that China faces or is likely to face.

Employment matters largely because it affects personal and family income: its level, its distribution among individuals and groups, and

* This chapter draws mainly on Background paper No.6 by Cai Fang, Richard Freeman and Adrian Wood: "China's Employment Policies in International Perspective" and Background paper No.17 by Paul Romer: "Notes on Optimizing China's New Pattern of Growth" .

its stability. Wage and salary employment is particularly valued for the stability and predictability of the income it provides. Losing a job not only causes a fall in income but also has a huge negative effect on happiness or mental well-being—comparable to divorce, or to the death of a family member. In a market economy, however, almost everyone who needs to earn a living can find some way to do so: so what matters is not just having a job, but the level of earnings and conditions of work.

Employment is a more prominent policy objective in developed countries than in developing countries, and in middle-income than in low-income countries, because richer countries have fewer self-employed farmers and more people in jobs subject to labor regulations. For this reason, employment is likely to become an increasingly prominent policy issue in China as it continues to advance economically. Now largely the concern of the Ministry of Human Resources and Social Security, employment issues should move up the agendas of the Ministry of Finance, the People's Bank of China(PBOC) and the National Development and Reform Commission(NDRC).

One employment policy issue in all countries is the total number of wage jobs—both fluctuations related to unemployment and longer-term trends. This issue, however, is blurred in developing countries(and increasingly in developed ones)by the large share of jobs in the informal sector, whose number cannot be accurately measured and whose quality is often inferior to that in the formal sector.

A second employment policy issue is the quality of the wage jobs—which depends crucially on the quality of education and on skills development at all levels of the education system. In this regard, economic theory and experience from other countries provides many messages that are relevant for China.

Employment policies also invariably extend to more specific issues, including wages and conditions of work, motivated by two objectives. One is to increase economic efficiency by allowing the country's supply of labor and skills to move freely into industries, occupations and localities where its contribution to production is greater and out of those where its contribution is lower. The other is to reduce unfairness at work by ensuring that workers of similar skill in jobs of comparable attractiveness receive similar wages, that women and minorities are not discriminated against, and that people are not exposed unwittingly to health hazards. In some cases, efficiency and fairness considerations pull the same way, but in others they conflict, which requires governments to strike difficult balances.

Employment Growth, Sectoral Structure and Adjustment

Growth and Employment

In developing countries, faster growth is linked to faster shrinkage of the share of agriculture, where self–employment predominates. Shifts of labor from agriculture to non–agriculture thus raise the number of wage and salary jobs in the economy. They also tend to raise the quality of employment, partly because wages outside agriculture exceed those in agriculture and partly because wage and salary jobs in non–agriculture generally involve less arduous work and

yield more stable incomes than agricultural self–employment.

Consistent with this developing country experience, China's rapid growth since 1980, coupled with labor market reforms that have allowed workers to leave agriculture more easily, has made employment outcomes better than they would have been if growth had been slower and other features of the economy remained the same. Official statistics suggest that in 1978, the agricultural share of employment was almost the same in China as in India(71%), but by 2004 had dropped by 24 percentage points in China and by only 14 percentage points in India.

Looking forward, however, it would be a mistake to let concerns about employment determine policy choices between faster or slower growth. Employment in agriculture is already much reduced. Many agricultural workers are also relatively old. Thus the scope for further transfer of labor out of agriculture into wage jobs is becoming more limited. Moreover, in less than 10 years China's total labor force will cease to grow.

In this context, China will start to look much more like a developed country in which short–term fluctuations in output cause fluctuations in employment(usually proportionally smaller, because labor productivity varies pro–cyclically), but there is little connection between the trend rate of aggregate output growth and aggregate employment. In this context, the future challenge for China is to raise the quality, not the total number, of non–agricultural jobs, and to reallocate workers in non–agricultural sectors from lower to higher productivity activities.

It should also be noted that while the structural transition from agricultural to non–agricultural employment has proceeded rapidly and relatively smoothly in China, the related transition from rural to urban employment has been slower and more difficult, as emphasized in Chapter3. Completing the rural–urban employment transition in a satisfactory way over the next couple of decades is among the biggest challenges that China faces in building a harmonious society.

Economic Re–balancing and Employment

Both international and Chinese economists have suggested that China needs to rebalance its economy in various ways: reduce investment; reduce saving; increase household consumption; increase government consumption; and reduce the foreign trade surplus. All these adjustments would affect the demand for labor. Over the medium term, none would have a large effect on the aggregate level of employment—including self–employment and informal employment, as well as formal wage and salary employment. However, rebalancing could affect the structure of employment, wages and working conditions, and would need to be carefully managed to minimise adjustment costs for workers and employers.

One relevant question is how rebalancing would affect the share of formal wage and salary jobs in total employment. In this regard there would be differences between the two main sorts of rebalancing that have been proposed for China. The first rebalancing is of the composition of domestic expenditure. A shift from investment to household consumption would reduce the share of wage and salary jobs, particularly formal jobs, because most investment involves this sort of employment(in machine–making or construction), whereas quite a lot of household spending is on goods produced by self-employed or informally-employed workers in agriculture, light industry and services.By contrast, a shift from investment to government consumption would not affect the share of wage and salary jobs and would increase the share of formal jobs, since almost all government employment is formal.

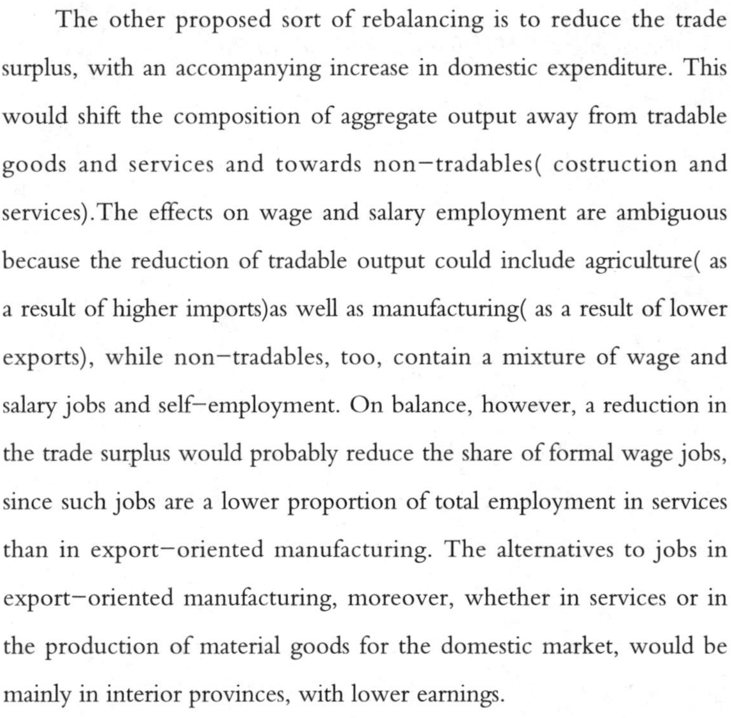

The other proposed sort of rebalancing is to reduce the trade surplus, with an accompanying increase in domestic expenditure. This would shift the composition of aggregate output away from tradable goods and services and towards non-tradables(costruction and services).The effects on wage and salary employment are ambiguous because the reduction of tradable output could include agriculture(as a result of higher imports)as well as manufacturing(as a result of lower exports), while non-tradables, too, contain a mixture of wage and salary jobs and self-employment. On balance, however, a reduction in the trade surplus would probably reduce the share of formal wage jobs, since such jobs are a lower proportion of total employment in services than in export-oriented manufacturing. The alternatives to jobs in export-oriented manufacturing, moreover, whether in services or in the production of material goods for the domestic market, would be mainly in interior provinces, with lower earnings.

But although in these ways reducing the trade surplus might lower the quality of employment in China, it would probably increase the total amount of non-agricultural employment. This is because the trade surplus is one of the main reasons why China's service sector remains small by comparison with other countries, and because at present in China services generate more than twice as many jobs per

unit of output as manufacturing. For example, complete elimination of the trade surplus could increase the service sector's share of employment in China by three to four percentage points.

If implemented too rapidly or without supporting policies, shifts in the structure of demand for labor can inflict heavy adjustment costs on workers, forcing them into inferior jobs or unemployment. The workers released from contracting activities may also lack the skills needed in expanding activities. The implication for policy is that rebalancing should be done gradually, so that changes in the structure of employment can occur mainly through different rates of expansion of different activities, rather than by growth of some activities and absolute shrinkage of others. Adjustment costs for workers can also be reduced by government action, especially to improve labor market information.

Absorbing China's Surge of College Graduates

The number of students in higher education has greatly increased in recent years, with the number of higher education graduates rising from 1.1 million and 1.5 million in 2002 to 6.3 million in 2009. They have entered the job market with career expectations that will be hard to fulfill and the employment prospects of college graduates has become a matter of concern for the government. Over time the situation should ease. With the increase in supply of university graduates, the pay premium they command in the job market should fall, increasing demand for their services. More important than this movement along the "demand" curve is the potential shift in the curve as a result of the economy's transition to highly skilled, technologically complex activities.

Korea provides the closest parallel to China's recent rapid and massive expansion of university education. Korea increased the number of higher education graduates at phenomenal rates from the mid-1950s through the 1990s. The Korean labor market absorbed the huge numbers of graduates fairly smoothly, partly through large declines in the relative earnings(and thus cost to employers)of graduates. But their absorption was also eased by changes in the sectoral structure of the economy. Less skill-intensive manufactured export sectors, for example in clothing and footwear, contracted, and more skill-intensive ones, such as chemicals and semi-conductors, expanded, increasing the demand for engineers and other workers with a college education, relative to less educated workers.

This will also happen in China. Rising education levels will make skilled workers relatively cheaper and shift the country's comparative advantage into more skill-intensive manufactures and services, absorbing part of the increased skill supply. Korea also provides another lesson. Despite the rapid growth of its high tech sector, most of its expanded supply of college graduates found employment in jobs that had traditionally used less educated workers. There was an upgrading of the education levels of occupations and industries across the board.

Education and Skills Development

Importance of Education for Growth

Nations set great store by their physical wealth: their factories, plants, roads and ports. But economists have shown that differences in the size of the physical capital stock can explain only a small fraction of the vast gaps in productivity between countries. Of greater importance is human capital—the skills of the population.

A 2004 study by the Nobel Laureate James Heckman[1], since confirmed by several more recent studies, shows the return to investment in human capital in China is much higher than the return to investment in physical capital. Moreover, the returns in poorer regions are higher than in richer areas. This means that China has been investing too much in physical capital, relative to the human kind. Indeed, the single strongest conclusion to emerge from the analysis of China's recent growth is that China should invest more in human capital, especially in young people underserved by current patterns of education spending. The economic case is compelling on its own. But the argument derives added force from the country's commitment to a harmonious society.

The under–investment in human capital is partly attributable to mispricing: the wages, paid to skilled workers do not adequately reflect their contributions to the economy. This reduces the incentive to acquire skills. One way to fix this problem is to subsidize training and skill development more generously. Heavier outlays by the central government in underserved areas would contribute to efficiency as well as equity, because the returns to education are higher in poorer areas.

Another way to fix the problem is to correct the under–pricing of skill. This would require further liberalization of the labor market.

---

[1] James J.Heckman "China's human capital investment" in China Economic Review 16(2005)50–70.

Greater labor mobility, for example, would help equalize the rate of return to human capital across regions and between cities and the countryside. In a freer labor market individuals would be compensated for their skills more generously, thus motivating them to acquire more human capital. In addition, a student–loan market should be developed to allow students to borrow against future earnings. Otherwise, only the rich will send their children to university, transmitting inequality from one generation to another.

Upgrading Worker Skills

China must improve the skills of many workers and young people who have(or in future are at risk of having)low levels of education. Experience in the US, the UK and other developed countries has shown that an underclass of poorly educated people in a modern economy is both a massive waste of human resources and a major cause of income inequality and social polarization. China should make every effort to avoid this problem, and this effort should start now, because the children who are educated in the next decade will be in the labor force for the next half–century.

The clearest current problem is the low quality of much education in rural areas. This problem is exacerbated by the unsatisfactory situation of the huge numbers of migrant workers(discussed in Chapter 3 : "Urban and Regional Development"), who are unable to obtain education for their children in the urban areas where they work, and therefore have to leave their children in their rural areas of origin. The educational prospects of these children are worrying: not only are many rural schools of low quality, but the children are living with grandparents whose educational level is low and may have emotional problems caused by the separation from their parents. Improving the quality of basic education, especially for schools and children in the lower part of the distribution of educational attainment, must be one of China's top priorities.

International experience with job–related education and training is more complicated. The economic returns to vocational schooling, as measured by the wages of its former students, tend to be lower than the returns to academic schooling. Government–run special training programs tend to have low returns, too, even in countries which have put large resources into them, such as Sweden. Vocational training seems to be most effective where it is run by employers, rather than by schools or government, and where it is in the form of apprenticeships. China needs to take account of this experience in developing its job–related education and training.

Reforming Higher Education

In recent years, China has rightly emphasized the need to expand higher education; with the result that the enrollment of college students has increased enormously. Spending by central and provincial governments on higher education has also increased greatly in recent years. However, there are now increasing concerns about the quality of higher education in China and its ability to meet the requirement of the economy and society. In particular, the higher education system remains one of the least reformed sectors in China, retaining many features of the planned economy. Government ministries intervene extensively in the academic and administrative affairs of the

universities, leading to inefficiency and low productivity. Within the universities, there is a lack of clear leadership and accountability under the current "system of president's responsibility under leadership of the party committee." There are also excessive restrictions on the establishment of private universities. Policies are needed that would include simple procedures for private universities to be registered, for them to obtain academic credit, and to provide tax exemption for financial contributions to private institutions.

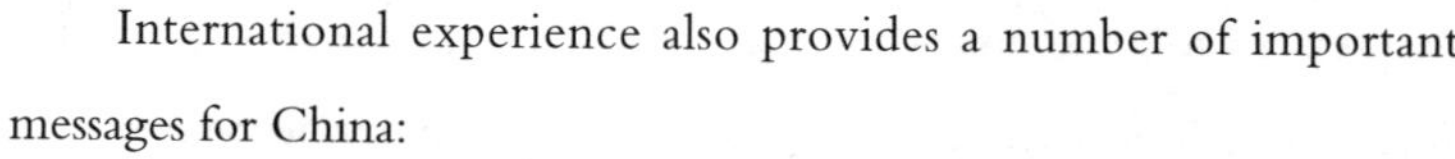

International experience also provides a number of important messages for China:

First, competition between universities is beneficial, though quality assurance is essential. A competitive environment creates incentives for universities to be more responsive to demand from both employers and students, most of whom are well–informed or potentially well–informed and hence best able to make choices which conform with their interests and those of the economy. In China's case, this suggests that the existing universities should be given much more autonomy in enrollment of students, in the choice of curriculum and learning environment, and in the mobilization and allocation of both human and financial resources within universities. The government should also issue its research grants in ways that encourage healthy competition between universities, for example by allowing professors who receive grants from an agency of the central government to take the grant to any university in China. The establishment of private universities should also be encouraged.

Second, universities should be financed by a mix of taxpayer support and variable fees. Higher education creates benefits beyond those to the individual, justifying taxpayer subsidies. However, graduates also receive significant private benefits—in terms of higher earnings and more satisfying jobs—so that it is efficient as well as equitable that they bear some of the costs. However, they should bear those costs when they can afford them—as graduates—not when they are students. A system of student loans is, therefore, essential.

Third, widening participation in higher education requires a range of' interventions, many of them earlier in a person's education. If student loans are income-contingent, experience from other countries(notably Australia, New Zealand and the UK) suggests that participation in higher education by students from poor backgrounds will not suffer. But efforts to increase the participation of students from poorer backgrounds needs to start much earlier and, most particularly, with measures that will improve a student's high school leaving grades.

Increasing Efficiency of Education Expenditures

More generally, experience around strongly suggests that China should rely much more on incentives and competition to drive improvements in the quality of education at all levels of the system and increase the efficiency of educational expenditures. Schools and universities that find better ways to teach pupils should be rewarded with more resources, so that they can teach even more students. The government might consider several measures to encourage this. By measuring educational outcomes—the skills students learn and the value of those skills in the marketplace—it could identify schools and universities that use resources well. The government could also require universities to make the salaries and job placements of their graduates available to prospective students. The disclosure of such information may increase competition to the benefit of society as a whole.

Insofar as they measure performance at all, most schools and universities test their students after they complete their studies. The institutions look good if their students do well. This encourages them to compete for the best students, but not necessarily to do a better job of teaching them. The government should instead test student knowledge at two points: before they begin an academic program and after they complete it. This type of testing captures the value that a school or university adds. The best educational institutions are not necessarily the ones with the best students but the ones that get the best out of the students they have.

To encourage competition among schools, students should be given more freedom to choose the school they wish to attend. Academic contests could award winners with fellowships, which would encourage students to excel and allow good students to choose their universities. State-controlled institutions should face competition from more private institutions, such as business schools and technological research institutes. Combined with rigorous measurement of student outputs, this would greatly enhance China's educational productivity.

Competition would also improve schooling at lower levels of education. As China continues to urbanize, it will need to build new schools, particularly at the primary and secondary levels. School buildings should be allocated first to the institutions that have performed the best. Instead of subsidizing schools, the government could offer school vouchers to target populations, such as the children of migrant workers. They could then "spend" these vouchers at the school of their choice.

By sharpening incentives and creating a competitive market for human capital, the government could do a lot to improve the effectiveness of the country's educational infrastructure, at no additional fiscal cost. International experience has shown that an effective way of improving basic education especially in poor regions is for the central government to take over responsibility for financing, while lower level governments continue managing schools. Thus local governments will have incentive to improve the quality of the education they provide and to attract more students, including the children of migrant workers (See Chapter 9 : "section on 'Reforming the Inter–Governmental Fiscal System'").

Labor Market Institutions and Regulations

Balance between Institutions and Markets

Every market economy needs labor institutions and regulations to protect worker rights at the job, to allow workers to form collective organizations to bargain with employers, and to limit labor–management conflicts. A good labor relations system provides workers with institutions of collective voice in the workplace and in the economy as a whole. It encourages employers and employees who engage in collective bargaining to reach efficient bargains—agreements that maximize output, as competitive markets are supposed to do, while producing a different division of output than in a market that lacks

such institutions. Efficient bargainers "leave no money on the table" . This usually occurs through labor–management cooperation, with infrequent strikes and considerable sharing of information, sometimes involving the assistance of neutral mediators or arbitrators.

Analysts categorize labor systems according to the extent to which wages and working conditions are determined by institutions–collective bargaining or regulations—rather than by market forces. Greater reliance on institutions lowers the dispersion of wages among observationally equivalent workers(that is, those who are similar in education, age and gender), and reduces the pay differential between ordinary workers and management. Advanced countries on average rely more on labor institutions than do developing countries, but there is wide variation among countries within both these groups in the degree of reliance on institutions.

International economic agencies differ in their opinions about the best combination of institutions and markets. The ILO favors "social dialogue" institutions because they create greater equity. The OECD, IMF and World Bank favor markets because they increase wage flexibility and give management the power to determine employment and working practices. In the 1990s, these three agencies favored the US labor market model, with its high turnover, limited regulation and weak unions, giving more weight to the US's high level of employment than to its high inequality and poverty. But evidence that some advanced countries—the East Asian and the Nordic countries in particular—have labor markets that diverge greatly from the US model but also produce high employment as well as the recent Wall Street implosion and rise in US unemployment have produced a

substantial change in thinking and a lot more uncertainty on the virtues of market determination of outcomes compared to institutional determination. Indeed, recent surveys of research on labor institutions in advanced countries, and on unions, regulations, and social protection in developing countries, stress that the only indisputable finding is that institutions reduce earnings inequality.

There is thus no ideal set of labor institutions or regulations that China might copy. The market–oriented policies that the OECD, IMF, and World Bank recommended for labor markets have not caused economic disaster(unlike laisser–faire policies for financial markets). But neither have the policies proved superior to policies in which government or collective bargaining play a greater role in the labor market. Rather than favoring any one set of policies or institutions, the evidence highlights trade–offs: institutions reduce earnings inequality and provide safety nets, but can reduce labor mobility and concentrate joblessness on disadvantaged groups of workers.

Knowing how countries around the world have responded to labor market problems can inform China about the range of possibilities for policies and their potential consequences in different circumstances, but there is no guarantee that what works in one setting in one period of time will work in another setting in a different period. Labor markets are idiosyncratic, so there is leeway for China to develop institutions and regulations with Chinese characteristics. The choice depends on the problems facing the country, the trade–offs the country wants to make between different goals, and the politics of enacting and implementing these decisions. A more flexible labor market has helped China to expand employment over the past thirty years, but

looking ahead, the goal of a harmonious society could be endangered by excessive inequality of earnings, which argues for increasing the role of labor market institutions.

Role of Unions

Countries vary widely in the nature of their labor laws and in the extent of the unionization of their workforces. There is a large gap between the EU and the US, for example, in the unionization rate, and an even greater gap in the percentage of workers covered by collective bargaining. There are also differences among countries in the ways unions operate. In some countries, unions bargain in a highly decentralized way with individual firms. This is common in the enterprise-based labor relations systems prevalent in parts of Asia—Japan, Korea, Malaysia and Hong Kong, for example—and in the US. By contrast, in many European countries bargaining is often between centralized industrial unions and employer federations in entire sectors. Economy-wide bargaining for wages by national union confederations has declined worldwide.

The variation among countries in union membership and how unions operate mainly reflects variation in national policies and institutional history rather than variation in the preferences of workers. Surveys of what workers want, in countries ranging from the US to Germany to Korea, and including one small survey in China, show striking similarity in worker desires for some independent representation inside their firms and for cooperative relationships with managements that pay attention to their views and interests.

China's 2008 Labor Contracts law(which instituted written

contracts of employment for all workers, including migrants, aimed at reducing wage arrears, and strengthened the ability of the All China Federation of Trade Unions(ACFTU)to organize workers in the private sector)and other recent changes in labor law regarding mediation are well up to world standards. Moreover, the role and impact of Chinese unions appears to have been qualitatively similar to that of unions in other countries: in unionized firms, wages are modestly higher, fringe benefits are more generous, and so on. The key issue going forward, therefore will be effective implementation of labor laws and effective support for those laws by the ACFTU—including pressuring firms to follow national labor laws, acting as a counterforce to the growing influence of wealthy business groups on policy decisions that affect workers, and helping migrant workers safeguard their rights.

Minimum Wage Policy

Virtually every government in the world sets minimum wages, though with wide variation in how exactly this is done. Some minimum–wage laws apply the same rate to all workers in a country, while others apply different rates for young workers or for workers in different regions, and so on. China introduced its first minimum wage regulation in 1993. In 2004, the Ministry of Labor and Social Security pressed each province, autonomous regions, and municipality to develop its own minimum wage, which resulted in higher minima in the more advanced areas, many of which set monthly rather than hourly rates, with greater monthly hours for migrant workers. Some people fear that regional minimum wages encourage a "race to the bottom" to attract investment, but in practice workers in areas with low minimum wages often press for increases. The US has a national hourly minimum wage, while states and municipalities can set their own minima. In 2008 enough localities had done so for most American workers to be covered by minimum wages substantially higher than the federal minimum.

Debates over minimum wages focus on how much they reduce employment. Most studies find modest effects (a 10 percent rise in the wage reducing employment by about 1 percent), and some find no effect at all. Some economists find these results surprising, but they can be reconciled with theory by recognizing that the elasticity of demand may be low, that governments pay attention to possible job losses when choosing the level of the minimum wage, and that firms can adjust labor practices to maintain employment while paying modestly higher wages. High minimum wages might well cause large job losses(or be unenforceable)but the cautiously chosen levels of minimum wages around the world do not appear to have significant adverse effects on employment, and benefit many workers, including those whose employers would otherwise have the power to hold their wages below the market level.

The key issue in minimum wages (as in other direct government regulation of labor outcomes)is again enforcement. Unions and workers themselves can play a vital role in enforcement by complaining to the government about illegally low wages and violations of laws on hours and other conditions of work. However, they are likely to complain only when they believe that enforcement would not cause job losses. Where workers or their unions believe that employers could not maintain employment if they complied with the law, the law will

be difficult to enforce(we return to this issue below in relation to the informal sector).

Unemployment Insurance

Unemployment insurance is another debated issue: it allows jobless workers to maintain a reasonable living standard, but it also tends to increase the length of time for which they are unemployed. Research shows that the adverse effect on the level of unemployment is related more to the duration of unemployment benefits than to their level relative to the worker's normal wage(the "replacement rate"). Thus in booms it may be desirable to reduce the length of time for which workers can receive unemployment benefits, and in major recessions to extend the duration of coverage, as the US has historically done. The best policy may be to combine varying duration of coverage with relatively high replacement rates.

A major task for China concerning unemployment insurance is to expand its coverage, which at present includes only urban areas, leaving the many employees of township and village enterprises uncovered. Even in urban areas, most migrant workers are not covered. These omissions debase the role of unemployment insurance in protecting workers, and make the system inefficient. In 2008, only 41% of urban resident workers were covered, and less than 4% of migrant workers living in urban areas for 6 months or more. The surplus of unemployment insurance revenue over spending has been increasing since 2002 and had mounted to 130 billion yuan by 2008. A growing surplus makes little sense in a program of this type, but it could perhaps be used to extend the coverage of the program.

The Informal Sector

"Informal" employment is hard to define or measure precisely, but is agreed by all to exist on a large scale in most countries. It includes wage and salary jobs in firms which are not registered with government agencies, and workers who lack formal employment contracts or are not enrolled in social security programs. The term is sometimes also extended to jobs which are casual, temporary, or home-based, and to the self-employed. Different countries use different definitions of "informal" , depending on their circumstances and on what information is collected by their household and establishment surveys.

On any and all of these definitions, there is currently a lot of informal employment in China. More than a third of the urban jobs measured by labor force surveys are not visible in establishment data, there is probably an even higher proportion of such jobs in rural areas, and roughly half of the workers surveyed lack contracts or social security provision. Since the mid-1990s, the government has endorsed "flexible" employment as part of the solution to job losses from unprofitable or overstaffed state enterprises. Over the same period, however, the government has developed a comprehensive system of employment law and introduced a market-compatible social security system in urban areas.

China's informal employment share is not unusual by international standards. More than half of all non-agricultural jobs worldwide can be considered informal. In developing countries, this share ranges from one-half to three-quarters, of which 30%-40% (and in Asia over 50%)

is wage employment and the rest is self–employment. As in China, the informal share of employment has either risen or remained stable over the past two to three decades in most countries, including developed countries and fast–growing developing countries such as South Korea. Worldwide, there is no sign in the data that the informal share of jobs in developing countries is likely to decline in the foreseeable future.

Policy towards informal employment raises difficult issues, because informality arises from a mixture of voluntary and involuntary decisions and has a mixture of desirable and undesirable results. Some unregistered firms are cheating the state and their workers out of taxes, wages and benefits that they could afford, or exposing their workers to unacceptable health risks. But some of the firms that avoid registration and taxation, and the jobs that they create, would not otherwise exist. Similarly, some workers accept jobs with no contracts or social security, or with health risks or wages below the legal minimum, because the alternatives for them are even worse jobs or no jobs at all. Others may find that the informal sector gives them greater opportunity to be entrepreneurial or to earn more(by avoiding taxes)than in the formal sector. In China informal employment, often of reasonable quality, has also helped to bridge the transition from planned to market–oriented allocation of labor.

There is thus an international consensus that the right policies lie somewhere in between two extreme and inappropriate approaches. It would be undesirable(and probably impossible)to suppress informal employment by draconian enforcement of laws and regulations. Such a policy would hurt many poor people by eliminating their jobs, as well as being administratively costly. But it would also be wrong to do

nothing, since some sorts of informal employment inflict unnecessary harm on poor people, as well as imposing costs on the state through lost tax revenues and through expenditure on health, pension and poverty problems caused by non–compliance with the law.

It is thus necessary to strike a difficult policy balance in this area, as China seems to have done quite successfully over the past decade. One strategic issue is the degree to which the governments should tacitly tolerate the avoidance of labor market regulations, especially in small firms and in backward areas. Some such toleration seems unavoidable.But too much toleration will make the problem of informal employment worse, subverting the basic objectives of improving the quality of employment and of making China into an efficient and fair rule–based society.

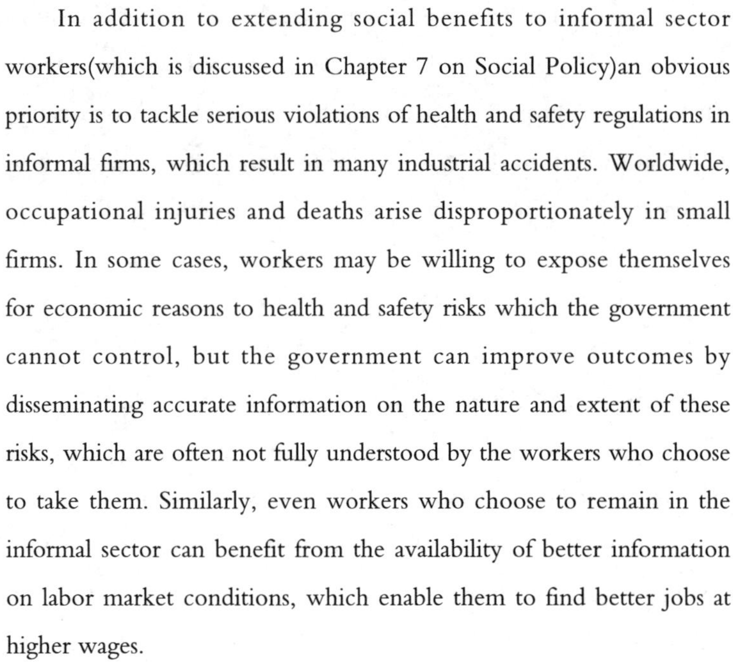

In addition to extending social benefits to informal sector workers(which is discussed in Chapter 7 on Social Policy)an obvious priority is to tackle serious violations of health and safety regulations in informal firms, which result in many industrial accidents. Worldwide, occupational injuries and deaths arise disproportionately in small firms. In some cases, workers may be willing to expose themselves for economic reasons to health and safety risks which the government cannot control, but the government can improve outcomes by disseminating accurate information on the nature and extent of these risks, which are often not fully understood by the workers who choose to take them. Similarly, even workers who choose to remain in the informal sector can benefit from the availability of better information on labor market conditions, which enable them to find better jobs at higher wages.

Another strategic issue concerning informal–sector employment is its implications for the standards that should be set by laws and regulations governing wages and working conditions in the formal sector. The existence of a big informal sector might suggest that the standards in formal–sector laws and regulations should be set at lower levels than would be ideal, to reduce the incentive to avoid them(which tends to enlarge the informal sector).However, a surprising finding of recent research is that government policies alter outcomes (and may improve the well–being of workers) in the informal sector even though they are not enforced there. In some respects, that is, informal workers and firms adhere to policies covering the formal sector(for example on minimum wages or the length of the statutory work week)as if those policies had established a social standard. This evidence is supportive of China's practice of making and enforcing labor laws.

Chapter 6 Strengthening the Pension System*

Over the past two decades, China has fundamentally reformed its pension system. In urban areas, a mandatory system is now in place that includes a basic pension and individual accounts. There is a separate system for public employees. Provision has also been made for voluntary pension arrangements. The Dibao system provides money to some of the elderly poor in both urban and rural areas. In addition, the government is piloting a pension scheme in rural areas which will include both a basic pension and voluntary individual accounts.

However, the pension system is still beset by problems. The mandatory system is highly fragmented and in most municipalities, the pension fund is in deficit. Mandated contributions are unevenly enforced; the system covers cities incompletely, because most firms in the informal sector do not participate; and it omits migrant workers and rural workers altogether. The system of individual accounts is also struggling. Funding has not occurred as planned(leading to the

* This chapter is a summary of Background paper No.4 by Nicholas Barr and Peter Diamond: "Pension Reform in China: Issues, Options and Recommendations" .

problem of so–called "empty accounts") and there are no institutions to help workers pick their portfolio and make direct investments in different assets. The pension system for public employees needs to be better designed. In addition, the rural pension system faces several strategic issues. One is whether the basic pension should be conditional on contributions. The second is whether such pensions should be confined to rural areas, or offered throughout the economy.

As part of China's overall effort to improve its social policies and programs, further reform of the country's pension system must remain a high priority.

Lessons from Economic Theory and International Experience

Core Objectives of a Pension System

Throughout the world, pension systems have the core objectives of consumption smoothing, insurance, income redistribution and poverty relief.

Consumption smoothing. Pensions allow a person to transfer consumption from his[1] productive middle years to his retirement years, so that he has money to spend even when he is no longer working and earning.

Insurance. A person does not know how long he will live.

[1] Throughout this chapter, the masculine pronoun is used to refer to an individual and his pension; but it is recognized that the pensioner may equally well be a woman.

Thus pension systems provide insurance in the form of annuities, i. e., weekly or monthly payments to the individual for the rest of his life. Such annuities are a form of risk pooling, enabling people to insure against the risk of outliving their pension savings. Pension systems can also protect spouses and young children if a worker dies before retirement.

Income redistribution. Pension systems can redistribute incomes within a generation: low earners, for example, can receive pensions that provide a higher replacement rate(i.e. a higher percentage of their previous earnings)than high earners receive. Pension systems can also redistribute income across generations. They can, for instance, impose a higher contribution rate on the present generation, thereby allowing future generations to enjoy more generous pensions or lower contributions. Similarly, pensions can redistribute income from future taxpayers to current retirees by giving them a better retirement income than their past contributions alone could finance.

Poverty relief. A general system of poverty relief for the entire population may not be affordable. It may also blunt the incentive to work. The elderly, however, are not expected to provide much labor, and are, therefore, a particular target for programs to reduce poverty, programs that would work less well across all age groups.

Of these four objectives, some are clearly the responsibility of the state; others can be addressed in different ways, so countries vary in their pension arrangements.

Pension Systems around the World

International experience and economic theory suggest that no

single pension system best serves every country(see Box 3).Rather, a number of different structures work pretty well. They include one or more of the following elements, in different degrees of importance and size.

Non–contributory pensions, minimum–income and minimum–pension guarantees (citizen's pension.) In many ways the simplest option is a tax–financed pension available to everyone beyond a given age, as in the Netherlands and New Zealand. This is commonly called a citizen's pension. As a variant, the citizen's pension can be affluence–tested, i.e., given to everyone except the best–off, as in Australia, Canada, Chile(since July 2008)and South Africa. Alternatively, there can be a guaranteed minimum income available to all poor elderly people on the basis of an income test, as in many countries.

Box 3

No Single Best Pension System for All Countries

Pensions have multiple objectives, notably the achievement of consumption smoothing, insurance, poverty relief and redistribution. They also face a series of constraints:

• Fiscal capacity:stronger fiscal capacity makes it easier for the system to find additional revenues for a pension system.

• Institutional capacity:stronger institutional capacity widens the range of feasible options for pension design.

• Behavioural parameters :these include the responsiveness of labour supply to the design of the pension system, and the effect of pensions on private saving.

• The shape of the income distribution, prior to transfers: a heavier lower tail of the income distribution increases the need for poverty relief.

There is no single best system for all countries for several reasons:

• Policy makers will weigh these objectives differently. They will differ in the importance they place on poverty relief and in their views about how risks should be shared within and across generations.

• The pattern of constraints, including the value of key behavioural parameters, will differ across countries.

• Politics: what is politically feasible in some countries, may be politically impossible in others.

• History bequeaths a set of institutions, which influence policies today. This institutional inheritance may be worth building on—or at least difficult to dismantle.

In sum, if the objectives differ and the constraints differ, the optimum is likely to differ. Thus:

• Different countries have different structures for addressing the multiple goals.

• Though no country's system is perfect, there are a number of different structures that work pretty well.

Defined-benefit(DB)plans. In a national DB plan, a worker receives a pension based on his earnings history and the age at which he first draws benefits. Though in many cases the pension benefit is based on the worker's wages in his final few years of work, it is now increasingly recognised that this design is problematical, and that it is better to base a person's pension on a longer period, up to his entire career. There may be a taxpayer subsidy from general revenues. Some national DB plans are partially "funded" which is to say they set aside financial assets in a trust fund in anticipation of future pension payouts. But most plans are largely "pay as you go" (PAYG), with pensions paid out of current revenues, with little or no prior funding.

Funded defined-contribution (FDC) plans. With funded individual accounts, pensions are paid from a fund built up over the years by members' contributions and actually invested in securities or other assets. The contribution rate is fixed. Upon retirement, the pensioner receives an annuity whose size is determined by the size of his lifetime pension accumulation, life expectancy and the rate of interest. Countries with DC systems can use publicly organised investment (as in Singapore) or private, regulated financial intermediaries (as in Chile).

Notional defined-contribution (NDC) systems[1]. A fairly recent innovation, pure NDC systems (sometimes also called non-financial defined-contribution systems) are hybrids, combining elements of both DC and DB. Like DC systems, they give workers individual accounts, which record the contributions workers make from their earnings and base benefits on contributions, not earnings. These systems also share some risk with the pensioner, since benefits vary with average wage growth and can rise or fall. But they are similar to DB pensions in that

[1] There are different Chinese translation of Notional Individual Account and the difference between fully funded and notional individual accounts is often not well understood. With a fully funded account, contributions are used each year to purchase individual assets—stocks, bonds, mutual funds and bank deposits. Thus, a fully funded account is similar to a private investment account. By contrast, a notional defined-contribution account is similar to a bank account. The returns credited to a NDC account are set by the government, based on the returns on the assets held and on the anticipated flow of new contributions. Thus, to the individual worker the only difference between the NDC and a funded account is that with the former, the rate of return is set by rules based on overall fund availability, as in a bank account, while with the latter, it depends on future market returns on the particular assets held in the account. The confidence of the worker that he will get his pension when he retires depends not on whether there are assets in the account or not, but on his confidence in the government. This is like in a bank account;the depositor only cares about the strength of the bank where he has the account and the sustainability of the rules determining benefit levels, not how the money he deposited was used. With funded accounts, the individual worker faces great uncertainty about how the markets will function, how much return he will get, and in the case of decentralized investment management, how competent and trustworthy is his investment manager.

they are not fully funded: workers' contributions go into a separate part of the state budget, and may or may not in part be separately invested in private financial assets. Pensions are paid to a greater or lesser extent out of current revenues, like a PAYG system. In place of market rates of return and market mortality projections for annuity determination, benefits are instead determined using legislated formulas, often tied to life expectancy and the growth of the payroll tax base. If they are in a separate part of the state budget, they are generally invested in financial assets, if only government debt.

Public employee pensions. Many governments set up pension systems for public employees. Most are DB systems, although some have been defined contribution or have offered DC as an option. Some public employees are included in the national mandatory system, with the government—their employer—providing a supplementary pension, just as a large corporation might provide a supplementary pension for its employees. Other countries exempt some or all public employees from the mandatory national system.

Voluntary pensions. These are separate from mandatory arrangements, and arise in two ways. An employer may choose to establish a pension fund even though the government does not require it. Such a pension scheme is voluntary for the employer, although he may require all of his staff to join the scheme as a condition of their employment. For workers covered by the mandatory national system, such voluntary pensions can be thought of as supplementary(the "enterprise annuities" in China fall into this category).In addition, in many countries, workers can choose to make contributions to a voluntary individual plan. Voluntary pensions of both types typically receive favoured tax treatment: contributions may, for example, be deducted from a person's taxable income. Countries vary widely in the size of their mandatory systems, and hence in the amount of room for voluntary arrangements.

Lessons from International Experience

The main conclusion to draw from experience worldwide is that there is a wide range of pension designs, with no single, dominant arrangement. There are many ways to design good pensions and so systems function reasonably well even in countries that have made very different choices from each other. This section discusses some of the other, central lessons.

Labor-market efficiency. It is very important to avoid unduly discouraging labor mobility, which is essential to the efficiency of the labor market and the growth of productivity. Pensions should be portable in the face of at least four types of movement by a worker: from one firm to another, from one geographical area to another, from the state to the private sector(including self-employment), and from the uncovered(rural)to the covered(urban)sector. Such portability is achieved most readily when the system has a uniform underlying structure, both across localities and across sectors, although parameters can vary.

Pensions can be provided to the self-employed and the intermittently employed. Even countries with very high pension coverage worry about people with incomplete employment histories, primarily women and informal workers. Countries generally have difficulty bringing these groups into the fold of pension systems that were created for employees of established firms. One solution is to provide a pension to the entire population above some age, paying the same benefit to everyone with lifetime residence in the country, and a pro–rated benefit to residents who have spent time abroad.

Gender and family. Should a basic pension be awarded to an individual or to his family? Such decisions can have major ramifications. Pension systems could focus primarily on workers, leaving arrangements between the worker and his family largely to his discretion. Alternatively, they could focus on the family by mandating protection, primarily for the surviving spouse(predominantly widows) and sometimes for young children as well. Pension arrangements can also differ in their consequences for each gender. A non–contributory pension, for example, will favor women more than a contributory pension, since women typically have more fragmented employment histories.

Funded individual accounts impose transactions costs; and may or may not assist capital markets. Funded individual accounts, which allow the individual to choose their portfolio or their fund provider, carry significant transactions costs. These costs can be reduced if the government selects the portfolio or limits the set of alternative investments. But in this case, the rate of return may be poor if the government chooses badly, or picks investments in pursuit of some goal other than the accumulation of retirement assets. It should also be noted that funded individual accounts may facilitate the development of capital markets, but this is not always or necessarily the case. Policy makers will need to ask themselves whether existing capital markets and financial intermediaries can meet the needs of funded accounts;

and if they cannot, whether funded accounts, by increasing the demand for financial instruments and intermediary services, can improve the functioning of both.

Finance and funding. An important feature of pension design is the degree of funding, i. e., whether contributions are used for current pension payments(Pay As You Go–PAYG), or to accumulate assets from which pensions in the future are paid(funding). Funding can affect the level of national savings and thus the rate of growth. Indeed, it is through increasing national savings that increased funding might conceivably raise economic welfare. Whether increased funding will actually improve welfare depends on the conditions in a particular country.

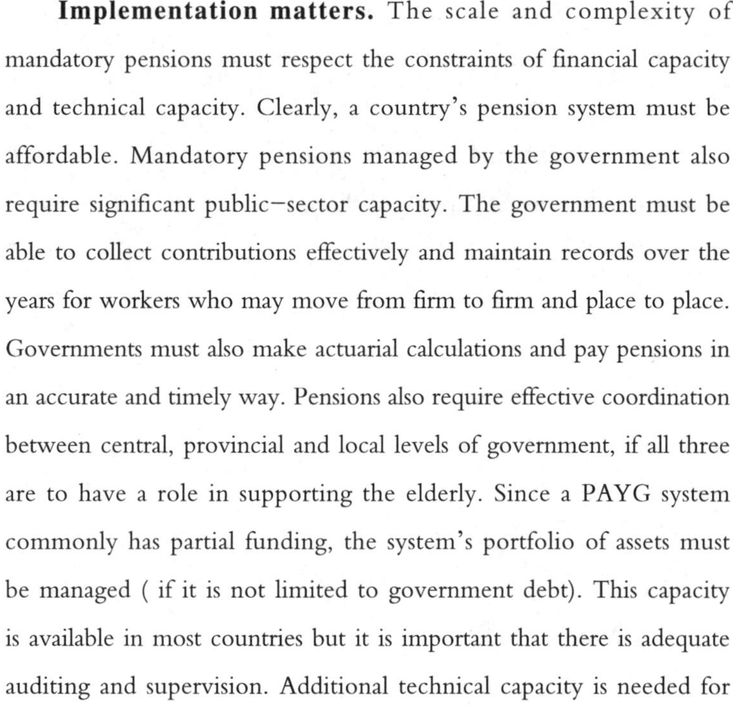

Implementation matters. The scale and complexity of mandatory pensions must respect the constraints of financial capacity and technical capacity. Clearly, a country's pension system must be affordable. Mandatory pensions managed by the government also require significant public–sector capacity. The government must be able to collect contributions effectively and maintain records over the years for workers who may move from firm to firm and place to place. Governments must also make actuarial calculations and pay pensions in an accurate and timely way. Pensions also require effective coordination between central, provincial and local levels of government, if all three are to have a role in supporting the elderly. Since a PAYG system commonly has partial funding, the system's portfolio of assets must be managed (if it is not limited to government debt). This capacity is available in most countries but it is important that there is adequate auditing and supervision. Additional technical capacity is needed for fully funded individual accounts.

Government matters. It is not only mandatory pension systems that depend critically on effective government. Voluntary pensions also depend on government to set rules and enforce them. Government must be able to enforce compliance with contribution conditions and protect asset accumulations. They must also maintain macroeconomic stability, without which households will not accumulate long–term financial assets, and ensure effective regulation and supervision of financial markets. Without government regulation and supervision, financial markets, including insurance and annuities markets, do not function well. Such regulation is therefore vital to protect individuals in areas too complex for them to protect themselves.

Capacity to evolve. It is also desirable for pension systems to have the capacity to evolve in a straightforward way as incomes rise, reforms proceed and administrative capacity grows. This principle is particularly relevant to China, a country in the midst of widespread change, where workers are moving from rural to urban areas and from the state to private sectors, where the age profile of the population is rapidly changing, and where labor markets and financial markets are undergoing significant reform.

Options for Further Reform of China's Pension System

The three elements of the present system—the basic pension, individual accounts, and voluntary pensions—provide a good basis for further pension reform. This reform needs to focus both on extending

coverage and on improving pension design.

Non-contributory Basic Pension(Citizen's Pension)

Even in a modern economy, contributory pension systems will have gaps. To fill these gaps and relieve poverty, governments in a number of countries, including some middle-income countries, offer a universal citizen's pension. Financed by taxes, without any contribution from the pension-holder, these pensions cover everyone—urban and rural, formal and informal, men and women. These pensions are often awarded at a flat rate to anyone who meets age and residence tests. Unlike contributory pensions, they can be extended to the informal sector without too many administrative difficulties. Such pensions help not just the retirees themselves but also other members of their family, including grandchildren.

In China, similar concerns about coverage have led to the recent introduction of a pilot pension scheme in rural areas. This is a very welcome development. The experiment should be institutionalized as quickly as possible, as part of a broader effort to introduce nationwide coverage and portable benefits. The government might also consider a number of refinements. It could separate the non-contributory part of the pension from the contributory part, so that all senior citizens in rural areas could benefit from a non-contributory basic pension. Tying the two parts together may increase contributions overall, but it also complicates the administration of the system and risks leaving many people out. The government might also consider expanding the non-contributory basic pension to cover city-dwellers as well as rural residents, thus making it a citizen's pension. This would end the tripartite distinction between rural, urban, and migrant, helping to integrate the system nationally.

Such a system clearly needs to be affordable. In that regard, policy makers need to give careful consideration to the size of the benefit; the age at which it is first paid; and the eligibility of better–off elderly people who can count on sufficient alternative sources of income. The full pension should be large enough to make a significant contribution to poverty relief, and to justify the administrative costs of delivering it. As examples, the Netherlands has a benefit equal to 70% of the net minimum wage and New Zealand a benefit set at between 65 % and 72.5 % of the net average wage for a married couple, and more per person for singles. To secure a uniform living standard across China's different regions, the benefit level should vary to reflect the cost of living in the beneficiary's place of residence. If a region chooses, it could supplement the benefit from its own resources to better reflect local living standards. The level of the non–contributory benefit should be indexed to prices and/or wages in the same way as the contributory pension.

The non–contributory pension should cover everyone who meets an age and residence test. The age for eligibility might well match the age for full benefits in the contributory system. Over the long run, as life expectancy increases, the age of eligibility should rise automatically in accordance with a measure of healthy life expectancy, although not necessarily in strict proportion. China should carefully study the trade–off between the generosity of benefits and the age at which people become entitled to them. A later starting age might be necessary to finance a sufficiently large benefit to make the pension worthwhile.

This trade–off obviously depends on the level of resources devoted to the system. China also needs to consider whether to reduce the benefit level for older people who have spent time abroad, as students or workers for example. It is likely that many such people would not have as large a financial need in old age, so this appears to be a good option.

Should the size of the citizen's pension be related to a person's income? There are several options. A flat–rate pension on the basis only of age and residence, and subject to income tax(as is the practice in the Netherlands and New Zealand)has the advantage of simplicity. But it is also the most expensive option(holding the size of benefits and age of retirement constant). If one wants to reduce or eliminate benefits for better–off people, they can be excluded on the basis of an income test. The test could apply to a person's total income, mandatory pension income or a combination.

Irrespective of these specific issues, it is appropriate that the level of benefits be quite low at first, until the system is working properly. However payments should increase thereafter, keeping pace with prices or wages in the same way as the contributory pension. The program should be introduced as quickly as possible and certainly over the course of the 12th Five–Year Plan.

Mandatory Contributory Pension

The mandatory contributory pension should also be gradually extended. It should first ensure that all large firms (referred to as the formal sector) in urban areas are covered. It should then be broadened beyond the cities to reach the formal sector in rural areas. This would represent a big step towards unifying the pension system and integrating

the nation's labor market. Eventually the mandatory contributory system should include small firms and the self–employed(referred to as the informal sector). But in China, as in every other country, this is a demanding task. In the short run it may not be the best use of China's administrative energies.

In the meantime, the danger is that the mandatory contributory pension will discourage firms from graduating to the formal sector from the informal sector. To avert this danger, the pension's net cost(that is, the cost of contributions minus the value of future benefits)must not be too large. China should take care to avoid the fate of some South American countries, where social security, which is closely associated with salaried labor, is resented as a tax by workers and employers[1].This damages productivity and deters informal firms from moving into the formal economy.

The contributions base also needs to be changed. Contributions are currently based on the standard wage, which encourages workers and employers to switch to other kinds of compensation. The contributions base should, therefore, be changed to a measure of earnings that approximates total compensation. The same measure of earnings should be used for both pension contributions and the income tax, thereby aligning the incentives of the income–tax authorities and the pension administration. Similarly, the calculation of basic benefits should be based on average local earnings using the same definition that is used for determining contributions. Thus benefits should vary with

[1] See Background paper No.13 by Santiago Levy: "Some Remarks on Social Policy of Latin America" for further discussion of this issue.

location, but within a formula set by a national authority.

Individual Accounts

The system of individual accounts could also work better. China introduced individual accounts as part of its pension reform in 1997. These were intended to be fully funded.However, funding has not occurred in line with the standard model. There are no institutions to help workers select individual portfolios or make direct investments indifferent assets. In addition, the need to pay current benefits has left the system unable to purchase assets as originally designed, seriously undermining its credibility.

China could follow the example of a number of other countries, such as Sweden, that offer "notional defined-contribution" (NDC) accounts. NDC pensions are a relatively recent innovation, used by countries seeking to retain the usefulness of a defined contributions approach without the necessity of full funding. Each worker has an account that records his cumulative contributions over the years; these contributions earn interest, credited to the account each year by the pension authority at a rate defined by law, for example, the growth rate of the payroll tax base. The recorded accumulation, therefore, increases each year by the amount contributed during the year plus the product of the notional interest rate and the level of the accumulation at the end of the previous year. Whether or not contributions are partially invested in private financial assets, the pension each worker receives is based quasi-actuarially on his accumulation, and paid for out of a combination of current revenues and returns on assets.

Such an arrangement would not preclude an eventual move

to full funding, should that suit China's future circumstances. The two arrangements can also coexist. For example, Sweden's 18.5% contribution rate is divided, 16% going to the NDC system and 2.5% to fully funded accounts. But even if China eventually moves to full funding, this should not be an objective for the 12th Five-Year Plan period. The circumstances under which funding might be attractive do not apply today. Funding is desirable if it leads to worthwhile increased national saving. But China already has a high savings rate that is more than enough to finance its current levels of investment. Funding might also be desirable if it could help improve the effectiveness of China's capital markets. But financial markets are still at an early stage of development in China. As a result, in the immediate term, funding individual accounts is likely to result in low returns or high risks. In addition the administrative requirements for mandatory funded accounts with individually chosen portfolios are stringent and do not seem now to be in place in China.

A more urgent and important objective is transparent accounting for individual accounts. At present, workers' contributions are not always recorded accurately, and the system's books are not open or accessible. To fix this, China will need to build stronger administrative systems so that all contributions to individual accounts are recorded and data is accessible. The rules that determine the rate of return on pension accumulations need to be made explicit and contributors should be told the annual rates of return on their funds. Contributors also need to be assured that their accounts are not "empty" accounts but obligations of the government/pension authorities. They should receive annual statements of their accumulation and the likely replacement rate(i.e.,

percentage of previous earnings)they can expect from the basic pension and their individual account.

Public Employee Pensions

Pensions for public employees—including civil servants and those, like teachers, who provide public services—are generous world–wide. In most countries, including China, the pension systems are DB, with benefits based on a short period of earnings at the end of a career. Such systems are poorly designed. They encourage gaming of the system and distort people's incentives for moving between public and private employment and retirement.

One can therefore applaud China's experiments with incorporating public employees who are not government employees into the mandatory contributory system. It's a decision that should be implemented fully and extended to government employees as well. This would not necessarily require a reduction in government employee pensions, since their participation in the national system can be supplemented by a government–provided pension, just as private firms are encouraged to supplement the mandatory system. Any supplementary system should endeavor to hold down administrative costs. This has been done successfully in the US with the Thrift Savings Plan for employees of the federal government.

Voluntary Pensions

In many countries, people complement their mandatory pensions with voluntary plans, provided by their employer or by themselves with approved institutions. In China both types of voluntary retirement plan are likely to grow and evolve in the coming years and should be encouraged. But China also needs better regulation and supervision to safeguard such arrangements for both individuals and firms. Stronger regulation is also needed for any insurance companies that provide benefits on an annualized basis. International experience strongly suggests that voluntary pension plans should be fully funded DC pensions, with income–tax treatment clarified and set on a consistent basis.

Overall Management of China's Pension System

The reforms outlined above will require major changes in the overall management of China's pension system. One issue is the need to raise the retirement age. Another key issue is the overall administration of the system, which needs strengthening and broadening to become nationwide in scope.

Raising the Retirement Age

Throughout the world, people are living longer. This is a wonderful thing, but it implies that if people continue to retire at the same age, the cost of a given monthly pension will rise. Moreover in China, longer life expectancy is currently combined with large–scale early retirement. This is because enterprises going through hard times encourage early retirement in order to shift the burden of compensation to the pension authorities. This is leading to even more pressure on pension finance.

In response to such pressures, a number of countries have

increased the earliest age at which pension benefits, in part or in full, can be claimed. Even more are now considering such changes in the light of current fiscal constraints. For example, the US passed legislation in 1982 increasing the age for full benefits in stages with delays and slow phasing. The age was 65 in 1982; it is now 66 and will reach 67 in 2022. In the UK, recent legislation phases in an increase in the state pensionable age, which will rise from 65 to 66 in 2020 and thereafter by one year each decade. Japan is slowly increasing the official age for benefits from 60 to 65. Also many countries that had different retirement ages for men and women have legislated increases in the ages for women so that retirement ages are equalised.

Although the labor market in China is not yet working efficiently, the pension system needs to be set up for the long term. In that context China needs to raise the retirement age, which is presently 60 for male SOE workers and 50 or 55 for women. It also needs to avoid encouraging or even mandating early retirement. Increasing the retirement age does, however, need to be done very carefully. It should follow a number of key principles. These include ensuring that the rules relate to date of birth and not date of retirement, that changes are made annually, and that as far as is sensible, rules for changing benefits are made explicit(see Box 4 for further elaboration of these principles).

Box 4

Principles for Adjusting Pensionable Age

An increase in pension age should be based on three principles.

• The rules should relate to a person's date of birth(which a person cannot change)and not to their date of retirement(which he can choose strategically). Otherwise there will be a wave of retirements just before any changes to benefits go into effect. Such an incentive to retire is inefficient. Mere consideration of raising the retirement age may prompt people to retire too early for fear that the pension age will change for anyone not yet retired.

• Changes should be made annually, to avoid large changes in benefit levels across nearby cohorts. Large changes are inequitable and politically difficult, since benefits could differ significantly between people born in successive years, sometimes only days apart. The combination of large changes and rules determined by date of retirement would exacerbate the inefficient incentive to retire early.

• As far as is sensible, rules for changing benefits should be explicit. The public should have little difficulty understanding the rationale for adjusting benefits as life expectancy changes. Automatic adjustment in line with explicit rules leads to greater predictability and decreased political pressure. Automatic adjustments may function better if based on actual mortality outcomes rather than projections. Nevertheless, there always remains the option of legislation to change whatever the automatic rules produce. Legislators around the world have, for example, intervened to alter income-tax brackets that rise automatically in line with prices.

Many people in China worry that raising the retirement age would increase unemployment. This is based on the belief that if workers stay in their jobs longer, there will be fewer job openings for new entrants to the labor force. Apart from temporary, short-run effects, that view is erroneous. In a market economy, there is not a fixed number of jobs. As discussed in Box 5, the number of jobs in the economy is responsive to the availability of labor.

Box 5

Unfounded Worries: Earlier Retirement and Unemployment

*Early retirement.*If the number of jobs in an economy were fixed, inducing an older worker to retire would create an opening for some other worker. In that ease, early retirement could ease unemployment. But that view is generally mistaken since the number of jobs in an economy is not fixed. Consider the experience of developed countries, where the average retirement age has decreased substantially over recent decades, without any parallel decline in unemployment rates. Empirical evidence for a number of developed countries over a 10-year period shows no systematic relationship between encouraging early retirement and lowering unemployment. There is no reason to think that this basic insight is different in developing countries.

It is wrong for several reasons to think of market economies as producing a fixed number of jobs. First, additional workers exert downward pressure on wages and make it easier for firms to find suitable workers, thus encouraging the creation of new jobs. The number of jobs is therefore variable, and is influenced by the number of workers. Second, taking a pension early frequently does not remove workers from the labor force, since some workers continue to work

elsewhere while receiving a pension from a previous employer. Third, the large pool of rural workers is potentially a much greater source of unemployment.

Thus it is mistaken to encourage early retirement or mandate retirement as a palliative response to unemployment. Retirement, after all, has long-term effects, often taking a worker out of the labour force for good, whereas unemployment is generally a short-term problem. It is better to focus on unemployment benefits and creating incentives for long-run growth, rather than distorting the labor market in the vain hope that retirement will have a large impact on unemployment. Similarly, disability benefits should be awarded on the basis of disability, not as a response to unemployment.

Raising the retirement age. The corollary to the previous argument is that slowly raising the retirement age in China will not have a significant effect on unemployment.

Administration of the Pension System

The government also needs to reform key aspects of pension administration.

Establishment of a national pension administration. Without a unified national system, pension rights will not be portable, compromising labor mobility. The mandatory contributory pension should be subject to a single set of regulations, with room for regional variations in benefit levels. All pension contributions, for both the basic pension and the individual accounts, should flow into a single pool, i.e., a national trust fund. Record-keeping and pension payments should be the responsibility of a single nationwide pension administration. It should manage a national database containing information on each worker's account and use a single system of record keeping. Such a National Pension Administration should be capable of making projections of the financial position of mandatory pensions and carrying out broader research. To boost confidence in the system, it should also inform the public about changes in the system, once they have been decided.

Separation of the Contributory pension system from the state budget. The contributory pension system should continue to be financially separate from the state budget. These pensions should be financed from dedicated revenue sources. Surplus revenues could be transferred to the National Social Security Fund(NSSF); deficits could be financed out of earnings on the Fund's assets, or, if necessary, out of the assets themselves. Pension contributions should be collected by the tax authority and delivered promptly to the pension administration. Under the current dual system, collections are made both by the Ministry of Labor and Social Security and by the tax authorities. This makes collections more costly and less accurate than they need to be.

Management of legacy obligations. At the time of the 1998 pension reforms, China had to meet two legacy obligations: the pensions of workers who retired before 1998 and the pension entitlements that contemporary workers had accrued up until 1998. In recognition of these legacy obligations, the government decided in 2003 to transfer some of its shares in SOEs to the NSSF. However, progress has been slow and only a small quantity of shares have been transferred. Given the extent of legacy obligations, continuing the transfer of state shares to the NSSF offers two potential advantages. Shifting the dividend flow to the pension system will improve the system's finances and reduce the fiscal subsidies it requires.Adding the NSSF as a long–term shareholder could also improve the corporate governance of the SOEs.

Administration of the non–contributory basic pension. This can build on different institutions in the short run and the long run. In the long run, the administrators of the non–contributory basic pension have much the same task as the administrators of the contributory pension: to deliver pensions accurately and in a timely fashion. As the coverage of the contributory pension spreads, the population covered by the two systems will become more and more similar. The administrators of the contributory system will then become the natural administrators of the non–contributory system as well, because they will be serving an increasingly similar clientele. Right now, however, the contributory pension benefit is not paid throughout the country. In the near term, therefore, it may be more appropriate to distribute the non–contributory pension through the Dibao facilities, which administer poverty relief throughout the country.

Concluding Remarks

The strategy outlined above is intended to provide a pension for everyone, to address problems in the existing system, and to integrate the two.

The strategy is coherent and fits the economy and society of China today. Some elements are directly relevant to the next Five–Year Plan:

putting into place a consistent set of rules for a nationwide system; creating an administrative structure to deliver a "citizen's" pension, and beginning to deliver such a pension; reforming "empty accounts" by introducing an explicit system of NDC individual accounts; extending the mandatory urban system to large firms in rural areas and to public employees; improving the regulation of voluntary pensions and of the asset markets in which they invest; and strengthening the administration so that it can support a national framework.

The strategy is also compatible with longer–term economic and social developments. It begins a process that will eventually cover all workers in all sectors and localities, avoiding the problems of categorical systems (e. g. ill–defined borderlines, people that fall into none of the categories, a person's category changing over time, some categories becoming obsolete, etc.). This arrangement supports efficient labor mobility. It is also compatible with a future move towards funding the individual accounts in the mandatory contributory system if that becomes worthwhile.

More generally, the strategy is compatible with moving towards a high–income country.

Chapter 7 Social Policy*

Tackling Income Inequality

China's economic reforms over the past 30 years have helped to lift more than half a billion people out of poverty. The country has also made great strides on broader measures of "human development", extending beyond income. Poverty nonetheless remains a major issue in China, and the country's social programs remain limited in their range and quality, with many groups (such as migrant workers) largely excluded. In addition, income ine quality has risen rapidly in recent decades, both between urban and rural areas and within them. China's overall Gini coefficient, for example, has increased from about

* This chapter draws mainly on the Background paper no. 15 by Li Shi: "Issues and Options for Social Security Reform in China"; Background paper No. 5 by Nicholas Barr and Howard Glennerster: "Social Policy: A Central Element in China's Development"; Background paper No. 2 by A. B. Atkinson: "Issues in the Reform of Social Policy in China"; Background paper No. 3 by Judith Banister, David E. Bloom, and Larry Rosenberg: "Population Ageing and Economic Growth in China"; Background paper No.19 by Christine Wong: "Public Sector Reforms toward Building the Harmonious Society in China"; and Background paper No. 13 by Santiago Levy: "Some Remarks on Social Policy of Latin America".

0.3 to 0.45, with corresponding increases in both the rural and urban coefficients (See Figure 5) . If not addressed, such disparities risk fueling greater social conflict and instability.

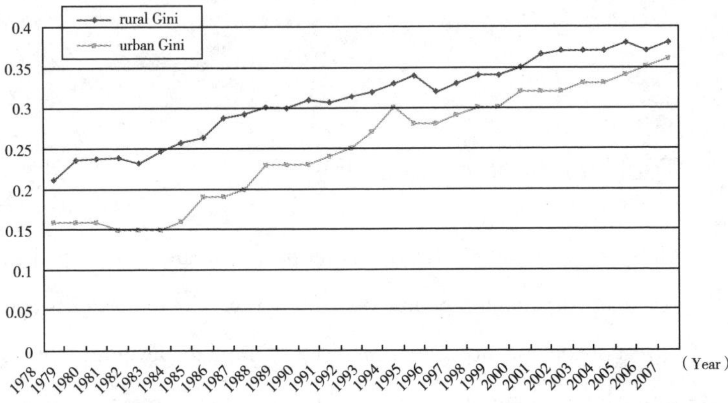

Figure 5 Changes in Income Inequality in Urban and Rural China, 1978—2007

Source: Annual Report of Household Income Distribution in China, 2008.

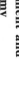

How should policy makers tackle inequality? One option is to suppress it at source: governments can intervene in the market, redirecting the rewards that it bestows. The government could, for example, dramatically raise the minimum wage. However, such measures can introduce damaging distortions into the allocation of resources. While some strengthening of labor market regulations is frequently desirable, the experience of other countries shows that inequality is best reduced through the broad gamut of social policies. In the UK, for example, inequality was reduced from 52 to 31 (as measured by the Gini coefficient) by benefits in cash and in kind, for education and health[1]. A similar reduction was achieved in Sweden and Denmark through cash benefits only. In the United States, inequality was reduced by 20% through social programs. These large gains in equality need not come at great cost to efficiency. In fact, well–designed social policy can raise productivity and growth.

China is certainly very focused on such issues. Both the 11th Five–Year Plan (FYP) and the guidelines for the preparation of the 12th FYP clearly state the government's objective of reducing inequalities and improving social programs. As part of this endeavor to build a harmonious society, the government has introduced several important new policies and programs in recent years, including free rural education, a cooperative medical scheme in rural areas, and a program to guarantee a minimum standard of living for hard–pressed households, But China's social programs remain much smaller relative to GDP than those in high–income countries or even many middle–income countries. Its programs also suffer from limited scope, patchy coverage, a very uneven distribution of benefits, and a lack of portability. Indeed the programs that do exist have mixed implications for inequality. Because their benefits are more generous in the cities than in the rural areas, and in richer rural areas than in poorer ones, they are increasing inequalities between localities even as they may narrow inequalities within a given area.

Social policy can be a powerful instrument to achieve the government's objective of reducing inequality. But to do this the

[1] Background paper No. 5 by Nicholas Barr and Howard Glennerster: "Social Policy: A Central Element in China's Development" .

existing programs require major reforms in their design, scale, and financing, as well as a redistribution of responsibilities between the central and local governments.

Common Principles of Reform[1]

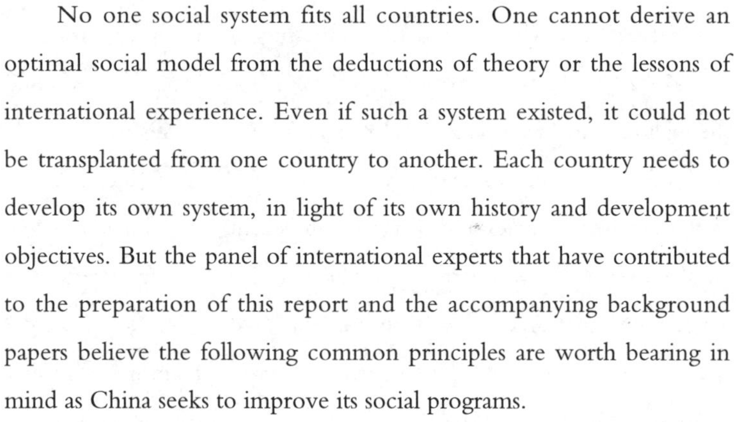

No one social system fits all countries. One cannot derive an optimal social model from the deductions of theory or the lessons of international experience. Even if such a system existed, it could not be transplanted from one country to another. Each country needs to develop its own system, in light of its own history and development objectives. But the panel of international experts that have contributed to the preparation of this report and the accompanying background papers believe the following common principles are worth bearing in mind as China seeks to improve its social programs.

- **Social policymaking must be tightly integrated with economic policymaking.** Social policy and economic policy can complement each other, or conflict with each other. These synergies and frictions should be recognized and accommodated upfront, with a view to maximizing the positive economic effects of social programs. One synergy was starkly illustrated by the world financial crisis. After it struck, many economies benefited from social safety nets, which cushioned the impact and hastened the rebound.

- **Strike the right balance between the market and the state.** The division of labor between the state and the market should be

[1] Background paper No. 2 by A. B. Atkinson: "Issues in the Reform of Social Policy in China" provides a more detailed discussion of these principles.

decided on the basis of rigorous analysis. Before the state intervenes, it should pinpoint the market failure it hopes to correct. And once the state has determined whether to step in, it must then consider how to intervene. Should it provide the service in question, pay for it, regulate it or give people the money to buy it, if they so wish? Answers to these questions can sometimes be gleaned from international experience and theory. For example, the production and distribution of food can be left more or less to the market, guided by regulation. The market cannot, however, reliably provide poverty relief, unemployment insurance, or primary education without substantial government involvement. In other areas, such as pensions and health care, the proper division of labor between the state and the market is less clear–cut. The country will have to make up its own mind in light of its particular circumstances.

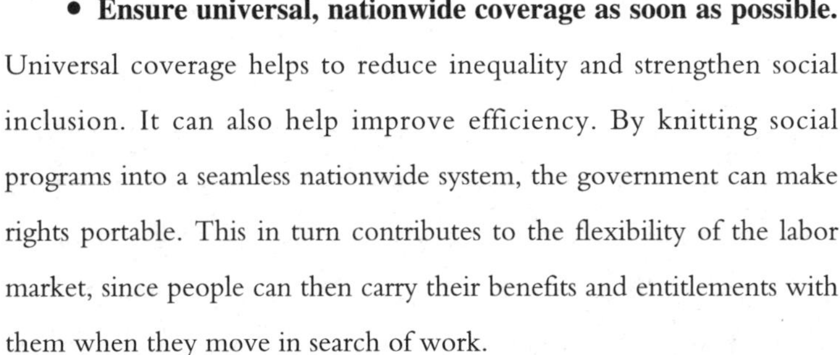

- **Ensure universal, nationwide coverage as soon as possible.** Universal coverage helps to reduce inequality and strengthen social inclusion. It can also help improve efficiency. By knitting social programs into a seamless nationwide system, the government can make rights portable. This in turn contributes to the flexibility of the labor market, since people can then carry their benefits and entitlements with them when they move in search of work.

- **Institutional flaws are best prevented, because they are hard to fix.** Once an institutional structure is in place, people quickly acquire a vested interest in its preservation. The flawed structure then becomes surprisingly resistant to reform, as the US health–care system clearly demonstrates. The design of social programs needs to pay particular attention to the dichotomy between the formal and the informal sectors.

- **Programs should be easy to expand as resources allow.** The size of a social program must, of course, be sustainable in terms of the financial resources available. But the program should also be easily "scalable" , able to grow, without fundamental changes in shape or design, as more resources become available. The resources available depend on a country's fiscal constraints, which themselves depend on the country's economic wherewithal and political disposition. A country with an individualistic ideology and little aversion to risk (such as the US) will tend to support a more parsimonious welfare state, whereas countries that prize solidarity and recoil from risk will support wider and deeper welfare states (e. g. Sweden) .

- **Share the financial burden fairly between the central government, local governments and individuals.** Services should be managed with an optimal level of decentralization, taking into account the nature of the service and the importance of being responsive to local needs. Imposing a fee (if only a small one) on the beneficiaries of the services may also contribute to more optimal utilization. However, many social programs, including primary education, basic health, and poverty relief, have spillover effects on the wider economy and on social cohesion. They qualify as national public goods. In recognition of this, national governments in developed nations have become increasingly involved in the design, financing and monitoring of such programs in recent years. They have established minimum standards of service, provided the resources necessary to meet those standards, and then enforced them from the center.

- **Decide who can best manage and deliver the program.** National programs are sometimes better delivered by provincial or local governments. Sometimes the secret of successful delivery lies outside the government altogether: programs benefit from the engagement of non–governmental organizations, grassroots organizations, and the poor and socially excluded themselves.

- **Make sure the program can be monitored, measured and evaluated.** Too often, governments do not know whether their social programs are succeeding or not. Programs should be designed so that their impact can be measured. Governments must identify the right indicators, collect the necessary figures, and monitor them diligently. They also need to develop a strong research and evaluation capacity.

These broad principles apply to the whole range of social policies and programs. Some of these programs have been discussed in earlier chapters—for example Chapter 5 looked at unemployment insurance and some aspects of education and Chapter 6 examined pension. This chapter will focus on other important social policies and programs, beginning, however, with some further reflections on the critical importance of education to equity as well as economic growth.

Education

The roots of economic inequality in China lie, in substantial part, in education. The rich and poor are divided by large gaps in schooling. They also reap different returns on the educational investments they have made. Making education affordable and accessible is rightly a priority for the government. It has successfully extended primary schooling to almost every child, even in the poorest areas. It has also expanded secondary education. Books are provided without charge to poorer families, who also receive a subsistence grant to defray the opportunity cost of keeping their children in school.

Unless everyone receives a reasonably good education, growth will slow and the economy will develop a "dual" character, with unproductive, unskilled activities coexisting alongside modern, skill–intensive production. This danger is starkly illustrated by the experience of Latin America and, to some extent, Africa, where a poorly educated subgroup of the population struggles to find employment in the modernizing part of the economy. In essence, this subgroup gets left behind. As the richer section of society approaches OECD levels of income, growth will eventually slow down, but poverty will linger. China does not yet have this problem. Its literacy rates are higher than virtually all other developing countries. Nevertheless the risks of slippage in access or quality should not be underestimated.

China has decentralized school finance, forcing each school to rely on local funding. As a result, the wide variation in local economic circumstances is translated into wide differences in school quality. According to economic principles, basic education should be publicly financed on the whole. Theory gives less guidance on whether it should be financed locally or nationally. But in the advanced countries, the central government is taking a growing interest in improving the performance of pupils and narrowing the gaps between them. The leveling up of standards is increasingly seen as a national public good, which cannot be achieved unless the central government devotes substantial funds to education and instills the right incentives in schools.

What does this mean for China? It suggests that if the central government wants to improve standards and close the gaps between pupils, it must commit more of its own resources to supporting education and motivating schools. There are various ways to do this. The government could, for example, offer block grants that take account of a locality's prosperity and population. But to raise the quality of education, this money must have strings attached so that local governments or schools improve the standard of schooling or the performance of pupils.

The experience of other countries suggests that the goal of raising standards can conflict with another worthy aim: keeping children in school for longer. It is harder to maintain high standards over many years of schooling. If there is a trade–off between duration and quality, governments should err on the side of quality. It is important not to extend the length of schooling if that risks reducing the spread of good schooling. If China nonetheless wishes to extend the duration of secondary education, it might profit from studying countries that have created vocational courses for children over 14, who may get "turned off" academic schooling.

China might also benefit from laying more emphasis on pre–school education, as well as the nutrition and care of very young children. According to recent research, the foundations of intellectual as well as social and emotional development are mostly laid by the age of five. Early childhood development is therefore crucial. In response, many countries have passed legislation requiring employers to offer parental leave at the time of birth. They have also expanded pre–school facilities, extended the school day, or linked schools with day–care and after–school facilities that match the varied working hours of parents. Many countries now offer health checks and parental advice through family support centers. Some have also offered cash payments to parents who vaccinate their children or keep their children in school.

Human capital is crucial to China's economic strategy. Safeguarding the welfare and intellectual development of children represents one of the best investments in human capital. It would therefore seem appropriate to gradually extend pre–school facilities in China as resources allow. In the medium term, China might also consider following the lead of many other countries by introducing child benefits: a weekly cash payment per child, frequently paid to the mother, often regardless of income.

Health

China's health–care system was once a leading example of comprehensive coverage, especially for a country at its stage of economic development. That is no longer the case. In health, China may have taken the market a stage too far. It gave responsibility for health care to local governments with meager resources. Its old system of primary–care clinics largely collapsed, taking preventive health care with it. Hospitals became the dominant providers of health care at much higher costs. As a result, progress in health has slowed, the private costs of health care have risen dramatically (even for those who are insured) and inequalities in income have been transmitted to inequalities in health.

These problems have not escaped the government's notice. Since

1998, it has introduced various reforms, including compulsory medical insurance for urban workers, a basic insurance scheme for other city-dwellers, and a new cooperative medical scheme for rural residents. These moves are all welcome, but worries still remain. Access to health care remains very unequal, varying by location, work status, and age. Hanging over many people is the possibility of catastrophic medical bills, relative to their incomes. Primary and preventive care, which could cut costs and reach the whole population, is neglected. The finance of hospitals is complex and focused on inputs rather than outcomes. The rural health-care initiative is clearly a move in the right direction. But it still saddles its beneficiaries with significant out-of-pocket payments, relative to their incomes, if they fall seriously sick.

Any discussion of health care must begin from an essential analytical distinction between finance and delivery. Almost every advanced country has adopted some form of collective finance of health care, and increasingly the money comes from taxes rather than employers. Many countries have also introduced and increased co-payments, or user charges, but their aim is more to cut costs, by discouraging irresponsible use of services, than to raise money.

This international practice chimes with economic theory, which suggests that health-care finance should be mostly public. This is particularly true for health insurance. The reason is that health risks differ across people and time. Purely private insurance provision always goes in the direction of segmenting the market by risk category. That is how you make money in insurance underwriting. The effect is to make insurance and hence certain kinds of care unaffordable or unavailable for those who are high risk at birth, and those who become high risk later in life (after suffering an episode of cancer for example) . Even worse, if health care is closely related to employment, as in the US, then those with higher health risk lose access to health insurance and health care, whenever they quit an employer or lose their job. Further, they may have trouble finding employment if their health risk is high.

But public finance does not necessarily imply public delivery. In the UK and Scandinavia, delivery is mainly public, but in Canada it is mainly private, and in France and Germany, it is a mix. However health care is delivered, there is also wide agreement that good primary care is the best way to promote health, prevent illness, and control acute medical costs.

There is a powerful case for China to show more ambition in health care. International experience suggests it should consider moving to a system that is more uniform, universally available and largely tax–financed. It needs to reform hospital management to contain costs and it could also benefit from sharpening incentives for good professional practice, by measuring clinical outcomes, waiting times, and compliance with quality standards. The government's health targets should be raised, its spending increased. Although health outlays have grown consistently in recent years, they are still low by international standards. Consideration could also be given to having a private component to the health delivery system to create at least some competition and consumer choice.

The Dibao Program

Better health care and education will help alleviate some of the poverty that still persists in China, despite the dramatic reductions in poverty since the end of the 1970s. But the government is not relying on such programs alone. In the late 1990s, it introduced the Dibao program, which guarantees a minimum standard of living to eligible persons. Extended to rural areas in 2005, the program now benefits about 70 million people (See Table 3) .

Table3 Urban and Rural Population Supported by MLSG in China, 2000—2008 (million)

	2000	2001	2002	2003	2004	2005	2006	2007	2008
Urban	4.0	11.7	20.6	22.5	22.1	22.3	22.4	22.7	23.3
Rural	3.0	3.0	4.1	3.7	4.9	8.3	15.9	35.7	43.1

Source: Ministry of Civil Affairs of China: Statistical Report of China's Social Development in 2008.

Poverty relief can contribute to economic efficiency, as well as equity. Investments in schooling, for example, will go to waste if pupils are distracted by hunger. Moreover, economic development will face greater resistance if those dislocated by it have no safety net to catch them, as policy makers in Central and Eastern Europe discovered when they liberalized their economies. A further strong conclusion from the theory of fiscal federalism is that welfare for the poor should not be financed locally. This is partly because poor localities have fewer resources, but also because localities are vulnerable to common shocks, such as the closure of a major industrial enterprise, which touch everyone.

This suggests a number of areas for improvement in the Dibao program, if it is to be the backbone of China social-assistance program for the future. Coverage of the program needs to be extended to all those eligible, including migrant workers and those in the informal sector. Eligibility should be determined more rigorously, benefits simplified, and inconsistencies in implementation ironed out. The Dibao standard must also be set more systematically, based on a more accurate assessment of poverty, which keeps pace with the cost of living. To make the program fair across regions, the central government should consider playing a bigger role in paying for it. Implementation, however, should involve all levels of government, the grassroots administration, and communities. To track the execution of the program and assess its impact, a monitoring framework should also be established.

Population Policy

China's population is aging. The proportion of the population aged 15–64, which grew rapidly over the past few decades, has reached its peak and is slated to decline quickly in the coming decades. According to demographic projections more than 30% of the population will be 60 or over by 2050[1]. The roots of population aging in China are the same as elsewhere: a low fertility rate, rising life expectancy, and the cumulative effect of past changes in birth and death rates. Another central factor in China is the one–child policy.

There is widespread concern in China that these future

---

❶ See Background paper No. 3 by Judith Banister, David Bloom and Larry Rosenberg: "Population Ageing and Economic Growth in China", Executive Summary.

demographics will damage growth and impose a heavy burden on the working population. China is not alone in this. Similar worries can be found in other aging societies. China might therefore consider some of the policy responses other countries have identified. These include policies to raise the retirement age, help those caring for children to work, increase the labor–force participation of women, and raise the productivity of the people remaining in the workforce. If implemented, such measures would go a long way to offset the economic consequences of an aging society.

An easing of the one–child policy is not essential to preserve economic growth in China. But such a change would allow the working–age population to rise gradually as a proportion of the whole. More importantly, an easing might help reverse the highly skewed ratio of males to females in the Chinese population. This ratio reflects selective prenatal abortions and the neglect, or worse, of girl babies. It prevents millions of men from marrying and leaves them bereft of the support of a spouse, children or grandchildren in their old age.

Overall Planning and Governance of Social Policy

The government's initiatives under the 11th Five–Year Plan are consistent with many of the principles proposed by the panel of international experts assembled for this report. But it is also clear that much more can and should be done to ensure that China has a well designed, governed and monitored system of social policies that effectively addresses inequality and supports economic growth.

Social policy should be better integrated with economic policy. China gives social policy due importance in its 11th FYP and in the guidelines for the 12th FYP and it can claim considerable progress towards its social objectives. But Plans themselves are not an adequate mechanism for integrating social and economic policy. While they list guiding principles and development objectives, these lists are not backed up by strong policy content. The Plan's legal status is unclear and it carries insufficient weight with the line ministries and provinces responsible for implementing policies. Moreover, the situation on the ground in China is changing rapidly, requiring more frequent monitoring. To integrate social and economic policy during the next plan period, China should consider alternative mechanisms. These alternatives should effectively translate broad objectives into specific action plans at national, provincial and local levels, with clearly defined indicators to monitor performance.

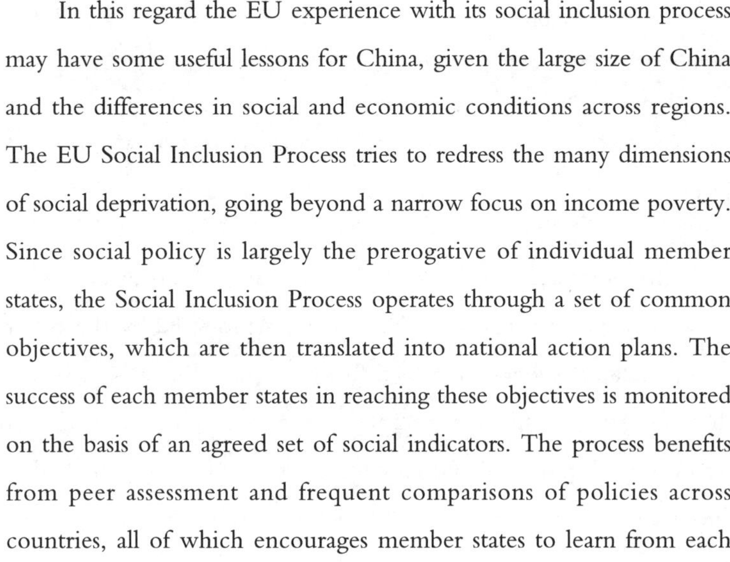

In this regard the EU experience with its social inclusion process may have some useful lessons for China, given the large size of China and the differences in social and economic conditions across regions. The EU Social Inclusion Process tries to redress the many dimensions of social deprivation, going beyond a narrow focus on income poverty. Since social policy is largely the prerogative of individual member states, the Social Inclusion Process operates through a set of common objectives, which are then translated into national action plans. The success of each member states in reaching these objectives is monitored on the basis of an agreed set of social indicators. The process benefits from peer assessment and frequent comparisons of policies across countries, all of which encourages member states to learn from each other. Progress is tracked with commonly defined social indicators, applied to internationally comparable data. This makes it possible to cross–check a nation's assessment of its own performance. A similar process may be useful to monitor effectiveness of social policy in difference provinces or regions in China.

China's social programs remain fragmented and partial. Although their coverage has increased, they still serve the formal labor force in urban China far better than any other slice of the population. Many programs leave out the large rural population, or the growing number of migrants and other workers in the informal sector, who account for about half of the urban labor force. As the government expands programs, it tends to take a piecemeal approach, adding schemes to cover discrete groups in need of support, such as landless farmers or rural migrants. This approach fails to pool risks efficiently. More importantly, it limits the portability of entitlements and impedes the mobility and flexibility of labor. It would be better to cover these new groups under existing schemes.

China can afford to scale up its social programs. Compared with other countries, China's government currently spends significantly less in this area. For example, its budgetary outlay on education (3.2% of GDP) is far below that of Vietnam, or the average lower middle–income country, let alone the OECD (See Figure 6) . China's public spending on health, at 1.8% of GDP, is also well below most lower middle–income countries (See Table 4) [1]. China's fiscal position is

[1] Data on education and health spending come from Background paper No. 19 by Christine Wong: "Public Sector Reforms toward Building the Harmonious Society in China" .

very strong by international standard and it could spend much more on health, education and other social priorities.

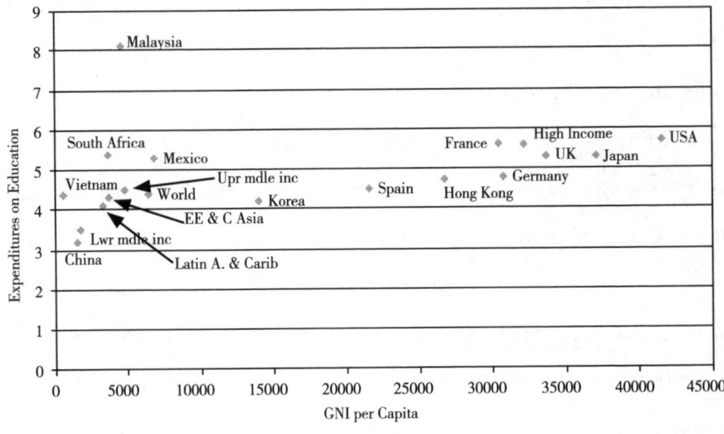

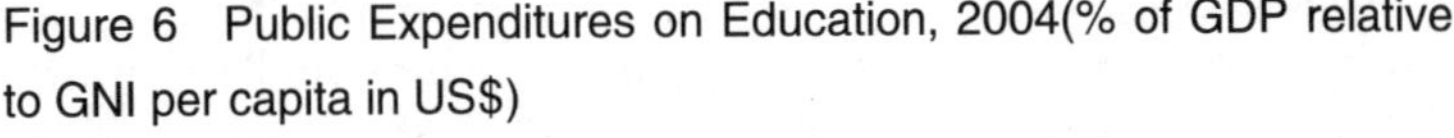
Figure 6 Public Expenditures on Education, 2004(% of GDP relative to GNI per capita in US$)

Source: Dahlman, Zeng and Wang, The Challenge of Life Long Learning for Education Finance in China; paper prepared in 2006 for conference organized by Ministry of Finance and World Bank.

Table 4 Public Expenditures on Health, China and Comparator Countries/Regions

Countries/Economies/Regions	1990—1998 年 *	2005 年
CHINA	2.0	1.8
High income	6.2	7.0
Middle income	3.1	2.9
Lower middle income		2.2
Low income	1.3	1.2
Low and middle income countries in:		
East Asia & Pacific	1.7	1.8

Continuation table

Countries/Economies/Regions	1990—1998 年 *	2005 年
Europe & Central Asia	4.0	4.1
Latin America & Caribbean	3.3	3.3
Middle East & North Africa	2.4	3.0
South Asia	0.8	0.9
Sub-Saharan Africa	1.5	2.6

* Data are for the most recent year available in period.

Source: World Bank, World Development Reports 1998—2006, and 2008 World Development Indicators.

China has devolved responsibility for most basic services to lower levels of government. This devolution is understandable in such a vast country, overseen by a relatively small central-government machine. But in keeping with the traditional Chinese principle of local self-reliance, China has taken it further than any advanced country and most developing ones. As a result, poorer areas, especially in the countryside, have far less to spend on their social programs. Indeed the government spends almost four times as much on social welfare in urban areas as it does in rural areas, although the urban population is smaller than the rural population. If China wants to ensure national minimum standards, in education or health, for example, its central government must provide more significant funding, as well as setting standards and motivating local agencies to meet them.

The central government should play a greater role in the design, financing and monitoring of social programs. But its capacity to play that role must first be strengthened. China cannot move to national systems until it builds the administrative capacity to support such systems. As the central government's role expands, the responsibilities of other levels of government must adjust accordingly. And their capacity must match their new duties.

Assuming the state apparatus is able to deliver social programs, officials must also be willing to make them work. Their incentives must be aligned with the overall objectives of the programs they are implementing. This will require better gathering and sharing of information on a program's performance and results. It may also include consultations with the public, who are, after all, the intended beneficiaries of social programs. It is often the people themselves who are the best judge of whether or not policies are "putting people first" .

Chapter 8 China's Role in the Global Economy*

Like the other post-war examples of catch-up growth, China's economic success was made possible by globalization, including the confluence of lower tariffs, cheaper transport, and frictionless communications. The open global economy provided two critical ingredients for China's growth: knowledge and markets. China absorbed technology, knowhow and ideas from the rest of

* This chapter draws on a number of Background papers, including Background paper No. 1 by K. Y. Amoako: "What African Countries Expect from China?" ; Background paper No. 8 by Barry Eichengreen: "What Kind of Economic and Financial Leadership does the World Expect of China?" ; Background paper No. 7 by Andrew Crockett: "China's Role in the World Economy: Looking forward to the 12th Five-Year Plan" ; Background paper No. 9 by Mohammed A. EL-Erian and Ramin Toloui: "What Does the World Expect from China, and What Should China Provide?" ; Background paper No. 16 by Jean Pisani-Ferry: "China and the World Economy: A European Perspective" ; and Background paper No. 18 by Andrew Sheng: "China's Approach to Networked Globalization—an Institutional Response" ; as well as the Commission for Growth and Development (Chairman: Michael Spence) 2009 "Post-Crisis Growth in Developing Countries" .

the world, assimilating this knowledge and, in many cases, adding to it. This learning contributed to rapid gains in productivity, enlarging the supply–side powers of its economy. But supply is of no use without demand, and China also took full advantage of deep global markets, which provided a reliable outlet for the fruits of its industrial revolution. Even as China has benefited handsomely from globalization, it has also contributed hugely to it. Its outward turn, culminating in its accession to the World Trade Organization (WTO) in December 2001, warrants a chapter in the annals of globalization all by itself.

Having recently surpassed Japan as the second largest national economy, China's economy is now of systemic significance. Its growth has a sizeable impact on global relative prices, ranging from commodities to manufactured goods. The deployment of its foreign–exchange reserves, the largest in the world at 2.85 trillion dollars, also has a significant impact on the global financial system. In addition, China is playing a growing and crucial role in a multitude of developing countries, by virtue of its demand for their goods and its investments in their assets, especially their natural resources. The remarkable post–crisis recovery in the developing countries is due in no small measure to China's resurgent growth and its longstanding openness.

The aftermath of the Financial Crisis

The open, global economy that underpinned China's success has just suffered its biggest shock since the Great Depression. The financial crisis of the past three years was the result of debt–fuelled asset inflation, resulting in excess consumption, deficient savings and persistent current–account deficits. This process came to a "sudden stop" in the fall of 2008, causing great damage to balance sheets throughout the economy and in many parts of the world. The damage quickly spread to the real economy via drops in consumption, investment, employment, and of course trade. The epicenter was the US financial sector. But the disaster was rapidly transmitted far beyond US shores, leaving no country untouched.

The balance sheets of America's households and banks are still under repair, even as the US government is rapidly adding to its debt. It is true that credit spreads in US financial markets have narrowed and growth has resumed. But even with the Federal funds rate near zero, output has not rebounded as vigorously as many people hoped. And what growth there has been has created surprisingly few jobs. Nine percent of the labor force remain unemployed in us, and the figure would rises to over 16% if you add everyone who takes a full–time job when it available, but who now works part–time or has given up looking for a job altogether. The longer high unemployment persists, the more analysts wonder whether the divergence between growth and employment may have deep structural causes, reflecting the rising competitiveness of major emerging economies in a subset of the global supply chain.

The Euro area, for its part, has suffered from repeated bouts of instability caused by the sovereign–debt woes of some of its members. The European Union's institutions have stepped in to help these countries meet their immediate financing needs. But there remains the threat of a debt restructuring in one form or another. That cannot disappear until the EU faces the politically difficult decision of how to share the burden among its members.

The advanced countries, which account for about two–thirds of global GDP (measured at market exchange rates), are likely to face an extended period of slower growth and, in many places, stubbornly high unemployment. Many emerging economies, by contrast, have weathered the storm remarkably well. They benefited from prudent macroeconomic policies and strong, heavily regulated financial sectors that steered clear of toxic assets.

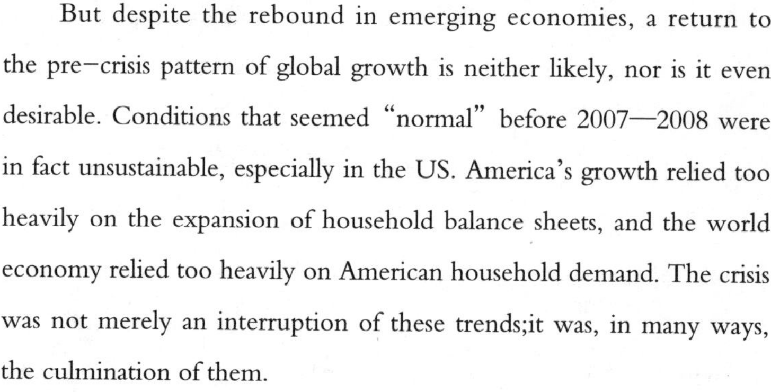

But despite the rebound in emerging economies, a return to the pre–crisis pattern of global growth is neither likely, nor is it even desirable. Conditions that seemed "normal" before 2007—2008 were in fact unsustainable, especially in the US. America's growth relied too heavily on the expansion of household balance sheets, and the world economy relied too heavily on American household demand. The crisis was not merely an interruption of these trends;it was, in many ways, the culmination of them.

So the global economy needs to move to a "new normal". But what kind of "new normal" will emerge? This is difficult to predict, because it is still very much a work in progress. It will be influenced by the choices governments make as they exit from the crisis, revive demand, reform their financial systems, contend with protectionist pressures, squabble over exchange rates and trade imbalances, and confront structural impediments to growth hidden by the pre–crisis dynamics. The new normal is, then, something to build, not just something to predict. China, by adapting its growth pattern and exercising its new influence in multinational policymaking, will be one of its architects.

The Realignment of the World Economy

The implosion of the advanced economies and the resilience of the emerging markets have hastened the ongoing realignment of the global economy. As the US struggles to recover from debt exhaustion, it has turned inwards, devoting less energy to global issues that require cooperation and compromise, including trade talks and the international dimensions of financial reform. With luck, its focus on these international issues will increase, as its domestic economy improves. Europe is a natural champion of global governance. But it too faces domestic economic challenges and its economic significance in the global economy is diminishing. Japan's relative position in the global economy is also declining and it has usually refrained from playing a prominent role in the management of the world economy and the global financial system.

On the other hand, a number of emerging economies have reached critical economic mass, giving them greater influence on the rest of the world economy and even a measure of insulation from it troubles. China's economy, in particular, is now of systemic significance (See Figures 7 to 9 on shares of global GDP and exports). It is no longer merely a "price–taker" in the world economy. Its asset purchases have a material impact on yields. Its appetite for oil, iron, copper, and so on has a marked effect on commodity markets. Its manufacturing output puts downward pressure on the relative prices

of those goods and the relative wages of the people who make them. From being a marginal player, China has become central to the world economic and financial system. Therefore Chinese economic policies and performance have a significant impact on other countries including both developed and developing. As a consequence, they also expect to see the leadership of China.

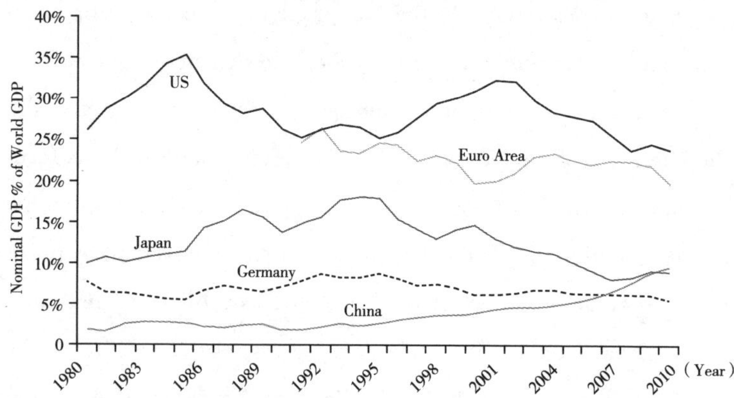

Figure 7 Shares of Global GDP at Current Exchange Rates

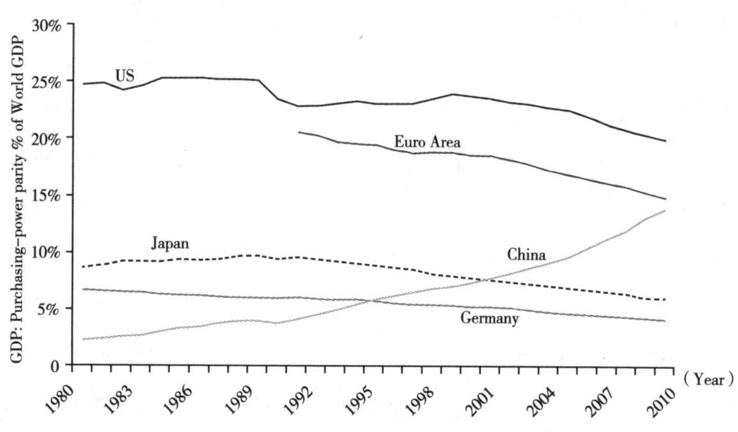

Figure 8 Shares of Global GDP in PPP Terms

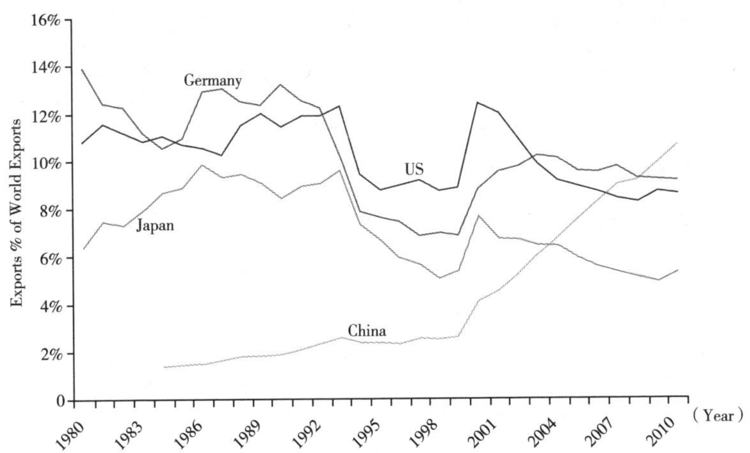

Figure 9 Exports as a Share of World Exports

Source of Figure 7 to 9: IMF.

Having achieved critical mass, the emerging economies now appear capable of growing at a healthy pace despite the slow recovery and lingering instability in the advanced countries. This is partly the result of their increased size. But it is also attributable to a shift in the composition of demand in these economies. As their incomes have risen, several emerging economies have become sizeable and attractive markets in their own right. A related element is the rising trade between emerging economies. A whole range of countries, from Korea to India, now count China as a big, and in many cases the biggest, trading partner.

This new pattern, absent even 10 years ago, has increased the resilience and economic independence of emerging markets. It does not, however, represent complete decoupling. The advanced countries are still an important component of external demand. To get a sense of how important, suppose the advanced countries were to suffer another downturn (an unlikely scenario, but certainly a possible one) . It is hard to imagine that the emerging economies would escape unscathed.

As their reliance on the advanced countries has diminished, the emerging economies' dependence on China has increased. If China's growth were to slow sharply, the other developing economies would immediately feel the effects. It is of no secret, for example, that a key ingredient in the restoration of Latin American growth has been trade with China.

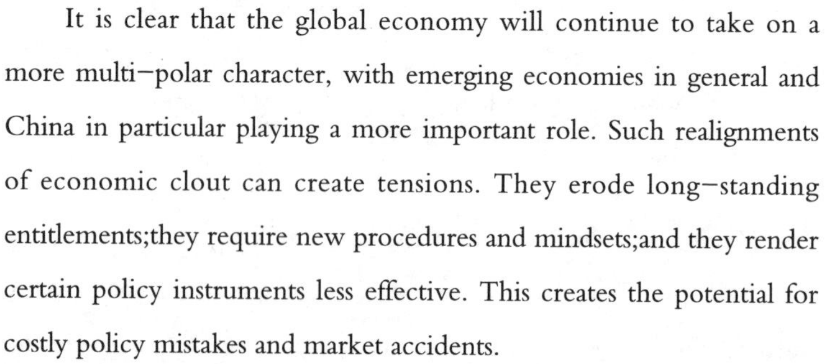

It is clear that the global economy will continue to take on a more multi–polar character, with emerging economies in general and China in particular playing a more important role. Such realignments of economic clout can create tensions. They erode long–standing entitlements;they require new procedures and mindsets;and they render certain policy instruments less effective. This creates the potential for costly policy mistakes and market accidents.

These tensions will be exacerbated by the world economy's multi–speed recovery. Countries growing at different rates may pursue inconsistent policies. Lagging economies may try to revive growth with unconventional policies, such as quantitative easing. Faster–growing economies may respond with unconventional policies of their own, including macro–prudential regulations and capital controls. A multi–speed recovery also raises the threat of escalating protectionism, as political sentiment in countries suffering from high unemployment turns hostile to trade.

Since the Second World War, the United States's position as the world's leading economic power has carried with it a number of privileges and responsibilities. It has been expected to provide what are often referred to as global public goods. These have included:

- Acting as a consumer of last resort
- Helping on occasion to co–ordinate macroeconomic policies through agreements such as the Plaza Accord
- Providing a reserve currency
- Acting as a lender of last resort in a financial crisis, providing liquidity to emerging markets short of dollars
- Helping to lead global trade talks and supporting multilateral institutions, such as the WTO

The US economy's weight in the world is declining and its capacity to perform these roles was significantly damaged by the crisis. It would struggle, for example, to resume its role as consumer of last resort. With the erosion of the US's dominant role, it is far from clear how these critical global public goods will be provided in the future. The world now faces the prospect of a period of leaderless global governance just at a time when major global issues—including rebalancing and restoring global aggregate demand, promoting global trade and investment, and combating climate change—require urgent and collective attention.

Some now expect China to shoulder global responsibilities commensurate with its new economic weight. But despite the size of China's economy, its per capita income is still relatively low. It is home to millions of people who have yet to leave the countryside and enter the modernizing economy. Because China is still a relatively poor country, and it cannot afford to take anything else other than its responsibilities. It is preoccupied with its domestic agenda, and would prefer to defer any responsibility for the global system until it reaches higher income levels. There is perhaps no historical precedent for an economy that attains such systemic significance at such an early stage in its own development.

Rebalancing Global Demand

Of the global duties the US now struggles to perform, the most pressing is that of consumer of last resort. The rebalancing and restoration of global demand in the medium term is much discussed within the G20, but it has not really gotten underway.

As a result of higher savings in the US, global aggregate demand is deficient. The US believes it cannot restore full employment without raising its net exports. Reviving America's export industries will entail some awkward supply–side adjustments, as resources leave the construction industry and enter tradable sectors. In making these adjustments, the US might draw inspiration from Germany, which has enjoyed an export boom thanks to impressive wage restraint and admirable productivity gains. But supply–side adjustments are only part of the story. As a matter of arithmetic, the US cannot raise its net exports unless the rest of the world increases its combined demand.

With their aging demographics, Europe and Japan are unlikely to do much to revive global demand (although a reduction in Germany's large current–account surplus would help) . The world is therefore looking to Brazil, Russia, India and China (the so–called BRICs) . The onus is falling on China in particular to do more to stimulate consumer spending and reduce its current–account surplus. This is consistent with the new growth pattern that China is itself keen to promote, so there is no fundamental conflict of objectives. The disagreements have more to do with the means of adjustment and the speed, with China's critics urging it to cut its surplus faster. It is, however, important to note that no one would benefit if hasty efforts to cut China's excess savings jeopardized its stability and growth. This point is often overlooked in international commentary.

Some critics of China's current–account surplus seem to believe that trade is a zero–sum game, in which one country's gain is another's loss. This line of thinking shows little grasp of the substantial external benefits of China's growth. But although such critics are ill–informed, they can be influential in political circles. Their complaints might sour the politics of international trade and foreign investment, including cross–border acquisitions and technology transfer. However, once the discussion gets beyond the mistaken perception of a zero–sum game, China's interests and the rest of the world's are largely aligned. China should narrow its surplus, because it would benefit its own economy, as well as the broader global economy.

Rebalancing China

Combined with substantial FDI and other less desirable capital inflows, China's current–account surplus is contributing to large increases in foreign–exchange reserves. For a country at China's level of development, it is wasteful to devote as much as 10% of GDP in some years to the accumulation of foreign assets. Most of these reserves are held in US Treasuries. Given the US's fiscal profile and prognosis, these assets are vulnerable to inflation and further depreciation of the dollar. They would seem to offer high risks, for low returns. That said, as a byproduct of its policy of managing the appreciation of the renminbi, China's accumulation of reserves may bring wider benefits to China beyond the coupon on a Treasury bond.

China's surplus reflects its high savings and its prodigious exports. But exports are likely to be a less powerful engine of growth in the future, as China's traditional markets in the advanced economies endure a period of protracted stagnation. One country's exports can, of course, grow faster than the overall market. But that would mean further enlarging China's market share, which might create tensions with its trading partners in both advanced and developing countries. Even if a large trade surplus were in China's interest, all else equal, it would cease to be so if it provoked a damaging trade war.

China should, therefore, rely less on developed markets and more on emerging markets—including especially its own. Beyond the fiscal stimulus of its crisis response, China would benefit from making maximum use of the domestic market to drive growth. This would not be to the exclusion of the evolving export sectors, but rather in addition. It is prudent at this stage to diversify as much as possible across markets to spur economic transformation and mitigate the risks to growth.

In fact, one of the objectives of China's 11th Five-Year Plan (2006—2010) was to achieve a basic balance between export and import. The critical question is how should it do so? One school of thought regards China's surplus and its exchange rate as closely tied. This view

is quite widespread, as reflected in numerous recent commentaries by influential analysts and journalists. They think of the exchange rate as the principal cause of the surplus and the main policy instrument for dealing with it. In their view, a stronger renminbi would be sufficient to eliminate the surplus.

While the exchange rate is relevant to restoring external balance without impairing growth, it is not sufficient. In fact it isn't even the main event. China's previous round of exchange rate appreciation from 2005 to 2008 was accompanied by an expansion in the current-account surplus rather than the reverse. Many outside commentators simply conclude that the appreciation was not fast enough. But they underestimate the structural changes China must undergo if it is to contain its excess saving. That excess saving has deep roots (just as the US saving shortfall has deep roots)—it is not an exchange rate issue alone.

Unless China's policies change the structural parameters of income, consumption and savings, a further strengthening of the exchange rate may not help. Nonetheless, there is a good argument for an appreciation as part of an overall program to increase consumption and upgrade the industrial structure, while maintaining internal balance. A stronger yuan would create pressure for beneficial microeconomic and structural changes in the tradable sectors of the economy. It would also slow the accumulation of reserves and probably help prevent overheating of the domestic economy.

China's real exchange (properly measured) is rising much faster than its nominal rate, because wages in some of China's export sectors are rising faster than productivity. This is a beneficial change. Higher wages should help to boost consumption, weaning the economy off its dependence on investment and exports. On the supply side of the economy, higher wages will impel productivity to catch up, shifting the economy towards higher value–added activities.

China fears that a decline in the competitiveness of export–oriented manufacturing will undermine the job creation needed to support migration from rural to urban areas. International experience, particularly in Latin America, suggests that China is right to be concerned about a pattern of growth and development that leaves large numbers of people stranded outside the modernizing part of the economy. But no one inside or outside of China thinks the country's long–term future lies in low value–added manufacturing processing. As incomes rise, this sector will move inland (assuming the country's infrastructure allows it) and then decline. In economies like Korea's, which have successfully navigated the route from middle–income to high–income, the domestic market grew in importance as the economy's purchasing power increased. As the growth of export jobs slowed, industries serving the domestic market contributed a bigger share of new employment.

As discussed in earlier chapters, China should therefore give priority to (1) the expansion and integration of the domestic economy and (2) education (increasing its quantity and quality) . By fostering the domestic market, China will create fresh sources of demand for labor. And by increasing the quality and quantity of education, it will give its people the skills they need to thrive in higher value–added industries. This would relieve the exchange rate of the burden of preserving the labor–intensive export sector.

Promoting Global Trade and Investment

If China agrees to narrow its surplus, it will also derive an indirect benefit. By doing its bit to restore global demand, it will strengthen the cause of free trade and multilateral co–operation, which benefit China and other countries enormously in the long run. It is in the interest of all countries, but especially China, to preserve an open global trading and investment system.

China went to great lengths to gain membership of the World Trade Organization in 2001. It now has a big stake in preserving the credibility of the WTO as the guardian of an open trading system. It is therefore important for China, and indeed all member countries, to abide by the WTO's rules and dispute–settlement mechanisms. It is widely, and probably correctly, believed that multilateral trade liberalization can quickly shift into reverse if forward momentum is not maintained. Given the role of open trade in China's development strategy, few countries have a greater interest in combating protectionist tendencies.

In practice, China's record of trade liberalization is generally good. This is not to say, however, that there are no areas of concern. Issues that merit continued attention include (i) intellectual property rights, which are not always enforced as vigorously as they should be; (ii) export incentives, in the form of tax rebates in certain industries; (iii) hidden subsidies for the exports of state–owned enterprises, and (iv) energy subsidies which often create distortions that hamper growth in the longer term. In general, since China's economy still has a substantial element of central planning, the government has an additional need to demonstrate that export prices reflect true costs.

The rules and policies that govern international investment are also coming under greater scrutiny. As far as possible, China should allow market forces to determine the allocation of investment, both within and across borders. Not only does capital mobility permit savings to travel across borders, it also facilitates the transfer of managerial and technological knowhow.

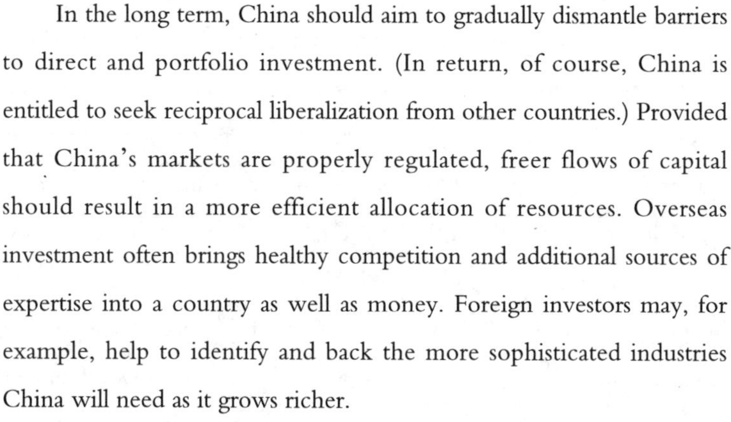

In the long term, China should aim to gradually dismantle barriers to direct and portfolio investment. (In return, of course, China is entitled to seek reciprocal liberalization from other countries.) Provided that China's markets are properly regulated, freer flows of capital should result in a more efficient allocation of resources. Overseas investment often brings healthy competition and additional sources of expertise into a country as well as money. Foreign investors may, for example, help to identify and back the more sophisticated industries China will need as it grows richer.

However, in circumstances like the present, capital inflows can be excessive and destabilizing. The surge of foreign portfolio investment in emerging economies in 2010 represents one of the distortions introduced by the West's response to the crisis: investors are fleeing rock–bottom yields at home in search of richer pickings abroad. In these circumstances, governments have every right to intervene to curb capital flows in order to keep control of inflation and asset prices. But a commitment to the goal of gradual liberalization, backed up by regular steps in this direction, would provide a valuable signal, both to domestic industry and to external trading partners.

China is not only a favored destination for inward investment, but also a growing source of outward investment. Its large trade surplus, coupled with substantial inflows of portfolio capital, has given China the financial means to make large overseas investments. Thus far, the bulk of this has been in the form of liquid claims on governments (particularly US Treasury securities) . But, for understandable reasons, China is seeking a higher return on its foreign assets. Unfortunately, its attempts to diversify into longer–term equity–type assets have provoked protectionist reactions in receiving countries. These reactions are mostly unjustified, but it will be important for Chinese policy not to give cause for legitimate concern. Such concerns could arise if it was believed that foreign investments were motivated by political and strategic, rather than commercial, considerations. Overseas acquisitions by state–owned enterprises are likely to encounter particular resistance, because these companies remain under the control of the Chinese government. Over time, China can alleviate some of these concerns by making sure its investment decisions conform to commercial criteria that are clearly specified and communicated to host countries. Singapore, which makes substantial equity investments through its sovereign–wealth fund without much controversy, shows that this can be done.

When foreign investment brings managerial control, particular care is required. China should be prepared to demonstrate that such control has a clear commercial rationale. Its investments in the raw materials of emerging and developing countries also require tact. Such investments are a legitimate outlet for a country's excess savings, but they should not bring privileged access to natural resources at the

expense of other countries. In other words, control of the sources of raw materials should not interfere with the principle that commodities are sold into a global market, supplying all customers at a more or less uniform price. This is an important principle that should be supported by the collective voice of the G20.

The IMF now hosts a dialogue between sovereign–wealth funds and the countries in which they invest. China can and should use this vehicle to promote greater acceptance of cross–border investment based on commercial criteria, and to allay exaggerated fears on the part of receiving countries. China can work with financial institutions in receiving countries to identify opportunities for investment that benefit both China and the host country.

Shifting to a Low–Carbon Economy

One of the highest priorities for the global economy over the period of the 12th FYP and beyond will be mitigating climate change and shifting to energy–efficient, low–carbon economies. The effects of climate change are starting to be felt around the globe, not least in China where extreme weather events (floods, droughts, etc) are becoming more frequent, endangering its progress and economic achievements. It is therefore imperative that China give due weight to climate change in formulating its growth strategy. Not doing so would lock China into industrial structures and urban forms that may become significant liabilities in a low–carbon world.

China has already begun an aggressive shift towards a lower–carbon economy. Indeed the transformation of the development pattern discussed in earlier chapters and the energy–efficiency objectives articulated in recent planning documents together represent one of the biggest efforts to reduce emissions by any country. However the 12th FYP will need to flesh out the policies that will achieve these objectives. In particular it will need a strategy for shifting from the use of coal in power generation towards low–carbon fuels.

Given the level of its per capita income, China's per capita emissions are rather high. Brazil, for example, has a much higher income per head of about $8100 at market exchange rates, compared with China's $3,800. And yet Brazil's emissions of 1.9 tons per person are well below China's current level of 4.9 tons. The implication is that China has ample room to increase energy efficiency and lower CO_2 emissions, relative to income, over time without impairing its growth.

China's global partners hope and expect that it will make progress in mitigating climate change. This outside scrutiny can be uncomfortable for China. But it should be able to meet international expectations without compromising its growth strategy, for the following reasons.

- Reducing greenhouse gases and increasing energy efficiency is consistent with the wider rebalancing under way in the Chinese economy (and, for that matter, the rebalancing required at the global level) . Over the medium term, the shift is likely to be beneficial—even essential—for the development of a sustainable economy for the mid 21st century.
- China is in many ways better placed to fight climate change than most other countries at a similar stage of development. It has strong state institutions, which can implement and enforce the targets

that the government sets. It also has strong public finances, which means it can afford to make the necessary public investments.

- Cutting carbon will increase transitional costs on China. But those costs can be minimized if the government shows a clear sense of direction and a credible commitment to future emissions cuts. That will give firms the right signal and sufficient time to plan for costlier carbon. Conversely, the longer China delays, the worse the transitional costs will become, because while it procrastinates, firms will be busy in investing plant and machinery that may be incompatible with a low–carbon future.

- The shift will not compromise energy security and could even enhance it.

These points bear further illustration. Take rebalancing, for example. At a global level, this implies a fall in US imports, including imported industrial products, combined with a shift in China from exports, which are largely industrial goods, towards domestic demand, of which a large proportion should be services. Thus rebalancing should reduce the carbon intensity of the global economy.

Cutting emissions will not, however, be easy. As noted above, China's economy is relatively carbon–intensive for a country at its level of development. This is mainly because industry is such a big part of China's GDP;energy is such an important input for industry ;and coal is such a big component of China's energy production. As a result, it may not be enough for China to improve the energy–efficiency of its current industries ;it may also have to change its industrial mix, moving into less energy–intensive activities.

Such changes will inevitably entail transitional costs. Companies and regions which have depended on coal–intensive industrial production will suffer;and the cost of pow er will probably rise for all users as the economy moves to more expensive, lower carbon energy sources.

The composition of growth will change, but the rate of growth need not slow. Faster expansion in services and higher value–added industrial production can offset the slowdown in more carbon–intensive industries. Even coal–based industrial output could continue to grow, albeit more slowly than in the past, as long as it can reduce energy intensity as quickly as it increases production.

Although the 11th FYP clearly aimed to change China's pattern of growth, it was not entirely successful. China proved to be better at expanding output than at rebalancing it. The 2008 stimulus package did increase social spending, but did not otherwise represent a significant break with China's past growth model. It will therefore be necessary to announce a new course, supported by a set of new policy commitments and instruments, if China is to move towards a low–carbon economy.

To bring about these changes, energy–intensity targets will not suffice. China will also need to create incentives for the economy to adopt low–carbon fuels and less carbon–intensive activities. Market–based instruments—such as carbon taxes, cap–and–trade schemes, or both—could be introduced. They encourage firms and households to reduce carbon as cheaply and conveniently as possible, as well as providing incentives for innovation.

By putting a price on the external costs of energy use, carbon taxes correct an economic distortion, confronting energy users with the full cost of their decisions. This gives carbon taxes great theoretical appeal. They are also comprehensive, falling on anyone who uses carbon throughout the economy. But this is also a major drawback in practice, since carbon taxes inevitably produce a comprehensive range of losers—including everyone who uses electricity. This disadvantage can however be offset:

- The taxes can start at a low level, increasing in stages;or they can begin with limited coverage, which is gradually widened. As long as there is a credible long–term commitment to increase the tax, or broaden its coverage, it can be wise to start small, thereby minimizing the tax's short–term costs while still providing longer–term incentives for appropriate investments.
- A carbon tax should induce a range of novel, and cost–reducing, responses. It would, for example, give impetus to the exploration of unconventional energy sources and to efforts to improve energy efficiency.
- A carbon tax raises revenues which could be used to ease any transitional problems. Compensation could be paid to low–income consumers, for example, to offset higher electricity costs. Subsidies could also be provided for insulation and other energy–conservation measures.

Another policy instrument that could be used—on its own or in tandem with a carbon tax—is a cap–and–trade scheme. By allowing firms to buy and sell the right to emit greenhouse gases, the cap–and–trade system imposes a hard limit on emissions, while allowing great flexibility in how that limit is reached. China's participation in the carbon–credit mechanisms of the Kyoto Protocol has started to lay the

institutional foundations such a system will need to function effectively. Depending on how such a trading scheme is set up, it could also raise revenue through the sale of emissions allowances. Over the medium term, an emissions trading system in China could possibly link to other carbon markets elsewhere in the world, accelerating China's shift to a low-carbon economy.

In addition to putting a price on carbon emissions, China should also consider some more specific measures, such as vehicle-efficiency standards and building codes, as well as zoning laws to combat urban sprawl and demarcate parks and other green areas that might sequester carbon.

Such policies need not compromise China's energy security, for the following reasons:

- By raising prices and efficiency in transport and other sectors, these policies will reduce China's demand for imported fossil fuels, such as oil, thereby easing China's dependence on the insecure regions of the world that produce these fuels.
- China's domestic coal industry has contributed to its national security for many decades. But the sector is already under some strain (as shown by the need for imports in some recent years) and it probably cannot keep pace with China's economic ambitions. China will therefore have to draw on a wider range of resources and use them more efficiently.
- Incentives for the production of alternative fuels (like shale gas) and for greater efficiency will improve the resilience and diversity of the energy sector.

- A shift to more renewable energy would increase China's energy security, because renewable energy can be generated domestically. Nuclear energy also raises few concerns regarding security of supply, not least because nuclear fuel can be readily stockpiled if necessary.
- Cutting carbon will require a number of supporting measures, such as the introduction of smart grids for distributing electricity. Many of these ancillary measures will also improve security, adding to the country's energy efficiency and contributing to the modern infrastructure that an advanced economy will require.

China can therefore cut carbon emissions while preserving energy security. Indeed, a continued dependence on carbon may itself prove risky, and not just environmentally. By mid–century, the world economy may have shifted to a low–carbon model. Goods and services incompatible with that model may be spurned;low–carbon goods prized. China has already shown that it can turn its traditional manufacturing skills to advantage in green industries such as wind and solar power. It could also play a pioneering role in the technologies and industries that will define the low–carbon economy, from carbon capture to electric cars. But China's firms will find it harder to thrive in these industries, if their home market is still wedded to a high–carbon model.

Global Governance

Rebalancing global demand, promoting global trade and investment, addressing climate change and reforming the exchange–

rate system are four of a much longer list of major global issues that developed and developing countries need to address together. These global issues—whether they are economic, social, ecological, or broader issues of security—are increasingly interconnected. But the international institutions that exist to tackle these issues remain patchy and fragmented. Policy makers must work through a loose collection of institutions and ad–hoc committees lacking any coherent design or any consistency in their representation of developing countries. This ungainly architecture has evolved in response to various past events and crises. It is now in urgent need of reform. The world would greatly benefit from China's active participation in discussions on how best to accomplish such reform.

The international frameworks in most obvious need of reform are those governing the world's financial system. Some of the chief tenets of that system have been thrown into question by the financial crisis of the past three years. The turmoil demonstrated that unfettered financial markets are not self–regulating and that their ructions can in fact disrupt the global economy. Although financial markets do have some self–stabilizing properties (greed is tempered by fear;rewards are accompanied by risk ;high prices can be a signal to sell;low prices an invitation to buy) these properties fail, disastrously, if risk is misperceived and mismeasured. A debate is therefore underway in international as well as domestic fora on whether the financial system can be stabilized by incremental changes to current financial arrangements, or whether wholesale change is required.

Emerging markets such as China have every reason to participate in this debate. On the one hand, emerging markets have often suffered

the consequences of global financial disruptions (although much less so on this current occasion) . On the other hand, emerging markets have been among the major beneficiaries of open capital markets and the free flow of investment. Their views deserve to be heard when it comes to striking the right balance between new controls on global finance and preserving the benefits that globalization can bring.

Another question of direct interest to China is how to broaden participation in international economic, decision–making, without making those deliberations too unwieldy and inefficient. As the weight of the emerging economies rises dramatically, Europe's overrepresentation on the board of the IMF and World Bank is increasingly anomalous. That has prompted the IMF in particular to carry out some piecemeal reallocation of votes and voices. It is also important that developing countries be adequately represented in groups such as the Basel Committee on Banking Supervision and the International Accounting Standards Board, which now play a much more important role in global governance. The emergence of the G20 (which also convenes the Financial Stability Board) as a powerful body for international cooperation could well spell changes in the prevailing balance of power among individual countries. But it is too soon to tell if this expanded group of large, systemic countries can be effective in setting international priorities and coordinating policies.

So what will the G20 and other international groupings ask of China? What does the world want of this rising power? At the most general level it wants China to recognize that its domestic policy choices have cross–border repercussions, and to take those repercussions into account when taking decisions. It also wants China

to cooperate with other countries in making mutually advantageous adjustments that might not be advantageous if made in isolation. It wants China to help strengthen the institutions, such as the IMF, that broker such agreements, even as those institutions take steps to accommodate it. But, above all, the rest of the world wants China and the rest of the BRICs to articulate a vision of how the world should accommodate their rise. Without that vision, the rest will not follow.

Beyond this general, shared aspiration, countries differ in their expectations of China. Among developed countries, the US is particularly concerned about its huge trade deficit with China, especially now that it is struggling with high unemployment. In contrast to the US, Europe is a natural champion of global governance. Although the rise of the emerging economies will erode Europe's influence in the Bretton Woods institutions, the gradual emergence of a multi-polar world is otherwise less of a threat. Europe is likely to share China's aspirations for a multi-currency reserve system that includes the euro and the renminbi as well as the US dollar. Europe and China also share an interest in regional integration. The ASEAN Plus Three grouping which includes China, Japan and Korea can perhaps learn from the EU experience. In the coming decade the economic rise of China is likely both to generate friction with Europe and create the potential for fruitful cooperation. The question for policy makers on both sides is how to prevent zero-sum dimensions from dominating and running the show. This requires high-quality dialogue that acknowledges the potential for friction while emphasizing the potential for fruitful cooperation.

Developing countries have a somewhat different interest in

China's active involve ment in global governance. They are keen to learn from China's remarkable development experience. They also appreciate China's reluctance to interfere in the domestic affairs of other countries and its willingness to invest and provide aid without lectures and conditions. They benefit from China's increasing trade, investment and aid and hope that China will not repeat the mistakes of some of the richer countries.

In this regard, developing countries are likely to encourage China to consider[1]:

- Increasing access to its markets for manufactured goods from developing countries. To some extent this will happen automatically as China's domestic market grows and its firms exit the extremely labor-intensive components of global supply chains.
- Encouraging joint ventures between Chinese firms and domestic companies, so that they can acquire technology and knowhow.
- Untying its aid and providing flexible financing.
- Providing support through regional and sub-regional institutions.

Although countries may differ in their expectations of China, almost all are keenly interested in China's domestic policies, because

[1] A more specific account of what African countries would like from China is provided in Background paper No. 1 by K. Y. Amoako "What African Countries Expect from China?"

those policies have an impact on them. As a result, they will read the 12th Five-Year Plan for clues about China's aims and intentions. China should not resent this outside scrutiny. It is, in fact, a compliment. China now attracts the attention that befits an economy of systemic significance and rising importance. The government should feel under no great obligation to seek international approval for its policies. But it should make its economic objectives clear to partner countries (and make its policies consistent with those objectives) .

International experience suggests, however, that it will not be easy for China to play the global role expected of it. The US and Europe (particularly the UK) still dominate global discussions of international finance and other issues, based on their long experience in international policy formulation, and the skills they have built up, not just in core government agencies but in their legislatures and in a broad range of think tanks. Japan by contrast "punches below its economic weight" for a variety of reasons. Japan's method of coordinating its policies internally gives its negotiators little room for maneuver in international negotiations. Because Japan rotates its staff so frequently, they struggle to match the networks of contacts and depth of institutional experience accumulated by their counterparts from some other countries. In addition Japan suffers from a relative shortage of high-quality think tanks and universities supporting international policy work. Finally, Japan suffers from a language barrier, given that international communication puts a premium on English language skills.

To improve its engagement with the global community, China must invest in people: it needs highly trained negotiators and interlocutors with a deep and detailed understanding, not only of

Chinese realities, but also of the realities of other countries. These intermediaries should represent China to the rest of the world, and represent the rest of the world to China: it needs to be a two-way affair. They should be able to present the Chinese case eloquently and convincingly, while also being able to interpret global perceptions and present the international case to the Chinese community clearly, effectively and objectively.

China must also establish international think tanks as interfaces with the rest of the world. These think tanks should enable foreign scholars and policy analysts to work in China and Chinese scholars to work overseas. Staff-exchange programs with international and regional institutions will also be very important. China should also broaden its circle of communications. It needs to talk more with other emerging markets. It also needs to recognize the importance of interacting with a wide range of stakeholders around the world, including governments, the private sector, civil society and community institutions that all have a role to play in global governance.

There will be a time when China and eventually India have global roles similar to those of the United States and Europe now. How the global economy fares when we get there will depend a lot on how these two economic giants deploy their resources and influence. China's transition over the next five years is part of a longer journey to that destination. As it makes this transition, China will have to negotiate, cooperate and occasionally compromise with other countries and international institutions. The valuable lessons it learns during this period will help prepare it for the global responsibilities it will shoulder in the future.

Chapter 9 System Reform*

This report has provided an international perspective on the challenges China will face as it evolves from middle–income into an advanced and prosperous nation. In the coming decade, China's economy must cope with at least five transitions: it must a) change its growth model, as its labor costs rise;b) rebalance demand, from investment and exports to consumption;c) accommodate a rapidly urbanizing population;d) build the social infrastructure necessary for a harmonious society;and e) take on international responsibilities, such as steering the world economy and tackling climate change, commensurate with its growing size and global impact. Few countries have successfully managed this transition;no country of China's size and diversity has ever done so.

China has long recognized these challenges. The need for a new growth model was acknowledged as far back as the 9th FYP and reiterated in successive plans. Hardly any of the issues discussed in the preceding sections were not identified in the 11th FYP, or in recent policy announcements by the senior leaders and the Party Congress.

* The discussion of fiscal reform in this chapter draws on Background paper No. 19 by Christine Wong: "Public Sector Reforms toward Building the Harmonious Society in China" .

But it is easier to recognize these problems than to solve them and, in practice, China has struggled to make many of structural changes envisaged in past plans. Growth is still led by investment and exports, services continue to lag, and, most important, big disparities of income, education and health remain between urban and rural Chinese, and between the coastal and inland regions.

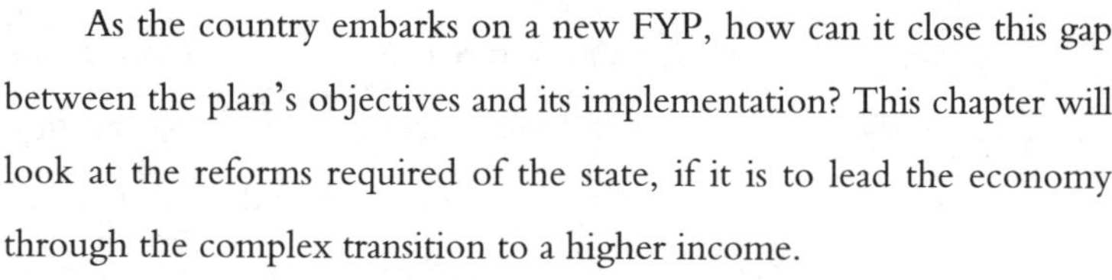

As the country embarks on a new FYP, how can it close this gap between the plan's objectives and its implementation? This chapter will look at the reforms required of the state, if it is to lead the economy through the complex transition to a higher income.

These reforms will require both the central government and sub–national administrations to rethink their roles and strengthen their capacities. The reforms should also extend to the State–Owned Enterprises (SOEs) , which should pay higher dividends and face stiffer competition in the markets they now dominate. China will also have to reform its fiscal arrangements, particularly the division of revenues and responsibilities between the central government, the provinces and the counties. Without reforms in these three areas, the state will struggle to play its part in realizing the ambitions of its development plan.

Enhancing the Effectiveness and Accountability of the Government

International experience suggests that China may have to alter the balance between planning and markets in the years ahead. To realize the plan's objectives, the government will have to draw on a wider range of market–based instruments. It will also have to pay close attention to the incentives faced by governments in the provinces and counties, where the plan's success will ultimately be decided. It may profit from reaching out more to the general public, and from ensuring that high-quality data and information is available to help it monitor progress and appraise its own performance.

Comprehensive Policy Planning

In a centrally planned economy, the government hands down a set of targets, quotas, obligations and entitlements that directly guide the behavior of enterprises and households. In the complex, mixed economy that China has become, planners must find other ways to exert an influence. The key to successful implementation is "policy planning" : that is, translating the plan's objectives into a set of policies that directly and indirectly guide the country's development. These policies can employ a variety of instruments to influence the decisions of market participants, bringing their incentives into line with the plan's aims.

To be successful, these policies cannot be formulated independently of each other;they must fit together as a coherent and internally consistent package. Governments are not monolithic and interpretations of the plan's objectives may differ among ministries and between central and local governments. Policy planning thus requires extensive coordination within the government.

Moreover, since policies cannot be expected to succeed immediately, policy planning must have a 3–5 year horizon. Policies will need to be phased in over time;they may also need revisions and refinements as results appear and circumstances change. Examples

abound in China and the rest of the world of economic policies that worked well for several years but eventually outlived their usefulness. These past successes have often ended up as stumbling blocks for future reform.

Judging by the experience of many countries, planning works best when it relies more on the price and other market–based mechanism. By working with the grain of market incentives, planners can achieve more lasting, sustainable result—and achieve them more efficiently. The next five–year plan, for example, aims to reduce China's consumption of energy per unit of GDP. It will improve its chances of success if it changes the way energy is priced and taxed. (see Box 6) .

Box 6

Energy Efficiency Plan

China's energy efficiency plan, a top priority of the 11th FYP, is impressive in its scope and detail. It comprises five major programs, ranging from the closure of small power plants and obsolete factories to the renovation of industrial boilers. In practice, however, government officials have often felt obliged to meet plan targets by administrative measures, such as arbitrarily cutting off power supply to heavy industry, or closing selected plants temporarily to reduce energy use. Such measures may work in the short term but they are neither efficient nor sustainable. They are, indeed, reminiscent of traditional central planning methods.

In order to meet its energy–efficiency objective, the government needs to rely much more on policy planning. A priority should be reforming energy prices so that they reflect the full costs of supply, including the scarcity value of energy resources and the costs of environmental externalities. At present, electricity prices, for instance, remain heavily regulated and well below generation costs, thereby providing poor signals to industries and consumers. Market prices would discourage waste, and promote energy-saving innovations over the longer term. The government could also rely more on taxes and subsidies to promote the development and dissemination of energy-efficient products.

This kind of planning is analytically demanding. Potential policies must be formulated, compared, monitored and evaluated. None of the issues discussed in this report can be resolved with a single instrument or a short-term fix. There are, moreover, alternative ways of addressing them, each with its own costs and benefits. In choosing between these alternatives, policy makers should be able to draw on a comprehensive analysis of a policy's strengths and weaknesses under a full range of scenarios.

With China's emergence in the world economy, its policy choices also affect other countries. To be fully informed in their policy making, China's leaders will want to know the nature and magnitude of these spillovers.

China's research on specific areas of economic policy is much stronger than it was. But the government still lacks a single agency with the necessary analytical breadth to support policy planning. It needs an internal "think tank" , capable of pulling together the different strands of policy, so that all of the agencies concerned with an issue can base their decisions on a shared body of evidence and analysis. Other countries have benefited from the work of "reform teams" , with the requisite expertise, clout and autonomy (see Box 7) on Reform Teams. International experience indicates that to be effective, such an agency should be free of administrative responsibilities, but enjoy direct access to the highest level decision makers.

Box 7

Reform Teams

The business of "feeling for the stones" in fast-growing economies was often carried out by highly qualified technocrats in small, dedicated "reform teams" . Singapore had its Economic Development Board, Korea had its Economic Planning Board, and Japan had its Ministry of Trade and Industry.

Reform teams were not burdened with administrative duties, but they were given direct access to the top of the government. Malaysia's Economic Planning Unit reported directly to the prime minister. The Council for U. S. Aid in Taiwan, China, which began in 1948 and evolved into the Council for Economic Planning and Development, reported directly to the president. Indeed, several future heads of government sprang from their ranks.

From this unique position—ensconced in government, but distanced from day-to-day administrative burdens and immediate political demands—the reform teams helped coordinate the government's efforts and overcome administrative opposition and inertia.

Although technocrats unchecked by political forces can fail to balance economic with political and social concerns, political forces unchecked by technocratic knowledge can be disruptive.

Source: Commission on Growth and Development (Chairman: Michael Spence) : The Growth Report: Strategies for Sustained Growth and Inclusive Development, p. 28.

Reform of Structure and Roles of Sub–National Governments

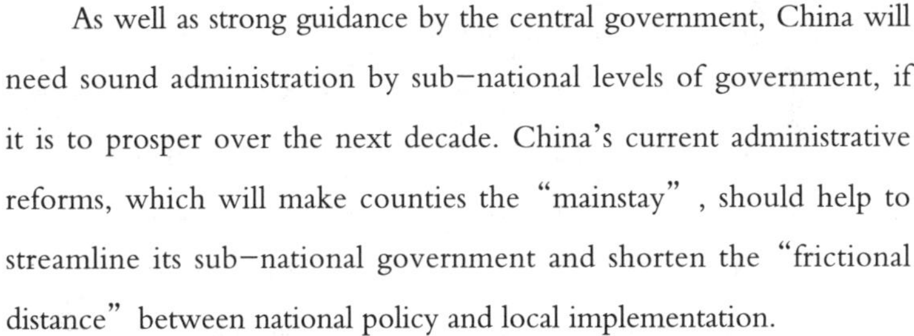

As well as strong guidance by the central government, China will need sound administration by sub–national levels of government, if it is to prosper over the next decade. China's current administrative reforms, which will make counties the "mainstay" , should help to streamline its sub–national government and shorten the "frictional distance" between national policy and local implementation.

But the reforms also run the risk of overburdening provincial and county governments. Provinces may have too many counties to budget for, and counties may have too many schools or medical facilities to supervise. Provinces differ greatly in the size of their population and the number of counties they contain. Counties themselves also vary widely in size, from 31, 000 people to 2.15 million. For this reason, a one–size–fits–all strategy for managing schools, clinics and other local services is unlikely to succeed. The government might consider redrawing some administrative boundaries to create units that are of a more manageable size. It might also consider organizing some services along different geographical lines, creating functional districts of a size appropriate for that service, rather than working solely within existing administrative boundaries.

China should also consider reforming the administrative hierarchy of cities, so that cities, regardless of size, can compete on an equal basis. As thing stand, higher–level cities in China "oversee" the governance of lower–order cities. They also enjoy greater autonomy in decision–making, more fiscal resources, and greater access to transport corridors, rail capacity, and so on. In place of this hierarchy, each city, regardless of size, should be given full autonomy over a well–defined area. All cities and towns should be granted the same tax bases and charged with the same expenditure responsibilities. It will, of course, take longer for smaller cities to make full use of all of the available sources of finance. In the interim, they may need more money from higher levels of government to put them on an equal footing with larger cities.

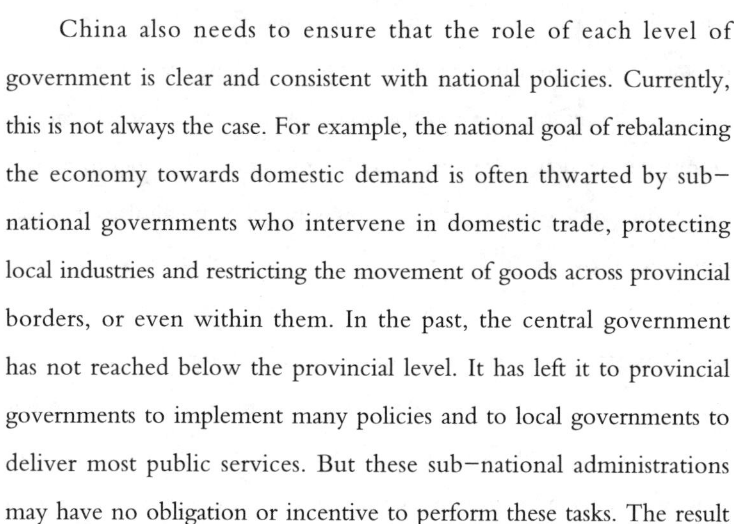

China also needs to ensure that the role of each level of government is clear and consistent with national policies. Currently, this is not always the case. For example, the national goal of rebalancing the economy towards domestic demand is often thwarted by sub–national governments who intervene in domestic trade, protecting local industries and restricting the movement of goods across provincial borders, or even within them. In the past, the central government has not reached below the provincial level. It has left it to provincial governments to implement many policies and to local governments to deliver most public services. But these sub–national administrations may have no obligation or incentive to perform these tasks. The result has been uneven implementation.

The relationship between central, provincial and local governments should, therefore, be a key focus of reform. One approach would be to hold provinces accountable for making sure that local governments implement national policies. Alternatively, China could follow the example of many countries, where the central government is more hands-on, stationing its own staff in local areas to monitor services directly.

Incentives for Public Officials and Public-Service Units

It will also be important to ensure that the incentives of public officials and public-service units (PSUs) are aligned with national priorities. For example, mayors should be judged not only on the basis of industrial production and GDP in their cities, but also on other indicators, such as the quality of transport and other public services provided to city residents. The government could also consider soliciting feedback from the public and other stakeholders on the performance of public officials, asking the public to judge how well public officials have met certain clearly defined goals.

Public service units (PSUs) should also be held accountable for the services they deliver, not the profits they make. International experience suggests that PSUs are most efficient and responsive when they are granted a clear mandate, given the resources they need to deliver on it, and held accountable for doing so. In China, however, PSUs now enjoy too much leeway to charge for services without supervision. Nor are they held accountable for results. They have consequently become more profit-oriented than service-oriented.

Reform of the PSUs will also require revamping the remuneration system to sever the link between the revenues a unit collects and the pay its employees receive. User charges and other revenues should be properly managed and accounted for. And the PSUs should also face competition from private providers of the services they offer. Better management and stiffer competition will both help to keep the PSUs focused on serving the public.

Reaching Out to the General Public

Other countries have benefited from consulting the public on the design of policy, the choice of social indicators and the monitoring of progress. Through devices such as "citizen's report cards" , the public can help the government raise the quality of public services and reduce corruption. The need to reach out to the general public and invite its participation in the design and implementation of social policies is well recognized by the European Union (see Box 8) , although experience shows it is not necessarily easy to do in practice. In China, the process of preparing the 12th Five–Year Plan has already involved extensive gathering of views from the public in every province, autonomous region and municipality. The government should now carefully consider how to extend this public involvement to monitoring plan implementation.

Improvements in Measurement, Information and Supervision

Accountability and information go hand–in–hand. The quality of China's statistics needs improvement. Even though a huge amount of information is routinely reported, China lacks a system for vetting and reconciling the figures produced by different ministries and agencies, which can vary widely. To plan the transition to a high–income economy, China will also need new indicators that truly reflect China's development strategy, objectives and performance. Reliable, timely data would also help the government evaluate the performance of the

nation's policies, service providers and public officials.

Box 8

Inclusion Process in the European Union

The EU's experience over several decades suggests that governments alone cannot secure social inclusion. This cause must also be championed by civil society, including grassroots organizations and the socially excluded themselves. To generate this kind of support, governments have to enter into partnerships with other actors, in accordance with national traditions and community arrangements. The active involvement of the public helps to ensure that the government's efforts are transparent and its objectives widely known. All work on social inclusion should therefore be as open as possible to the active participation of the regional and local public authorities, non–governmental bodies involved in the fight against poverty and social exclusion, and the poor and socially excluded themselves. The experience of the EU suggests such broad engagement is both crucial to success and difficult to achieve. In particular, it can be hard for civil–society groups to deliver services or advocate for change across local and national boundaries.

Source: Background paper No. 2 by A. B. Atkinson: "Issues in the Reform of Social Policy in China" .

Changes in the Scope and Functioning of the SOEs

China's rapid growth over the past three decades is attributable in large part to the dynamism of the non-state sector. A recent study by the OECD compared Chinese SOEs with its non-state enterprises. It found that thanks to "improved governance and other reforms, SOEs are, in some ways, operating more like private-sector firms". However, their performance still lags their private counterparts. The OECD derived estimates of total factor productivity, taking into account a firm's capital intensity, size, location and industry. It found that productivity is highest in private firms. This result is consistent with a long list of previous studies that use a wide range of methodologies and generally conclude that China's SOEs are significantly less efficient than enterprises with other ownership forms. "With capital accumulation a key driver of GDP growth and SOEs responsible for a large share of total investment, low capital productivity in the state enterprise sector amounts to a significant drag on economic growth" [1].

SOE reform has been a key element of the reform process in China for many years. In the pre-reform era, SOEs completely dominated the urban economy. Their scope and function has changed substantially since then. But SOEs remain a sizeable force in today's economy. In 2008, according to the Industrial Survey, the net fixed assets of SOEs outside the financial sector amounted to RMB 7, 593 billion, double the amount in 2001 and more than the assets of private and foreign-invested companies combined (See Table 5). Their profits were also higher, at RMB 906 billion. Moreover, SOEs benefited disproportionately from the recent stimulus program, which

[1] OECD Economic Survey: China, 2010, pp. 109-118.

concentrated on the construction and infrastructure sectors they dominate. This suggests that the share of the SOEs in the economy today is even larger than it was in 2008.

Table 5 Selected Industrial Statistics, 2001 to 2008 (billion Yuan)

	2001	2005	2008
Industrial Net Fixed Assets			
State enterprises and holding companies	38638	49140	75927
Private companies	2039	9587	23945
Foreign companies (a)	11112	21419	36871
Total Profit			
State enterprises and holding companies	2389	6520	9064
Private companies	313	2121	8302
Foreign companies (a)	1443	4141	8243

(a) Includes Hong Kong, Macau and Taiwan investments

Source: CIEC.

The continued dominance of the SOEs in today's Chinese economy is largely attributable to government policies—despite the government's emphasis on fair competition among different ownership types. In December 2006, the State Assets Supervision and Administration Commission (SASAC) announced its intention to maintain absolute control in seven sectors declared to be "strategic" (defense, electrical power distribution, oil and petrochemicals, telecommunications, coal, civil aviation, shipping); as well retaining controlling stakes in a long list of sectors described as "basic or pillar industries" . These include machinery, automobiles, information technology, construction, steel, base metals and chemical

industries.

Must this list be so long? By granting monopolies or oligopolies to SOEs in quite so many industries and services, China may struggle to improve its efficiency and sustain stable growth. It should consider re–examining which industries or activities really require state ownership. After all, the state does not need to own large swathes of an industry—even a strategic industry–in order to steer its development. Both economic theory and extensive international experience show that the state can guide strategic industries and enterprises more effectively through regulation, competition policy and market incentives.

In the early days of China's reforms, state ownership was a bulwark of stability. China was careful not to repeat the chaotic privatizations of Eastern Europe and the former Soviet Union. But conditions in China are now quite different. An orderly reduction in the scale and scope of the SOEs is now possible. The state's shares in SOEs can be transferred to the "public" , through the capital markets at home and abroad. In some SOEs, the state could sell its entire holding, transforming the enterprise into a public company. In other cases, the state could substantially reduce its stake, without relinquishing it altogether.

In many sectors, ownership may be less important than competition. The government can erode the monopoly power of the SOEs by removing barriers to entry and other impediments to competition, including the favorable access to credit that SOEs enjoy. Opening up the service sector to private participation will be of particular importance. These reforms would generate much needed

economic dynamism during the difficult period of transition.

In the SOEs that remain, corporate governance should be reformed. In the state's industrial enterprises, unlike its financial institutions, corporatization remains incomplete. It has been extended only to second–level companies, not to their group or mother companies. This has resulted in an anomalous situation, where corporatized companies are supervised and owned by parent companies with inferior corporate governance.

The state sector should be accountable to its ultimate owners—the whole people. This will require the corporatization of all SOEs, including the group companies, and the reform of their internal governance. The whole people cannot be active owners, of course. But any institution exercising ownership rights on their behalf, whether it be SASAC or another body, should be responsible for safeguarding the people's interests and holding SOEs accountable to them.

The owners of a company enjoy a residual claim on its profits. But SOEs in China pay virtually none of their net profit to the government, either through dividends or by any other means. This is a most unusual practice, with no international precedent. Many of the second–level enterprises that are listed do pay dividends, but they pay them to their group or mother companies who do not then pass them on to the government. Allowing the SOEs to retain their entire net profit was an exigency introduced in the mid–1990s when many SOEs were in financial distress. But this practice has continued despite the huge profitability of SOEs today.

According to economic principles and international practice, all the net profit of SOEs should belong to the state. In most countries, these profits are paid directly into the state budget;in some instances, they are paid indirectly through a fund, but the state remains the ultimate beneficiary. In China, recent discussions suggest SOEs might remit more of their profits to the state, but the amounts being considered are extremely small, between 0% and 15%.

Logically, the debate should start at the other end. The assumption should be that the bulk of the net profit of SOEs should go to the state budget. The SOEs could then try to make a case for partial exemption, i. e. for special legacy costs they may bear. The SOEs could also bid to retain some of their earnings for their own investments, but this would have to be justified against all the other investment needs of the state sector as well as other demands on the state budget, such as education and health expenditures. There are many examples internationally of firms that have retained too much of their profit, plowing it into inefficient investments. Higher dividends would also improve the SOEs'corporate governance by removing the over–investment bias, especially in large industrial enterprises.

Reform of the Fiscal System

Strengthening Public Finance

In a market economy, the fiscal system (i. e. the government's ability to tax and spend) is one of the most effective tools for redistributing income and opportunity. At present, the size of the state budget in China is modest by international standards. In recent years, fiscal revenues have amounted to only around 20% of GDP.

Adding extra–budgetary revenues would increase the ratio to 25%. But this is still smaller than the ratio in the United States where public expenditures are relatively small (federal revenues amount to about 20% and state revenues add a further 10%, bringing the total to 30% of GDP) . In European countries, where expenditures on public services are higher, fiscal revenues are 40% of GDP or more.

If China is to foster a harmonious society and a more prosperous economy, its government will need a bigger budget. Despite the progress made in the 11th FYP, China needs to increase government spending on social protection, health and education, where it still spends significantly less than average for a lower middle–income country. By taking on a greater share of the cost of social programs, such as health, education and social security, the government will relieve the burden on household budgets, increasing their disposable income. The additional public spending should also ensure that poor families and poor regions enjoy better services.

Public spending per person differs greatly across China's localities, contributing to large geographical variations in the standard of public services, such as basic health, education and the minimum income guarantee. The central government has tried to narrow these disparities during the 11th FYP, by increasing its transfers to local governments. But the disparities remain very high by international standards and are inconsistent with the objectives of a harmonious society.

Fiscal revenues should therefore be increased in the near future to at least 30% of GDP, which is the current standard of the United States and below the standard in most other developed countries. This should be achieved with only minimal additional taxes on households, except for the very rich, so as not to defeat the goal of increasing the share of household income in GDP. If China's SOEs were required to remit their net profits to the state budget, as happens in almost every other country in the world, China's fiscal revenue would increase immediately to over 30% of GDP.

As well as raising revenues overall, China should also seek to redistribute the tax burden. At the moment, manufacturing and investment are unduly favored by the fiscal system. Removing that distortion would help to rebalance the economy, as is well known within China. Other useful changes would include expanding the VAT to cover the service sector and levying VAT at the point of consumption, not the point of production.

The mechanics of budget-making also need strengthening at all levels of government. At the national level, the central government needs to improve its ability to design and analyze policy. This will help it to prepare realistic budgets and monitor programs rigorously. The U. S. , for example, entrusts these tasks to two main agencies: the Office of Management and Budget (OMB) in the executive branch and the Congressional Budget Office (CBO) in the legislative branch. The OMB has a staff of 500 and the CBO 250, of which most are economists and public policy analysts with advanced degrees (See Box 9) . Managerial and analytical skills of this kind are in even shorter supply at the sub-national levels of China's government. These layers of government need the technical knowhow to match their important roles in formulating and implementing China's fiscal policy.

Box 9

Budget preparation and evaluation in the USA

The Office of Management and Budget (OMB) is the largest body within the US President's Executive Office. It has 500 staff, a budget of $ 70.9 million (in 2008) and its director sits in the cabinet. Its predominant mission is to help the President in preparing the federal budget and supervising its implementation in executive–branch agencies. In helping to make the President's spending plans, OMB evaluates agency programs, policies, and procedures;assesses competing demands for money;and sets funding priorities. OMB ensures that agency reports, rules, testimony, and proposed legislation are consistent with the President's budget and policies. In addition, OMB oversees and coordinates the administration's procurement, financial management, information, and regulatory policies.

OMB also tries to improve managerial standards in the government, including its use of information technology, its financial management, its procurement procedures and its staffing practices. The performance of federal agencies is rated (green, yellow, or red) on score cards prepared by OMB staff. OMB also oversees the efforts of government agencies to evaluate their programs, spot successes and failures and learn from the results.

Approximately half of all OMB staff is assigned to the four Resource Management Offices, the majority of them as program examiners. Program examiners may monitor a federal agency or a topical area, such as U. S. Navy warships. These staff monitor both

spending and management. They are also responsible for giving expert advice.

Each year they review the budget requests submitted by federal agencies. They help to decide which requests will be sent to Congress as part of the President's budget. They perform in-depth program evaluations, review proposed regulations, read agency testimony and analyze pending legislation. They are also often called upon to provide analysis and information to staff members of the President's office.

Source: Background paper No. 19 by Christine Wong: "Public Sector Reforms toward Building the Harmonious Society in China" .

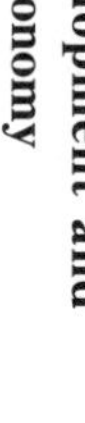

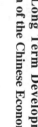

Reforming the Inter-Governmental Fiscal System

As discussed in earlier sections, if China is to narrow regional disparities and encourage balanced growth, its government needs to increase its social spending in the poorer regions. Under China's decentralized system, it falls to local governments to implement many of the components of social programs, such as improving education, widening health-care coverage, strengthening social-safety nets, and so on. Indeed, for the majority of the Chinese population, these services are provided by rural local governments at the county and township levels. The prospects for improving these services depend, therefore, on the willingness and capacity of local governments to take on the task. Under the present inter-governmental fiscal system, however, the average local government appears to have neither the resources nor the incentive to meet their responsibilities for social spending. To implement the social programs in its development plan, China will need to allocate more central funds to social spending, reduce disparities among localities, and initiate a substantial reform of the inter-governmental fiscal system.

As shown in Table 6, sub-national governments in China are responsible for almost 80% of public spending, but raise less than half of the tax revenues. This is not an unusual phenomenon among large countries. In a big country with large disparities between regions, it is also desirable that the central government receives surplus revenue, so that it can use these funds to help the poorer regions. In China, however, local governments are dependent on transfers to meet their spending needs to a degree unprecedented in international experience. These transfers impose a heavy administrative burden on the central government, which must budget for and monitor a trillion-yuan program of earmarked grants. This issue needs to be reviewed as part of further reforms of inter-governmental fiscal relations.

Table 6 Share of Sub-national Governments in Total Government

	Developing Countries	OECD Countries	Transition Countries	China (2008)
Sub-national share of Government Tax Revenues	9	19	17	47
Sub-national share of Government Expenditure	14	32	26	79

Source: World Bank 2006, CSY 2009, quoted in Background paper No. 19 by Christine Wong: "Public Sector Reforms toward Building the Harmonious Society in China" .

Note: data for other countries is from various years.

An immediate priority is to clarify and rationalize the spending responsibilities of different levels of government. The current assignments are largely inherited from the era of central planning and do not suit the highly decentralized, mixed economy that China has become. As China's population becomes more mobile, many local public goods now have significant inter–local or even national spillovers. Two good examples are public health, in a country where contagious diseases can spread by high–speed rail, and the education of migrant children, who may slip through the cracks of the country's fragmented school system. Under these new circumstances, it no longer makes sense to leave the responsibility for education and public health entirely in the hands of local governments. Similarly, assigning pensions and unemployment insurance to local governments hinders population mobility.

Economic principles and international experience suggest three approaches to reforming the inter–governmental fiscal system:

(i) The central government should take over both the financing and management of programs that require a national perspective. One clear example is the basic pension system (See Chapter 6:"Strengthening the Pension System") . Unifying the current patchwork of schemes into a nationwide pension system would serve the cause of both efficiency and equity. It would ensure labor mobility throughout the country (thus improving efficiency) and equalize pension standards (thus promoting equity) , after allowing for local differences in the cost of living (ref to earlier sections on pension reform) . The same would be true for the unemployment insurance scheme.

(ii) For some other programs, a better solution is to de–link

finance and delivery, so that local governments provide the service, but higher levels of government pay for it. In most developed countries this is now the arrangement for basic education. The schools are managed by the lowest level of government, to gain the benefit of having decision–makers close to the students and their families. The costs of the program, however, are met by higher levels of government, to ensure equal standards throughout the country. In China, in contrast, counties are responsible for the bulk of spending on basic education. Because they differ greatly in the resources they can spare, the quality of education also varies greatly between regions. To narrow these gaps, the central government should pay more of the costs of basic education, even if counties continue to provide it. The same is true for other social programs such as basic health, Dibao, etc. , where the country aims to achieve universal coverage with equal standards. As discussed earlier, investment in human capital in the poorest regions is the best investment China can make to promote growth and reduce inequality.

(iii) In most countries, the central government's transfers to lower levels of government are tied to particular streams of revenue. The central government may, for example, commit to share a given percentage of some tax or duty, distributed according to an agreed formula. This ensures a stable source of revenues for local governments, allowing them to plan ahead and manage their budgets with greater confidence. China already has very large formula–based transfers. But many local governments feel that these constitute too small a proportion of total transfers. If local governments were relieved of some of their spending responsibilities, as suggested above, then rule–

based transfers would then represent a much larger proportion of their remaining transfers.

It is also worth considering whether local governments should be given some formal revenue–raising powers of their own, as happens in many other countries. This could help make local governments more accountable and responsive to the needs of citizens. According to economic principles, local taxes should fall on property and natural resources, i. e. , immobile assets whose values depend on the quality of the environment created by the local authorities. Natural resource taxes would be of particular benefit to underdeveloped regions rich in ores, hydrocarbons and so on.

In summary, a reformed fiscal system should give all levels of government the resources they need to further the country's development, and the incentives to do so.

Concluding Remarks

This chapter's over–riding question is how to reduce the gap between the ambition of China's plans and their uneven implementation. Just as reform of the economic system and openness to the outside world were the key factor behind China's remarkable achievements over the past 30 years, so too will achieving China's development objectives in the coming decades depend on deepening reform and continued openness. This is an extremely complex and challenging question for any country, and this last chapter should be seen as the beginning of the thinking on this topic rather than the end.

Introduction to Authors

K. Y. Amoako

K. Y. Amoako is the founder and president of the African Center for Economic Transformation (ACET). He began his career in 1974 at the World Bank, where he became one of the first Africans to rise to a senior position. He served as the World Bank's Division Chief for programs in the Africa Region and also Division for programs in the Latin America and Caribbean Region, as well as Director of the Education and Social Policy Department. From 1995—2005, Amoako served as Executive Secretary of the Economic Commission for Africa (ECA) of the UN. In 2006, he became a Distinguished African Scholar at the Woodrow Wilson International Center for Scholars, in Washington, DC.

A.B. Atkinson

A.B. Atkinson is a fellow of Nuffield College, of which he was Warden from 1994 to 2005. He is currently a lifetime Professor of London School of Economics. He has been the President of Royal Economic Society, of the Econometric Society, of the European Economic Association, and of the International

Economic Association. He has served in the UK Royal Council for the Distribution of Income and Wealth, the UK Pension Law Review Board, and the Commission on Social Equity. He has been a member of the French Economic Analysis Committee and an economic adviser to the French Prime Minister. He was knighted in 2001 for services to economics. His most recent book is *The Changing Distribution of Earnings in OECD Countries.*

Judith Banister

Judith Banister is a Senior Demographer who specializes in the demography of China. Her research focuses on population and related socio-economic trends. Dr. Banister's ongoing projects include research on China population aging and economic growth, health and mortality trends in China, employment and labor compensation in China manufacturing, and the evolving status of women in China. Her Ph.D. is from Stanford University. Her career has spanned the public sector—Chief of the International Programs at the U.S. Bureau of the Census; private sector—Director of Global Demographics at the Conference Board; and the academic sector—Professor at Hong Kong University of Science & Technology. She works as a Consultant in Silicon Valley, California, and with Javelin Investments in Beijing.

Nicholas Barr

Nicholas Barr is a Professor of Public Economics at the London School of Economics and the author of numerous books and articles including *The Welfare State as Piggy Bank*, *The Economics of the*

Welfare State, and *Reforming Pensions: Principles and Policy Choices* (with Peter Diamond). He is a member of the Editorial Board of the *International Social Security Review* and an Associate Editor of *CESifo Economic Studies* and the *Australian Economic Review*. Alongside his academic career is wide–ranging involvement in policy. He had two spells at the World Bank, working on the design of income transfers and health finance.

David E. Bloom

David E. Bloom is "Clarence James Gamble" lecture Professor of Economics and Demography at Harvard University, Chair of the Department of Global Health and Population at the Harvard School of Public Health, and Director of Harvard University's Program on the Global Demography of Aging. He is a research associate at the National Bureau of Economic Research and a fellow of the American Academy of Arts and Sciences. Bloom received his Ph. D. in economics and demography from Princeton University in 1981. He has worked extensively in the areas of health, labor, development of economics, and demography and published a lot of articles.

Cai Fang

Cai Fang successively graduated from Renmin University of China, Graduate School of Chinese Academy of Social Sciences (CASS), where he received his Ph. D degree in Economics. He is currently the Director of Institute of Population and Labor Economics of CASS,

the Member of the Standing Committee of the 11th NPC. He also serves as the Vice President of China Population Association and Member of the National Planning Expert committee. Mr. Cai's research focuses on theories and policies of agricultural economics, labor economics, population economics, China's economic reform, economic growth, distribution of income and poverty, etc. His publications include *The Chinese Economy, The Development and Transition of China's Labor Market, China's Population and Labor Issues Report* (serial books, edited).

Andrew Crockett

Andrew Crockett is the Special Adviser to the Chairman and a member of the Executive Committee of J.P. Morgan Chase & Co. He also serves as a member of the International Advisory Council of China Banking Regulatory Commission, and the International Council of the China Development Bank. Before joining JPMorgan Chase&Co., Mr. Crockett had been General Manager (CEO) of the Bank for International Settlements from 1993—2003 and was the first Chairman of the Financial Stability Forum (now the Financial Stability Board) from 1999—2003. Earlier in his career, Mr. Crockett had held senior positions at the Bank of England and the International Monetary Fund.

Peter Diamond

Peter Diamond is an Institute Professor and professor of economics at the Massachusetts Institute of Technology. He has been the President of American Economic Association, of Econometric Society, and of National Academy of Social Insurance. He has won 2010 Nobel Prize in Economic Sciences. He first consulted to the US Congress about Social Security reform in 1974 and has been actively engaged on this topic ever since. He has twice written reports on pension reform in China, in 2004—2005 and 2009—2010. His recent publications include *Reforming Pensions: Principles and Policy* (with Nicholas Barr)

Barry Eichengreen

Barry Eichengreen is respectively the George C. Pardee and Helen N. Pardee Lecture Professor of Economics and Professor of Political Science at the University of California, Berkeley. He is a Research Associate of the National Bureau of Economic Research (Cambridge, Massachusetts) and Research Fellow of the Centre for Economic Policy Research center (London, England). In 1997—1998 he was Senior Policy Advisor at the International Monetary Fund.

Professor Eichengreen was awarded the Economic History Association's Jonathan R.T. Hughes Prize for Excellence in Teaching in 2002 and the University of California at Berkeley Social Science

Division's Distinguished Teaching Award in 2004. He is the 2010 recipient of the Schumpeter Prize from the International Schumpeter Society. He is President of the Economic History Association in the 2010—2011 academic year. His most recent books include *Exorbitant Privilege: The Rise and Fall of the Dollar and the Future of the International Monetary System*, etc.

Mohamed A. EL-Erian

Mohamed A. El-Erian is CEO and co-CIO of Pacific Investment Management Corp. the global investment management firm with $13 trillion of assets under management as of December, 2010. Prior to rejoining PIMCO at the end of 2007, EL-Erian was President and CEO of Harvard Management Company (HMC—from February, 2006), the entity managing Harvard's endowment and other related assets. He was also a faculty member of the Harvard Business School. Dr. EL-Erian earned a B.A./M.A. in economics from Cambridge University and doctorate and master's degrees in economics from Oxford University. He was ranked 16th in *Foreign Policy*'s list of "Top 100 Global Thinkers" .

Shenggen Fan

Shenggen Fan is the Director of International Food Policy Research Institute (IFPRI). After joining IFPRI in 1995, he led IFPRI's program on public investment and conducted extensive research on poverty-relief development strategies in developing countries in Africa, Asia, and the Middle East. Before joining IFPRI, he held positions at the International Service center for National

Agricultural Research in Netherlands and the Department of Agricultural Economics and Rural Sociology at the University of Arkansas. He received his Ph.D. in applied economics from the University of Minnesota and his bachelor's and master's degrees from Nanjing Agricultural University in China.

Richard B. Freeman

Richard B. Freeman holds the Herbert Ascherman Chair in Economics at Harvard University. He is currently serving as Faculty co–Director of the Labor and Worklife Program at the Harvard Law School. He directs the National Bureau of Economic Research / Sloan Science Engineering's Workforce Projects, and is a Senior Research Fellow in Labour Markets at the London School of Economics' . Professor Freeman is a fellow of the American Academy of Arts and Science. Freeman received the Mincer Lifetime Achievement Prize from the Society of Labor Economics in 2006. In 2007, he was awarded the IZA Prize in Labor Economics.

Howard Glennerster

Howard Glennerster is a Professor Emeritus at the London School of Economics where he taught social policy, the economics of health, education and social security for many years. He has published widely on these topics and been an advisor to the Department of Health and Treasury of UK.

J.Vernon Henderson

J.Vernon Henderson is the Chair Professor of Political Economy and Professor of Economics and Urban Studies at Brown University, and a Research Associate of the National Bureau of Economic Research. He has conducted research on aspects of urbanization and local government finance and regulation of USA, Brazil, Canada, India, China, Korea and Indonesia. He is currently doing research on systems of cities, industrial location, urban productivity, environmental regulation, and development of urban sub–centers, as well as tax and public service competition among cities. His Ph.D. is from the University of Chicago .

Homi Kharas

Homi Kharas is a Senior Fellow in Global Economy and Development at The Brookings Institution in Washington D.C, also a Non–Resident Fellow of the OECD Development Center; and a member of the National Economic Advisory Council to the Malaysian Prime Minister. He was ever a member of the Working Group for the Commission on Growth and Development, chaired by Professor A. Michael Spence. Previously, Homi served as the Chief Economist for the World Bank's East Asia and Pacific region and as the Director for Poverty Reduction and Economic Management, Finance and Private Sector Development, responsible for the Bank's advice on

structural and economic policies, fiscal issues, debt, trade, governance and financial markets. His research interests are now focused on global trades, East Asian growth and development, and international aid for the poorest countries. He holds a Ph. D. in economics from Harvard University.

Ravi Kanbur

Ravi Kanbur is T. H. Lee Chair Professor of World Affairs, and Professor of Economics at Cornell University. He holds an appointment Chair Professor both in the Charles H. Dyson School of Applied Economics and Management in the College of Agriculture and Life Sciences, and tenured in the Department of Economics in the College of Arts and Sciences. Ravi Kanbur has served on the staff of the World Bank, as a Economic Adviser, Senior Economic Adviser, Resident Representative in Ghana, Chief Economist of the African Region of the World Bank, and Principal Adviser to the Chief Economist of the World Bank. He has also served as the Director of the World Bank's *World Development Report*. He holds a doctorate in economics from the University of Oxford. His main areas of interest are public economics and development.

Santiago Levy

Santiago Levy is the Vice–President at the Inter–American Development Bank. From August 2007 to February 2008, he served as General Manager and Chief Economist for

the IDB Research Department. Previously, he was General Director at the Mexican Institute for Social Security (IMSS) from December, 2000 to October, 2005. From 1994 to 2000, Levy served as the Deputy Minister at the Ministry of Finance and Public Credit of Mexico. He holds a Ph.D. in economics and a Masters in Political economy from Boston University. He was a post–doctoral fellow at Cambridge University. His recent published books include: *No Growth without Equity? Inequality, Interests and Competition in Mexico* (with Michael Walton).

Li Shi

Li Shi is a Professor of Economics in the School of Economics and Business, doctoral supervisor, and Acting Director of the Institute for Income Distribution at Beijing Normal University. He is a member of the Advisory Committee of Ministry of Human Resources and Social Security, member of the Advisory Committee of Ministry of Agriculture, and member of Advisory Committee of Poverty Alleviation Office of State Council, China. He is Non–Resident Senior Research Fellow at UNU–WIDER and Research Fellow at IZA. He was Professor and Research Fellow at the Institute of Economics, Chinese Academy of Social Sciences from 1996 to 2005 and a research fellow at the University of Oxford in 2001 and professor at Hitotsubashi University, Japan in 2002. His current studies focus on income distribution, poverty and rural migration in China. He has published in journals such as Journal of *Comparative Economics*, Journal of *Population Economics*, *Review of Income and Wealth*,

Oxford Bulletin of Economics and Statistics, *Economic Development and Cultural Change*, *Oxford Development Studies*, Journal of *Development Economics*. His publications include several edited volumes such as *China's Retreat from Equality* (2001, with R. Zhao and C. Riskin, M.E. Sharpe: New York), *Unemployment, Inequality and Poverty in Urban China* (2006, with H. Sato, Routledge: London and New York), *Income Inequality and Public Policy in China* (2008, with B. Gustafsson and T. Sicular, Cambridge University Press) and *Rising Inequality in China* (2013, with H. Sato and T. Sicular, Cambridge University Press).

Edwin R. Lim

Edwin R. Lim joined the World Bank in 1970 and in the following 30 years, was responsible for the Bank's work in a number of developing countries, including Ghana, Nigeria, Indonesia, Thailand, Vietnam, India and China. He retired as a Director of the World Bank in 2002. From 1980 to 1990, he was the World Bank's Lead Economist for China and established the World Bank's office in China and served as the first Chief of Mission from 1985 to 1990. In 1994, Mr. Lim took two years external leave from the World Bank. He proposed to the State Council and participated in the founding of China's first international investment bank — China International Capital Corporation (CICC) and served as CICC's first CEO. As of 2003, Mr. Lim directed China Economic Research and Advisory Programme. He was educated at Princeton University (B.A.) and Harvard University (Ph. D. in Economics).

Jean Pisani–Ferry

Jean Pisani–Ferry has been since January 2005 Director of BRUEGEL (for *Brussels European and Global Economic Laboratory).* He is also a professor of economics with University Paris–Dauphine. Pisani–Ferry has made his career in research and policy. After having held positions in research and government in France, he joined the European Commission in 1989 as an economic adviser to the Director—General of DG ECFIN. From 1992 to 1997 he was the Director of CEPII, the main French research centre in international economics. In 1997, he became senior economic adviser to the French minister of Finance and was later appointed Executive President of the French Prime Minister's Council of Economic Analysis (2001—2002). From 2002 to 2004, he was senior adviser to the director of the French Treasury.

Ian Porter

Ian Porter spent most of his career at the World Bank, including assignments as Country Director for South East Asia, Manager of Policy Support for the Board of Directors, Division Chief for Population and Human Resources in West Africa and Resident Representative for Tanzania. Earlier in his career with the World Bank he worked on economic and sectoral reform issues in China, Thailand and Vietnam. He is currently focusing on east Asia and southeast Asia, working with a number of international institutions

and think tanks, including the Asian Development Bank, the World Bank, the United Nations, on a range of development issues and the China Economic Research and Advisory Programme. He holds a B.A. in Philosophy, Politics and Economics from Oxford University and an M.A. in Development Economics from Sussex University.

Paul Romer

Paul Romer was the President of Charter Cities, a research institute non-profit focused on the interplay of rules, urbanization, and development. Charter cities are special reform zones. He is a senior fellow at the Stanford Institute for Economic Policy Research.

While teaching at Stanford's Graduate School of Business, Romer took an entrepreneurial detour to start Aplia, an education technology company dedicated to increasing student effort and engagement. To date, students using the Aplia software have submitted more than half a billion answers to homework problems in economics and other related courses. He is a pioneer of endogenous growth theory and set up the model in 1986. He is also non-resident follow at the Center for Global Development in Washington, D.C. He is a member of the Board of Trustees of the Carnegie Foundation. He is also the Henry Kaufman Visiting Professor at the New York University Stern School of Business.

Andrew L. T. Sheng

Andrew Sheng is currently the Chief Adviser to the China Banking Regulatory Commission and a Board Member of the Qatar Financial Centre Regulatory Authority, Sime Darby Berhad and

Khazanah Nasional Berhad, Malaysia. He is also Adjunct Professor at the Graduate School of Economics and Management, Tsinghua University, Beijing and the University of Malaya, Kuala Lumpur. He was Chairman of the Securities and Futures Commission (SFC) of Hong Kong from 1 October, 1998 to 30 September, 2005. Between October 1993 and September 1998, Andrew was the Deputy Chief Executive responsible for the Reserves Management and External Affairs Departments at the Hong Kong Monetary Authority. Between 1989 and 1993, he was Senior Manager, Financial Sector Development Department at the World Bank. From 1976 to 1989, he held various positions with Bank Negara Malaysia, including Chief Economist and Assistant Governor in charge of Bank and Insurance Regulations.

Michael Spence

Michael Spence received the Nobel Prize in Economic Sciences in 2001. He served as the Chairman of Commission on Growth and Independent Development (2006—2010, the life of the commission), Professor Emeritus of Management in the Graduate School of Business at Stanford University, a Senior Fellow of the Hoover Institution at Stanford and Professor of Economics at the Stern School of Business at New York University. He serves on the boards of Genpact and Mercadolibre, and a number of private companies. Prof. Spence earned his undergraduate degree in philosophy at Princeton summa cum laude and was selected for a Rhodes Scholarship. He was awarded a B.S.and a M.A. from Oxford in mathematics and earned his Ph.D. in economics at Harvard.

Ramin Toloui

RaminToloui is an executive vice president and emerging markets portfolio manager based in the Newport Beach office of PIMCO. Prior to joining PIMCO in 2006, Mr. Toloui spent seven years in the international division of the U.S. Department of Treasury, most recently as the director of the Office of the Western Hemisphere, managing a team of economists and advising senior U.S. government officials on financial policies in Latin America. He previously served as senior advisor to the Under Secretary for International Affairs during the crises in Argentina, Brazil, Uruguay, and Turkey in 2001—2003.

Christine Wong

Christine Wong is currently Senior Research Fellow and Chair of Chinese Studies in the School of Inter-disciplinary Area Studies, University of Oxford. She has worked in advisory capacities on China's fiscal reform and decentralization for the World Bank, the Asian Development Bank, the OECD, UNDP, UNICEF, and DFID. Christine was previously the Professor of International Studies at the University of Washington's Henry M. Jackson School of International Studies (2000—2007), and had also taught

in the University of California, Santa Cruz and Berkeley and Mount Holyoke College. She has written extensively on China's public finance and public sector reform. She works closely with several Chinese research organizations and sits on the academic advisory boards of the National Institute for Fiscal Studies, and the Center for Industrial Development and Environmental Governance, both at Tsinghua University, Beijing.

Adrian Wood

Adrian Wood was educated at Cambridge and Harvard Universities. From 1969 to 1977, he taught at Cambridge, where he was a Fellow of King's College and a lecturer in the Faculty of Economics. From 1977 to 1985, he was a senior economist at the World Bank in Washington D.C, working on China, Turkey and writing *The 1980 World Development Report*. From 1985 to 2000, he was a Professorial Fellow of the Institute of Development Studies at the University of Sussex. From 2000 to 2005, he was Chief Economist of the UK's Department for International Development. He is now Professor of International Development at the University of Oxford and a Fellow of Wolfson College.

Yves Zenou

Yves Zenou is professor of economics at Stockholm University and Senior Research Fellow at the Research Institute of Industrial Economics. His research interests include: Social interactions and network theory, urban economics, segregation and discrimination of ethnic minorities, criminality and education. Yves Zenou was previously a Professor of Economics at the University of Southampton, UK, and a Visiting Professor at the University of California, Berkeley, the European University Institute and Tel Aviv University. He is currently the Editor of *Regional Science and Urban Economics*, and Associate Editor of the Journal of *Public Economic Theory*, the Journal of *Urban Economics*, the Journal of *Urban Management*, the Scandinavian Journal of *Economics*, and Annals of *Economics and Statistics*.

Zhang Xiaobo

Zhang Xiaobo is a senior research fellow at the development strategy and governance division of the International Food Policy Research Institute (IFPRI) and a co-editor of *China Economic Review.* He earned B.S. in mathematics from Nankai University, China; M.S. in economics from Tianjin University of Economics and Finance, China; and M.S. and Ph.D. in applied economics and management from Cornell University. He was selected as the president of Chinese Institute of Economics in the united states from 2005 to 2006. He has published widely on topics ranging from regional development, public investment, rural industrialization to demographic change in China.

Li & Fung Group and Li & Fung Research Center

Li & Fung Group was found in 1906 in Guangzhou as a traditional export trading company of family business, and registered in Hong Kong as Lee Fung Hong (1937) Co. Ltd. in 1937 with solely private capital. It's now a controlling shareholder of Lee Fung Hong Group.

Striving on operation and business expansion for years, Li & Fung Group has developed into a multinational business group, based in Hong Kong and managing three core businesses: export trade, distribution, wholesale and retail—Export business through Li & Fung Co., Ltd. while Lihe responsible for distribution and Wholesale; Liya retailing chain convenience stores and cake stores; Trinity Holdings Limited engaged in senior men's clothing retail; Toy R & D City business toys and children's products retailing and so on.

By 2009, Li & Fung had been seized more than 35000 employees in more than 70 cities worldwide, with a turnover of more than $16 billion. Harvard University, Stanford University together with Wharton Business School have conducted a number of case studies on Li & Fung's supply chain management, network operations and value chain business models.

Founded in 2000, Li & Fung Research Center is dedicated to providing research and analysis on macro economy and China business to the management layers and customers of Li & Fung Group for decision-making purposes.